Possible Worlds,
Artificial Intelligence,
and
Narrative Theory

Possible Worlds, Artificial Intelligence, and Narrative Theory

Marie-Laure Ryan

Indiana
University BLOOMINGTON & INDIANAPOLIS
Press

The paper used in this publication meets the minimum requirements of American
National Standard for Information Sciences—Permanence of Paper for Printed Library
Materials, ANSI Z39.48-1984.

MANUFACTURED IN THE UNITED STATES OF AMERICA

Library of Congress Cataloging-in-Publication Data
Ryan, Marie-Laure, date.
     Possible worlds, artificial intelligence, and narrative theory / Marie-Laure Ryan.
          p.   cm.
     Includes bibliographical references and index.
     ISBN 0-253-35004-2 (alk. paper)
     1. Fiction—Technique.   2. Possibility in literature.   3. Artificial intelligence.
     4. Narration (Rhetoric)   5. Literature and semiotics. I. Title.
     PN3355.R93 1991
     808.3'014—dc20   91-6825

1 2 3 4 5 95 94 93 92

Contents

Glossary

System of reality A set of distinct worlds. The system has a modal structure, and forms a modal system, if it comprises a central world surrounded by satellite worlds. The center of a modal system is its actual world, the satellites are alternative possible worlds.

Textual universe The image of a system of reality projected by a text. The textual universe is a modal system if one of its worlds is designated as actual and opposed to the other worlds of the system.

Semantic domain A concept slightly more general than textual universe. The set of concepts evoked by the text, whether or not these concepts form a system of reality (i.e., whether or not the text asserts facts and makes existential claims).

AW The actual world, center of our system of reality. AW is the world where I am located. Absolutely speaking, there is only one AW.

APW An alternative possible world in a modal system of reality.

TRW Textual reference world. The world for which the text claims facts; the world in which the propositions asserted by the text are to be valued. TRW is the center of a system of reality comprising APWs.

TAW Textual actual world. The image of TRW proposed by the text. The authority that determines the facts of TAW is the actual sender (author).

TAPW Textual alternative possible world. An alternative possible world in a textual universe structured as a modal system. TAPWs are textually presented as mental constructs formed by the inhabitants of TAW.

NAW Narratorial actual world. What the narrator presents as fact of TRW.

Principles
  $=$ identity
  $<>$ nonidentity
  $=>$ accurate representation
  $\sim$ not
  $\square$ necessity
  $\lozenge$ possibility

In nonfiction, TRW $=$ AW
In fiction, TRW $<>$ AW
In fiction, TAW $=>$ TRW
In accurate nonfiction, TAW $=>$ TRW

In accurate nonfiction, TAW => TRW
In inaccurate nonfiction (lies and errors),
~ (TAW => TRW)
In fiction told by reliable narrator, NAW = TAW
In fiction told by unreliable narrator,
~ (NAW = TAW)

Possible Worlds,
Artificial Intelligence,
and
Narrative Theory

Introduction

In the thinking of literary theorists, the concepts of narrative and of fiction are magnetically attracted to each other. This affinity is witnessed by the number of books using the phrase "narrative fiction" in their title, or one term in the title and the other in the subtitle. Does the longtime popularity of the composite category of "narrative fiction" stem from an inability to distinguish its components, or is it due to the tacit belief that narrativity and fictionality can only reach their full potential in conjunction with each other?

Almost as powerful as the affinity between narrative and fiction is the mutual attraction exerted by the categories literary and fictional. A culture with no fiction but a literature appears as unlikely as a culture with fiction but no literature—no texts consumed for the sake of pleasure. Many literary scholars implicitly regard fictionality as the trademark of literariness, and scrutinize the problem of fictional discourse in the hope of finding there a key to the understanding of literary communication (cf. Herrnstein Smith 1978, Martínez-Bonati 1981a). But while it may be true that most of literature belongs to the category fiction, that the prototypical examples of fictionality are narrative texts, and that the fullest variety of narrative techniques is displayed in fiction, the three features literary, narrative, and fictional remain distinct, and do not presuppose each other. Every one, or nearly every one, of their combinations is represented in Western culture.

(1) *Literary Narrative Fiction* (+ + +): Novels, short stories, drama, epic poetry. In the "low" literary domain: jokes, romances, thrillers.

(2) *Literary Narrative Nonfiction* (+ + −): Works of autobiography and history acknowledged as literature: Rousseau's *Confessions,* Gibbon's *Decline and Fall of the Roman Empire,* Michelet's *Histoire de France.*

(3) *Literary Nonnarrative Fiction* (+ − +): Postmodernist antinarrative texts (regardless of the fact that they may be titled novels: the evolution of the genre has made the label "novel" separable from the feature of narrativity).

(4) *Literary Nonnarrative Nonfiction* (+ − −): Collections of aphorisms, such as La Rochefoucauld's *Maxims* and Pascal's *Pensées;* or some classics of science or philosophy honored as literature, such as the writings of Freud and Rousseau. To either (3) or (4)—depending on the definition of fiction—also belongs lyric poetry.

(5) *Nonliterary Narrative Fiction* (− + +): Admittedly unusual, this category is represented by the following text, published in the advertising section of *Time* magazine (October 1987):

> Once upon a time there was a man named Rupelstiltskin who could spin straw into gold. An odd but lucrative occupation. One day he set out on a journey, lugging his spinning wheel, straw, and gold. Alas, Rumpelstiltskin tumbled down a hill. His gold tumbled, too—right into the mouth of an enchanted frog. Magically, the frog transformed into the Gold Bankard from First Interstate Bank, the nation's largest bank system.

(6) *Nonliterary Narrative Nonfiction* (− + −): News reports, works of history, narratives of personal experience, live play-by-play broadcasts of sports events.

(7) *Nonliterary Nonnarrative Fiction* (− − +). This class is, together with the third, the hardest to illustrate—arguably because the features narrative and fictional present special affinities: a fiction may presuppose at least an embryo of narrativity. Potential candidates include the imaginary situations offered to children as mathematical problems: "A merchant buys fifty pairs of shoes at $10.67 a pair. He sells half of them at $17.96, one-tenth at $13.66. For how much does he need to sell the rest to make a 45% profit?" In elementary schools, however, these problems are known as "story-math." The philosophical dialogues of Plato would fit into this category if they had not been elevated by cultural tradition to literary status. Since they have not yet been canonized as literature, the dialogues between the imaginary couple Ralph and Wanda on human sexuality, published in the early eighties in *Time* magazine, provide what may be the best example of the category.

(8) *Nonliterary Nonnarrative Nonfiction* (− − −): Advertisements (except for the case mentioned in [5]), recipes, interviews, textbooks, literary criticism and theory (despite deconstructionist claims to the contrary), laws, organized debates, sermons, conducting business, saying hello and goodbye, exchanging opinions.

While literary theorists have been traditionally reluctant to separate the issues of narrativity and fictionality, other disciplines have recently taken positive steps toward their distinction. Work in sociolinguistics (Labov), discourse analysis (Sacks, Polanyi), textual linguistics (van Dijk), folklore (Bauman, Young, Shuman), and cognitive psychology (Rumelhart, Mandler and Johnson) has paid attention to nonliterary nonfictional narrative, outlining the pragmatic principles governing its conversational use, and stressing its formal similarities to the narratives of literary fiction. Conversely, philosophers working in the analytical tradition, such as Kripke, Searle, Lewis, Howell, Goodman, Wolterstorff, Woods, Parsons, and Walton have devoted their attention to the logic and semantics of fiction as an autonomous field of investigation.

Following this trend, I propose to explore fictionality and narrativity as distinct properties, and to address both issues from an interdisciplinary perspective—a perspective which may be called semiotic, since my approach is largely formalist, and my concern is signification in all kinds of texts, not just in literary ones. The first part of this book is devoted to a definition of fictionality, while the second investigates the semantics of narrativity. The common denominator of the two sections is provided by the conceptual framework and its two sources of inspiration: the theory of possible worlds, and artificial intelligence. Through this choice of models, I hope to address the growing dissatisfaction with formalist approaches to literature and the current feeling of a crisis in narratology (as voiced in Rimmon-Kenan 1988). Rumors of the demise of formalism and narratology may be greatly exaggerated, but it is undeniable that many of the gold mines on which they have lived for the past twenty years are no longer productive. Traditional topics, such as point of view and narrative technique, have been largely exhausted; standard models, such as the semiotic square or generative grammar never kept their promise of providing a universal and scientific account of textual meaning. The crisis of formalism and of narratology is an urgent need for new sources of ideas.

The theory of possible worlds is a formal model developed by logicians for the purpose of defining the semantics of modal operators—primarily those of necessity and possibility, but other operators have been suggested. The theory has two concepts to propose to textual semiotics: the metaphor of "world" to describe the semantic domain projected by the text; and the concept of modality to describe and classify the various ways of existing of the objects, states, and events that make up the semantic domain.

The metaphor of world is of course nothing new to literary critics. An expression such as "the world of Virginia Woolf" is a neutral cliché so traditional in literary parlance that it does not commit its user to any particular approach or assumption. Philosophers acknowledge this debt to literary thinking in their attempts to define the concept of world: Alvin Plantinga (1976) assimilates a possible world to a "book," Robert Merrihew Adams (1974) calls the formal definition of a world the "story" of that world. But in being borrowed and returned by philosophers, the dead metaphor receives a new influx of life. The concept comes back to textual semiotics sharpened by a repertory of analytical tools which reveal new territories to be explored. As Pavel (1976:9) observes, the main legacy of possible-world theory to textual semiotics is an interest in the problem of truth in fiction and in the relations between semantic domains and reality—two questions considered heretic by orthodox structuralism.

The interest of literary semioticians in the concept of possibility predates, however, any systematic involvement with modal logic and the theory of possible worlds. It originated in Todorov's 1969 attempt to design a formal coding—what he calls a grammar—for the plots of *The Decameron*. He discovered that events considered possible by characters, but never enacted, had as much impact on the development of the plot as events presented as facts. To distinguish the various types of possibility he introduced a repertory of operators which modified entire narrative propositions in the same way a modal verb, such as "may" or "could," modifies a sentence. In his coding system, narrative propositions could appear either unmodalized or modified by one of four operators: obligatory, optative, conditional, and predictive.

The first systematic attempts to apply the conceptual framework of modal logic to textual semiotics are those of Vaina (1977) and Eco (1978). Vaina's paper provides the main inspiration as well as the logical foundations for chapters 6 and 7 of this book. Her definitions suggest a self-embedding property of possible worlds: on the one hand, a possible world is a "complete state of affairs," on the other, a "course of events," made out of a succession of complete states. In addition to these distinct states, the semantic domain of the narrative text contains a number of subworlds, created by the mental activity of characters. The semantic domain of the text is thus a collection of concatenated or embedded possible worlds. This idea of recursive embedding of possible worlds in what I call the textual universe is a recurring theme in the chapters of this book.

While Vaina's paper remains on a purely abstract level, Eco provides a bridge between theory and practice by applying the concept of possible worlds to the reading of a short story by Alphonse Allais, "Un Drame bien parisien." He introduces the idea of an opposition real world/possible world within the plot (*fabula*, in his terminology) of the narrative text. This contrast allows him to study the interplay of narrative facts, characters' representations of these facts, and their beliefs about other characters' beliefs. He also applies the concepts of modal logic to the dynamics of the reading process, by assimilating possible worlds to the inferences and projections built by readers as they move through the text. These possible worlds may be actualized, thrown away, or remain in a virtual state, depending on whether the text verifies, disproves, or leaves undecided the reader's rationalization of the narrative events.

Other landmarks in the possible-world approach to narrative and to fiction include David Lewis's formulation of truth conditions for fictional discourse (1978); Lubomir Doležel's development of a catalog of modal operators including not only possibility and necessity, but other categories more directly relevant to narrative semantics, such as the modalities "good/bad," "prohibited/obligatory," or the epistemic categories "known/unknown" (1976a); Doreen Maître's study of the relations between textual worlds and reality and her classification of fictional genres according to the possibility of their verification in the actual world (1983); and finally Thomas Pavel's multiple and varied contributions, among which I will single out two topics: the exploration of the migration of individuals from one world to another, which invokes Kripke's theory of names to define the conditions of trans-world identity, and the description of the multiple subworlds and conflicting ontologies that make up a cultural landscape (1986). All of these contributions have been essential to the development of the ideas proposed in this book, and in due time many will be presented in greater detail.

Yet for all the recent activity in the area of possible worlds and literature, I feel that most of this work has not gone beyond this rather superficial and inaccurate generalization: fictional texts represent possible worlds, nonfictional ones represent the real world. The first part of this book seeks a more sophisticated application of the theory of possible worlds to the definition of fictionality.

While fiction is a mode of travel into textual space, narrative is a travel within the confines of this space. In the second part of the book, the idea of a semantic domain consisting of a plurality of worlds will be developed into a theory of narrative conflict, and lead to an account of the forward movement of plot.

Artificial intelligence, the second influence on this work, is only beginning to emerge as a source of inspiration for literary theory. As the simulation by computer of mental processes, AI lives largely from imports. The most important contributions in the field are not made by pure computer scientists, but by representatives of other disciplines who use the computer as an instrument of research. To claim allegiance to AI, then, is to put at one's disposal a wide repertory of possible sources: discourse analysis, speech-act theory, cognitive psychology, the theory of graphs, and various types of logic, including predicate calculus, the logic of actions, and the theory of formal languages.

The direct offerings of AI to narratology and to the theory of fiction stem from two areas of research: the cognitive processing of texts, and automatic story generation. Two chapters of this book are directly devoted to these topics. Chapter 10, "The Formal Representation of Plot," examines a problem crucial to the cognitive processing of the narrative text, since understanding a text as narrative involves the extraction of information and its storage in memory in a pattern yet to be elucidated. Chapter 11, "The Heuristics of Automatic Story Generation," presents a survey of work accomplished in this domain, outlining an imaginary (and to some extent not yet programmable) program to take care of the deficiencies of existing proposals.

As a source of ideas, however, AI extends its influence far beyond these two chapters. The potential contributions of AI to literary theory and textual semiotics fall into five categories: a fundamental belief; a lesson in methodology; a set of questions defining a particular approach; a repertory of analytical tools; and a source of analogies.

The fundamental belief is that the creation of meaning is not a mysterious brainstorm caused by a random meeting of circumstances—a unique individual in an ephemeral state of mind, nurtured to some immeasurable extent by a culture whose boundaries remain fuzzy, and bringing to the text a deeply private experience of the world—but the predictable output of definable processes operating on a variable input. Interpretation, writes Jerry Hobbs, is "a mathematical function of two arguments: a text and a set of beliefs" (1988:78). The ambition of AI is to make explicit the function—this is to say, the set of cognitive processes—which, given *this* text and *these* beliefs as arguments, yields a determinate interpretation.

The lesson in methodology derives from the very stupidity of the computer. The inability of the machine to guess the intent of its human partner forces researchers to explicate their assumptions, and unmasks what lies hidden under the cloak of self-evidence. In a story-generating program, for instance, putting a cheese in the mouth of a fox is not sufficient to save him from starvation: the computer must be told that cheese is edible, that the fox has knowledge of this fact, and an inference mechanism must be available to make the fox aware of the location of the cheese. The painstaking task of specifying knowledge that we take for granted leads to an appreciation of the complexity of semantic representations and provides an antidote to the solipsism of literary criticism. When the reader is a computer of limited knowledge, there is no way to mistake one's own interpretation for an exemplary reading—a danger against which reader response criticism has found no protection. While the Model Reader of reader response criticism slavishly fulfills the critic's expectations, the computer is quick to rebel against the will of its master when the master's reasoning presents deficiencies. As programmers are used to say: garbage in, garbage out.

But if the narrow-mindedness of the computer can teach literary critics how to explore and formulate their assumptions, and discourage them from unfounded claims, grandiloquent generalizations, or hasty conclusions, the lesson should not be heeded to the point of becoming stifling. The disadvantage of dealing with machines to which everything must be taught is the necessity of limiting implementations to extremely reduced microenvironments: computers can only work on very short texts composed from a small subset of linguistic structures, and concerning a fixed topic. To the literary critic, much of the work in AI presents a discrepancy between the complexity of its formal apparatus and the triviality of the results. A reasonably sophisticated reading by computer of a complex literary narrative is out of the question for the foreseeable future. The main problem will not be solved by faster computers, parallel machines, or better algorithms, since its resides in the entry of a sufficient database of presupposed knowledge—and the entry of this kind of data proceeds mainly at human speed. Automatizing data entry would require a program able to scan texts and extract information—but this would be the very program whose development forms the goal of text-centered AI. Because of this limitation, the most interesting work in AI is speculative and not actually implemented by computer—almost as speculative, in fact, as literary theory.

Among the concerns of AI, the most profitable for narratology is its insistence on the question: "What does it do?" (The it can be replaced with any kind of semantic or discourse unit.) This question echoes the preoccupation of reader response criticism (Stanley Fish formulated it more than a decade ago), but AI offers concrete steps toward its solution, by translating it into a search for problem-solving schemes. Under the influence of robotics, AI researchers approach the text as a means to perform a certain task:

> The standard view in AI of the agent's procedure for generating utterances and other actions is that it is some sort of planning mechanism. . . . The agent starts with a goal (an intention) and develops, or begins to develop, a plan of action, that is, a decomposition of the goal into subgoals, and these into further subgoals, ultimately yielding a sequence of actions, such as utterance, which is believed will achieve the goal. As the actions are executed, the environment is monitored, and when unanticipated conditions arise, the plan is modified to accommodate them. (Hobbs 1988:82–83)

While the utterance of a text is a verbal act, a narrative text is a report of acts, both verbal and physical. The title of an article by Jerry Hobbs, "Text Plans and World Plans in Natural Discourse" (1981), emphasizes the versatility of the concept of problem-solving: the notions of goals, plans, and moves are not only applicable to the rhetorical structure of the narrative text (what Seymour Chatman calls the level of discourse), but, in a more literal manner, to its semantic content—the level of story. On the discourse level, goals and plans are those of the speaker, but on the semantic level they relate to characters. Narratives are supported by plots, and plots live from characters plotting against each other. As I will try to show in chapter 7, our understanding of the dynamics of narrative action can be greatly enhanced by the work performed in artificial intelligence on the logic of plans and the interaction of competing schemes (Wilensky 1983a, Bruce and Newman 1978).

The analytical tools proposed by AI to narratology and text theory consist of conceptual units and of data structures. The question "what does it do" presupposes a delimitation of the "it" and a catalog of the possible "whats." A good example of segmentation and categorization on the level of discourse is the system proposed by Reichman in *Getting Computers to Talk Like You and Me* (1985). The boundaries of conceptual units are set by clue words, such as "but," "incidentally," "by the way," "but look," and their strategic function is defined in terms of speech act and conversational moves: challenge, support, opening and closing of context, concession of argument, development, statement of point. On the level of story, the search for units and functions continues a tradition that goes back to Propp's *Morphology of the Folktale.*

The most significant and original contribution of AI to narratology is arguably Wendy Lehnert's concept of plot-unit. Briefly defined, plot-units are configurations of narrative events that mediate between the so-called "affect states" of characters: being pleased, being displeased, and striving toward a goal. While the boundaries of plot-units are provided by the three affect states, their function is captured by such conceptual categories as problem resolution, failure, request, promise, threat, coercion, and double-cross. A higher narrative unit, subsuming several of Lehnert's plot-units, is proposed by Michael Dyer (1983) under the name "Thematic Abstraction Unit" (TAU). These higher units illustrate an adage or an idiom which defines their function: hidden blessing, caught red-handed, close call, dire straits. Chapter 10 will explore in greater detail the concept of plot-unit, and assess its significance for the semantic representation of plot.

Data structures are the visual models through which AI organizes and manipulates its conceptual units. Of particular interest to narratology are two types of structure: the tree and the stack. A stack is a data structure built and unbuilt in an order opposite to the formation of queues: whereas in a queue the first to arrive is the first to be served, in a stack the last element added is the first one to be processed. Stacks have been used by AI to model the flow of conversational moves and the shifts between contexts in the realm of discourse (Reichman 1985, Polanyi 1988), but so far they have not been applied to the study of narrative. Chapter 9 explores the stack as an alternative to the traditional metaphors of framing and embedding in visualizing and explaining the phenomenon of boundary-crossing in the textual space. Trees are familiar to literary theorists through Chomsky's generative grammar and the attempts of narratologists such as Prince and Pavel to design a version of the linguistic model adapted to the description of narrative structures. Tree-shaped diagrams will be used in chapter 7 to map the plans of characters, and their value for the semantic representation of plot will be discussed in chapter 10 in conjunction with the concept of story grammar.

Thinking is not only methodical but also intuitive, not only logical but also analogical. Discoveries are made by focusing on certain metaphors and following their ramifications. For years, the leading analogy in literary thinking has been the linguistic one: literature is a language (as well as, metonymically, an artifact made of language); the text is a "system of signs." Involvement with AI and computer science suggests another metaphor: the text as a machine. Or if the text is a language, why not a computer language? This idea is playfully pursued in chapter 9.

Analogies derived from the computer field shape my approach to narrative in more general ways. Computer aficionados share with literary semioticians and avant-garde authors a predilection for puns, trompe-l'oeils, paradoxes, serial constructs, Chinese boxes, permutations, transformations, in short, for any game played with symbols—be they bits, bytes, pixels, numbers, letters, words, or sentences. Many of the formal structures and textual phenomena that fascinate practitioners and theorists of postmodernism have parallels in computer languages, computational theory, or computer architecture. The literary practice of *mise-en-abyme* finds an echo in recursivity, the process by which a computer program activates a copy of itself. Self-reference, the favorite idea of deconstruction, is used in the theory of computation to prove the unsolvability of the so-called "halting problem": designing an automaton which, taking as input a program P and a string i, will tell for any P and any i whether P operating on i will terminate or end in an infinite loop. The proof, inspired by Gödel's famous theorem, consists of turning a program into input data and making this program operate on itself.

An even more fruitful analogy between computers and textual structures resides in the idea of discrete levels and hierarchical organization. In narrative theory, we have the concept of a "pyramid of narration" (Martínez-Bonati, 1981:30), formed by various speakers quoting each other and transporting the reader to a new subworld with each change of narrative voice. In computer architecture, we have the concept of a series of different machines stacked upon each other. The programmer who feeds instructions to the computer in a high-level language, such as LISP, PASCAL, D-BASE, PROLOG, or LOGO, does not communicate with a real machine but with a virtual one. The user's access to the real machine—which understands only binary code—is mediated by a hierarchy of imaginary ones, each speaking its own language and defined by its own set of instructions. The message sent by the user is successively translated into the language of each one of these virtual machines, until it becomes executable by the hardware of the real machine. The idea of hierarchical organization thus leads into the concept of virtuality. And in the emphasis placed throughout this book on virtual constructs—virtual events, virtual narratives, virtual plans—the influence of the theory of possible worlds converges with the inspiration derived from artificial intelligence.

The chapters of this book have been kept largely autonomous, and need not be read in the order suggested in the table of contents. Every reading should, however, begin with chapter 1, where the conceptual framework of the whole book is presented. Chaper 1 introduces a list of abbreviations that are used over and over again and are gathered in a glossary at the beginning of the book. A definition of fiction is proposed in chapter 4, and forms, together with the concepts developed in chapter 1, the prerequisite to chapter 5. Chapters 2 and 3 can be read any time after chapter 1. The reader primarily interested in narrative semantics can skip directly to part 2 after the first chapter—though most of the issues discussed in part 1 are as relevant to narratology as to the theory of fictionality. In part 2, chapters 6 and 7 form the prerequisite to all the others except for chapter 9, which can be read all by itself. It is also helpful to read chapters 8 and 10 before turning to chapter 11.

Earlier versions of some of the chapters of this book appeared in article form, and I am indebted to the following periodicals for permission to reuse the materials: *Poetics* for "Fiction, Non-Factuals, and the Principle of Minimal Departure," which forms the source of chapter 3, for "The Heuristics of Automatic Story Generation," condensed in chapter 11, and for "The Pragmatics of Personal and Impersonal Narration,'' which provides some materials to chapter 4; *Poetics Today* for ''Stacks, Frames, and Boundaries, or Narrative as Computer Language,'' reproduced in chapter 9, for ''The Modal Structure of Narrative Universes,'' upon which chapters 6 and 7 are built, and for ''Possible Worlds and Accessibility Relations,'' a version of chapter 2 of this book; and finally *Style* for ''Embedded Narrative and Tellability,'' expanded as chapter 8, as well as for ''Fiction as a Logical, Ontological, and Illocutionary Issue,'' whose arguments are scattered throughout the first part of the book.

Many people—whether they know it or not—were influential on the completion of this project. To the teaching of Jean Rousset at the University of Geneva I owe my initiation into narratology, and my lasting interest in what wasn't yet known as textual semiotics. For their sustained interest in my work, comments on earlier drafts, challenging discussions, or for planting the seeds of the papers which eventually led to this book, I am indebted to Thomas Pavel, Teun van Dijk, Lubomir Doležel, Uri Margolin, Gerald Prince, Harold F. Mosher, Ross Chambers, Katharine Young, Monika Fludernik, and Sigrid Mayer. For doing their best to pry me away from the word processor I also wish to thank my children Caitlin and Duncan, strong adherents to the referential theory of fiction (it's just a story, Mom, isn't it?), and my husband Philip, whose personal definition of fiction encompasses whatever I write or say.

Part I THE FICTIONAL GAME

1 Fictional Recentering

Fictional, fictive, fictitious: the variety of adjectives derived from the noun "fiction" is matched by the variety of terms proposed as antonyms. If it is not fiction, is it then fact, truth, or simply nonfiction? And if not fictional, fictive, or fictitious, is it natural, serious, real, or historical? The choice of derived adjectives and of antonyms reflects an implicit position on the nature of fiction. Some terms apply to discourse, others to objects, and still others are compatible with both categories. We may speak of fictitious or of real situations; of fictive or historical events; of fictional or real objects; of fictive or natural discourse; of fictional or true stories; of fictive or serious utterances. The semantic classes represented in this series of expressions suggest two possible answers to the question of fictionality: to be fictional is a mode of being, an ontological status specific to certain entities; or a mode of speaking, an intent constitutive of a type of communicative act. A definition of fiction based on the first possibility generates what I shall call a referential theory, while a definition based on the second leads to an intensional theory, involving a phenomenological and illocutionary approach.

The Referential Theory of Fiction

What I mean by referential theory of fiction is the development of a formal definition out of the most common and intuitive use of the term fictional. In everyday language, we call an object or a situation fictional when it does not exist objectively, when it is a creation of the imagination, and we classify a text as fiction when it is primarily concerned with such entities. As antonyms to "fictional," the above definition suggests "real" or "factual." When true of the real world, a statement yields facts; but what does it yield when false? A strict adherence to the referential criterion leads to the answer: false statements yield fiction. But we do not want to accept errors and lies in the realm of fiction. For the referential definition to be tenable, we must find a way to distinguish fiction from errors and lies without invoking the speaker's intent.

 A conceivable solution to this problem invokes the fact that in lies and false statements, the speaker still refers to objectively existing entities. The failure of the propositional act is a matter of predication. A property is incorrectly attributed to an existing object, but the reference to the object is itself successful, since it picks out and makes identifiable to the hearer a specific member of the world. It should then be feasible to distinguish lies and error from fiction, without invoking intent, by adopting a Fregean position on the matter of reference. According to Frege (1892), one of the first philosophers to have considered fiction as a logical issue, a sentence about an imaginary entity does not refer, and this sentence is automatically false (or indeterminate, in a three-value system). Statements about fictional entities could then be excluded from the set of true statements on grounds of referential failure, while errors and lies would illustrate the case of faulty predication.

 Implicit to the Fregean position are three propositions: (1) Reference can only be made to that which exists; (2) "To exist" is synonymous with "to occur in the real world"; and (3) Only one world exists, the world we regard as real. (This last proposition was actually advanced by Russell [1919].) Under these assumptions, deciding whether or not reference is successful means deciding whether or not the entity denoted by a proper name belongs to the inventory of the one and only existing world, whether or not the proposition "[proper name] exists" has extension (= is true) in reality. Most of us would agree that the answer is positive for the names Napoleon, Flaubert, and Marilyn Monroe; negative for Emma Bovary and Little Red Riding Hood, but what about Santa Claus, the monster of Loch Ness, Zeus or Aphrodite? For the child who believes in Santa Claus the name refers to a jolly fellow who brings presents to good children on Christmas Eve, and this story yields facts, but for the adult who tells it to the child the story consists of imaginary events. Hence the question of fictionality would be resolved in a potentially contrasting manner by sender and receiver.

 Through its strict distinction between referring and nonreferring sentences, however, the Fregean position encounters the challenge of mixed uses of language, such as these sentences:

(1) Conan Doyle created Sherlock Holmes.
(2) Susan is like Emma Bovary: she cannot distinguish fiction from reality.

According to the three theses I have mentioned before, the truth value of the propositions expressed by these sentences could never be positive. But obviously, such sentences are used, and used as potentially true. For the literary critic, an even more disturbing consequence of the Fregean position is that it turns any attempt at interpreting fiction into a ludicrous activity. If their lack of referent makes all sentences about Emma Bovary false or indeterminate, it becomes impossible to distinguish—in the words of Felix Martínez-Bonati—"the true statement that she was (or is) married to a small town physician, and the false statement that she was the chaste mother of numerous children" (1981b:26). If there is no logical difference between these two statements, criticism itself cannot be truth-functional, and there is no point in debating the respective merits of conflicting interpretations.

To avoid this dead end, we must abandon the claim that reference to an object presupposes its existence in the actual world. When we use the name "Emma Bovary," we do indeed refer to a specific individual: the two readers who exchange their opinion of Flaubert's heroine have the same object in mind. Remaining within the referential perspective, could we then say that it is the ontological status of the referent, rather than the ability to refer, which spells the difference between fictional and nonfictional language? The thesis of Russell limiting existence to the real world determines what Thomas Pavel (1986) calls a segregationist ontology: there are two types of entities, those that are found in the real world and therefore exist, and those that cannot be found in reality, and are consequently deprived of existence. The second type is inherently fictional, and its presence as textual referent decides the question of fictionality. The segregationist ontology presents errors and lies as false statements about real entities, while it presents fiction as true statements about imaginary beings. But in linking fiction to imaginary beings, it loses the distinction between fiction and literary criticism, which also refers to nonexisting entities. The contrast between the factual statement "Unicorns do not exist in the real world" and the fictional sentence "Once upon a time there was a unicorn" adds further evidence against the view that fiction is simply discourse about imaginary objects. Moreover, while Frege's theory of reference stumbled on the problem of mixed uses of language, the segregationist ontology not only faces the same difficulty, but encounters the additional challenge of ontologically hybrid textual worlds. If objects are inherently fictional or real, how can one explain the presence of historical individuals and real locations in a work of fiction? How can the invented Sherlock Holmes live on the geographically real Baker Street, or the imaginary Natasha of *War and Peace* lose her fiancé in a war against the historical Napoleon? These examples suggest that the attribute of fictionality does not apply to individual entities, but to entire semantic domains: the Napoleon of *War and Peace* is a fictional object because he belongs to a world which as a whole is fictional. How do we decide that this world is fictional? The only answer compatible with the referential approach states that the semantic domain of the text is recognized as fictional when it departs through at least one property from the actual world. As a collection of propositional functions, the text has no extension in the actual world—the actual world does not fulfill its specifications. This argument, however, leads us back to our initial problem. If fiction creates a semantic domain differing on some point from reality, so do errors and lies, and so do the embellishments and exaggerations which are so common in narratives of personal experience. (I take these narratives to be nonfictional.) Since we have in the meantime given up the idea of blocked reference for fictional discourse, its distinction from errors, lies, and embellishments becomes once again dependent on the sender's intent, and we can dismiss the referential theory in favor of a phenomenological approach. The universe of *War and Peace* is fictional not because of its intrinsic properties (such as inventory and history), but because of the gesture through which it came into being, and is offered to the reader.

Following a route pioneered by literary theorists such as Thomas Pavel, Lubomir Doležel, and Umberto Eco, I propose to characterize the fictional gesture in the framework of modal logic and the semantics of possible worlds. This model will offer answers to problems such as the relation between the actual world and the semantic domain of the fictional text, or the possibility of making truth-functional statements about fictional universes. Chapter 4 will complete this characterization by defining in illocutionary/intensional terms the rules constitutive of the fictional gesture.

Possible Worlds

The Leibnizian concept of possible worlds was rediscovered by twentieth-century philosophers as a convenient tool in building a semantic model for the modal operators of necessity (symbolized as $\square$) and of possibility ($\lozenge$). It will be remembered that according to Leibniz, an infinity of possible worlds exist as thoughts in the mind of God. Of all these possible worlds, only one is actual: the best of them all, chosen by the divine mind to be instantiated. This privileged world is the one we live in, what we call reality.

Facing the task of defining truth conditions for sentences such as:

(1a) Napoleon could have won the battle of Waterloo
(2a) Napoleon could not have been Robespierre
(3a) A bachelor cannot be married
(4a) 2 + 2 cannot equal 5

which translate logically as

(1b) $\lozenge$ Napoleon won the battle of Waterloo
(2b) $\square$ Napoleon is not Robespierre
(3b) $\square$ If x is a bachelor, then x is not married
(4b) $\sim\lozenge\ 2 + 2 = 5$, or $\square\sim 2 + 2 = 5$

logicians such as Montague, Hintikka, and Kripke have proposed semantic models shaped like a universe, that is, like a system of worlds. The best known of these models, the propositional modal system or M-model of Saul Kripke, is presented as follows by Michael J. Loux:

> Kripke defines what he calls an M-model structure, telling us that "this is an ordered triple (G,K,R)," where K is a set of objects, G is one of the objects belonging to K, and R is a relation defined over the members of K. Intuitively, Kripke tells us, we are to think of K as the set of all possible

worlds; G is to be thought as the actual world; and R represents a relation which Kripke calls relative possibility and others have called accessibility. (1979:21)

In such a model, the truth value of a proposition is assigned separately for each possible world. For the modal operators of necessity and possibility, Kripke proposes the following rules:

(a) ◇ A is true in W if and only if there is at least one possible world, W', such that W' is accessible to W and A is true in W'.

(b) □ A is true in W if and only if for every world, W', such that W' is accessible to W, A is true in W'.

By assimilating K, G, and R to the set of all possible worlds, to the actual world, and to accessibility relations respectively, Kripke makes the model relevant to the semantics of modal operators. It will take a further concretization of the three key notions to extend this relevance to the problem of fiction. We must now ask: how is a possible world defined? What is its mode of existence? Wherein resides—if we don't accept Leibniz's solution— the difference between the actual world and merely possible ones? What are the various types of accessibility relations?

The relevance of the conceptual apparatus of modal logic to the theory of fiction finds an early expression in Aristotelian poetics: "It is not the poet's business to tell what happened, but the kind of things that would happen—what is possible according to possibility and necessity" (*Poetics* 9,2). "In other words," writes Thomas Pavel about this passage, "the poet must put forward either propositions true in every alternative of the real world (things possible according to necessity), or propositions true in at least one alternative of the actual world (things possible according to probability" (1986:46).

As already noted in the introduction to this book, a converse borrowing of metaphors from the domain of poetics occurs in the work of adherents to the theory of possible worlds. For Alvin Plantinga, to each possible world corresponds a book: "The set of propositions true in a given world W is the book on W. Books, like worlds, have a maximality property: for any proposition p and book B, either B contains p or B contains -p, the denial of p. The book on (a), the actual world, is the set of true propositions" (Loux 1979:259). Robert Merrihew Adams replaces the notion of book with that of story:

Let us say that a world-story is a maximal consistent set of propositions. That is, it is a set which has as its members one member of every pair of mutually contradictory propositions, and which is such that it is possible that all of its members be true together. The actual world differs from the other possible worlds in that all the members of its world-story (the set of all the propositions that are true in it) are true, whereas the stories of all the other possible worlds have false propositions amongst their members. (Loux 1979:204)

While Plantinga's books and Adams's stories offer a rather formal account of the notion of possible worlds, David Lewis argues in favor of their existence by appealing to intuitive beliefs: "It is uncontroversially true that things might be otherwise than they are. I believe, and so do you, that things could have been different in countless ways. I therefore believe in the existence of entities that might be called 'ways things could have been.' I prefer to call them 'possible worlds' " (Loux 1979:182). For Lewis, the existence of possible worlds presents an absolute character. In a position known as "realism about possible worlds," he takes them to be "respectable entities in their own right" (183). This position denies any ontological difference between possible worlds and the actual world:

> Our actual world is only one world among others. We call it alone actual not because it differs in kind from all the rest but because it is the world we inhabit. The inhabitants of other worlds may truly call their own worlds actual, if they mean by actual what we do; for the meaning we give to "actual" is such that it refers at any world *i* to that world *i* itself. "Actual" is indexical, like "I" or "here," or "now": it depends for its reference on the circumstances of utterance, to wit the world where the utterance is located. (184)

In Lewis's indexical theory, every possible world is real, and every possible world can be actual, but these two terms, so often used interchangeably, are not synonymous. "To be actual" means: "to exist in the world from which I speak." Alternative possible worlds (APWs) cannot be actual for me, since I consider them from another planet in the universe of possibilities. I may therefore speak of unactualized possible worlds and of unactualized possibilities. But insofar as they exist absolutely, APWs are real, and every possibility is realized in some world.

An interesting consequence of the position defended by Lewis is that the total universe of possibilities contains an infinity of subuniverses, each organizing its constituent worlds into a different system of reality. If we regard the actual world as the center of a modal system, and APWs as satellites revolving around it, then the global universe can be *recentered* around any of its planets. From the point of view of an APW, what we regard as the actual world becomes an alternative. We can make conjectures about what things would be like if Hitler had won the war; conversely, the inhabitants of the world in which Hitler won the war may wonder what would have happened if the Allies had triumphed—just as they have in actuality.

The indexical theory is a convenient way of distinguishing the actual from the possible, but for many philosophers the loss of the privileged ontological status of the actual world is too high a price to pay. Though it takes its point of departure in an intuitive view of possibility, Lewis's account leads to a counterintuitive view of actuality. Against the view of recentering I have just presented, it can be argued that the relation between the actual world and its alternatives is not reversible. I can think about a world in which Hitler wins the war, but the Hitler of this world cannot, on his own initiative, think about the APW in which he lost the war. The second victorious Hitler is a creation of my imagination, and so is the third, defeated Hitler who I think as thought by the second one. The third Hitler is not identical to the one I regard as actual; he owes his existence to the recursivity, rather than to the reversibility, of the relation of alternativeness. If we travel to an APW, and from there to one of its alternatives, we will never return to the actual world.

The uniqueness of the actual world, as well as the synonymy of the terms actual and real, is restored in Nicholas Rescher's proposal to regard possible worlds not as absolutely existing entities but as constructs of the mind. The facts of the actual world, Rescher maintains, can "unqualifiedly be said to exist" (168). They have "an objective foundation in the existential order" which renders them "independent of minds" (173). The facts of unactualized possible worlds, by contrast, "exist in a relativized manner, as the objects of certain intellectual processes" (168). In the case of actual existence, Rescher observes a dualism:

> There is
>   (1) The actually existing thing or state of affairs (for example, with "that dog have tails" we have tailed dogs) and
>   (2) The thought or entertainment of this thing or state of affairs.
> But with nonexistent possibilities (such as, that dogs have horns) the ontological situation becomes monistic since item (1) is altogether lacking. And this difference is crucial. For, in the dualistic cases of actual existence, (1) would remain even if (2) were done away with. But with nonexistent possibles there are (*ex hypothesi*) no items of category (1) to remain, and so category (2) is determinative. Exactly this is the basis of the ontological mind-dependence of nonexistent possibles. (169)

If possible worlds are constructs of the mind, we can classify them according to the mental process to which they owe their existence. (I use the term "to exist" as applicable to both actual and nonactual entities, without commitment to their reality.) A convenient point of departure for this classification is what James McCawley calls "world-creating predicates" (1981:326): verbs such as to dream, to intend, to believe, to consider, to fantasize, to hypothesize. Various types of possible worlds, with either implicit or explicit predicate, are illustrated in the following sentences:

(1) *Reports of dreams:*
    I dreamed that I had caught a wild horse and named it "Hurricane."
(2) *Hypotheticals (counterfactuals):*
    If Grouchy had arrived before Blücher, Napoleon would have won the battle of Waterloo.
(3) *Projections:*
    There is a real possibility that Oscar will be fired.

(4) *Fantasy:*
Surrounded by the bubbles of her jacuzzi, Syndi imagined herself floating in Gardenia-scented, rainbow-colored clouds.

(5) *Wishes:*
She wished she would never have to leave this garden of delights.

(6) *Intents:*
John plans to study at Blarney University and to become a talk-show host.

(7) *Beliefs, knowledge:*
Until the Renaissance, people thought that the earth was flat.

Among these mental constructs, the objects of the first seven fail Rescher's criterion of actual existence. The mental construct as a whole can thus be regarded as a possible world. The objects of the last type of representation—knowledge and beliefs, to which I shall globally refer as epistemic world—present, however, a problem for Rescher's classification. When knowledge is accurate, it makes sense to postulate an "actually existing state of affairs" and to distinguish it from its mental image. On the other hand, when beliefs are inaccurate, the dualism observed by Rescher disappears: the thought of the states of affairs is alone constitutive of their existence. The objects reflected in epistemic worlds may thus present either actual or possible existence. But the reflecting subject is unaware of the difference: it takes an external point of view to assess the accuracy of a mental representation. From the perspective of the reflecting subject, objects of firm beliefs all have actual existence: I cannot distinguish the real world from my representation of it. The internal perspective classifies epistemic worlds as actual, while the external perspective classifies them as possible. If epistemic worlds are possible worlds in their own right, there will be nearly similar planets in the total universe of possibilities: the actual world, and its potentially accurate (though always incomplete) reflections in the mind of its inhabitants. In a sense, however, epistemic worlds are more than singular possible worlds. We not only form beliefs about reality, we also reflect on the possible worlds created by the mental acts of other individuals, and the universe formed by this plurality of represented worlds is a modal system in its own right.

Insofar as they owe their existence to an act of the mind, the entities found exclusively in possible worlds differ in ontological status from the objects of the actual world. Is this difference limited to the question of origin, or does it extend to the feature of logical completeness? According to logicians, an object x is logically complete if for every property p, the proposition "x has p" is either true or false. David Lewis would answer the question of completeness in the positive for the members of both actual and possible worlds. Logical completeness is arguably an attribute of real objects, and as we have seen, Lewis regards the furniture of possible worlds as no less real than the objects found in the actual world. Through their notions of world-book and world-story, Plantinga and Adams also take the side of completeness. Rescher's position leads him to the opposite solution. An object created by a mental process is specified in its features by this very process. "Thinking up an object" amounts to providing its mental description. But a description, verbal or mental, is always incomplete. When we think up an entity, we only specify a subset of its potential properties. It would take a divine mind to run through the list of all possible features and to think up an object into logical completeness. If such a feat could be achieved, the object would arguably receive the attributes of both reality and actuality. This is the suggestion made by that great dreamer of possible worlds, Jorge Luis Borges, in his short story "The Circular Ruins": "He wanted to dream a man," writes Borges of the hero, "he wanted to dream him with minute integrity and insert him into reality" (1983:46).

Recentering

Of Rescher's and Lewis's contrasting views of the nature of possible worlds, which one is the most promising for a theory of fiction? Rescher's position invites us to regard the universe of a fictional text as a possible world created by a mental act. Like all types of merely possible worlds, fictional worlds lack autonomy, reality, and actuality. This conclusion corroborates our intuition that there is a fundamental ontological difference between a human being like Flaubert, and a creature like Emma Bovary. Flaubert was made of flesh and blood, and was born of a mother. Emma is made of language, and owes her existence to Flaubert's imagination. And while Flaubert possessed the faculty of creating Emma Bovary, Emma is unable to return the favor. The acts of fictional characters are entirely specified by the text, and Flaubert's novel never shows us Emma engaged in the Borgesian activity of trying to invent the mind to whom she owes her existence.

Rescher's position may account for what we know objectively about fictional worlds, but the indexical theory of David Lewis offers a much more accurate explanation of the way we relate to these worlds. Once we become immersed in a fiction, the characters become real for us, and the world they live in momentarily takes the place of the actual world.

The pseudoreality that characters have for the reader of fiction is demonstrated by the natural tendency to empathize with them. Would we hope for an outcome favorable to our favorite characters, would we worry that the villain's schemes might succeed and the hero be defeated, would at least some of us be terrorized by horror stories and moved to tears by romance, if we regarded characters—as structuralists used to do—as mere collections of textually defined features? The ontological ambiguity of literary characters and the discrepancy between what we know about them and how we relate to them is captured in these remarks from a book review by Paul Gray:

> Literary critics and academicians have been insisting for a long time now
> that characters who appear in novels and plays do not exist outside the

words and works that create them. Foolish to wonder whether Rhett ever came back to Scarlett or how many children had Lady Macbeth, lecture the professors. Such killjoys are technically right, of course, but imaginatively out to lunch. One of the principal pleasures of reading stems from the illusion of eavesdropping on unguarded lives, of getting to know people better than they may know themselves. Small wonder that vivid characters seem to go on living after their stories end. (Gray 1989:66)

As for the pseudoactuality of the fictional world, it is demonstrated by the absence of any specific world-creating predicate associated with fictionality. The presence in a sentence of a world-creating operator builds a bridge between the actual world and the alternative possible world represented by the propositions that fall under the scope of the operator. The subject of the world-creating predicate is located in the actual world, and the mental activity described by the verb is a historical event within this world. But the propositions embedded under the predicate yield the facts of the created world. While they mediate between two spheres, world-creating predicates maintain an extraneous perspective on the created world: speaker and hearer contemplate it from the point of view of the actual world. In fiction, by contrast, speaker, hearer, and speech act are relocated within the created world. Nothing indicates a foreign perspective on the sphere focused upon, nothing records its birth in a mental event. The first sentence of Proust's *Remembrance of Things Past*, "For a long time I went to bed early," could be used as well in a genre devoted to the description of real-world events. Formal markers of fictionality admittedly exist, but they operate conventionally rather than logically—through stylistic connotations rather than through literal meaning. The formula "once upon a time" has become such a marker because of its traditional use in fairy tales, not because of its reference to a remote past. The time it points to may be distant, forgotten, legendary, but it remains logically the past of the world in which the speech act takes place. And according to the indexical theory of actuality, speech acts always take place in the actual world for their participants.

For the duration of our immersion in a work of fiction, the realm of possibilities is thus recentered around the sphere which the narrator presents as the actual world. This recentering pushes the reader into a new system of actuality and possibility. As a traveler to this system, the reader of fiction discovers not only a new actual world, but a variety of APWs revolving around it. Just as we manipulate possible worlds through mental operations, so do the inhabitants of fictional universes: their actual world is reflected in their knowledge and beliefs, corrected in their wishes, replaced by a new reality in their dreams and hallucinations. Through counterfactual thinking they reflect on how things might have been, through plans and projections they contemplate things that still have a chance to be, and through the act of making up fictional stories they recenter their universe into what is for them a second-order, and for us a third-order, system of reality.

To account for this organization of semantic substance (whether fictional or not) into an actual world surrounded by the satellites of APWs, I propose the term of textual universe to refer to that which is conjured by the text. What I have so far called "fictional world" can now be paraphrased as the actual world of the textual universe projected by the fictional text.

Make-Believe and the Dual Nature of Fiction

Incompatible though they may seem, Rescher's mentalism and Lewis's indexical actualism both yield valuable insights into the nature of fictional universes. If what we know objectively about these realms conflicts with what we take them to be when we fall under their spell, then a valid theory of fiction should account for the discrepancy between belief and behavior, rather than deciding in favor of either one of these two perspectives. An elegant solution to this dilemma is Kendall Walton's assimilation of fiction to a game of make-believe (1978 a and b). When children engage in make-believe, they agree on a certain number of rules of substitution. These rules are instituted through an operator indicating pretense: "Let's pretend these buckets full of sand are cakes, and the flowers on them are the frosting, and I am the saleslady, and you are the customer, and these seashells are money." In fiction the rule simply states: "Let's pretend the facts told by the narrator are true, and the world he describes is the actual world." (This rule will need to be refined, in order to take into account the possibility of unreliable narration.) As long as the world-creating predicate "let's pretend" is used, the children maintain an extraneous perspective on the world of the game. As soon as they begin to play, the operator is dropped. "Here is a delicious cake," the saleslady will say. In make-believe as in fiction, stepping into the game means erasing the linguistic signs of its status as game. Even though they *know* that the bucket is full of sand, and that it is covered with flower petals, the children act *as if* the sand were dough, and the petals were sugar frosting. Similarly in fiction: we know that the textual universe, as a whole, is an imaginary alternative to our system of reality; but for the duration of the game, as we step into it, we behave as if the actual world of the textual universe were *the* actual world. As inhabitants of the one and only actual world, we realize that the textual universe is created by the text, but as players of the fictional game, we agree to regard it as preexisting to it, as being merely reflected in the narrator's declarations. Contemplated from without, the textual universe is populated by characters whose properties are those and only those specified by the text; contemplated from within, it is populated by ontologically complete human beings who would have existed and experienced certain events even if nobody had undertaken the task of telling their story. Through its double perspective on the textual universe, the make-believe approach to fiction reconciles our intuitive belief in the unique character of the actual world and in the privileged character of our point of view with our willingness to suspend the disbeliefs entailed by this belief. There is only one *actually* actual world, but there is an infinity of potentially *pretended* actual worlds. And if only the inhabitants of the actual actual world can say "I am real," and speak the truth absolutely, fictional characters can nevertheless say "I am real," and speak the truth for their own world.

The idea of a plurality of systems of reality makes it possible to use the notions of actual and possible world in the characterization of fiction without resorting to this tempting but fallacious generalization: nonfictional texts describe the actual world; fictional ones describe alternative possible worlds. This generalization is confounded by the presence of an actual world in the universe of fictional texts, and the presence of possible worlds in the universe of nonfictional ones. Because of the common modal structure of most textual universes,[1] both fictional and nonfictional discourse may contain factual statements, referring to the actual world of the system, and nonfactual ones, representing its alternatives. In a nonfactual statement, the speaker describes an APW from an external point of view, while in fiction, the writer relocates to what is for us a mere possible world, and makes it the center of an alternative system of reality. If this recentering is indeed the gesture constitutive of fiction, the above generalization can be replaced by the following: nonfictional texts describe a system of reality whose center is occupied by the actually actual world; fictional ones refer to a system whose actual world is from an absolute point of view an APW.

Recentering and Discourse Typology

The concept of fictional recentering presupposes a distinction between three modal systems, centered around three distinct actual worlds. The first is our native system, and its central world is the actually actual world (or more simply, the actual world), to which I shall henceforth refer as AW. The second system is the textual universe, the sum of the worlds projected by the text. At the center of this system is the textual actual world, abbreviated as TAW. As a representation proposed by the text, the textual universe must be distinguished from the system it represents, which I shall call the referential universe. And just as the textual universe is offered as an image of the referential universe, the textual actual world TAW is proposed as an accurate representation of an entity external to itself, the textual reference world, abbreviated as TRW. The following axioms concerning the three types of actual world provide the basis for a possible-world definition of fictionality:

(1) There is only one AW.
(2) The sender (author) of a text is always located in AW.
(3) Every text projects a universe. At the center of this universe is TAW.

(4) TAW is offered as the accurate image of a world TRW, which is assumed (really or in make-believe) to exist independently of TAW.

(5) Every text has an implied speaker (defined as the individual who fulfills the felicity conditions of the textual speech acts.) The implied speaker of the text is always located in TRW.

The three types of actual world open the possibility of three types of divorce. TAW may either reflect accurately or misrepresent AW. The text may either be presented as a representation of AW, or as the image of an APW made actual through a recentering (TRW <> AW) (see Glossary for relational symbols). And finally, TAW may be either compatible or incompatible with TRW, the world it is supposed to represent. The above distinction between an actual sender (AS) and an implied speaker (IS) opens a fourth possible divorce: either the sender stands behind the implied speaker and accepts responsibility for the claims, or their respective beliefs differ, and the actual sender establishes distance, either privately or publicly, from the implied speaker.

The four distinctions just outlined generate the table shown in figure 1 for the classification of mimetic discourse. Under this label of *mimetic discourse* I understand utterance acts fulfilling the following conditions:[2]

(1) A mimetic utterance act makes singular existential claims ("there is an x," rather than "for all x");

(2) It describes particular facts and individuated entites;

(3) It is proposed (really or in make-believe) as a version of a world existing independently of the discourse that describes it;

(4) It is meant to be valued as either true or false in this world.

The semantic value of the equal sign is not the same for all columns of figure 1. Insofar as TAW is a textual representation of a world external to itself—a "version of a world," Nelson Goodman (1978) would say—a + in the first and third column means similarity or compatibility between the two members of the equation. In the second column, the interpretation of the + sign is strict identity: TRW = AW when the speaker means to describe AW. And finally, a + in the fourth column means solidarity between speakers, while − means distantiation. The interpretation of this distantiation differs, depending on whether or not it occurs in conjunction with a recentering. Coupled with a + in the second column (i.e., in the absence of recentering), a − in the fourth column means that the distantiation is hidden to the hearer, while coupled with a − it expresses an overt act of role-playing.

Of the sixteen possible combinations of values, only six—or possibly seven—are represented. Eight are eliminated for logico-semantic reasons. Four of the exclusions are due to the fact that if the second feature receives a positive value, then by the law of associativity the first and third must share the same value: if TRW is strictly identical to AW, then the symbols AW and

TRW are interchangeable, and assigning different values to the first and third column would lead to a contradiction. This constraint eliminates combinations $-+++$, $++-+$, $++--$ and $-++-$. (Note that a $+$ in the first or third column does not trigger the same constraint, since in these cases $+$ means similarity and not identity of worlds.) Two other combinations are eliminated by the definitions stated in axioms (2) and (5). If AW differs from TRW, then the implied speaker must be distantiated from the actual speaker, since one resides in AW, and the other in TRW. This principle eliminates combinations $+-++$, $+--+$, $--++$, and $---+$, two of which are also eliminated by the other constraint. Finally, the combinations comprising a $-$ in the second and third column are eliminated for pragmatic reasons to which I shall return below.

The first combination expresses the unmarked case of sincere and truthful mimetic discourse. Senders present the text as a representation of the actual world, and this actual world, which functions as world of reference, is correctly represented.

Error differs from the unmarked case through the divorce between the facts of AW/TRW and their textual representation. Since senders are unaware of this divorce, they share the beliefs of the implied speaker.

The difference between errors and lies resides in the duplicity of the sender, expressed by a $-$ in the fourth column. Senders are aware of the conflict between the facts of AW and their representation, but they keep the conflict hidden, covertly playing the role of the implied speaker.

Through misinformation, a would-be liar could inadvertently propose an accurate representation of reality. A $+$ in the first column distinguishes these accidentally true lies from the regular false ones.

Fiction is characterized by the open gesture of recentering, through which an APW is placed at the center of the conceptual universe. This APW becomes the world of reference. The world-image produced by the text differs from AW, but it reflects accurately its own world of reference TRW, since TRW does not exist independently of its representation. TAW thus becomes indistinguishable from its own referent. This phenomenon—which makes the concepts TAW and TRW largely interchangeable when discussing fiction—explains the fashionable doctrine of the self-referentiality of the literary text.[3] The $-$ in the fourth column is due to the fact that the relocation of senders into a new actual world necessitates the sacrifice of their identity. To become citizens of the recentered system they step into the role of narrator, and to gain an audience they extend to receivers an invitation to follow them in their relocation. The "fictional pact" is concluded when hearers (readers) become in make-believe temporary members of the recentered system, thus shifting their attention from AW to TAW/TRW.

As target of their relocation, senders of fictional texts could select a world similar to the actual world in nearly all respects—similar, but not identical. The result is true fiction, a genre commonly defined as the reporting of historical facts through techniques normally associated with narrative fiction (more about this genre in the next chapter). True fiction tends toward the situation of a TAW/TRW similar to AW, but senders decline responsibility for any accuracy-in-AW of TAW by refusing the identification of TRW to AW, thus distantiating themselves from the narrator who resides in TRW.

To the extent that in fiction TRW collapses with TAW, a − in the second column ("recentering") precludes a − in the third. This eliminates the two combinations not yet discussed: + − − −, and − − − −. Due to an ambiguity inherent in the concept of TAW, however, there is a sense in which the four − could be represented. The concept of TAW can be interpreted in two ways: it could mean either that which the text as a whole describes as actual; or that which the narrator presents as such. In the first case, TAW must be distinguished from NAW—the narrator's declarations, outlining a version of TRW. In the second, TAW and NAW are one and the same construct. The case of unreliable narration demonstrates the possibility of a lack of coincidence between NAW and TRW. In unreliable narration, the authority of the narrator is undermined by internal contradictions, and the reconstruction of the facts of TRW necessitates the rejection or the correction of some narratorial declarations. Assimilating TAW to the narrator's declarations would lead to a combination of four − for unreliable narration. But it could be argued that in unreliable narration, the narrator's version of TRW is invalidated by a text-internal logic. Now if TAW is "that which the text presents as actual," it is constituted by this internal logic, which overrides the narrator's declarations. In this case, TAW differs potentially from NAW, and unreliable narration receives a + in the third column, just like the regular case of authoritative fictional narration. Or rather, unreliable narration is represented as the combination characteristic of lie or error *within the domain of the implied speaker's discourse*. An effect of the fictional recentering is indeed the creation of a recursive structure. The matrix of features of figure 1 is assigned from the point of view of the actual sender. When the sender in AW steps into the role of the narrator and selects a new actual world, the utterance act of this narrator must be analyzed for the new system of reality. Within this system, the narrator can produce accurate representations, lies, errors, or fiction.

If TAW is regarded as potentially distinct from the narrator's declarations, the only possible realization of the combination with four negative values would be through a radical lack of narratorial authority. In some modern novels, such as *The Unnameable* by Samuel Beckett or *La Place de l'étoile* by Patrick Modiano, the narrator's discourse is perceived as pure rambling, and the facts of TRW become totally inaccessible. Since the truth-value in TRW of the narrator's declaration is undecidable, there is

	TAW=AW	AW=TRW	TAW=TRW	AS=IS
Nonfictional accurate discourse	+	+	+	+
Errors	−	+	−	+
Lies	−	+	−	−
Accidentally true lies	+	+	+	−
Standard fiction	−	−	+	−
True fiction	+	−	+	−
Unreliable narration in fiction	−	−	−	−

AW=Actual world   AS=Actual speaker
TAW=Textual actual world   IS=Implied speaker
TRW=Textual reference world

Figure 1
A typology of mimetic discourse

no text-internal logic which delineates a textual actual world. In the absence of a TAW, this type of text could receive by default a − in the third column.[4]

By characterizing nonfiction as referring to AW, and fiction as referring to a TRW indistinguishable from TAW, the present proposal may appear to revert to the referential account which was rejected earlier in this chapter. But there is an important difference between the two views of reference. In the so-called referential theory of fiction, reference was conceived as an intrinsic property of words, independent of the speaker's intent: some expressions "have reference in AW" and some others do not. "Having reference in a world" meant "having extension in that world," a phrase philosophers define as "expressing a propositional function that is true of an object in that world." (To fit into this account, proper names have to be regarded as propositional functions asserting existence; "Santa Claus" has no extension in AW because "There is an x named Santa Claus" is false in AW.) According to the rejected proposal, if sentences have no extension in AW, the text is fictional, and fiction cannot not be distinguished from other types of inaccurate representation. While the old proposal regards reference as synonymous with extension, the new proposal regards reference as an act. Reference is now conceived in intensional terms, as the gesture of selecting a world and making propositional acts about this world. A proposition may refer to a world without necessarily being true in this world. Lies and errors refer to AW, just as accurate discourse does. And conversely, a proposition may be true in a world even though it does not refer to it: the sentence of *War and Peace* "On the twenty-ninth of May [1812] Napoleon left Dresden" is verified in AW, but its reference world is the world of *War and Peace.*

One may wonder how the system represented in figure 1 would characterize the type of discourse I have described as nonfictional nonfactual: counterfactuals, descriptions of dreams, or summaries of literary works in which the narrative text is implicitly or explicitly modified by the prefix "in text t, p." Insofar as it evokes an APW from the perspective of AW, nonfactual discourse remains referentially rooted in AW. It evokes an alternate possible world in its quality of satellite, emphasizing its otherness rather than putting this world in the place of AW. When I narrate a dream or summarize a novel, I state a truth valid in the actual world: the existence of a mental act whose content is that of the dream or the novel. Similarly, counterfactual statements are used to express truths about AW (provided they are not expressed in a fictional context). Nonfactual discourse thus differs from factual discourse through the world it evokes, but it maintains the same world of reference, and is described on figure 1 through the same matrix of values. The distinction of factual and nonfactual discourse would require an additional feature, specifying whether or not discourse remains focused on the world in which it is valued.

Discourse Types and Possible Worlds: A Summary

The logical differences between the various types of discourse discussed in this chapter are graphically represented in figure 2. Discourse can be classified according to whether it focuses on the center of a speaker's system of reality (factual, a) or on a world at the periphery (world-creating, all other cases). Within world-creating utterances, a distinction can be drawn between discourse describing peripheral worlds from the point of view of the center (nonfactual, b) and discourse involving a relocation of the speaker and a consequent recentering of reality (c, d, and e). Once the leap to a new system has been taken, the same repertory of moves becomes recursively available. The relocated speaker of a fiction may utter factual statements (c), fictional nonfactuals (d), or fiction within fiction (e), as either the main narrator or one of the characters (small figure in the diagram) jumps the ontological boundary into yet another system of reality.

Factual discourse   **World-creating discourse**

A: Factual discourse

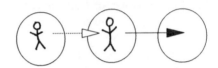

C: Fiction (fictional
factual discourse)

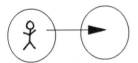

B: Nonfactual discourse

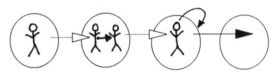

D: Fictional nonfactual discourse

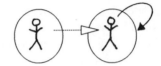

Speaks about

Impersonates

E: Fictional fiction

Figure 2
The relation of speaker to described world
in factual and world-creating discourse

2 Possible Worlds and Accessibility Relations: A Semantic Typology of Fiction

The use of the concept of possible worlds to describe the spheres of a fictional system of reality calls for an inquiry into the nature of possibility. Since there are no limits to the human imagination (or rather, since the human imagination cannot conceive itself as limited), in a fictional universe everything can happen, whether at the center or at the periphery. One may then be tempted to conclude that there is no such thing as an impossible world. If this is the case, what sense does it make to invoke the concept of possibility? To avoid a trivialization of the terminology of modal logic, we must address the question of what makes a world possible by exploring the various types of accessibility relations through which APWs can be linked to the actual world AW. This chapter will develop the concept of accessibility relations into a system of semantic classification that should offer a basis for a theory of genre.

Accessibility Relations

According to Kripke, possibility is synonymous with accessibility: a world is possible in a system of reality if it is accessible from the world at the center of the system.

When philosophers speak of possible worlds, they usually interpret the accessibility relation as a logical one. A world is possible if it satisfies the logical laws of noncontradiction and of excluded middle:

(p or ~p AND NOT (p AND ~p)
(A proposition must be true or false, and not both at the same time)

According to the strictly logical definition of possibility, a world in which Napoleon dies on St. Helena and successfully escapes to New Orleans is not possible, since it entails "Napoleon did and did not die on St. Helena." But there is nothing inconsistent about either one of these facts taken individually, and both are verified in some logically possible world (the second in a drama by the German expressionist playwright Georg Kayser). It can be argued that under a logical interpretation of possibility, the only necessary propositions are mathematical truths ("two plus two makes four") and analytical statements ("bachelors are unmarried").

It is obvious, however, that the logical interpretation of accessibility relation is not sufficient for a theory of fictional genres. Texts such as nonsense rhymes, surrealistic poems, the theater of the absurd, or postmodernist fiction may liberate their universe from the principle of noncontradiction. If we want to avoid the embarrassment of speaking about the impossible possible worlds of fiction, we must accept a much wider range of accessibility relations. Some of these will be looser than the logical laws, others more constrained: in historical novels, for instance, TAW entertains much closer relations to AW than logical compatibility. These closer relations determine the semantic difference between the genre of the historical novel and other types of texts obeying the law of noncontradiction, such as fairy tales and science fiction.

Since a text projects a complete universe, not just an isolated planet, two domains of transworld relations should be distinguished: (1) the transuniverse domain of the relations linking AW to TAW, and (2) the intrauniverse domain of the relations linking TAW to its own alternatives (TAPWs). The relations of the first domain determine the degree of resemblance between the textual system and our own system of reality, while the relations of the second determine the internal configuration of the textual universe. Or to put it another way: transuniverse relations function as the airline through which the participants in the fictional game reach the world at the center of the textual universe, while intrauniverse relations make it possible for the members of TAW to travel mentally within their own system of reality. In the following discussion I will mainly focus on the relations AW/TAW, but the conceptual repertory that describes transuniverse relations also finds applications in the intrauniverse domain.

In decreasing order of stringency, the relevant types of accessibility relations from AW involved in the construction of TAW include the following:

(A) *Identity of properties* (abbreviated A/properties): TAW is accessible from AW if the objects common to TAW and AW have the same properties.

(B) *Identity of inventory* (B/same inventory): TAW is accessible from AW if TAW and AW are furnished by the same objects.

(C) *Compatibility of inventory* (C/expanded inventory): TAW is accessible from AW if TAW's inventory includes all the members of AW, as well as some native members.[1]

(D) *Chronological compatibility* (D/chronology): TAW is accessible from AW if it takes no temporal relocation for a member of AW to contemplate the entire history of TAW. (This condition means that TAW is not older than AW, i.e., that its present is not posterior in absolute time to AW's present. We can contemplate facts of the past from the viewpoint of the present, but since the future holds no facts, only projections, it takes a relocation beyond the time of their occurrence to regard as facts events located in the future.)

(E) *Physical compatibility* (E/natural laws): TAW is accessible from AW if they share natural laws.

(F) *Taxonomic compatibility* (F/taxonomy): TAW is accessible from AW if both worlds contain the same species, and the species are characterized by the same properties. Within F, it may be useful to distinguish a narrower version F′ stipulating that TAW must contain not only the same inventory of natural species, but also the same types of manufactured objects as found in AW up to the present.

(G) *Logical compatibility* (G/logic): TAW is accessible from AW if both worlds respect the principles of noncontradiction and of excluded middle.

(H) *Analytical compatibility* (H/analytical): TAW is accessible from AW if they share analytical truths, i.e., if objects designated by the same words have the same essential properties.

(I) *Linguistic compatibility* (I/linguistic): TAW is accessible from AW if the language in which TAW is described can be understood in AW.

A combination of relations A/properties and B/same inventory (which between themselves entail all other relations) makes the textual universe similar on all counts to our own system of reality (see figure 3 for a summary of the following discussion).[2] Absolute compatibility with reality is of course the ideal of nonfictional texts presented for the sake of information, such as works of history, journalism, and biography. If the receivers decide that the sender's intent is informational, and that relations A and B obtain, they will complete their representation of reality on the basis of the new information they gather from the text. The invitation to use the text in such a way is what makes AW the referent of TAW.

Can principles A/properties and B/same inventory hold in fiction as well? This would imply that the sender of the text recenters the system of reality around a world which is on all points similar to AW. This seems not only pointless but also impossible. Fictional universes always differ through at least one property from our own system of reality: even if the sender of the fictional text recenters the textual universe around a world TRW in which everything is supposed to be exactly the way it is in AW, TRW differs from AW in that the intent and act of producing a fiction is a fact of AW but not of TRW. (Similarly, when children pretend that everything is the way it is, the real world differs from the world of make-believe through the presence of children playing that very game.)

On all points other than its own existence as fiction, however, a fictional text may offer an exact reproduction of reality. Novelists are aware of the possibility when they warn the reader that all resemblance to actual individuals and events should be regarded as entirely coincidental. But as the increasing popularity of what has been called "true fiction" indicates, a fictional universe may be deliberately conceived and presented as an accurate image of reality. The difference between nonfiction and true fiction is that the former claims to represent reality itself (TRW = AW), while the latter represents a world TRW distinct from but very similar to AW. True

	A	B	C	D	E	F/F'	G	H	I
Accurate nonfiction	+	+	+	+	+	+	+	+	+
True fiction	+	+	+	+	+	+	+	+	+
Realistic & historical fiction	+	−	+	+	+	+	+	+	+
Historical fabulation	−	−	+	+	+	+	+	+	+
Realistic fiction in "no-man's land"	−	−	−	+	+	+	+	+	+
Anticipation	+	−	+	−	+	+	+	+	+
Science fiction	+/*	−	+/−	−	+	F + F'−	+	+	+
Fairy tale	*	−	−	+	−	−	+	+	+
Legend	−	−	+	+	−	−	+	+	+
Fantastic realism	+/*	−	+/−	+	−	+	+	+	+
Nonsense rhymes	*/−	−	−/+	#	−	−/+	−	+/−	+
Jabberwockism	*	−	−	#	−	−	?	+	−$
Sound poetry	*	−	−	#	−	−	−	−	−

*: non-applicable because of a − on C
#: non-applicable because of a − or ? on G
−$: incompatibility restricted to most nouns and verbs

A = identity of properties
B = identity of inventory
C = compatibility of inventory
D = chronological compatibility
E = physical compatibility
F = taxonomic compatibility
   (natural species only)

F' = taxonomic compatibility
   (for both natural species
   and manufactured objects)
G = logical compatibility
H = analytical compatibility
I = linguistic compatibility

Figure 3
Genre and accessibility relations

fiction includes such mimetic practices as dramatized history, romanced biographies, and what has paradoxically come to be known as "nonfiction novels," i.e., stories about true facts that use the techniques of narrative fiction. (The best-known example of this genre is Truman Capote's *In Cold Blood*.) True fiction exploits the informational gaps in our knowledge of reality by filling them in with unverified but credible facts for which the author takes no responsibility (as would be the case in historiography). The textual world is epistemically accessible from the real world, insofar as everything we know about reality can be integrated into it. In a romanced life, for instance, the narration respects all available historical information about the hero, but it completes this information with undocumented dialogues and reports of private thoughts which could conceivably have occurred as described. In a nonfictional text, these details would have to be presented in a hypothetical mode, as true of some set of possible worlds to which the real world may or may not belong. The point of presenting the text as a fiction is that unverifiable facts can be directly asserted for TAW without being asserted for AW, and therefore without compromising the credibility of the author.

While the undocumented facts of romanced lives, dramatized history, and nonfiction novels exclude a strict application of principle A/properties, we find a much closer adherence to it, at the expense of B/same inventory, in the journalistic practice exemplified by the Ralph and Wanda dialogues of *Time* magazine. (Ralph and Wanda are an imaginary couple who report and discuss the latest theories of sexual behavior.) Other examples of this genre of true fiction: Plato's dialogues, and Rousseau's Prosopopée de Fabricius in *Discours sur les lettres et les arts*. In these texts all the facts are (ideally) verified, but the speech act through which they are presented is imaginary, either because the speakers do not belong to the inventory of AW (Ralph and Wanda), or because they never actually uttered the words attributed to them (Socrates, Fabricius). Since the speech act is imaginary, these texts are not uttered from within AW, but involve the relocation constitutive of fictionality.

If we relax A/properties, but maintain B/same inventory, we get imaginary stories about real people. An example of this category is (arguably) the legend of George Washington and the cherry tree. In the nonfictional domain, this combination of accessibility relations is exemplified by the stories of tabloids: "President Truman inspected UFO crash in 1947."

A converse case is presented by realistic and historical novels, such as *War and Peace*, the stories of Sherlock Holmes, or *The French Lieutenant's Woman*: A/properties is maintained as far as logically possible, but B/same inventory is replaced by C/expanded inventory. TAW contains some individuals who have no counterpart in AW (Natasha, Sherlock Holmes, Sarah Woodruff), but presents otherwise the same inventory and the same geography as AW at the same point in time. The properties of the common members are the same for both worlds: the London of Sherlock Holmes is the capital of England, and the names of its streets are identical to those of the real London. The Napoleon of *War and Peace* was born in Corsica in 1769, the son of Charles Bonaparte and Laetitia Ramolino, and he has (had) twelve brothers and sisters. These facts may not be directly relevant to the plot of the novel, but they play an oblique role in assessing the truth value of interpretations, since all valid statements about the textual universe must be compatible with them. When A/properties and C/expanded inventory are respected, the only differences between the members of AW and their counterparts in TAW reside in their interaction with the members native to TAW: the London of Sherlock Holmes has the property of having a resident named Sherlock Holmes; the real London of the end of the nineteenth century does not. Logically speaking, A and C make AW a subset of TAW: all the propositions true in AW are also true in TAW, but the propositions concerning individuals specific to TAW are indeterminate in AW (or false, in a two-value system).

In a genre one might call historical fabulation, A/properties is much more openly transgressed than in the preceding class. Once again, the inventory of TAW includes the inventory of AW, but the properties of the common members differ in ways not necessarily connected with their involvement with noncommon members: Napoleon escapes to New Orleans, Hitler wins the war, and Anne of Austria foolishly gives to her lover, the Duke of Buckingham, the jewelry she received as a present from her husband King Louis XIII. In this situation, some proposition will be true in TAW and false in AW even under a three-value system.

When C/expanded inventory no longer holds, but from D/chronological on all other relations still do, TAW is located in a geographic and historical no-man's-land. The laws of nature are in force, and TAW is populated by the same kinds of objects as AW, but the representatives of the classes are different individuals. None of the proper names in use in AW have reference in TAW. This rather unusual combination of relations creates the eerie atmosphere of the taxonomically ordinary yet absolutely foreign world of Kafka's novels *The Trial* and *The Castle*.

Severing relation D/chronology results in either anticipation or science fiction, depending on which other relations are maintained. The point of anticipation novels is to show what may become of the actual world given its present state and past history. For the demonstration to be convincing, all relations other than B/same inventory and D/chronology must be in force. (B in fact could be maintained.) The London of Orwell's *1984* once had a King named George VI, a prime minister named Churchill, and was involved in a war against Hitler. From today's point of view, however, lifting rule D is no longer necessary to contemplate a world dated 1984. Strictly speaking, *1984* is no longer anticipation, but a strange breed of imaginary history. The history of England follows a common course in AW and TAW up to 1950, then branches toward Margaret Thatcher in one world, and Big Brother in the other. Margaret Thatcher does not exist in the TAW of *1984*, and neither does any inhabitant of the post-1950 AW. For the contemporary reader, the novel illustrates the rare case of an intersection between AW's and TAW's population. But from Orwell's point of view AW's population was a subset of TAW's. The novel was composed around 1950, approximately the time of the historical split, and it does not explicitly eliminate any historical character known at the time of the writing.

In science fiction proper, the focus is on the changes brought about by technological advances. Since technology must respect mathematical and natural laws, relations E/natural laws, F/taxonomic, G/logical, H/analytical, and I/linguistic will be maintained, but all others may be severed. The trademark of the genre is its respect for the wide version of F but its transgression of the narrow version F'. TAW typically contains the same natural species as

AW, but different manufactured objects and different individuals. An interesting problem occurs when technological advances lead to interplanetary travel. In this case, the taxonomic repertory of the planet earth remains that of the earth of AW, but the other planets may contain extraterrestrial beings. These planets are also part of the actual world of the textual universe: modal logic uses the term "world" metaphorically, and metaphorical worlds may encompass a plurality of literal worlds. (If they could not, AW would be limited to the earth, and the sun and the moon would be deprived of actuality.) When interplanetary travel achieved through technological means leads to the discovery of extraterrestrial beings in TAW, F/taxonomic is no longer in force, though TAW and AW still observe the same physical laws. Alternatively, space travel could lead to planets where the laws of physics no longer hold. This would be a case of split ontology, to be discussed below.

An opposite divorce of E/natural laws and F/taxonomy is found in the realistic fantasy of Kafka's *Metamorphosis*, or Marcel Aymé's *Le Passe-Muraille*. In these works, TAW is populated by the same species as AW, yet the laws of nature are broken. The heroes are not knights, dragons, and princesses, but ordinary people engaged in the familiar pursuits of everyday life. Yet these ordinary people can walk across walls, or discover one morning, without excessive surprise, that they have been metamorphosed into an equally ordinary species of repulsive insect.

A very productive situation in textual matters is a TAW linked to AW by only G/logical, H/analytical, and I/linguistic, and optionally D/chronological. Lifting F/taxonomy introduces fairies, ghosts, dragons, unicorns, and witches into the textual world, while lifting E/natural laws makes it possible for animals to talk, people to fly, and princes to be turned into frogs. When D/chronology is still in force, TAW is located in some mythical past, and its taxonomic similarity with AW will be limited to the classes of objects characteristic of preindustrial societies: cottages rather than condominiums, swords rather than guns, and horses as a primary mode of transportation. If D is lifted as well, TAW will include computers and time-travel, robots and interplanetary vessels, and its heroes will be Spider Man and Wonder Woman rather than knights and princesses. When E/natural laws and F/taxonomy are lifted, so is usually C/expanded inventory: fairy tales have their own geography and population. An exception to this is the genre legend ("How Paul Bunyan Created the Grand Canyon"): supernatural beings roam through TAW, and miracles are common occurrences, but the main characters or locations have counterparts in AW. A similar inclusion of the geography and population of AW is found in some fantastic tales such as *Frankenstein*, whose hero was born (as well as mentally conceived) in Geneva.

Emancipation from relation G/logical opens the gates to the realm of nonsense. As Susan Stewart (1978) observes, nonsense is characterized by its rejection of the logical law of noncontradiction. P and ~p can be true, not just in separate worlds of the textual universe, but in its actual world as well.

Transgressions of G occur not only in folklore forms such as children's rhymes, but also in so-called postmodernist fiction (McHale 1987). When we read in Robert Pinget's *Le Libera* that a certain character is dead, and thirty pages later that he is alive, the contradiction is not meant to be resolved by assigning the second assertion to an earlier point in time. The character is simultaneously dead and alive in TAW. This radical break with the laws of logic should be distinguished from the much more common textual practice of presenting contradictory statements as possibilities, without introducing contradiction within the boundaries of TAW. An example of a logic-preserving use of contradiction is the following rhyme:

> A bottle of pop, a big banana
> We're from Southern Louisiana
> That's a lie, that's a fib
> We're from Colorado. (Quoted in Stewart 1978:72)

Here the speakers are not simultaneously from Colorado and Louisiana, but from Colorado in one possible world, and from Louisiana in another. The text makes it impossible to decide between the two alternatives (for there is no reason to believe that the first statement is really a lie), and a blank world is left at the center of the textual universe.

Other types of nonsense are produced by transgressions of H/analytical. Some texts are based on a systematic denial of some of the essential properties that define a concept. Consider this French rhyme:

> Un jeune vieillard, assis sur une pierre en bois
> Lisait son journal plié dans sa poche
> A la lueur d'un réverbère éteint.

> (A young old man, sitting on a wooden stone, was reading a newspaper folded in his pocket, under the light of a street light which had been turned off.)

This text cancels the property "old" from *vieillard*, the property "mineral" from *pierre*, and the property "dark" from *réverbère éteint*. Each of these canceled properties belongs to the definition of the word. But other definitional properties are left untouched: under *vieillard* we still understand a human being, rather than a machine, under *pierre* a solid object rather than a fluid. A complete transgression of H/analytical would lead to an obliteration of I/linguistic: if the entity named "horse" could have all the properties of a computer in TAW, AW and TAW would not follow the same linguistic conventions, and TAW would remain as inaccessible to the reader as the universe of a text in a foreign language. Linguistic incompatibility can also result from a lack of overlap in the taxonomic repertory of AW and TAW. If the species of TAW differ radically from those of AW, their names will be deprived of semantic content, unless the text offers its own lexical definitions. Taken as a self-sufficient entity, Lewis Carroll's poem "Jabberwocky" illustrates this type of obscurity:

> Twas brillig, and the slithy toves
> Did gyre and gimble in the wabe
> All mimsy were the borogroves
> And the mome raths outgrabe. (Carroll 1975:130)

Replaced in the wider context of *Through the Looking Glass*, however, the poem becomes linguistically accessible through Humpty Dumpty's translations: brillig means "four o'clock in the afternoon," "slithy" means "lithe and slimy," and toves are "something like lizards, something like badgers, and something like corkscrews" (Carroll 1975:187). While "Jabberwocky" retains some taxonomic/linguistic overlap with AW (there are jaws and claws and swords in this world, and they have presumably the same properties as what we call jaws and claws and swords in AW), all connections are severed in this sound poem by Hugo Ball (quoted by Stewart 1978:92):

> gadjiberi bimba glandridi lonni cadori
> gadjaina gramma beriba bimbala glandri galassassa
> laulitalomini
> gadji beri bin glassa glassala laula lonni cadorsi
> sassala bim
> Gadjama tuffm i zimzalla binban gligia wowolimai bin
> beri ban

With the last linguistic connection to AW vanishes the possibility of knowing and saying anything about TAW. Vanishing with this possibility is the very notion of textual universe.

Undecidable Relations

The evaluation of accessibility relations from AW to TAW presupposes the text's ability—that is, the implied speaker's willingness or authority—to establish the facts of TAW. When epistemic access to these facts is denied, the world at the center of the textual system fails to solidify—to borrow the felicitous expression of Felix Martínez-Bonati (1981:115)—and accessibility relations become wholly or partially undecidable. Variations on this situation include:

(A) The empty center. The text limits its assertions to worlds at the periphery, avoiding the representation of an actual world. This effect can be achieved by modalizing propositions with adverbs of possibility ("maybe," "perhaps"), or by linking them through an "or" operator, so as to leave in doubt which ones of them hold true in TAW. Both techniques are characteristic of the work of Georg Trakl, a poetry of the virtual if there ever was.

(B) The unknowable center. The text blurs the distinctions between TAW and the worlds at the periphery (i.e., the private worlds of characters) by leaving it unclear who is speaking, or by preventing the reader from identifying the reference world of sentences. In Robbe-Grillet's *Dans le labyrinthe*, we never know for sure whether the text describes a factual reality or a character's dream-world or hallucination.

(C) Radical lack of authority. In texts such as Beckett's *The Unnameable*, the narrator undermines his authority by withdrawing previous statements as lies, without giving valid reasons to believe the denial rather than the original statement. The narrator's discourse is regarded as "just discourse," as incoherent rambling expressing an inner world of transient perceptions.

Between the extremes of a completely solidified and a radically inaccessible TAW lies the possibility of a partially defined center. In works such as Robbe-Grillet's *La Jalousie* and Nabokov's *Pale Fire*, we know little that is definitive about the individual facts of TAW, but the text manages nevertheless to outline the general laws by which this world is constructed. The TAWs of *La Jalousie* and *Pale Fire* are basically realistic worlds respecting relations D/chronological through I/linguistic for the former, and C/expanded inventory through I/linguistic for the latter: fairies and time travel, nonsense and strange jargons are obviously not possible in these domains. How do we get an intuition of the principles by which these worlds are put together? We apprehend TAW through its reflection in the mind of characters, and even though we do not trust the details of the reflection, or cannot identify the reflecting mind, we assume that the mental image respects the basic configuration of the reflected reality. If the character's subjective view of TAW is linked to AW through a certain cluster of relations, we assume by a law of transitivity that the same relations hold objectively between AW and TAW.

Multiple Relations and Split Ontologies

One set of accessibility relations is not always sufficient to categorize the actual world of a textual universe. The text may present what Thomas Pavel (1986) calls a "dual" or "layered" ontology: the domain of the actual is split into sharply distinct domains obeying different laws, such as the sacred and the profane in medieval mystery plays, or the visible world (everyday reality) versus the world of the invisible (the Court, the Castle) in Kafka's novels (Doležel 1983). Unlike the private worlds of the characters' mental constructs, "the Sacred" or "the Invisible" are not alternative possible worlds located at the periphery of the textual system, but complementary territories within the central world. In Kafka's novels, TAW is split between a realistic sphere, obeying all relations except for A/properties, B/same inventory, and C/expanded inventory, and a sphere of undecidable relation to AW. The case of myth and medieval mystery plays must be assessed from two different vantage points: the perspective of the believer in the sacred who professes a dual ontology, and the perspective of the non-believer who adheres to a unified, profane ontology. For nonbelievers, the sacred in these texts is reached by lifting relations E/natural laws and F/taxonomy while the profane respects these relations. But how do members of the original community categorize the text? Claiming that adherents to the system of beliefs projected by the text regard TAW as globally compatible with E and F would miss the fact that their own conceptual system is based on a dual ontology. For believers in the sacred, the "supernatural" belongs to "the possible in the actual," though not to "the possible in the ordinary." Their conceptual system distinguishes a profane from a sacred set of laws, species, or individuals, and they regard the divisions of TAW as consistent with the divisions within AW.

The discrepancy between the believer's and the nonbeliever's point of view demonstrates the historical relativity of the assessment of accessibility relations, and its dependency on explanatory models such as scientific theories and religious revelation. A text may be judged as conforming to E/natural laws at some point in history, and as breaking E at a later point: in the Middle Ages, a story about witches could be told as true of AW. Conversely, a text such as Jules Verne's *Twenty Thousand Leagues under the Sea* broke D/chronology and F'/taxonomy (narrow version) for the nineteenth-century reader, but the passing of time and the invention of submarines makes it fully compatible with these relations for the modern reader. From a contemporary perspective, the semantic type of the text is more akin to the genre of the adventure thriller than to the genre of science fiction, as which it was originally proposed. I would not, however, go as far as saying that the text has shifted genre: as long as the origin of *Twenty Thousand Leagues under the Sea* is remembered, the reader regards it as science fiction (just as *1984* will forever remain a novel of anticipation).

Multiple Relations and the Ubiquitous Center

The (actual) existence of texts with an empty center raises the question of the reverse case: a text that would absorb *all* possible worlds within the boundaries of TAW. In the semantic universe of this text, the center would be everywhere and the circumference nowhere, since the domain of the nonactual would be drained of its substance. While no such text has ever been written in AW, one "exists" in a recentered system of reality: the novel of the Chinese author Ts'ui Pen, as described by an English scholar in the short story "The Garden of Forking Paths" by Jorge Luis Borges:

> In all fictional works, each time a man is confronted with several alternatives, he chooses one and eliminates the others; in the fiction of Ts'ui Pen, he chooses—simultaneously—all of them. *He creates*, in this way, diverse futures, diverse times which themselves also proliferate and fork. (Borges 1983:26)

Under a narrow conception of accessibility, the forking paths of this think-able but unwriteable fiction lead into all the futures allowed by logical and physical laws. All the worlds respecting E/natural laws, F/taxonomy, and G/logic will then be combined in TAW, but since these worlds may be mutually contradictory, G will not hold for TAW as a whole. Under the diversified notion of accessibility proposed in this chapter, the forking paths may lead into worlds of any semantic type, and by simultaneously actualizing them all, TAW is linked to AW through all existing subsets of relations.

Intra-Universe Relations

As already stated, a semantic universe consists of a plurality of worlds, and its semantic description requires a recursive application of the taxo-nomic system within its own confines. In *Alice in Wonderland*, for instance, TAW is a realistic world related to AW through all relations except for A/properties and B/same inventory. (The passage through this world is too swift to decide whether or not C/expanded inventory holds.) From the world originally designated as TAW, however, the text takes a trip to the dream world of Wonderland by lifting E/natural laws and F/taxonomy, and this dream-world momentarily takes the place of an actual world through an internal gesture of recentering (internal as opposed to the external recenter-ing through which Lewis Carroll makes the entire textual universe come into being). This internal recentering sets the text apart from both standard realistic novels, in which dream-worlds exist only at the periphery of the textual universe (dreams are recounted as dreams, not lived as reality), and from the fantastic universe of fairy tales, in which E/natural laws and F/taxonomy are broken in the central world of the system.

To capture the semantic characteristics of a genre it may be necessary to assess the peripheral worlds of the system in their relation to both AW and TAW. A case in point is the genre of the fantastic, as defined by Todorov (1975). According to Todorov, the fantastic atmosphere arises from a hesita-tion between a rational and a supernatural interpretation of the facts. Typi-cally, a character is confronted with events that cannot be accounted for by the character's model of "the possible in the actual." The character there-fore tries to explain them away by rejecting them to a peripheral world, such as dream or hallucination. When compared to AW, the TAW of the fantastic text breaks relations E/natural laws and possibly F/taxonomy, but the char-acters conceive TAW as respecting these relations. What the hero originally believes to be possible in TAW corresponds to what AW's adherents to a profane ontology believe to be possible in AW. At the end of the text, how-ever, the character is forced to revise his or her model of reality by adhering to a dual ontology. In their initial state the epistemic worlds of characters are conformant to AW but in conflict with TAW; in their final state they are aligned on TAW but deviate from AW.

The inner discrepancy which Todorov labels as fantastic stands in striking contrast to the epistemic homogeneity of the fairy tale: here the supernatural is spontaneously accepted as part of TAW, and the characters' representation of reality is not regulated by the laws of nature. A slightly different type of harmony between a supernatural AW and its reflection in the character's mind occurs in *The Metamorphosis*, a text which Todorov rightly excludes from the fantastic. Being transformed into a bug is for Gregor Samsa a totally unprecedented event, one neither foreseen nor explained by his private worldview, and therefore not to be experienced by any other individual. Yet he has no choice but face the evidence ("this was not a dream" is the first thought to cross his mind), and in his representation of TAW the actuality of the metamorphosis is never called into question.

Genre and Accessibility Relations

As the preceding discussion has suggested, accessibility relations are involved in the differentiation of genres. But the taxonomic classes yielded by computing the various combinations of relations does not necessarily correspond to the generic labels in use in a given culture. In some cases the labels are narrower and in others wider. Tolstoi's *Anna Karenina* and Robbe-Grillet's *La Jalousie* both contain a "realistic" element, though the former respects C/expanded inventory and the latter does not: *La Jalousie* makes no reference whatsoever to individuals or locations of AW. On the other hand, pastoral romances are anything but realistic, yet their system of reality can be reached through the same accessibility relations as the universe of *La Jalousie*: in both cases the inventory of TAW does not contain that of AW, but TAW respects the laws of physics and logic.

To refine the categories provided by the various combinations of accessibility relations into a taxonomy corresponding to accepted generic labels we must introduce additional factors of semantic diversification. I would like to propose three of these factors: thematic focus, stylistic filtering, and probabilistic emphasis.

Thematic focus is the principle by which the text selects setting, characters, and events from the history and inventory of the textual universe to form a plot or a message. The generic labels "psychological," "detective," or "historical" novel all concern types of thematic focus within the systems of reality accessible through relations C/expanded inventory through I/linguistic.

While thematic focus guides the selection of that which is to be shown, *stylistic filtering* determines in which light these objects will be presented, the impression they will create on the reader. Generic labels such as comic, tragic, or idyllic refer to various types of stylistic filtering. The distinction of the pastoral romance from *La Jalousie* within the set of physically possible TAWs involves both thematic focus and stylistic filtering: the former selects the bucolic as thematic focus, and out of the bucolic filters the idyllic; the latter selects a landscape of colonial life, and paints it in neutral colors.

Probabilistic emphasis has to do with whether the text dwells on the ordinary or the marginal within the horizon of possibilities determined by the relevant accessibility relations. Through probabilistic emphasis we can differentiate what Doreen Maître (1983) calls "escapist fiction," such as adventure thrillers or historical romance, from the realistic novels of Zola or Flaubert, even though both types respect the same set of accessibility relations. Escapist fiction depicts glamorous lifestyles, thrilling adventures, incredible coincidences, agonizing dilemmas, burning desire, everlasting passion—all of which are logically, economically, psychologically, and physically possible in AW, though highly unlikely.

The generic labels in use in a culture may involve various combinations of the three types of semantic criterion. (They may of course also cover nonsemantic features, such as formal constraints and pragmatic requirements.) "Detective" or "historical," when applied to novels, refer to a type of thematic focus that presupposes a certain cluster of accessibility relations. "Idyllic" is a stylistic filtering, "pastoral" a thematic focus, and the label "pastoral romance" covers both of these features. Some labels are ambiguous between two types of criterion. "Realistic" is understood by some as referring to accessibility relations: a text is realistic if it respects all relations from E/natural laws, and if the facts it describes are economically and psychologically possible in AW. For others, the events depicted in the realistic text must also fall within the statistically probable. Still another use of realistic emphasizes thematic focus: the text is realistic if it concentrates on everyday life among the regions of TAW. In this third sense, realistic no longer implies acceptance of E/natural laws. Kafka's *Metamorphosis*, or *Le Passe-Muraille* by Marcel Aymé, can be said to combine a fantastic and a realistic element. The label "fantastic" is another example of potential semantic polyvalence. In its broadest and most intuitive use "fantastic" is synonymous with transgression of E. But in the narrower definition proposed by Todorov, this transgression is not regarded as a sufficient condition. The fantastic text must create an epistemic uncertainty by making the relation AW/TAW at least temporarily undecidable with respect to E. If we accept this definition, then the label "marvelous" may be substituted for fantastic for those texts in which the transgression of E/natural laws is taken for granted, such as legends and fairy tales.

Expanding the Repertory

The preceding catalog of semantically relevant accessibility relations is anything but definitive. The need for expansion will undoubtedly arise, as more texts are processed through the model, as new genres come into being, or as we fine-tune the analysis of individual texts to distinguish them from other representatives of the same genre. The list of candidates for addition to the model includes the following:

(1) *Historical coherence*: TAW is accessible from AW if TAW not only includes AW's population, but contains no anachronisms with respect to AW. Through this relation, it becomes possible to distinguish standard historical narratives, as well as what I have called historical fabulation, from works of fantasy which allow the meeting of characters, objects, and preoccupations from different periods: Joan of Arc coming back into the modern world and starting a war against sexism, or prehistoric man watching soap operas on television. (See McHale [1987] on the creative role of anachronism in postmodernist fiction.)

(2) *Psychological credibility*: TAW is psychologically accessible from AW if we believe that the mental properties of the characters could be those of members of AW. This means that we regard the characters as complete human beings to whom we can relate as persons. The relation of psychological credibility can be broken in many ways: through the symbolic unidimensionality of allegorical figures; through the rudimentary inner life of fairy tale or science fiction characters; or through the madness of the marginal creatures who populate the theater of the absurd. For madness to break the relation, however, it must be generalized to all the members of TAW. Presented in the context of a "sane" environment, madness is only an extreme on the scale of psychological possibility.

When a text breaks the relation of psychological credibility, it usually breaks some other, more salient relation, which makes the specification of the psychology relation somewhat superfluous for the semantic description of the genre. Among the aforementioned examples, fairy tales also break E/natural laws, science fiction breaks D/chronology, and the theater of the absurd transgresses G/logic. But from a redundant property, the question of psychological credibility can be elevated into a distinctive feature by a text presenting an innovative combination of accessibility relations. Such a text could be a fantastic tale combining supernatural events with a plausible portrayal of human psychology.

(3) *Socio-economic compatibility*: TAW is accessible from AW if both worlds share economic laws and social structure. By adding this relation to the catalog it becomes possible to distinguish the "realistic" world of Robbe-Grillet's *La Jalousie*, where at least some people work for a living, from the Edenic landscape of the pastoral romance, where the availability of goods is taken for granted.

The main reason for including relations of psychological credibility and of socio-economic compatibility in the catalog resides in their hermeneutic importance. A text respecting psychological credibility makes psychoanalytical theories literally applicable as interpretive models, while a text transgressing the relation can only justify a figural application: characters in fairy tales may allegorize the Oedipus complex, but they do not suffer from it. Along the same lines, a text respecting socio-economic compatibility makes Marxist doctrine available as potential explanation, while a pastoral romance does not.

(4) *Categorial compatibility*: Under this label I understand the respect for distinctions between basic logical categories. Through this relation, it is possible to explain the semantic difference between TAWs containing allegorical characters such as Death and Beauty, and TAWs excluding such entities. Insofar as an allegory is the incarnation of an abstract idea, it transgresses the categorial distinction between particulars and universals. Another example of categorial transgression is the statement that concludes the television program "Sesame Street": "This program has been brought to you by the letter Z and the number 6."

Accessibility Relations and Fictionality

The preceding discussion reveals a close connection between fictionality and the strength of the relations between AW and TAW. In nonfictional texts, the breaking of relations must be either concealed (deceit), or inadvertent (error). For TAW to depart from AW in these cases, the textual referents must fall within a zone of disagreement as to whether or not they are covered by the relation: you cannot tell lies or make errors about facts unanimously recognized as true. The nature of the various relations is such that the last ones listed create much greater unanimity than the higher-ordered ones. E, F, G, H, and I are consequently much less likely to be broken unbeknownst to either sender or receiver than A or B. We all agree in principle on the laws of language and logic. If in the reader's opinion a text breaks these relations, he or she will assume that the violation was not only intentional, but meant to be recognized, and that consequently TAW can only be reached through a ludic relocation to another system of reality. Our opinion of physical laws and of taxonomic classes are less unanimous: some of us believe in ghosts, UFOs, ESP, miracles, etc. Even if readers reject these entities from their personal representation of reality, the possibility remains that the sender regards them as real, and so their occurrence in a text does not constitute an absolute sign of fictionality. Still greater is our disagreement concerning the inventory of the real world, and the properties of its members. It is consequently easy for a text to misrepresent facts or introduce nonexisting individuals, while claiming nevertheless that TAW reflects AW.

The distance between AW and TAW, as measured by accessibility relations, thus provides a fairly reliable indicator of fictionality, but not an absolute criterion. What looks like a surrealistic poem breaking the logical law of noncontradiction could very well be an entry in the diary of a schizophrenic patient; what looks like a fantastic description of former lives could be the autobiography of a famous actress; conversely, what looks like the genuine love letters of a Portuguese nun could be the invention of a seventeenth-century French author. The question of fictionality is decided neither by the semantic properties of the textual universe nor by the stylistic properties of the text, but is settled a priori as part of our generic expectations. We regard a text as fiction when we know its genre, and we know that the genre is governed by the rules of the fictional game. And we enter into this game when our concern for the textual system of reality momentarily displaces our existential concern for the affairs of our own native system.

3 Reconstructing the Textual Universe: The Principle of Minimal Departure

One of the greatest theoretical advantages of the possible world approach to fiction is that it provides a convenient method for assessing the truth value of statements describing or interpreting the universe of a fictional text. This method was developed by David Lewis (1978) as an extension of an earlier proposal on truth conditions for counterfactuals (1973).

The pragmatic purpose of counterfactuals is not to create alternate possible worlds for their own sake, but to make a point about AW. When we say: "If the catcher had not dropped the ball after that third strike the Cubs would have won the game," our purpose is to suggest how close the Cubs came to victory: a dropped ball measures the distance between the possible world in which the Cubs win, and the actual world in which they are losers. To the above statement, a Cardinal fan may reply: "No way, because the Cardinals would have scored anyway in the next inning," thus demonstrating that the acceptance or rejection of a counterfactual is a matter of truth value. The logical characteristic of counterfactuals is that their global truth value (which is assessed for the actual world) cannot be computed on the basis of the individual AW truth value of their antecedent and consequent. In versions (a) and (b) of the example below, neither antecedent nor consequent capture facts of AW; yet (a) is widely regarded as true as a whole, and (b) as false. Conversely, a counterfactual with a false antecedent and a true consequent (what Reichenbach [1976] calls a counterfactual of noninterference) may be false, like (c), or true, like (d). (The propositions under consideration are those yielded by the expressions within brackets, with the verb changed to the indicative mode, e.g., "Napoleon has not escaped from Elba" for the antecedent, and "Napoleon did not die on St. Helena" for the consequent (a). The individual truth value of component propositions are in parentheses; the global truth value of the statement appears on the right, without parentheses.)

If [Napoleon had not escaped from Elba] (F)
    (a) [he would not have died on St. Helena] (F) T
    (b) [he would have lived until 1850] (F) F

(c) [he would have died in 1821] anyway (T) T
(d) [he would have lost the battle of Waterloo] anyway (T) F

To determine the truth value of these statements, Lewis (1973) proposes to take into consideration the notion of relative similarity between possible worlds. His analysis can be presented as follows:

> There is a set of possible worlds A where the
> antecedent holds and the consequent holds.
> There is a set of possible worlds B where the
> antecedent holds, but the consequent does not.
> Of all these worlds, take the one which differs the
> least, on balance, from AW. If this world belongs
> to set A, the counterfactual is true. If it
> belongs to set B, the counterfactual is false.

To extend this analysis to the case of fiction, Lewis proposes to regard statements of truth in fiction as counterfactuals. The facts yielded by the fictional text are implicitly cast in the role of the antecedent, and the interpretive statement functions as consequent. When we say "Sherlock Holmes was definitely not a ladies' man" we mean something like "If Sherlock Holmes existed, and the plot of the story were enacted in AW, then Sherlock Holmes would definitely not be a ladies' man." If we accept this statement as a whole in AW, we implicitly accept its consequent as true in the textual universe. This analogy permits the following analysis:

> A sentence of the form "In the fiction f, p" is nonvacuously true iff [if and only if] some world where f is told as known fact and p is true differs less from our actual world, on balance, than does any world where f is told as known fact and p is not true. (1978:42)

While I basically endorse this analysis, I find some problems in its formulation. The use of the term "fiction f" is ambiguous. In the expression "In the fiction f, p [is true]," f refers to the world TRW in which p is valued; but in the expression "where f is told as known fact," f stands for a story, this is to say, for a *textual* universe, whose center is TAW. Moreover, the expression "told as known fact" disregards the problem of the teller, and suggests an unproblematic relation between the text and the facts of TAW and TRW. Narratologists will be quick to point out that what counts as fact in TRW depends on who asserts these facts: the declarations of a character, or of a personal narrator, do not necessarily yield truths for TRW. To avoid these difficulties, and to stress the analogy with the counterfactual analysis, I propose the following formulation. (In the formula, TRW can be interpreted as also standing for TAW, since the two constructs, as we have seen in chapter 1, are always analogous in fiction.)

There is a set of modal universes A, which are constructed on the basis of a fictional text f, and in whose actual world the nontextual statement p is true.

There is a set of modal universes B, which are constructed on the basis of a fictional text f, and in whose actual world the nontextual statement p is false.

Of all these universes, take the one which differs the least, on balance, from our own system of reality. If it belongs to set A, then p is true in TRW, and the statement "in TRW, p" is true in AW. Otherwise, p is false in TRW, and "in TRW, p" is false in AW.

This algorithm would not be complete without a procedure for picking the closest universe. Insofar as the distance between systems of reality is a function of the distance between their respective centers, the same algorithm should measure the difference between individual worlds and entire universes. It should therefore apply to both the case of counterfactuals and of statements about fiction. To go back to the counterfactual "If Napoleon had not escaped from Elba he would not have died on St. Helena," we want to know how we decide that the closest of the worlds of set A, which all comprise the propositions

> Napoleon does not escape from Elba
> Napoleon does not die on St. Helena

differs less from reality than the closest of the worlds of set B, comprising

> Napoleon does not escape from Elba
> Napoleon dies on St. Helena

The distance cannot be computed on the basis of the number of differing propositions: set A differs from reality through at least two propositions while set B has only one proposition specified as contradicting AW, yet if the statement is true, a world of set A is closer to reality than any world of set B. To evaluate distance, we must take into consideration not just the textual propositions, but the context of a logically complete and consistent environment. The closest world of set A is reached by copying into it the history of AW and the properties of the actual Napoleon up to the exile on Elba, changing the truth value of the proposition "Napoleon escaped from Elba," and from this situation, letting events follow their most predictable course. If Napoleon had not escaped, the entire causal chain which eventually led to his death on St. Helena would have been avoided, and unless some event of low probability had intervened, he would indeed have died on the island of Elba. To make him die on St. Helena despite his refusal or failure to escape, we must further alter the history of the world, for instance by postulating this event:

Afraid that the new Royalist government would attempt to assassinate him, Napoleon asked England to move him to St. Helena.

This amendment to history is not a logical consequence of the antecedent, nor a probability attached to it, but a bridge introduced for the sole purpose of making the antecedent compatible with the proposition "Napoleon dies on St. Helena." In forming this second world, we depart from AW in a somewhat gratuitous way. The Napoleon of the first world is basically the same individual as the real Napoleon, minus the will to escape. The Napoleon of the second world loses not only his fighting spirit but other features of what we take to be his real personality such as pride and dignity. Any other way to link "not escaping from Elba" to "dying on St. Helena" will similarly result in the postulation of superfluous departures from AW.

Our knowledge of reality is put to similar use in the valuation of statements of fact about fiction. It is stated nowhere in *Madame Bovary* that Emma's husband has two legs, yet theorists of fiction (i.e., Châteaux 1976 and Doležel 1980) agree that the statement "Charles Bovary is one-legged" is to be taken as false in the universe of the novel. The reason is that the text presents Charles as a human being, and the normal number of legs for a human being is two. Since we regard "the real world" as the realm of the ordinary, any departure from norms not explicitly stated in the text is to be regarded as a gratuitous increase of the distance between the textual universe and our own system of reality. This procedure extends to the valuation of interpretive statements. Accepting the explanation "In Coleridge's 'Christabel,' the heroine's conscious mind has repressed the Oedipal feeling" (Spatz 1975:113) means entertaining the opinion that a universe in which a person can behave like Christabel does in the poem, and be said to repress her desire for her father, is more consistent with our ideas of psychological laws than a universe in which the heroine's behavior is compatible with the statement that she has surrendered to the Oedipal feeling. Or to put it in a simpler way: it means that readers who agree with the interpretation would accept this statement of a real-world person about whom they had similar information.

From the preceding analysis, we can derive a law of primary importance for the phenomenology of reading. This law—to which I shall refer as the principle of minimal departure—states that we reconstrue the central world of a textual universe in the same way we reconstrue the alternate possible worlds of nonfactual statements: as conforming as far as possible to our representation of AW. We will project upon these worlds everything we know about reality, and we will make only the adjustments dictated by the text. When someone says "If horses had wings they would be able to fly," we reconstrue an animal presenting all the properties of real horses, except for the presence of wings and the ability to fly. We perform the same operation when we read about a flying horse in a fairy tale, when a child tells us "Last night I dreamed about a flying horse," and when a poet writes about the flying horse of imagination.[1]

The need for the principle of minimal departure in interpreting fiction is made particularly compelling by historical narratives. If it weren't for the principle, a novel about a character named Napoleon could not convey the feeling that its hero is *the* Napoleon. The resemblance between the Napoleon in the novel and the Napoleon of AW would be as fortuitous as the resemblance between a certain John Smith, and any other person answering to the same name. Under the principle, the Napoleon of TAW is regarded as a counterpart of the Napoleon of AW, linked to him through what David Lewis calls a line of transworld identity. Whether this Napoleon escapes to New Orleans or dies on St. Helena, he remains the individual picked out in all possible worlds by the name "Napoleon."[2]

It is by virtue of the principle of minimal departure that readers are able to form reasonably comprehensive representations of the foreign worlds created through discourse, even though the verbal representation of these worlds is always incomplete. Without the principle, interpretation of verbal messages referring to APWs would be limited to the extraction of strict semantic entailments. The reader of a fiction containing the sentence "Babar the King of the elephants went to a restaurant" would be entitled to reconstrue the proposition "at time tn Babar was at a restaurant," but not to draw the pragmatic inference: "Babar was hungry, and he went to the restaurant to eat." To come to this conclusion, we must assume that in the anthropomorphic world of Babar, where elephants have kings and are able to talk, they are attracted to restaurants for the same reason we are.

The dilemma between a method of reading invoking the principle of minimal departure and a reading narrowly determined by textual propositions is exemplified in chapter 3 of *Don Quixote*. In the words of Felix Martínez-Bonati, whose position opposes minimal departure in nonrealistic genres:

> The innkeeper asks Don Quixote whether he is carrying money, to which the hero replies that he has none and has never read in books that a knight errant uses it. The author will not write it, explains the innkeeper, because it is taken for granted that they do. Don Quixote accepts the argument (and promises to take money with him in the future), but we may doubt it. Do knights errant carry money to pay for services such as lodging? It belongs to the style of the genre that the question is undecidable. . . . Certain imprecisions are essential [to the world of the chivalric novel]—not just to the manner of its presentation or to its actualized aspects. (1983:193)

As a textual fundamentalist, Don Quixote follows a strictly incremental algorithm in his reconstruction of the textual universe of chivalric romances. Starting from a blank system of reality, he populates it with facts and objects, as these facts and objects are introduced by the text. As an adherent to the principle of minimal departure, the innkeeper proceeds both substitutionally and incrementally, starting from a preconceived image of a full universe, and amending it or adding to its population according to textual directions. For the textual fundamentalist, the question whether knights errant carry money is undecidable because of ontological incompleteness. When they are not busy rescuing damsels or defeating enemies, knights errant live in a vacuum in which they neither sleep nor eat nor find use for money. For the adherent to the principle of minimal departure knights errant need to sleep and eat and pay for services unless otherwise specified, and the text's failure to report these activities is strictly a matter of thematic focus. The gaps in the representation of the textual universe are regarded as withdrawn information, and not as ontological deficiencies of this universe itself.

Martínez-Bonati's uneasiness with the existence of money in the world of chivalric romances suggests that an unrestricted application of the principle of minimal departure may be too powerful for most fictional genres. If statements of the type "x's exist" (generic) and "x exists" (particular) fall under the scope of the principle, the inventory of TAW will by necessity include all the species and individuals found in AW. There will be computers in the world of "Jabberwocky," Paris will be part of the geography of *The Trial,* and the writings of Aquinas will be potentially available to the characters of "Little Red Riding Hood." While I accept the fact that knights errant, living in a world patterned after the Middle Ages, have access to money, I find the above statements highly counterintuitive. To prevent the invasion of textual universes by unwanted species and individuals, we must give special treatment to existential propositions. A proposition of the type "x's exist," where x refers to a species, will be transferable from AW to TRW if:

(1) x's existed in AW in the stage of its historical development that corresponds to the stage at which TAW is shown, and

(2) the appropriate environment for x's is set up in TAW.

Moreover, a proposition of the type "x exists," where x refers to an individual or geographic location, will be transferable to TAW if it fulfills both (1) above, and

(3) the text names as member of TAW at least one individual or geographic location belonging to AW.

Rule (1) excludes computers from the universe of fairy tales on the basis that the stage of AW serving as model for its reconstruction is roughly the medieval world. Rule (2) excludes them from "Jabberwocky" on the basis that the text actualizes none of the frames in which they are likely to be found: technology, business, bureaucracy, etc. And rule (3) excludes Paris and Napoleon from *The Trial,* as well as from "Jabberwocky" and "Little Red Riding Hood," because none of these texts presents individuals belonging also to AW. When members are indeed held in common, minimal departure instructs us to accept the entire inventory of AW in TAW: if a novel has Rouen, it also has Paris; if it has Napoleon, it also has Josephine and Marie-Louise in its background, as well as Charlemagne and Louis XIV among the figures of its past. The solidarity of a world's inventory explains why in chapter 2 I have excluded from the catalog of accessibility relations the case of a textual universe accepting only a subset of AW's population. George Orwell's *1984* may form an exception by including Churchill and Hitler, while excluding Margaret Thatcher, but its case is so odd that it confirms the rule: the history of the real world had to catch up with the anticipated year 1984 for a textual universe to be selective in its hospitality toward historical figures. (Alternatively, the modern reader could assume that Margaret Thatcher exists in the world of *1984* but became a housewife, a chemist, or a member of Big Brother's police.)

Minimal Departure and Intertextuality

Through its reliance on the reader's experience of reality, the principle of minimal departure may seem at odds with one of the key concepts of contemporary literary theory: the doctrine of intertextuality. Whether it is defined as the emergence of meaning from a horizon of expectations created by other texts of the same genre, or as a ludic transformation of foreign textual material, intertextuality replaces the world with the written word as frame of reference of the reading process. I would argue, however, that the two principles are not incompatible but complementary: the functioning of minimal departure depends as much on intertextual relations as the functioning of intertextuality relies on minimal departure.

The dependency of minimal departure on texts takes two forms, one general and one particular. Texts exist in the world as a potential source of knowledge, from which we draw information in building our representation of reality. The frame of reference invoked by the principle of minimal departure is not the sole product of unmediated personal experience, but bears the trace of all the texts that support and transmit a culture. Through an inversion of the principle of minimal departure, knowledge about the real world may be derived not only from texts purporting to represent reality, but also from texts openly labeled and recognized as fiction. If we reconstrue fictional universes as the closest possible to the real world, why not reconstrue the domains of the real world for which we lack information as the closest possible to the world of a certain fiction? Trusting the scholarship of Umberto Eco, many readers regard *The Name of the Rose* as a reliable treatise of medieval theology. Don Quixote and Emma Bovary are famous fictional examples of this tendency to invert the principle.

As a part of reality, texts also exist as potential objects of knowledge, and this knowledge may be singled out as relevant material for the construction of a textual universe. The principle of minimal departure permits the choice, not only of the real world, but also of a textual universe as frame of reference. This happens whenever an author expands, rewrites, or parodies a preexisting fiction, or whenever a fiction includes the universe of another fiction in its system of reality. When we read the Sherlock Holmes stories written by the son of Conan Doyle, we reconstrue the textual universe as coming as close as possible to the universe of the original Sherlock Holmes stories, which itself is assumed to have been already constructed as coming as close as possible to AW. The Sherlock Holmes of the new stories bears the same relation to the original Sherlock Holmes as the Napoleon of *War and Peace* to the actual Napoleon: they are counterparts of the same individual, presenting somewhat different properties, and inhabiting different possible worlds. Minimal departure may select not only one, but several different textual universes as frame of reference, thus permitting the migration of fictional characters out of their native environment. In some conceivable systems of reality, Sherlock Holmes matches wits with Arsène Lupin, Dracula meets Frankenstein, and Faust falls in love with Helen of Troy.

Like minimal departure, intertextuality involves a rejection of the view that textual universes are created *ex nihilo,* and that textual meaning is the product of a self-enclosed system. One version of the doctrine tells us that TAW is a priori populated, not with the objects found in AW, but with the creatures characteristic of what may be called a "generic landscape." Reading a fairy tale, we know right away that we may find dragons and flying horses, foxes and frogs, but no catfish, mosquitoes, or sparrows. People will not suffer from diseases, except for princesses who may linger from some mysterious condition, and queens who may die in childbirth. We expect some animals to be able to talk (foxes, frogs, owls, golden fish, deer) and some others to be deprived of this ability (cows, pigs, flies). Whether or not a character is turned into a stone, we regard as a law in effect the possibility of metamorphosis. On the other hand, we expect some suspension of the real world laws of human psychology: the princess and the hero may have many children, but their love is Platonic, and they are free from the urges of sexuality. Marital infidelity is as incongruous in the world of fairy tales as it is *de rigueur* in the world of the soap opera.

Generic landscapes solidify through a process of filtration: we gather their elements from the themes and objects characteristic of a certain corpus. Since they are extracted from fully reconstituted textual universes, these objects have already been preprocessed according to the principle of minimal departure. Generic competence tells us that flying horses belong to the landscape of fairy tales, while knowledge of the world enables us to visualize them as creatures with four legs, a mane and a tail. Not explainable through minimal departure, however, is the absence of certain features in the description of some objects. We enter princesses as [+human], [+female], [+beautiful] in the intertextual database, but what do we do about their sexuality? Minimal departure tells us that some kind of sex drive, whether high or low, is part of human nature, but the behavior of princesses in typical fairy tales shows no trace of this impulse. If we enter princesses as [−sexual] we depart from reality in a way not explicitly prescribed by any text of the corpus, but if we specify them as [+sexual] we do not do justice to their behavior. Moreover, any valuation other than indeterminate introduces the theme of sexuality in the generic landscape: [−sexual] would mean that fairy tales may insist on their lack of sex drive. The description of objects in the generic landscape should reflect, not so much the full range of their inherent properties, as those features which may be thematized in the texts of the genre. As an abstraction from many texts, the prototypical fairy tale princess is an incomplete entity, lacking determination on the feature of sexuality, but the princesses of individual fairy tales are ontologically normal human beings, who simply reveal nothing of their sexuality in the events shown in the text. By the same principle, the prototypical knight errant of chivalry romances is not preoccupied with financial matters, even though money exists in the world of specific representatives of the genre. Minimal departure thus operates on the individuated characters of particular texts, not on the abstract classes of generic landscapes.

In another respect, however, minimal departure does remain operative in the formation of generic landscapes. If these landscapes are not frozen but evolving entities, if new genres can develop out of old ones, rather than being created *ex nihilo*, then we must assume an intertextual application of minimal departure. A modern writer may for instance decide to parody the world of fairy tales by focusing on the sexual preoccupations of knights and princesses. If the text initiates a genre of its own (let's call it the erotic fairy tale), the new landscape will be obtained by taking over all the features characteristic of fairy tales, and adding sexuality to the relevant properties of characters.

As complementary sources of information, minimal departure and generic landscapes both contribute to the reader's reconstruction of the textual universe. If reading were exclusively conditioned by minimal departure from reality, TAW would comprise all the objects and features of AW (under the restrictions stated above), and entities foreign to AW would only be accepted under explicit textual direction. If reading were wholly conditioned by generic landscapes, TAW would accept all the objects constitutive of the landscape, whether or not they are explicitly mentioned in the text, as well as all the additional objects introduced by the text, but it would exclude the elements of reality not included in these two sets. But if reading is a compromise between minimal departure and intertextuality, the furniture of TAW will be the union of the sets respectively defined by the text, and the two principles. Under the first proposal there are no dragons in the world of "Snow White," but money in chivalric romances; under the second, no money in chivalric romances, but dragons in "Snow White"; under the third both dragons in "Snow White" and money in chivalric romances. It may be objected that these questions are irrelevant to anyone not enamored with the logic of possible worlds: if dragons and money play no part in the plot, does it really matter whether or not they do exist in TAW? Fortunately, the usefulness of minimal departure and of generic landscapes is not limited to Byzantine philosophical questions: minimal departure explains the very possibility of making truth-functional statements about fiction, as well as the (pretended) ontological completeness of fictional beings, while generic land-scapes predict what will be shown and hidden in a certain type of text, what will be given or denied significance.

Challenging Minimal Departure

A potential objection to the principle of minimal departure resides in its naturalistic bias: if fictional universes are drawn into the orbit of the real world, will not the strange be reduced to the ordinary, and the uncanny to the commonplace? Do we do justice to the resources of human imagination by pressing the variety of fictional universes into the same ontological mold? It appears reasonable to claim that Emma Bovary and Stephen Daedalus, characters of realistic novels, are regarded by the reader as fully individuated and logically complete human beings, but it seems counterintuitive to say that Anna Karenina and Anna Livia Plurabelle, Jabberwocky and Alice, Godot and d'Artagnan, Sleeping Beauty and the allegory of Beauty in a medieval novel participate in the same mode of existence. We would blatantly misread *The Trial* if we filled in the gaps in the representation of the Court according to our knowledge of real world institutions; and we would grossly misunderstand the law of Wonderland if we expected the Queen of Hearts to play croquet by the same rules as the members of the Lawn Tennis and Croquet Club of Wimbledon, England. My reply to these objections is that every text is placed under the authority of the principle of minimal departure, but that it is textually feasible to challenge this authority by either frustrating or subverting the principle.

Frustration occurs when a text offers the principle no substance to feed on. In *The Trial*, as Doležel (1983) has shown, TAW is split into two sharply distinct realms, one ordinary, well-known, and visible, the other one invisible, epistemologically inaccessible, and impenetrable to the members of the visible world. The information about the Court is so sparse and contradictory, the logic of its operations so arcane, that assimilation with familiar institutions never takes root. The principle of minimal departure is fully operative in the visible world, but it comes up empty when it casts its net in the world of the Court. Objects like Jabberwocky are similarly protected from the principle through their radical strangeness: we lack any model to complete the picture. As for allegories, they resist assimilation to normal human beings because of their categorial impossibility. How could one expect "human density" and psychological verisimilitude of a creature whose very existence transgresses the logical difference between individuated existence and abstract, universal concepts? In contrast to allegories, witches and dragons present the ontological fullness of a real object. The universe of fairy tales may be different from everyday reality, but there is no radical otherness about its inhabitants.

The other way of challenging the principle is to subvert it through systematic inversion or contradiction. The worlds of dreams and of madness, of ritual and of nonsense may be patterned according to what Thomas Pavel (1986:93) calls a principle of *maximal* departure. The reader of *Alice in Wonderland* quickly learns the futility of real-world knowledge (while Alice never fully assimilates the lesson). In a game of croquet, the balls are hedgehogs, the mallets are flamingos, the arches move around, and the players may hit any "ball" they choose at any time they want. In a trial held by the King and Queen of Hearts, witnesses stand accused, and sentences precede verdicts. Rules are created on the spot for nobody to follow them, orders are issued never to be executed, conversations constantly violate Grice's principles of cooperation, and the only thing left to expect is the unexpected. In *Ubu Roi* by Alfred Jarry, the subversion of the principle is suggested by these comments of the author on his own play:

> The curtain rises on a set which is supposed to represent Nowhere, with trees at the foot of beds and white snow in a summer sky; the action also takes place in Poland, a country so legendary, so dismembered that it is well qualified to be in this particular Nowhere, or in terms of a putative Franco-German etymology, a distantly interrogative somewhere. (Quoted in Krysinski 1987:145)

Bearing no counterpart relation to the historical country, this Poland of Nowhere contains a character named Stanislas Leczinski who is not an exiled eighteenth-century king, but a simple peasant. In a work subjected to minimal departure, we would regard this peasant as "what Stanislas Leczinski would have been like, had he not been born into a royal family." But in a Poland of Nowhere, none of the properties of the historical Stanislas can be carried over. Though they were deliberately introduced in the textual universe, resemblances to AW are meant to be processed as purely fortuitous. The point of the text is to call to mind the principle of minimal departure—only to block its operation.

The Scope of Minimal Departure

In the preceding discussion, minimal departure has been described as a principle applicable not only to fiction, but to all kinds of statements describing APWs: counterfactuals, reports of dreams, commands to the imagination (as found in a book by Dr. Seuss, *Oh the Thinks You Can Think:* "Think up a white sky. Think of bloogs blowing by" [1975, no page]). Yet fiction is not another kind of nonfactual discourse: while the various types of nonfactual statements constitute mutually exclusive categories, the feature of fictionality can be superimposed upon any one of them. Counterfactuals, reports of dreams, and commands to the imagination can all appear in the context of both fiction and nonfiction. If the principle of minimal departure is to provide a valid criterion for a definition of fiction, it should capture not only the similarity, but also the difference between fiction and other types of world-creating discourse.

This difference appears whenever indexical elements, more particularly first- and second-person pronouns, are involved in a proposition. In nonfactual discourse, these pronouns refer to a counterpart of the speaker or hearer in an alternate possible world. When somebody tells us, "If I were elected president I would do away with all forms of government including my own office," the referent of the pronoun "I" is reconstrued by the hearer as presenting the speaker's own identity and personality, but as differing from the speaker through the accidental feature "having been elected president." A similar projection of the hearer's properties would take place if the sentence were in the second person. When the use of a proper name projects the I into a foreign identity (e.g., "I dreamed that I was Marilyn Monroe," "If I had been Napoleon"), this foreign identity is only a superficial disguise. When we hear somebody say in the context of a conversation "If I had been Napoleon, I would not have invaded Russia," we imagine an individual with the speaker's fundamental identity, and most of his accidental properties, but who lived in 1812 and was the emperor of France. If the referent of the pronoun "I" were reconstrued as presenting the complete identity of Napoleon, this "I" would have no choice but act like the real Napoleon did, and the statement would be pointless. This extension of the principle of minimal departure to first and second pronouns, and the possibility of adopting some of the features of another individual while retaining one's basic identity explains why we can express personal opinions by means of nonfactual statements.

Let us now consider what would happen if the referents of first- and second-person pronouns fell under the scope of the principle of minimal departure in the case of fiction. The use of a first-person pronoun in a fiction would automatically invoke a counterpart of the author. If a certain John Smith wrote a tale narrated by a gnome, the reader would imagine a gnome corresponding as much as possible to the real John Smith, as when John Smith says "If I were a gnome." Or to take an actual literary example: in the novel *Jane Eyre,* which is narrated in the first person, Charlotte Brontë would project herself in the role of a governess, and through her novel, she would be telling us how she would have felt and behaved if she had met somebody like Mr. Rochester. Such an identification of an author with a fictional speaker is of course possible, at least indirectly, but authors can project themselves into *any* character, not just into the referents of first-person pronouns. (Consider Flaubert's declaration: "Madame Bovary, c'est moi!") Even when an author identifies emotionally with a first-person narrator, the bonds between author and narrator are very different from those linking the speaker of a regular type of nonfactual to the referent of first-person pronouns. If the pronouns "I" and "you" fell under the scope of the principle of minimal departure in the case of fiction, narrators would be the direct speakers for the author, and narratees would be counterparts of the reader.

We would then have a foolproof procedure at our disposal for determining the author's personal position, and fiction would lose most of the uncertainty which makes its interpretation such a challenging activity.

The only case in which the referent of a first-person pronoun in a fiction may be interpreted as a counterpart of the author is when the narrator is explicitly referred to by the author's name. The rigid designator of the name confers upon the narrator the status of a historical character and places him or her under the scope of the principle of minimal departure. A narrator named "Borges" in a fiction by Jorge Luis Borges is no less an immigrant from AW than would be a character, or, for that matter, a narrator named Napoleon. When the narrator of "Funes the Memorious" is identified as Borges, we are entitled to assume that this Borges presents all the properties of the real Borges, except for the property of relating to Funes as creator to creature: within the textual universe, Borges the narrator regards Funes as a real person. The fictional protection of first-person pronouns from the principle of minimal departure is overridden by the principle itself, when a proper name restores the lines of transworld identity from author to narrator. But fiction and nonfiction remain nevertheless distinct through the default status of counterpart relations: in counterfactuals or reports of dreams, the hearer assumes by default the existence of transworld identity between actual speaking subject and textual I; in a discourse framed as fiction, the hearer assumes the absence of relation, unless a proper name explicitly identifies the textual I as counterpart of the author.

4 Voices and Worlds

The referential divorce between the I of the actual world and the relocated I of the textual universe in fictional communication invites us to reconsider the problem of fictionality in terms of the relation between the two subjects and their respective discourse. The doubling of the I creates a layered illocutionary structure whose parameters are described as follows by David Lewis: "Here at our world we have fiction *f*, told in an act *a* of storytelling; at some other world we have an act *a'* of telling the truth about known matter of fact; the stories told in *a* and *a'* match word for word, and the words have the same meaning" (1978:40).

If the dual-world, dual-intent, single-text structure is indeed constitutive of fictional communication, the author's implicit utterance in AW frames, embeds, and relays the discourse attributed to the speaker in TRW. It is the task of the illocutionary approach to define in intensional terms the setting of this frame.

In the best-known illocutionary account of fiction, John Searle's "The Logical Status of Fictional Discourse," the intent of the actual sender is defined in largely negative terms. Explicitly rejecting the idea that storytelling constitutes a speech act in its own right, Searle builds his proposal on the observation that the sentences representative of the various classes of illocutionary acts may appear in both fiction and nonfiction. When a sentence is uttered in a nonfictional context, the pragmatic rules governing its use are in effect, and the hearer is entitled to make certain assumptions concerning the speaker's intent. For the speech act of assertion, Searle formulates these rules as follows (1975:322, also 1969, chap. 3):

(1) The essential rule: the maker of an assertion commits himself to the truth of the expressed proposition.

(2) The preparatory rule: the speaker must be in a position to provide evidence or reasons for the truth of the expressed proposition.

(3) The expressed proposition must not be obviously true to both the speaker and the hearer in the context of utterance.

(4) The sincerity rule: the speaker commits himself to a belief in the truth of the expressed proposition.

When a sentence presenting the formal properties of an assertion occurs in a novel, however, these rules are not in force. In writing at the beginning of *The Red and the Green* "Ten glorious days without horses! So thought Second Lieutenant Andrew Chase-White" (1965:3), novelist Iris Murdoch is not committing herself to the truth of the sentence, since she knows, and wants the reader to recognize, that there is no Andrew Chase-White. What she is doing instead is "pretending to make an assertion, or going through the motions of making an assertion, or imitating the making of an assertion." Searle distinguishes between a deceptive and a nondeceptive sense of "pretend" (pretending to be Richard Nixon in order to be let by the Secret Service into the White House versus pretending to be Nixon as part of a play or a game of charades), and he assigns fictional pretense to the second category. The author of a fiction thus engages in a "non-deceptive pseudo-performance" of illocutionary acts, normally but not necessarily of the representative type (1975:324–25).

Since Searle's account of fiction relies on his own concept of speech act, it is vulnerable to any valid objection raised against the theory. A criticism recently voiced by Mary Louise Pratt (1986:64) is that speech-act theory presupposes the existence behind every utterance of "an authentic, self-consistent, essential subject, a 'true self,' which does or does not want to know the answer to the question, does or does not hold the intension that the other is supposed to recognize, does or does not have evidence for the truth of p." Only such subjects would know for sure whether they are standing behind their utterances, or just "going through the moves." But to Pratt, as it is to Derrida, the existence of this subject is largely illusory. Following a similar line of reasoning, Thomas Pavel argues that the rules governing speech acts, more particularly the essential rule of assertion, are "exorbitantly severe":

> In order to follow the sincerity rule scrupulously, a speaker has to be transparent to himself with respect to his beliefs. . . . But the picture we get from actual situations indicates that we more or less believe a limited number of propositions, without knowing whether we believe their consequences or not, and for a large number of propositions we simply do not know, in any serious sense of the word, whether we believe them to be true or not. (1986:20)

Far from restricting our assertive acts to the propositions we deeply believe to be true, we frequently advance, for their intrinsic interest or just for the fun of it, propositions to which we are only loosely committed, or even not committed at all. Ludic uses of language are as widespread in everyday conversation as are serious utterance acts. Playing the devil's advocate, teasing, making aberrant claims in a spirit of contradiction, and talking to inanimate objects can all be described as a form of pretense. In many cases, the unstable character of our beliefs prevents us from assessing the extent to which we are sincere and the extent to which we are just pretending: sometimes we end up identifying with the role we thought we were only playing, sometimes we end up secretly distantiating ourselves from the positions we fought to establish. If fictional discourse is "pretending to accomplish speech acts," it is omnipresent in our daily verbal transactions, and there is a continuum rather than a qualitative difference between fiction and nonfiction. Many literary theorists endorse this fuzzy-set interpretation of the pretense analysis, even though Searle's intent was to discriminate rigidly between fiction and nonfiction. According to Pratt, we should regard as fictional not only novels, jokes, and fables but also hyperbole, teasing, "kidding around," imitations, verbal play, hypotheses of any kind, the "scenarios" in the Oval Office, the hypothetical situations used in mathematical problems and philosophical arguments, and assumptions made "for the sake of the discussion" (1977:91). (The list also includes some of the forms of discourse that have been characterized in chapter 1 as world-creating nonfactuals involving no recentering: imagining, planning, reporting dreams, wishing, and fantasizing.)

While I agree that a definition of fiction should accept a wider variety of discourse forms than the standard case of literary narrative fiction, I believe that there remain fundamental differences between forms of pretense such as kidding, teasing, playing the devil's advocate, and talking to inanimate objects, and the pretense of fiction proper.

The most important difference—as Searle insists—resides in the nature of the pretense. In spontaneous verbal play, pretense usually presents a slightly deceitful element. The games of teasing or playing the devil's advocate would miss their target if the hearer were not induced to believe, at least for a fleeting moment, that the speaker is acting seriously. No such ambiguity occurs in fictional communication: the pretense must be fully overt for the text to be recognized as fiction.

While the pretense of fiction lures the hearer into an alternative system of reality in order to contemplate it for its own sake, verbal play remains much more firmly rooted in AW. The point of the devil's advocate who argues for a cause he or she does not believe in is to address real issues. And the point of a plant lover who exclaims in front of a favorite philodendron "Stupid weed, are you going to die on me?" is to express his or her real feelings for a real plant. As in counterfactuals, the evocation of an APW where aberrant principles hold true, or where plants can understand language, yields a message to be valued in the actual world.

Still another difference between fiction and the pretense of verbal play is the behavior discussed in the preceding chapter: the status of the I and you with respect to the principle of minimal departure. The plant lover who talks to a philodendron pretends to believe that the plant can understand language, but he or she retains in all other respects a real identity. Similarly, when I play the devil's advocate for arch-conservative politics in order to tease or challenge my humorless liberal friend, I pretend to be not one of the obtuse bigots who in my friend's opinion defend the position, but the intelligent and well-educated person I (think I) really am. The whole point of the game is to get my friend to contemplate a possible world in which adherence to the controversial policy is compatible with my own level of intellectual sophistication, and to challenge him or her to demonstrate that such a world could never be actualized. In the type of pretense exemplified by playing the devil's advocate or talking to inanimate objects the speaker plays the role of his or her own counterpart, while in fiction proper the sender adopts a foreign identity. One form of behavior is like pretending to be sick, the other like pretending to be Napoleon. Our incomplete transparency to ourselves may prevent drawing a distinct line between sincere utterances and speech acts accomplished in a game of self-pretense, but adopting a foreign identity is such a radical step that it constitutes a discrete category.[1]

While critiques such as Pratt's and Pavel's fault Searle for ignoring spontaneous forms of pretense, I would, on the contrary, fault him for accepting nonpretended speech acts into a discourse framed as fiction. According to Searle, when the author of a fiction speaks about real entities he or she does not engage in pretense, but performs the act of referring in a serious manner.

> Most fictional stories contain nonfictional elements: along with the pretended references to Sherlock Holmes and Watson there are in Sherlock Holmes real references to London and Baker Street and Paddington Station; again, in War and Peace, the story of Pierre and Natasha is a fictional story about fictional characters, but the Russia of War and Peace is the real Russia, and the war against Napoleon is the real war against the real Napoleon. The test [for what is fictional and what isn't] is what counts as a mistake. . . . If there never did exist an Andrew Chase-White, Miss Murdoch is not mistaken. Again, if Sherlock Holmes and Watson go from Baker Street to Paddington Station by a route which is geographically impossible, we will know that Conan Doyle blundered. (1975:330–31)

In Searle's analysis, then, the Sherlock Holmes stories are a patchwork of serious statements spoken by Conan Doyle, and of fictional statements spoken by the substitute speaker Dr. Watson. One wonders, however, what happens to Dr. Watson when the text refers to London, and who could be the speaker of a sentence like "Sherlock Holmes lived on Baker Street." If we attribute the reference to Baker Street to Conan Doyle, and the reference to Sherlock Holmes to Dr. Watson, the unity of the speech act will be broken up. But a postulate of speech-act theory states that the speech act is the most basic unit of verbal communication. If the unity of the speech act asserting that Holmes lived on Baker Street is to be maintained, we must attribute both references to the speaker, namely Dr. Watson. By analogy, we must assume that the impersonal narrator of *War and Peace* is able to refer to both Napoleon and Natasha. Contrary to Searle's claim, this speaker is under no strict commitment to report exclusively the historical truth about Napoleon: Georg Kayser did not blunder when he wrote a drama about the emperor's escape to New Orleans. At most one could invoke a kind of "rule of sportsmanship," through which authors of realistic historical fictions would be morally required to respect established fact on little-known subject matters. The reason for this moral commitment is the reader's tendency to invert the principle of minimal departure. Nobody will be misled by a novel describing Napoleon's escape to New Orleans, since the fact of his death on St. Helena belongs to general knowledge, but if a novel described him as a voracious reader of Marquis de Sade some readers would integrate this information into their representation of the real Napoleon. It is this convention of respecting little-known facts which opens the possibility for authorial blunders in fiction, and not a deep-seated logical difference between pretended and authentic speech acts in the fictional text.

The difficulties encountered by Searle in dealing with statements concerning members of AW derive from his neglect of the notion of possible worlds. For him, either an author speaks about imaginary entities, and he pretends to refer to them, or he speaks about AW, and he refers seriously. By combing the notion of pretense with the concept of possible worlds, and by assuming that the world at the center of a system of reality may present various degrees of overlap with AW, we can avoid the logical fragmentation of the text. Through fictional pretense, the author of a novel like *War and Peace* becomes a member of a world in which Napoleon and Natasha really exist, and this membership gives him or her the right to refer to both characters through factual discourse. Once the initial step into TRW has been taken, there is no logical difference between speech acts referring to Natasha and speech acts referring to Napoleon.

Another problematic point in Searle's analysis is its failure to protect the narrator from the principle of minimal departure in standard third-person impersonal narration. According to Searle, the author of an anonymously narrated fiction "pretends to perform illocutionary acts," while the author of a first-person narration "pretends to be someone else making assertions." Thus in the Sherlock Holmes stories, Sir Arthur Conan Doyle is "not simply pretending to make assertions," but *"pretending to be* John Watson, M.D." (1975:328). One wonders, however, who the actual speaker pretends to be in the case of impersonal narration. By opposing "pretending to perform speech acts" to "pretending to be the individuated narrator," Searle seemingly eliminates the need for a substitute speaker in impersonal fiction. But his formula hides the fact that the verb "perform" requires a logical subject. If the author of a classical third-person narrative fiction like *Anna Karenina* is not adopting a foreign identity, then this author must be pretending to be *him* or *herself* performing speech acts. Searle's analysis thus misses the distinction between impersonal narration and the rather unusual case of fictional self-impersonation.

The problem encountered by Searle with impersonal narration can be resolved by extending his analysis of personal narration to all forms of fiction. This extension requires the postulation of a dummy substitute speaker when the text prevents the individuation of the narrator. The function of this dummy substitute is to prevent any relation of coreference between the I of AW and the I of TRW, thus protecting the impersonal narrator from the principle of minimal departure. Since every speech act presupposes an addressee, a substitute hearer, or narratee, must be postulated as correlate of the substitute speaker. The slot of the substitute hearer will again be filled by a dummy when the narratee remains invisible. Thus completed to accept all forms of narration, Searle's analysis can be translated into a formula that reflects the dual-world, layered structure of fictional communication. This formula is shown in figure 4.

To each pair of speaker/hearer in figure 4 corresponds a distinct transaction, defined by its own pragmatic rules. The exchange in TRW can belong to any existing class of textual or sentential speech act, and it is governed by whatever felicity conditions relate to its illocutionary category. In a move which constitutes the point of the fictional game, the responsibility of fulfilling these felicity conditions is delegated by the actual speaker to the substitute speaker. By stepping into the role of the substitute speaker, the author can offer every conceivable string of linguistic signs to the reader's consideration, without accepting the normal consequence of uttering these words.

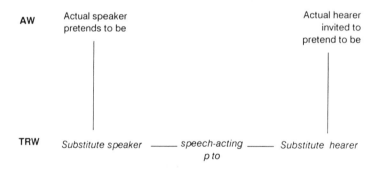

Figure 4
The structure of fictional communication
Version 1

The transaction of AW is the fictional communication proper. Since this transaction embeds the speech act of TRW, the fictional operator is not an ordinary illocutionary category on a par with such categories as question, command, and assertion, but a meta-speech act, an illocutionary modality ranging over speech acts. Just as a standard verb can appear in a sentence either by itself or modified by a modal verb (must, ought, could, etc.), a standard speech act may stand on its own, or be performed fictionally.

The No-Narrator Theory of Fiction

Before describing in detail the parameters of the formula depicted in figure 4, and proposing an intensional definition of the fictional gesture, let us consider a potential challenge to the present proposal: the case of impersonal and omniscient narration. (These two properties are commonly subsumed under the label "third-person narration," but they remain logically distinct: *The Old Man and the Sea* is told in the impersonal mode but makes no use of omniscience; *Remembrance of Things Past* has an individuated narrator but maintains access to the minds of other characters.)

In impersonal narration, discourse focuses away from the enunciating subject, and the question "who could legitimately utter such a discourse?" yields no answer beyond the minimal inference: a subject endowed with a mind and linguistic competence. The reader may be able to attribute some opinions, bias, stylistic idiosyncrasies, and a specific cultural background to the enunciating subject, but no definitive, computable physical properties. The narrator is not a specific member of TRW, and his or her lack of individuating features calls into question the validity of the concept of substitute speaker.

Omniscent narration challenges the notion of embedded speech act through what Ann Banfield calls "unspeakable sentences": free indirect report of thoughts, stream of consciousness, and the representation of subconscious processes. An example of an unspeakable sentence is this passage from Virginia Woolf's *Mrs. Dalloway:* "And then, thought Clarissa, what a morning—fresh as if issued to children on a beach" (1925:3). The sentence becomes even less speakable when considered in conjunction with another on the next page: "A charming woman, Scrope Purvis thought her . . . ; a touch of the bird about her, of the jay, blue-green, light, vivacious, though she was over fifty and grown very white since her illness" (4). By expressing a consciousness other than that of the enunciating subject, these sentences presuppose the supernatural ability of reading into foreign minds. Their sincerity conditions are consequently not fulfillable in the actual world. Rather than attributing free indirect reports of speech and thought to a ghostlike, absent speaker, Banfield invokes a linguistic principle of her invention—one self, one expression—to argue that since the represented self is referred to in the third person, there cannot be an implicit first-person speaker. If the reporting voice does not belong to an individuated human or human-like being, and if the narrative discourse is not a possible speech act, what is the point of invoking the parameters of standard verbal communication? Together with S. Y. Kuroda (1976), Banfield bypasses the categories of substitute speaker and embedded speech act by endorsing a "noncommunicative" theory of impersonal narration, according to which the text involves no narrator and no speech act. Following a tradition initiated by Käthe Hamburger (1957) and Emile Benveniste (1966), Kuroda and Banfield argue that in impersonal/omniscient narration "nobody speaks" and the events are simply "telling themselves." The sentences of this fictional mode imply no I-you relation and they are consequently "freed from the speech act" (Banfield 1978:445).

This account is supported by significant pragmatic differences between personal (first-person) and impersonal narration. Personal narrators are bound to their own point of view, impersonal narrators may speak from the perspective of any character. The discourse of personal narrators may be introduced by another narrator; impersonal narrators stand at the bottom of what Felix Martínez-Bonati calls "the pyramid of narration" (1981:30): the narratorial discourse may quote other speakers but cannot be quoted (unless the quoter belongs to another system of reality, as in my own quotes of literary fictions). Personal narrators may be unreliable; impersonal narrators may not: since they are not individuated, the gap between the truth and their declarations could not be justified on psychological grounds. From this it follows that the declarations of personal narrators stand in a variable relation to the facts of TAW/TRW, while impersonal narrators have absolute narrative authority: their declarations yield truths, either directly or after a metaphorical or ironic transformation. But what impersonal narrators gain in the domain of authority, they concede in autonomy. Personal narrators have their own verbal idiosyncrasies; the style of impersonal narrators cannot be distinguished from the style of the author. And while personal narrators are entitled to their own opinions, impersonal narrators can only relay the position of the implied author. When the narrator of *Anna Karenina* asserts that "All unhappy families are unhappy in their own, separate ways," we take this not only as narratorial judgment for TRW, but also as Tolstoi's pronouncement for AW. (Or alternatively, in Nabokov's ironic twist of the maxim in *Ada*, we take it to reflect neither a narratorial nor an authorial position.)

Another advantage of Banfield and Kuroda's proposal resides in its ability to account for the fact that fictional discourse displays a wider range of pragmatic possibilities than nonfiction, and is not constrained by the demands of real-world interpersonal communication. In which genre, if not in a novel or short story, would these two passages be compatible: "That day was to Akaki like a great festival. . . . He kept smiling to himself all during dinner"; "Unfortunately we cannot say where precisely the Civil Servant who was giving the party lives"? (Gogol, *The Overcoat*, 1965:253).[2]

These facts may speak in favor of the no-narrator theory, but it should be kept in mind that the proposal cannot account for the case of personal fiction. Should it turn out to be the best analysis of impersonal/omniscient narration, the price to pay would be the loss of a unified model of fictional expression. Under the pretended speech act proposal, discourse is divided into layered and nonlayered, fictional and nonfictional. Under the Banfield/ Kuroda proposal, the classes are communicative versus noncommunicative discourse, the former requiring a further division into real and fictional communication.

But in order to be maintained, even within a limited domain, the no-narrator/no-speech-act theory must explain how the sentences of impersonal fiction can convey meaning without projecting an intent (for if there is an intent, there must be a speaker addressing a hearer). In contemporary philosophy of language, meaning is usually defined in intensional terms. According to Grice, "x means something" is equivalent to "somebody means something by x," which in turn is equivalent to "somebody intended the utterance of x to produce some effect in the audience by means of recognition of that intention" (1971:442). If Grice's account of meaning is correct, we can dismiss right away the no-narrator theory of fiction.

Kuroda avoids the intensional account of meaning by claiming that a sentence can project a semantic content by being simply "made to exist as a real entity in this world" (1976:130). He calls this ability of sentences to evoke meaning without being actually uttered the "objective function" of sentences, and he contrasts it with their "communicative function," which is, roughly, the ability of sentences to express the speaker's judgment and opinions. It is, presumably, in virtue of this objective function that we are able to interpret such unuttered linguistic objects as the words in a dictionary or the examples of a linguistics article. Following this line of reasoning, it could be argued that in impersonal fiction, the author is implicitly telling the reader: "Extract propositions out of these sentences I have fabricated on the basis of their objective function, and imagine a world in which they are all true." Since the concept of objective function comes very close to the Fregean notion of sense, this could be reformulated as: take these sentences, and construct a world on the basis of their sense.

This proposal encounters two difficulties. First, in order to reconstruct the semantic universe of a text such as *Madame Bovary*, we must take the expressions Emma, Mme. Bovary, and Charles's wife as referring to the same individual, even though they differ in their sense or objective function. But referring is an act presupposing an actor, a context, and an intent. We must therefore imagine a narrator performing the referring act. This narrator is implicitly present in any mimetic use of language—in any text inviting its reader to imagine a world populated by individuals to whom the text is referring.

Another argument against the no-narrator account rests on the fact that the propositions yielded by the sentences of impersonal narration are not necessarily true in the fictional world. Consider the famous opening sentence of Jane Austen's *Pride and Prejudice*: "It is a truth universally acknowledged that a single man in possession of a fortune must be in want of a wife" (1933:231). What describes the world of *Pride and Prejudice* is not the proposition encoded in this sentence, but another proposition, something like: "It is a belief of every mother trying to find a rich husband for her daughter that a single man in possession of a fortune must be in want of a wife." The statement is obviously made in an ironic mood. But irony is not an objective property of sentences; it resides in the speaker's intent. The speaker of the above sentence cannot be Jane Austen, since "he" believes in the existence of the characters, so "he" must be a narrator performing an ironic speech act. (Referring to the impersonal narrator, "he" is used in this text as a genderless personal pronoun, indicating not "either gender" but no gender at all.)

The Parameters of the Embedded Transaction

The challenge of the no-narrator theory invites us to reconsider the parameters of the embedded transaction: substitute speaker, substitute hearer, and embedded speech act.

The Substitute Speaker

Substitute speakers come in two ontological varieties: personal/individuated narrators, who present what I shall call a psychological reality, and impersonal narrators, whose existence is postulated on purely logical grounds.

Narrators of the first variety function as an autonomous mind interposed between the mind of the author and the minds of characters. The worlds of their private domain form an integral part of the textual universe: the reader treats their beliefs, projections, wishes, and opinions as existing on a par with those of characters. The apprehension of the textual universe would remain incomplete without an assessment of the narrator's private domain. From an ontological point of view, the individuated substitute speaker can be described as accidentally incomplete. In accidental incompleteness, the gaps in specification are regarded as gaps in information. For every property p, the formula "either the narrator has p or does not have p" implicitly holds in TRW, regardless of whether or not the text specifies which one of the disjuncts holds true. Like other characters, whose ontological status he or she shares, the personal narrator is incomplete within AW but complete in TRW, incomplete objectively but complete in make-believe.

Speakers of the second category function as a mere speech position, a point of view on the textual universe, a "rental consciousness" for the author's relocation in TRW. Their existence is postulated for the sole purpose of relieving the author of the responsibility of fulfilling the felicity conditions of the textual utterances. Since anonymous speakers are deprived of human dimension, and cannot express subjective opinions divorced from those of the implied author, the reader may dispense with the reconstruction of their personality, beliefs, and judgments as an autonomous private domain. While personal narrators are implicitly complete in TRW, impersonal narrators achieve completeness in neither AW nor TRW. The ontological status of impersonal narrators is one of radical incompleteness, which cancels the validity of the formula "either the narrator has p or not p." It is not the case that the narrator of *Anna Karenina* is objectively either a man or not a man in TRW, no matter how symptomatically male or female "his" discourse may appear.

In most works of narrative fiction, the substitute speaker falls together with what I have called in chapter 1 the implied speaker: the substitute speaker can be regarded as the subject who fulfills the sincerity conditions of the textual utterance.[3] But in the case of deceptive narration, substitute and implied speaker must be dissociated—just as, in the lies of real-world communication, the implied speaker differs from the actual speaker. In the Jason section of *The Sound and the Fury* (as analyzed by Rabinowitz 1977:134), Faulkner impersonates a morally flawed individual who projects himself as an innocent victim. The implied speaker is the "innocent" Jason, while the substitute speaker is the whole person, the despicable individual. But whether or not substitute speakers stand behind implied speakers, they are the ones who are held personally responsible for fulfilling the felicity conditions of the textual utterance.

The Substitute Hearer

The distinction substitute/implied speaker is paralleled in the domain of the hearer, but the receiving side involves an additional construct. The laminations of the hearer include:

(1) The implied hearer: an individual who is able to use contextual information in order to decode irony and figural expression, but accepts uncritically the propositions expressed either directly or after the ironic/figural transformation.

(2) The substitute hearer or narratee per se: the audience "objectively" addressed by the substitute speaker, rather than implied by the narratorial discourse. The types of substitute hearer available to fictional discourse reproduce the types of addressee available to nonfictional communication: the hearer may be projected as a private individual (as in letters and conversation), as the general public (as in published texts), or it may remain unspecified (as in soliloquy, which I take to be addressed to nobody in particular, rather than to a hearer identical with the speaker). An instance of fictional

communication involving an unspecified substitute hearer is the solitary rambling of Beckett's narrator in *The Unnameable.*

(3) The role under which the actual hearer (or reader) is asked to step into TRW, i.e., the identity he assumes through his act of pretense. At this point one might wonder why it is at all necessary to postulate a hearer/reader's role in TRW, potentially different from the substitute hearer. Let me restate the reason advanced in chapter 1: playing the fictional game means regarding the text as the representation of an actual world TRW, while remaining aware that TRW is not objectively AW (the text does not refer to *the* actual world). And according to the indexical definition, I can only regard as actual the world in which I am located. If the reader is to pretend that the characters are real people, and that the events actually happened, he must project himself as a member of TRW. Kendall Walton (1978b) proposes a psychological motivation for the concept of reader's role in TRW, by arguing that it explains the phenomenon of fearing fictions. It is indeed from the perspective of a member of the fictional world that the reader is emotionally affected by the events that take place in this world.

In the standard case of impersonal narration, the three constructs of the receiver's side fall together. The narrator is reliable, an audience can accept uncritically all of his or her declarations, and since the utterance is offered to the general public, every member of TRW is legitimately included in the audience, including the member into whose identity the hearer is stepping.

In the case of personal unreliable narration addressed to the general public, (1) is divorced from (2), but (2) concurs with (3). This happens, according to Peter Rabinowitz, in *The Sound and the Fury:* the implied hearer (whom Rabinowitz calls ideal narrative audience) "believes that Jason has been victimized, and sympathizes with his whining misery" (1977:134) although the substitute hearer and the member of TRW into whom the actual hearer projects her or himself can only despise him. (Rabinowitz labels these two concepts collectively as "narrative audience.")

When the utterance of the substitute speaker is addressed to an individual, as in drama or epistolary novels, (2) is divorced from (3). While the substitute speaker can be individuated, the role assumed by the actual hearer is always that of an anonymous member of TRW. If the actual hearer pretended to be a specific individual, he or she would become a character, an agent in the plot. Rather than regarding her- or himself as an agent, the hearer plays the role of passive spectator. The reader of an epistolary novel does not project her- or himself as the recipient of the letters, switching role with each missive, but as an anonymous member of TRW who happens to have intercepted the correspondence. Similarly, the audience of a play does not pretend to be the addressee of the current speaker, but an outside observer who looks through the transparent fourth wall of the classical stage. To prevent the reader from becoming a full-fledged character in the fictional universe and taking over an active role in its elaboration, the author invites him or her to step into TRW as an anonymous, nonindividuated member. As Thomas Pavel puts it—explain-

ing the position of Kendall Walton—"when caught up in a story, we participate in fictional happenings by projecting a fictional ego who attends the
imaginary events as a kind of non-voting member" (1986:85). This mandatory
anonymity of the reader's role in TRW leads to the following relation with the
substitute speaker: When the utterance of the substitute speaker is addressed
to an anonymous hearer—the general public—the reader projects him or
herself as part of the legitimate audience. The group concept of substitute
hearer includes in this case the reader's alter ego. On the other hand, when
the utterance is addressed to an individual identified by a proper name, the
reader's role in TRW is that of an external witness of the transaction.

A potential distinction of (1), (2), and (3) occurs when a substitute
speaker tries to deceive an individuated addressee. In *Les Liaisons dangereuses,*
when Valmont writes a deceptive letter to Cécile, there are (a) the implied
speaker Valmont, a well-meaning friend of Cécile, and the implied hearer
Cécile, who trusts him; (b) the narrator Valmont, a liar trying to seduce Cécile,
and his addressee Cécile, who may or may not fall into Valmont's trap; and (c)
the anonymous member of TRW with whom the reader identifies.

The potential dissociation of the substitute speakers from the role
adopted in TRW by the actual hearer leads to the model of fictional communication shown in figure 5.

The Embedded Transaction

The communicative function of an utterance can be described on two
levels: on the textual, or macrostructural level, by labels corresponding to
genres (recipe, law, novel, biography), and on the sentential, or microstruc-
tural level, by illocutionary categories (assertion, command, question, prom-

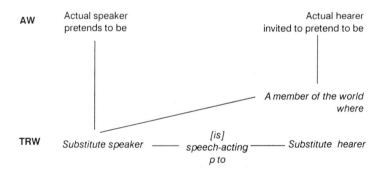

Figure 5
The structure of fictional communication
Version 2

ise). Both levels should be considered in describing the transaction between substitute speaker and substitute hearer.

A fairly widespread position among literary theorists inspired by speech-act theory regards the embedded transaction as the imitation of a nonfictional genre. According to Mary Pratt (1977: 201–10), novels mimic memoirs, letters, biographies, autobiographies, or, in the unmarked case, simply "narrative display texts" (i.e., stories told as true fact, for the sake of their intrinsic "tellability"). Barbara Herrnstein Smith, who regards poetry as fiction, bases this position on the claim that poetry is "a representation of spoken discourse, usually in verse" (1978:32). (The versified form provides, however, convincing evidence that the poem could never be uttered as spoken discourse.) By stressing the potentially "unspeakable" character of fictional sentences, Banfield and Kuroda's position offers a needed antidote against the reduction of fiction to an imitation of nonfiction. An epistolary novel may reproduce letters, and a first-person narrative fiction may read like an autobiography, but many fictional texts do not allow separate specification of embedded and embedding genre. What could be the embedded genre of a novel with stream of consciousness besides precisely novel, or of a nonsense rhyme besides nonsense rhyme?

The resistance to internal macro-level classification exhibited by these texts suggests that a theory of fiction must allow both "typed" and "untyped" embedded utterances. A typed utterance can be described on the macro-level by a generic label, while an untyped utterance can only be characterized as "text" (or as "narrative," a broad metageneric category). But whether or not the utterance is typed, its component sentences remain classifiable as microlevel speech acts such as command, assertion, and question. When the substitute speaker is not an individuated human being, or when the substitute hearer remains unspecified, the propositional content of the individual sentential speech acts is not subjected to the restrictions operative in normal human communication. There are simply no limits on what can be legitimately said by a nonembodied voice or by a mumbling speaker engaged in soliloquy.[4]

The distinction between typed and untyped utterances opens two possibilities on the lower level of the first two proposals for the structure of fictional communication:

(a) x g(t) to y, where t is a text with macrolevel communicative function g;
(b) x f(p1) & f(p2) & f(p3) to y, where the f's correspond to microlevel speech acts and the p's to the "speech-acted" propositions.

The Fictional Rules

The distinctions made above between types of substitute hearers and types of embedded transactions have led to a splitting of the analysis of figure 4 into several sub-cases. To subsume them all under the same model I propose the analysis shown in figure 6.

By replacing "pretends to be x doing something" with "pretends *that* x is doing something" (sending, receiving), the model of figure 6 says nothing explicit about roles being played in TRW by the actual speaker and hearer. But I take "sender pretends through the utterance of t that x is uttering t" to be synonymous with "sender pretends to be x uttering t." If, by uttering a text t, which implies an I, a speaker pretends that another I is uttering this text, then we can assume that the real I *speaks as* this other I.

This equivalence does not hold on the hearer's side: the actual hearer can pretend, on the sender's invitation, that t is addressed by x to y, without necessarily identifying with y. This difference between the two sides of the model is due to an asymmetry inherent to all communication: we can over-hear an act of verbal communication addressed to somebody else, eavesdrop on a conversation, intercept a letter, but we cannot sneak up in the same way into the role of speaker. We can receive without being the intended receiver, but we cannot send without being the intending sender. But whether or not actual hearers pretend to be part of the projected audience, they do witness in make-believe the transaction of TRW, thus pretending to be themselves members of TRW.

The rules of the fictional transaction specify the nondeceptive character of the pretense, the identity of substitute speaker and hearer, and the invitation extended to the reader to reconstruct a universe on the basis of the pretended speech act. My proposed formulation reads as follows:

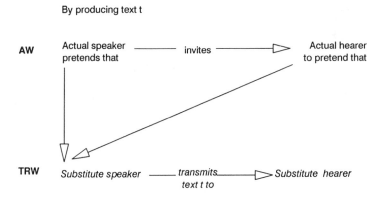

Figure 6
The structure of fictional communication
Version 3

Through the utterance of text T, the speaker S intends
(a) the hearer H to pretend that text T is an utterance of S' addressed to
H', where S' and H' are a pair of substitute speaker and hearer located
in a world TRW distinct from AW;
(b) H to assume that S' bears no counterpart relation to S unless explicitly referred to by the same name;
(c) H to "make-believe" the system of reality centered around TRW, on
the basis of the transaction between S' and H', by projecting him or
herself as an anonymous member of TRW. (This member will be included in H' if H' is a nonindividuated audience.)[5]

This set of rules, together with the model shown in figure 6, will be referred
to in chapter 5 as "the formula of chapter 4."

Reading as Fiction

A widespread position among theorists of fiction is that under certain
circumstances a nonfictional text can be read as fiction, or even objectively
become fiction. If this assumption is correct, a proper definition of fictionality should not only account for the possibility, but also elucidate the meaning of the expression "to read a text as fiction."

Under what I have called in chapter 1 a referential definition, the feature of fictionality depends on the relation between what is in AW and what
the text says there is in TAW. Since the relation AW/TAW may be assessed
differently by author and reader, a text meant as nonfiction may be received
as fiction, or vice versa. (It is hard, however, to find convincing examples of
the second possibility: I can only come up with the case of Don Quixote and
Emma Bovary, who significantly happen to be themselves characters in fictions.) This discrepancy makes fictionality, in the words of Thomas Pavel, a
"historically variable property" (1986:80). To support his position, Pavel
argues that the erosion of belief in Greek deities made their adventures
available for fictional treatment, such as tragedy and epic poems. The loss of
religious belief not only turns the gods into a suitable subject matter for
profane texts, it also leads to a new attitude toward the ancient myths:
"When a mythological system gradually loses its grip on a society, the ancient gods and heroes start to be perceived as fictional characters" (41).
Removed from their cultural context, the tales of the gods may still be appre-
ciated for their charm as stories, but no longer for their value as religious
revelation. Unable to extract sacred teachings because of what they regard
as referential failure, modern readers of myths expect from them the same
type of gratification they derive from such notoriously fictional genres as
novels and fairy tales. The literary theorist who claims that the status of
classical myths has switched from nonfiction in archaic Greek society to
fiction in contemporary culture demonstrates an implicit commitment to
the referential definition.

With an illocutionary/intensional approach, the feature of fictionality is not historically variable but fixed once and for all at the moment of the text's creation. Myth was meant as religious revelation, not as entertaining narrative, and no loss of religious belief can change the sender's intent. According to Searle, "'The Bible as literature' is theologically neutral, but 'The Bible as fiction' is tendentious" (1975:320). The first phrase acknowledges the poetic qualities of the Bible, which are compatible with religious significance, while the second suggests that the author rejects the truth-in-AW of the text. But if intents cannot be changed, they can be disregarded. In the framework of the above analysis, the phrase "read the Bible as fiction" could be interpreted as "read the Bible *as if* it had been conceived under an act of pretense," while remaining aware that it was not the case. Pretend, in other words, that the historical author was impersonating a substitute speaker, and taking no personal responsibility for the textual speech act. There is no doubt that this game can be played—the limits on what we can pretend coincide with the limits of human imagination—but what would be the point of pretending authorial pretense? When we read a myth as entertaining narrative, rather than as a source of religious knowledge, we do indeed disregard the sender's claim to represent a sacred reality, but we do not do so by imagining a substitute speaker, a substitute hearer, and a layered illocutionary structure. Our disregard of the author's religious intent does not lead us to "read the text as fiction" in the sense of the definition presented in this chapter. What we do with the myths of a foreign culture, rather, is read them for the sake of their aesthetic value.

Most uses of the phrase "read as fiction" in contemporary literary theory reduce the problem of fictionality to an aesthetic issue. According to Pavel, "texts which are nonfictional on semantic or pragmatic grounds can be read fictionally for purely textual reasons: well-written memoirs or romanced biographies are obvious examples" (1986:71). This statement equates the nature of reading fiction with textual qualities. But as we have seen, fictionality carries no mandatory stylistic properties. What Pavel means by the term "reading as fiction" is really "reading for the pleasure of the text," as opposed to reading for information. Conversely, what could be regarded as "reading fiction as nonfiction" (e.g., scrutinizing Proust's *Remembrance of Things Past* for biographical data about the author or looking for symptoms of mental disease in a story by Edgar Allan Poe) is really reading a pleasure-oriented text as informational document.

There is, however, an important similarity between reading nonfictional narratives for the sake of pleasure, and participating legitimately in the fictional game—a similarity which explains the blurring of the two issues in the mind of critics. Modern readers of myths realize that the textual universe departs from their native system of reality; yet by deciding to contemplate this universe for its own sake, rather than evaluating it as a representation of the system centered around AW, they accomplish the same gesture of recentering as the reader of a fiction. In both instances, readers project themselves into the role of a member of a world different from AW. The difference is that in fiction they respond to the sender's invitation, while in reading nonfiction for the sake of pleasure they perform a transgression. Whereas the legitimate audience of myth is native to TRW, the reader-for-pleasure reaches this world as immigrant.

Fiction and Textual Orientation

The confusion inherent to the concept of "reading as fiction" derives from the fact that most fictional texts do indeed carry what I shall call an aesthetic or pleasure orientation, as opposed to an informational purpose. The difference between these two pragmatic categories lies in the criteria by which the receiver is invited by the sender to evaluate the text. Information-oriented texts are offered to readers as material for building their knowledge of reality. The relevant evaluative criteria are truth-in-AW, and given this truth, the novelty of the contents. Pleasure-oriented texts are proposed by contrast for the sake of their intrinsic formal or semantic properties. They are not meant to transmit something worth extracting and using, but something worth experiencing. The success of the transaction is measured by the satisfaction derived from the event—or is it activity?—of receiving the text. The two orientations of pleasure and information are not mutually exclusive, nor are they exclusive of a third major pragmatic category: texts conceived as a means to incite readers to action (advertisements, sermons, political propaganda). A genre such as proverb is offered both for its didactic value and for the felicity of the formulation. A memoir, work of historiography, or autobiography may be proposed at the same time as a literary work and as a source of information. Directive texts invite readers to action by providing information. And while the primary orientation of a political speech is to control the behavior of receivers, the text will be more efficient if it satisfies the evaluative criteria of the pleasure category.

A text's pragmatic orientation (po) may be conceived as a mandatory operator specifying what the sender intends to achieve, by proposing a text with the global illocutionary force f, and the propositional content p. Every act of textual communication can be symbolized as po(f/p). On the other hand, the fictional operator (symbolized here by FI) is an optional modality affecting the textual communication: actual senders either speak for themselves (po(f/p)), or they delegate responsibility to a substitute speaker: FI(po(f/p)). Through its ludic character, the fictional operator presents strong affinities with the pleasure orientation, but the categories intersect rather than coincide. The features of fictionality and of nonfictionality are both compatible with any of the three orientations. Proverbs are nonfiction, but they carry a pleasure orientation; parables are fictional, but their main point is didactic; and many advertisements make use of imaginary situations represented through fictional discourse. Within the same text, distinct levels of meaning may carry a different fictional status, and embody distinct orientations: in didactic novels, the fictional representation of TRW is offered for the sake of pleasure, but the message of the work is an indirect statement about AW, uttered in the author's name, and meant to both enlighten readers, and influence their behavior.

5 The Fiction Automaton

A definition of fiction is a machine built for the purpose of telling fiction from nonfiction. The design of the machine reflects a priori decisions as to which kinds of input should be accepted and which ones rejected. The machine would be of little interest, however, if the designer were able to foresee all possibilities. The real usefulness of the automaton does not reside in its ability to tell us what we already know—that "Little Red Riding Hood" belongs to fiction, that the Constitution of the United States does not—but in its handling of marginal cases. In this chapter I propose to run various types of communicative acts through the automaton of the formula of chapter 4 (pp. 74–76, and fig. 6) in the hope of situating the phenomenon of fictional expression within an extended family of verbal and nonverbal activities. What matters, however, is not so much the label that comes out of the automaton for a given input as the ability of the three criteria used in the definition to explicitate similarities and differences among various types of communication. Fiction is not an immutable essence to be discovered, but an analytical concept whose justification resides in its usefulness. How broadly this concept should be defined depends on what the user wants to do with it. It does not really matter where we draw the line between fiction and nonfiction, as long as we are able to assess the relations between marginal forms of fiction and the prototypical case—and as long as this prototypical case is pleasure-oriented narrative fiction.

Verbal Play

As I have argued above, most forms of verbal play—be they teasing, playing the devil's advocate, or talking to inanimate objects—differ from fiction through their failure to satisfy criteria (a), (b), and (c): the speaker is assumed by default to impersonate a counterpart of her- or himself, if the pretense is overt at all; this counterpart does not invite the hearer to play a role, but rather challenges the actual hearer; and the point of the utterance is usually to make a statement about AW.

Of all forms of verbal play, the closest to fiction are spontaneous games of make-believe, such as a father telling his daughter "I am the fuzzy green monster, and I am going to eat the little purple heffalump." This form of behavior adheres to criteria (a), (b), and partly to criterion (c). The father is engaging in an overt act of impersonation, he adopts the foreign identity of a monster, and he invites the daughter to "make-believe" the world in which the monster is speaking. Both father and daughter relocate themselves in this world, and regard it for the duration of the game as the center of reality. The only difference with standard fiction resides in the identity and involvement of the substitute hearer (last part of criterion [c]): the daughter is not invited to pretend to be an anonymous witness of the monster's speech act, but to step into the role of the purple heffalump. In so doing she becomes actively involved in the creation of the world of make-believe.

Rather than impersonating a monster or a heffalump, father and daughter could pretend that the monster is chasing the daughter, or that the father is trying to catch a heffalump. This one-way pretense would be equivalent to the case of Borges pretending to be Borges in a different system of reality. Players who play their own role would select the identity of their counterpart as one of the roles made available by the inventory of the world of make-believe. Both sides could indeed select their own counterpart—or even switch identities. All these games would still differ from fiction on criterion (c).

Apostrophe

The rhetorical trope of apostrophe is a formal relative of the spontaneous verbal game of addressing inanimate objects. The plant lover who exclaims "Stupid weed, are you going to die on me?" expresses her real feelings for a real object. She does so by pretending to be herself, talking to an intelligent counterpart of the plant. This counterpart is a member of an APW, but the speaker does not relocate to that world, nor select it as referent. She remains in AW, tied to her own identity, talking about a member of AW while addressing its counterpart in an APW. Her discourse crosses an ontological boundary, without hope for a response, for communication can only take place between members of the same world. To reach an audience, the apostrophe must be intercepted by a member of AW: seemingly addressing a plant, the speaker is really displaying her utterance to a third party, or engaging in soliloquy. Whereas fiction and genuine games of make-believe create a quadrangular relation between two actual and two substitute participants, in apostrophe the relation is triangular: the distinction actual/substitute is activated only on the hearer side of the transaction.

The poet who writes "O Rose, thou art sick" plays the same language game as the dejected plant-lover. The function of literary apostrophe—as

Jonathan Culler (1981) observes—is to express an emotional relation between the speaker and the topic of his discourse. Do poets express their own feelings, as does the plant lover? The answer to this question does not reside in the nature of apostrophe but in the nature of poetry. As a rhetorical trope, apostrophe can occur in a number of genres: sermons, political speeches, novels, poems. Some of these genres are fictional, some others are not. In a fictional context, apostrophe involves a primary and a secondary pretense, generating two speakers and three hearers. Whether or not poets speak in their own name in exclaiming "O Rose, thou art sick," or impersonate an anonymous speaker (the "lyrical I" postulated by German theorists), depends on whether or not the genre of lyric poetry justifies the fictional analysis.

Metaphor

Metaphor, along with tropes in general, has never to my knowledge been openly regarded as fiction. At close examination, this exclusion is more puzzling than evident. Metaphorical expression is obviously a kind of world-creating activity; like most forms of fiction, metaphors are literally false in AW; yet they are uttered without deceptive intent. The semantic domain created by the literal meaning of metaphor could be regarded as a conceptually remote type of possible world, put together according to very liberal principles. The metaphor world would break not only the laws of nature, but also logical, analytical, and basic taxonomic principles. These transgressions would allow words to be winged, dawn to have rosy fingers, light to be obscure, and warriors to be lions and men at the same time, sharing mutually incompatible essences. If one accepts this account, metaphor could be defined as an extreme form of fiction, leading to the most remote territories of the global universe of conceptual possibilities. The distinction of metaphor from other forms of fiction would be mostly a matter of accessibility relations.

I believe, however, that there is an important functional difference between a full-fledged fictional universe, whether close or remote, and the semantic domain yielded by the literal meaning of tropes. A true fictional universe is an autonomous construct, and its actual world functions as reference world of the discourse which creates it. By relocating themselves into this system, hearers contemplate TAW for its own sake, and temporarily put aside their concern for AW. In metaphor, there is no relocation to a new system of reality. We may imagine a "world" in which the propositions yielded by the literal meaning of metaphors and other tropes are true, but this world does not function as the center of a system of reality. The meaning that originates in the metaphor world is reflected back toward AW. This world is not created for its own sake, but as a point of view allowing us to rediscover AW from a new perspective. Like counterfactuals, metaphors take a detour to an APW in order to express truths about AW. This return to AW excludes metaphor from the realm of fiction. Or rather, metaphor is not inherently fiction or nonfiction, but shares the fictional status of the surrounding discourse.

This view of metaphor as discourse retaining AW as primary reference world is supported by the theory developed by Paul Ricoeur in *La Métaphore vive*. According to Ricoeur, metaphorical expression is a way to redescribe a reality which would remain inaccessible to direct description (1982:13). Taking the strongest commitment to truth-functionality, Ricoeur speaks not only of metaphorical meaning, but also of "metaphorical referentiality" to designate this power of metaphor to push back the limits of language and capture aspects of reality that cannot be expressed literally.

But if being valued in AW disqualifies a mode of expression from being fiction, what about parables and didactic novels? Their difference from metaphor is that the semantic universe created by these texts must first be constructed as an autonomous and ontologically complete system of reality, before the truths that apply to this system can be transferred back to AW. The teachings of the didactic novel are interpretations of the facts of TAW whose potential field of applicability includes both AW and TAW. But the primary reference world remains the central world of the system reached through the fictional relocation. In metaphor, by contrast, the "world" yielded by the literal meaning does not function as referent. Contemplated in itself, this world is no more than a meaningless spectacle. We may imagine winged words or a rosy-fingered dawn, but these images only reach intelligibility when we translate them into descriptions of real-world phenomena. While AW remains a secondary reference world in didactic narrative fiction, it functions in metaphorical discourse as primary, as unique referent (unless of course the metaphor appears in a fictional context).

Lyric Poetry

Why should poetry be regarded as fiction, and not simply as words put together by the author according to some particular stylistic conventions? Because, argues Barbara Herrnstein Smith, poems presuppose a speaker, but they are not regarded as the utterance of a historical individual. The author is not taking full responsibility for what his poem says: "To the objection, 'But I know Wordsworth meant what he says in this poem,' we must reply 'You mean he *would have* meant them if he *had* said them, but he is not saying them' " (28). By transferring the responsibility of the utterance act to a substitute speaker, the fictional analysis supports the claim that Wordsworth is not really saying what the poem seems to say.

But why is contemporary literary theory so intent on silencing the voice of the author, so dead-set against the idea that he or she may be proposing a vision of AW? In many types of poems, the subject matter is such that the fictional analysis seems superfluous. In antiquity, poetry was often closer to modern scientific discourse than to any kind of fiction. There is no reason to believe that Lucretius engaged in an act of pretense when writing *De Rerum Natura*, a philosophical/scientific theory of the universe, or that Virgil's *Georgics*, a versified treatise about agriculture, involves a recentering of reality. Both works present a version of AW (TRW = AW), conceived by a member of AW. Similarly, when Baudelaire writes a sonnet about cats in general, Rilke a poem about a Roman fountain, or Francis Ponge a short lyrical essay about an oyster, there is no logical necessity to attribute the utterance to a substitute speaker, since there are cats, oysters, and Roman fountains in AW. Why couldn't these works be regarded as nonfictional utterances spoken in the poet's name and referring to AW? It may be objected that the poems are not "really" about cats, oysters, or a Roman fountain, but about more general—and dignified—themes, such as Art, Cosmic Order, Mind and Matter, Love and Death, if not simply about themselves (self-referentiality being generally regarded as the most elevated topic of all). But even these general topics are issues within AW, and addressing them does not necessitate pretense and recentering.

Against this position, one could argue that the semantic domain of a poem such as "Les Chats" is only accidentally compatible with AW—or rather, that this compatibility is unusual for poetry. Most poetic worlds depart openly from AW: there are blue deer in the poems of Georg Trakl, and the speaker of Baudelaire's "La Vie antérieure" lives in some kind of underwater grotto. Moreover, many poems are spoken by personae, such as the Persian lovers Hatem and Suleika in Goethe's *East-West Divan*, or an Irish airman foreseeing his death, in Yeats's poem by the same name. We certainly do not believe that Trakl is affirming the existence of blue deer, that Yeats is expressing his personal experience as an Irish airman, or that Goethe is talking in the name of some of his former selves. All this speaks in favor of a pretense analysis. Should one then split lyric poetry into fictional and nonfictional, depending on its content and the presence of a persona—or should a poem like "Les Chats" be assimilated to true fiction? Under a fictional analysis, poems would not be prevented from addressing real issues, but AW would be regarded as a secondary reference world. The potential universality of the poetic message would thus be assimilated to the case of parables and didactic novels.

I believe, however, that even those poems which openly depart from AW do not completely satisfy the requirements of the formula of chapter 4. There are deep-seated phenomenological differences between the semantic domain of lyric poetry and of a clearly fictional genre such as the classical novel. The decisive issues include how readers construct and experience the semantic domain, how they apprehend the images proposed by the text, and how they relate to the lyrical voice. The phenomenology of lyric poetry is best apprehended through negative statements. (I propose these principles as valid of lyric poetry, a basically meditative genre, and not of primarily narrative poems such as ballads and epics. From a phenomenological point of view, narrative poetry is a versified form of narrative fiction and falls on the same side of the fictional divide.)

(1) There is no speech act nor speech situation. Consider this poem by William Carlos Williams:

> This is just to say I have eaten the plums which were in the icebox and which you were probably saving for breakfast. Forgive me, they were delicious: so sweet and so cold. (Quoted in Culler 1975:175)

If this statement appeared as the first sentence of a novel, framed in quotation marks, we would imagine a concrete context of utterance: for instance, a note left on a kitchen table, addressed by a man to a woman; we would speculate on the relation between sender and addressee, and we would try to anticipate the future reaction of the addressee. But because the text is framed as a poem, the context loses its importance. As Jonathan Culler writes: "We deprive the poem of the pragmatic and circumstantial functions of the note," and we "supply a new function to justify the poem" (1975:175). The function provided by Culler's interpretation turns the poem into a praise of immediate sensual experience in the face of repressive social rules ("Do not eat the forbidden fruit!").

(2) The semantic domain has no history. We do not speculate about what led the speaker of Williams's poem to write the note, nor about how the addressee will react. By contrast, we are very interested in what will happen to Scarlett O'Hara after the end of *Gone with the Wind*.

(3) The creatures of poetry are not individuated. By uttering the words "Tyger, tyger burning bright," the speaker of Blake's "Tyger" does not address an individual feline, but conjures up to the reader's mind an abstract concept—the essence of tigerness. Similarly, a poem addressed to "My Coy Mistress" is about a general type of woman, not about a specific individual. The reader understands this to be a constitutive rule of the genre, and does not attempt to extract from the poem concrete biographical information.

(4) We do not relate to the "characters" as ontologically complete persons. They have no self nor destiny. We do not try to fill in the gaps in their portrait nor to provide psychological motivation for their behavior. I would go as far as saying that there are no characters in poetry, only allegories. We do not care, in reading the first line of Wallace Stevens's "The Idea of Order at Key West," "She sang beyond the genius of the sea" whether there is or isn't a female singer on a beach in some world including a Key West. "She" is perceived as the incarnation of an idea, not as a person made of flesh and blood. The creatures of poetry lack a basic existential dimension—the dimension of membership in an actual world.

(5) In a role-poem, the persona adopted by the author lacks the fullness of existence of the personal narrator. Like other creatures of poetry, the "persona" is not perceived in make-believe as a real person. This is obvi-

ously the case when the poem is uttered by the Muse or by Fate. But it is equally true of less openly allegorical speakers. The Irish Airman of Yeats's poem is not a fighter in World War I but man facing death in the sky; Hatem and Suleika are not individuals bound by particular circumstances and engaged in a specific love story, but prototypical lovers.

(6) All of the preceding observations support this general claim: the semantic domain of lyric poetry is not a system of reality, a modal universe organized around an actual world. The sentences of poetry are not truth-functional, and do not outline a factual domain. When Georg Trakl writes about a blue deer, we do not construct a world where there is a blue deer, member of the class of blue deer. When Baudelaire writes "J'ai longtemps vécu sous de vastes portiques" [Long years I lived under vast porticoes], we do not imagine a subject who in a former life really lived in TRW under the described circumstances. Nor do we attempt to naturalize the utterance as hallucination. The blue deer and the vast porticoes are perceived as verbal artifacts, as products of the poet's imagination. Like all creatures of poetry, they are not offered to the reader's contemplation as existents, but as the metaphorical expression of the poet's relation to AW.

The phenomenological differences between narrative fiction and lyric poetry are summarized by this principle:

Narrative fiction makes existential claims about TRW; its primary message is of the form:

In TRW, $(\exists x)\ f(x)$ [There is an x, such that f(x)]

When narrative fiction makes universal claims, they are based on singular existential claims. A novel must first assert "There was a woman named Anna Karenina," before it can claim "All unhappy families . . . ," etc.

Lyric poetry makes no individual existential claims but only universal ones. Its primary message is captured by the formula:

In TRW, $(\forall x)\ f(x)$ [All x are f(x)],

or

In TRW, $(x)\ f(x)$

(The unquantified x stands for an abstract concept, such as love, death, art, or the human condition.)[1]

Through its avoidance of existential claims, lyric poetry lacks the element of make-believe and the playful recentering of true fiction. It never asks its reader to regard any individual entity as real. The reader can contemplate the "creatures of poetry" without traveling to a new system of reality because they have no roots in an actual world. Poetry is essentially metaphorical, and as I have shown in the preceding section, figural language does not display a foreign world for its own sake. The poetic text translates into concrete images an inner experience of AW, which the reader is invited to share.[2] The utterance act is not meant to be witnessed, but appropriated by the actual reader. Experiencing poetry means: looking at AW under its directives, adopting the poet's vision, identifying with the lyrical I. "Hypocrite lecteur, mon semblable, mon frère" [Hypocritical reader, my same, my brother] writes Baudelaire of the lyrical relation between speaker-I and reader-I.

In summary, lyric poetry may or may not involve a substitute speaker, but even when the poem creates a persona, this persona does not engage in a linguistic transaction with a substitute hearer. The lyrical text never fully complies with the first criterion of the formula for fictional communication. And since lyric poetry does not extend an invitation to pretend belief in a foreign system of reality, it fails to fulfill the other conditions.

Drama

As text meant to be performed—composed by an individual, transmitted by another—drama generates two types of transaction in the actual world. Each of them allows in turn two different values for the slot of receiver. The written text of a play can be regarded as the object of an exchange between author and reader (theater as literature), or as a message from the author to the members of the performing cast (theater as script). The oral performance generates a transaction within the stage, linking actors among themselves, and a transaction across the stage, from the cast to the audience. Which ones of these transactions are fictional, and which ones are not?

In the first analysis, drama as literature, the reader treats the text as if it were narrative fiction. The author pretends, or rather, the reader pretends that the author pretends to be an anonymous narrator who represents events in some possible world for an anonymous hearer. Stage directions are processed as descriptive statements, and the speech of characters is regarded as directly quoted dialogue. This mapping satisfies the criteria of fictionality, but by assimilating drama to narrative fiction, it obscures its distinctive character.

In the second analysis, drama as script, the utterance of the author is a directive speech act addressed to the actors (dialogue) or to the director (stage directions), instructing them how to perform the play. As Searle observes, "the playwright's performance in writing the text is rather like writing a recipe for pretense than engaging in a form of pretense itself" (1975:328). On this account, dramatic texts involve no impersonation, and fail criterion (a).

The third transaction yields the mapping: "John Smith (an actor) pretends to be Othello addressing Desdemona, and invites Jane Doe (an actress) to pretend to be Desdemona." On this analysis, drama fails criterion (c), and only differs from spontaneous games of make-believe through the directed character of the pretense.

The only mapping of the dramatic speech situation compatible with the present definition of fictionality is the transaction by which the actor John Smith pretends for the audience to be Othello addressing Desdemona, thereby inviting the spectator to pretend to be an anonymous witness of the dramatic action.

Prefabricated Discourse

Another form of discourse involving more than one transaction in the actual world is what Barbara Herrnstein Smith calls "prefabricated utterances": verbal messages put together by an author and meant to be appropriated by a substitute speaker. The standard example of prefabricated discourse is greeting card messages:

> To Mother, with Love from Both of Us
>
> This world may change in many ways
> But you just grow more dear
> And closer, Mother, to our hearts
> With every passing year, etc.
>   (Quoted in Herrnstein Smith, 1978:58)

According to Smith, the utterance act of the author is fictional, while the discourse of the appropriator is not: "Though the statement is personal, it is not the statement of the person who composed it: it does not spring from or reflect *his* emotions and sentiments, it is not *his* mother who grows more dear; and he could not very well be 'the two of us' who are purportedly saying the fond message. . . . As the author's composition, the message is fictive; but once it is signed 'John and Mary' and sent to Mrs. Jones in Cincinnati, it *becomes* natural discourse and, the conventions having switched, will be taken, perhaps quite properly, to affirm their sentiments" (58).

Under Smith's analysis, greeting card messages invert the situation of dramatic discourse: in drama, as we have seen, the utterance of the appropriator is fictional, while the message of the author to the appropriator is not. Under the present definition, however, the utterance act of the author of the greeting card does not fully qualify as fiction. Admittedly, the I of the message bears no counterpart relation to the I of the author, but in crafting the text of the card the author does not invite the prospective buyer (= the actual addressee) to engage in an act of pretense. On the contrary: real-world addressees are asked to appropriate the message, to transmit it in their own name. In fiction proper, responsibility for the message is delegated by the author to the impersonated speaker, but in greeting cards, this responsibility is offered to the buyer/addressee, who in accepting it becomes a substitute speaker without adopting a foreign identity.

Parody

In Webster's dictionary, parody is defined as "a writing in which the language and style of an author is imitated or mimicked, especially for comic effect or in ridicule." The core of this definition is formed by the obligatory feature of imitation, and the optional, but almost imperative, feature of ridicule.

Parody comes in many species. One of them is the literary pastiche: authors publishing under their own names a text ostentatiously written in the style of another. An example of this type of parody is *A la manière de . . .* by Paul Reboux and Charles Muller, a collection of short imitations of famous French writers. Each pastiche bears a title: "Gide," "Proust," "Goncourt," so that there is never any doubt as to the target of the parody. At first glance this textual practice is easily analyzed as a case of fiction: the actual authors speak in foreign voices, pretending to be the authors they are imitating. They lose their own style and identity to the style and identity of the author being imitated.

This analysis would be appropriate for certain types of imitation: for instance, for a novel in which the author would select as narrator the counterpart of a real writer, and try to reproduce the style of this writer for the sake of verisimilitude. A text coming close to this case is *L'Allée du Roi*, a fictional autobiography of Mme. de Maintenon by Françoise Chandernagor. The author not only imitates seventeenth-century language, but integrates into the text segments of the letters of the real Mme. de Maintenon. This imitation is not performed with the intent to ridicule, but on the contrary, in an attempt to share the inner experience of the historical individual.

Analyzing a literary pastiche along the same lines as a text like *L' Allée du Roi* would fail, however, to capture its inherent mockery, its ironic distance. The author of a parody of Proust does not tell readers: "Pretend that I am Proust," but rather: "I am myself but I can write like Proust." The implication that somebody else could write like Proust suggests that style is not inner vision, not the spontaneous emanation of genius, but a collection of definable and repeatable procedures. From this downgrading of style from a mystical to a technical phenomenon stems the deprecatory effect of parody.

In distancing themselves from the parodee, parodists prevent their real-world addressee from relocating into TAW and engaging in make-believe. When the text projects a world and populates it with individuals, as in narrative parody (i.e., parody of plots and character types, rather than simply stylistic imitation), the reader does not regard these individuals as pseudo persons but as pseudo literary creations: "Mme. de Grand-Air," in a parody of Proust, would be perceived as "a character Proust could have invented," whereas

"Mme. de Guermantes," to the reader of Proust, is "a person who could have existed." If this analysis is correct, narrative parody, like literary criticism, is more closely related to nonfactual expression than to what I call fiction. The reader never loses sight of the implicit prefix which marks the alternativeness of the system of worlds projected by the text. Whereas literary criticism tells us "In the universe created by Proust, p," narrative parody suggests: "In a universe that Proust could have created, p."

Assimilating literary pastiche to nonfactual discourse leaves open the possibility of its distinction from a clearly fictional species of parody: the case of the narrator of a novel speaking or writing in an easily recognizable sociolect whose features are being exaggerated or twisted around for a comical effect. An example of this type of parody is the folksy, uneducated language of the narrator and main character in Ring Lardner's epistolary novel *You Know Me Al*. Another, the academic mannerisms in the "Acknowledgments, "Introduction," "Notes," and "Essays in Criticism" which compose the narrator's fictional scholarly edition of a fictional fiction in *Saul's Fall* by Herbert Lindenberger. In this type of parody, the author mimicks the language of an entire group behind the back of an individuated narrator who belongs to this group. The text is fiction since the author pretends to be the narrator and invites the reader to "make-believe" his persona and environment; but it is parody because of the ironic distance through which the author invites the reader to pass an amused judgment on the counterpart in AW of the group of TAW stylistically represented by the narrator.

In summary, the language game of parody is no more intrinsically fictional than metaphor or apostrophe, and like these other games it may be played in a fictional context without creating an additional layer of fictionality.

Fantasy Broadcasts

During strikes in professional baseball or football some radio stations broadcast "fantasy games" involving the local team, presented by the regular announcers, and interrupted by fantasy advertisements. Does this activity qualify as fiction? John Smith, announcer for the New York Mets, pretends to be the John Smith of a world in which the Mets are currently playing the Dodgers. Since the pretense is overt, this act of self-impersonation is analogous to Borges naming his narrator Borges. Radio broadcasts are public statements, and so are make-believe radio broadcasts. The actual hearer can thus follow the game by pretending to be any member of the fantasy world. This fulfills all the requirements of the above definition. The relation of the fictional world of fantasy broadcasts to the actual world is one of identical inventory, with only partial identity of properties: in the actual world Strawberry is on strike; in the fantasy game he strikes out with the bases loaded. An interesting case to be considered—though I have not heard of such an occurrence—would be the broadcasting of the regular ads during the fantasy game. Being embedded within a fiction, would they become fiction themselves—in which case the advertisers would decline responsibility for urging the listeners to consume their products—or would they constitute islands of nonfiction, in which case John Smith's act of pretense would frame a serious act? The mechanisms of advertisement are such, however, that the question of fictionality would not carry any pragmatic impact: what counts is exposure to the name of the product, which happens regardless of the communicative situation.

Urban Legends

Urban legends are those incredible stories which always happen to a friend of a friend (a FOAF, in the technical jargon of folklorists) and which we pass on by attributing them in turn to a personal acquaintance. Tales of horror or of stupidity (never of cleverness), urban legends include stories about "hitchhikers who vanish from moving cars, alligators lurking in New York City sewers, rats that get batter-fried along with the chicken in fast-food outlets, housewives caught in the nude while doing laundry, pets accidentally cooked in microwave ovens" (Brunvand 1984:ix), and skiers crashing down the mountain with their pants down (this last one must be true: it was told to me as fact). The stories transmitted as urban legends respect all but the first two of the accessibility relations discussed in chapter 2. This conformity to the laws of AW makes them plausible—this is to say, tellable about AW—despite their lack of probability. Urban legends illustrate the borderline of the possible-in-AW, and they derive their tellability from the principle "reality is stranger than fiction."

The case of urban legends exemplifies the difference between the common referential use of the term fiction and the present definition. According to the referential definition the stories are fiction, since they are false in AW. Jan Harold Brunvand, who pioneered the study of the genre, characterizes urban legends as "mainly fictional oral narratives that are widely told as true stories" (1986: ix). According to the definition presented in chapter 4, urban legends are clearly nonfiction, since the teller believes in their truth-in-AW, and accepts responsibility for their accuracy. Nothing is more insulting to the teller of an urban legend than having his gullibility exposed by comments such as: "Funny, the same story also happened in Texas to my sister's boyfriend's cousin."

The communicative function of the FOAF is symmetrically opposed to the function of the substitute speaker of fictional communication. Whereas the substitute speaker disengages the responsibility of the actual speaker, the "reliable source" of the FOAF imparts credibility to the current teller through the chain of personal contacts, and guarantees the authenticity of the story. In the typology proposed in chapter 1, urban legends illustrate the rare case TRW = AW but TAW <> AW.

Tall Tales

Exaggeration is an accepted part of many basically nonfictional narrative genres, such as conversational anecdotes and narratives of personal experience. These genres are characterized by a double communicative orientation: the story is offered as a source of information, but it is also told for the sake of pleasure. When the two goals conflict, tellers are granted some liberty with the criteria pertaining to the informational function. For the sake of tellability, they are allowed to embellish the facts. In their informational processing of the story, hearers set the record straight, accepting the narrator's declaration within the limits of common sense. In conversational narrative, then, TAW may depart from AW, but the emphasis is on the similarity between the two worlds. Hearers gather from TAW whatever they can accept as true in AW, and they retain AW as primary reference world.

In the folklore genre of the tall tale, exaggeration is no longer a tolerated device, but an imperative. The point is to see who can create the most incredible story, who can reach the farthest world in the realm of the possible. But the tale must respect a set of accessibility relations specific to the genre: there will be no witches and fairies in tall tales about fishing, but a fisherman may catch a thousand fish in his rubber boots. Since the emphasis is on the distance between AW and TAW, the truth of the story is not valued in AW. In this respect, tall tales fulfill one of the conditions of fictionality.

A difference with standard fiction, however, is that the persona of the narrator is regarded as a counterpart of the actual speaker, and falls within the scope of the principle of minimal departure. When Texas storyteller Ed Bell tells his audience about catching fish in the fog (a tall tale quoted and analyzed in Bauman 1986), the hearer regards the fisherman as an incarnation of *this* Ed Bell, even though he does not believe in the truth of the story. In written fiction, as we have seen, the counterpart relation is only allowed when the narrator is identified by the name of the actual speaker (Borges = Borges). But in oral storytelling, the physical presence of the actual speaker fulfills an identifying function equivalent to naming: if Ed Bell tells a story and uses the pronoun I, this I stands for the individual who was baptized Ed Bell. I do not know of any case of an oral storyteller using a first-person pronoun, and referring through this pronoun to an individual other than her- or himself (counterparts in other worlds being, of course, included in the concept of self).[3] An *individuated* first-person narrator divorced from the actual speaker is a purely written phenomenon.

The counterpart relation between actual speaker and narrator/protagonist allows an interesting effect—one that introduces a deceptive element, and brings the genre closer than standard narrative fiction to such verbal games as teasing or playing the devil's advocate. The tall tale may be camouflaged as a narrative of personal experience, and reveal only gradually its fictional features.[4] Compare the credibility of the introduction of Ed Bell's story about fishing in the fog:

> When I was stayin' over there by Houston for a few nights, we lived about a hundred 'n' thirty-nine miles from Houston, when we were on the coast, but I was stayin' over close to Houston. I don't remember what for. And one o' those Houston boys says, "Hey, Ed, let's go redfishin' tomorrow."

with the obvious fabrication of the events reported in the conclusion:

> Folks, we got sixteen o' those big reds, and the fog lifted, and we's fifteen miles from the bay. We'd been fishin' in a fog bank. (Bauman 1986:108)

The tale slips toward fictionality, and its true genre is revealed, as the distance between AW and TAW becomes too extensive to be bridged by the hearer's tolerance for exaggeration in narratives of personal experience. This generic shift demonstrates that the criteria of fictionality need sometimes to be evaluated both prospectively and retrospectively. In a prospective evaluation, the rules are recognized to be in effect at the onset of the transaction, and shape the hearer's expectations. In a retrospective evaluation, the fictional status of the text is determined for the hearer by his or her final apprehension of the sender's intent.[5]

Metafiction

Fictional texts, like nonfictional ones, may be surrounded by metatexts which comment upon them: prefaces, footnotes, notices to the reader, epigraphs, etc. The metatext of a fiction is a metafiction when it acknowledges the fictional status of its object text. Not all metatexts do this: the preface to *Les Liaisons dangereuses* introduces the correspondence of the characters as authentic documents; the footnotes of Jean Paul's novels *Hesperus* and *The Invisible Lodge* are uttered by the narrator of the main text. By denying the fictional status of the object text, such a metatext centers reality around the same world, and becomes itself fiction. On the other hand, when the metatext presents the object text as a fiction, its center is another world, and the speaker remains external to the object text's system of reality. An example of this situation is Racine explaining in the prefaces to his tragedies why he made his characters the way they are, and why he believes them to be true to life. We can assume that in this case Racine speaks in his own name, remains located in AW, and presents TAW as a reflection of AW. By staying outside the fictional game, the text of metafiction is itself nonfiction. The recursive nature of fictionality, however, opens a third possibility: a metatext presenting its object text as a fiction, but doing so from within the fictional universe. In *Pale Fire*, Kinbote's preface and footnotes to John Shade's poem are the fictional utterances of a substitute speaker. Kinbote admittedly fails to acknowledge the fictionality of the poem, reading it instead as autobiography, but this example suggests the theoretical possibility of fictional footnotes, prefaces, and postfaces to a fictional fiction.[6] In an essay appended to *Lolita* ("On a Book Called *Lolita*"), Nabokov plays with the idea that his own authorial declarations belong to this category: "After doing my impersonation of suave John Ray, the character in *Lolita* who pens the foreword, my comments coming straight from me may strike one—may strike me, in fact, as an impersonation of Vladimir Nabokov talking about his own books" (1955:313). By alluding to this act of self-pretense, without really admitting to it, Nabokov steps half-way into the fictional system, and wraps up his own novel in what could be, but is not for sure, a new layer of fictionality.

While metatexts reflect upon a text from the outside, the metatextual function can also be fulfilled by internal elements: storyteller interventions, addresses to the reader, comments on the truth of the facts, evaluative statements, or "signature" of the text through the self-identification of the speaker (a practice common in medieval epics). These internal metatextual elements (or metanarrative, when they comment upon a narrative text) display the same logical variety as external metatexts. A metatextual comment may or may not acknowledge the fictional status of the text; if it does, it may or may not be caught in the fictional game. When we read in *Jane Eyre* "Reader, I married him," the storyteller's intervention is addressed by the substitute speaker Jane Eyre to a reader located in TRW who regards her as a real person. The intervention, consequently, fails to acknowledge the fictionality of the text. On the other hand, when we read in *The French Lieutenant's Woman* "This story I am telling you is all imagination. These characters I create never existed outside my own mind" (1981:80), the speaker is not the narrator but the author himself, and the statement is literally true in AW. If it is at all possible for fiction to embed nonfictional statements, then there is no better example than this type of metanarrative comment.[7] Later in the novel, however, Fowles pulls the persona of the author into TRW by showing him sitting in a train across from Charles, the main character in the novel. Through this overt act of self-impersonation, Fowles paradoxically denies the ontological boundary between AW, where the characters of the novel are creatures of his own mind, and TRW, where they exist as autonomous individuals.

On the reader side, a similar transfer from AW to TRW occurs in Italo Calvino's *If on a Winter's Night a Traveler*. First the addressee of the metanarrative comment appears to be you or me, the reader in AW: "You are about to read Italo Calvino's new novel, *If on a Winter's Night a Traveler*. Relax. Concentrate. Dispel every other thought" (1981:3). The action ascribed to the reader by the first sentence is what the *actual* reader is *presently* doing. The next few sentences contain advice, rather then description of facts. They could again be literally addressed to you or me. As the narrative goes on, however, the actions and properties of the reader are more and more narrowly specified by the text, created by Calvino. As he loses the freedom to act as he pleases, the persona of the reader is drawn from AW into TRW. The relocation is completed in the final sentence when the reader is specified as a male character: "You stop for a moment to reflect on these words. Then, in a flash, you decide you want to marry Ludmilla" (259).

Through the fictionalization of author and reader Fowles and Calvino call into question the possibility of jumping out of the fictional game from within the game itself. Can a fiction really contain islands of nonfiction or does a so-called authorial intervention create a new layer of role-playing? Can the authors speak in their own names, advancing propositions for AW, or are they always pretending to be a counterpart of themselves in a world similar, but not identical to AW? The potentially infinite recursivity of the fictional game leads Brian McHale to the following conclusions:

> The metafictional gesture of sacrificing an illusory reality to a higher, "realer" reality, that of the author, sets a precedent: why should this gesture not be *repeatable*? What prevents the author's reality from being treated in turn as an illusion to be shattered? Nothing whatsoever, and so the supposedly absolute reality of the author becomes just another level of fiction, and the *real* world retreats to a further remove. (1987:197)

An alternative to creating an additional level of fictionality is for the metafictional comments to destroy the fictionality of the entire text. When the reader is constantly reminded that the text displays a verbal artifact and not a real world, a realm populated by constructs of the imagination and not by persons and material objects with an autonomous existence, the gesture of recentering is blocked and the reader contemplates the semantic domain from a foreign perspective. By implicitly or explicitly prefixing all of its statements with "in fiction f," the self-conscious modern literary text tends toward the status of nonfactual nonfictional discourse.

Visual Media

Is the concept of fiction applicable to nonverbal forms of communication, such as mime, painting, photography, and sculpture? And if yes, is the validity of the illocutionary approach threatened? Kendall Walton, who answers the first question in the affirmative, does indeed regard the existence of nonverbal fiction as evidence against the usefulness of speech-act theory and the notion of pretended speech act:

> The quickest way to see what is wrong with the pretense theory of fiction is to remind ourselves that *literary* works of fiction are not the only ones, and that a crucial test of the adequacy of any account of what makes fictional literature fictional is whether it can plausibly be extended to other media. The pretense theory fails that test.

Renoir's painting, "Bathers," and Jacques Lipchitz's sculpture, "Guitar Player," are surely works of fiction. But I doubt very much that in creating them Renoir and Lipchitz were pretending to make assertions (or to perform other illocutionary acts). . . . It is unlikely, I think, that either Renoir or Lipchitz imagined himself to be asserting anything. (1983:82)

As an alternative to a model based on the concept of pretended speech act, Walton defines fiction as "a prop in a game of make-believe" (1983:87). The players in the fictional game agree to regard an object as something else—a doll as a child, a glob of mud as a pie, splotches of paint on a canvas as a bather, a text as a description of facts—and through this something else they gain entrance into the world of make-believe. But what is "regarding as," if not an act of pretense? The putative existence of nonverbal fiction does not invalidate the concept of pretended speech act for literary fiction, only for the nonverbal forms. Pretense is the mechanism of make-believe, and the common denominator of an extended family of human activities. The members of this family differ from each other through the nature of the pretended event: verbal, physical, and perhaps visual. For the game of mud pies we can modify the formula of chapter 4 as shown in figure 7, retaining the two levels, the pretense, the invitation to pretend, and the substitute identities, but replacing the verbal action of transmitting a text with the physical action of making a pie. Depending on the game being played, A' and B' will be counterparts of A and B, or radically different individuals: children can pretend to make pies, or pretend to be x and y making pies.

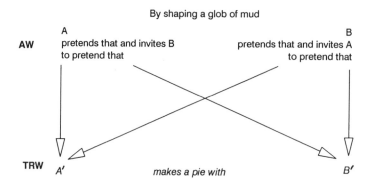

Figure 7
The communicative structure of games of make-believe

For mime, ballet, and the nonverbal aspect of theater I propose the analysis of figure 8. Notice, by comparison with figure 6 of chapter 4, the voiding of the slot of substitute hearer: a physical action is not addressed to somebody in the sense a speech act is. There may be beneficiaries, but unless the beneficiaries are themselves the agent they are not directly involved in the action. As in the formula of chapter 4, this analysis says nothing about the role of the addressee in TRW, but we can assume that by pretending that A', B', and C' perform a certain action, the spectator implicitly pretends to witness this action from the viewpoint of a member of TRW.

The question of fictionality is much more difficult to assess in pictorial and other types of visual communication (sculpture, cartoons, photography). There is an element of make-believe inherent to all pictures: the sender (artist, photographer, etc.) presents spectators with a surface covered with lines and colors, and asks them to regard these marks as an object—to pretend that they see this object. For Walton, this seeing something as something else forms the essence of both fiction and visual representation. His definition of pictorial depiction (P-depiction) reads roughly as follows (to emphasize the core of the analysis I simplify the formulation and leave out some rules which I find irrelevant to the present discussion):

A picture D is a depiction of an object P for a society S if there is in S a game of make-believe, such that
   (a) The propositions "O exists" and "O is a P" are true in make-believe in virtue of certain properties of D; and

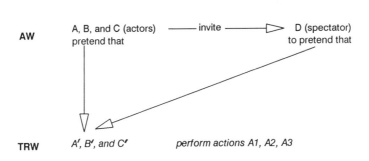

Figure 8
The communicative structure of nonverbal performing arts

(b) Some actions that the members of S perform in perceiving D count in make-believe as "seeing O," "recognizing that O is a P," and "examining the features of O." (1973:313)

To evaluate this formula properly one must bear in mind that while it is derived from Walton's own definition of fiction as "prop in a game of make-believe," its object is not fictionality in pictorial depiction, but pictorial depiction in general. From Renoir's "Bathers" to Whistler's portrait of his mother, from Botticelli's "Birth of Venus" to David's "Coronation of Napoleon," from the picture of a sunflower in a botanical treaty to Van Gogh's "Sunflowers," and from a snapshot of real-world events in the newspaper to an art photograph of a nude, Walton's analysis is indeed satisfied by all kinds of representational pictures and sculpture. Only abstract art fails to satisfy conditions (a) and (b). Thus while a narrow application of the speech-act account excludes the possibility of visual fiction, Walton's counterproposal excludes the possibility of visual nonfiction. It follows that for Walton, the category nonfiction is restricted to verbal communication.

Why this discrepancy between verbal and visual media? Walton does not address this question, but here is a conceivable explanation. Pictures, when compared to words, have a unique ability to conjure up the presence of their referent. The picture of an object can be mistaken for this object, while a word can never be mistaken for its referent. Pictures invite their spectators to pretend that they are seeing the depicted object, to pretend that this object exists in front of them. Words never do this: they invoke the thought of their referent, not its immediate presence. The referents of discourse either exist absolutely (nonfiction) or exist in make-believe (fiction), but the referents of pictorial representation, because of their pseudo-presence, always exist in make-believe. Hence the inherent fictionality of all pictorial representation.

This argument rests, however, on a confusion between pretended *presence* and pretended *existence.* Even if one admits that all pictures conjure up make-believe presence (a claim which I consider far from established: couldn't a picture be processed as a *sign* of an object rather than as this object itself?), the existence of the referent is not necessarily established by an act of make-believe. When we look at a portrait of Napoleon, we may face him in make-believe, but it takes no act of pretense to believe in his historical existence. Walton's inclusion of all pictures in the fictional category conflicts with our intuition that a photograph of Gorbachev is to a painting of a unicorn what a journalistic report of Gorbachev's dealings with Lithuania is to a Lithuanian fairy tale about a unicorn. This parallelism is essential to the concept of fictionality in visual repesentation, and the ability to account for it should be the primary criterion of validity for a definition of visual fiction.

The parameters we have used in the formula of chapter 4 are not easily applicable to visual representation. The notion of the substitute participant appears particularly problematic on the sender side of the model. In verbal fiction, the concept of substitute speaker is justified by the implicit or explicit presence of an I in TRW who transmits the text to another member, and who is not identical with the I of AW. In theatrical fiction, there is an I performing actions in TRW who is not the actor of AW. But in pictorial communication, the showing I of AW plays no role in TRW. The world of the picture appears unmediated to the spectator, and the artist remains absent from it. The spectator perceives an object in make-believe, but not somebody performing the action of showing this object.

What, then, is "fictionality" in visual communication? Here are three proposals accepting an increasing number of works:

(1) A picture is fictional when it is offered as the illustration of a fictional text (e.g., an illustration of "Little Red Riding Hood," as opposed to the illustrations of a cookbook or botanical treaty). Here, the fictionality of the picture is derived from the fictionality of the text, and presupposes an account of verbal fiction.

(2) A picture is fictional when it represents a nonexistent object located in an APW: "The Birth of Venus" by Botticelli as opposed to "The Coronation of Napoleon," or the picture of a unicorn as opposed to the picture of a bather such as Renoir's. This account suggests an adherence to what I have called in chapter 1 the referential definition of fiction. Why should the referential definition be more acceptable in pictorial than in verbal communication? Because pictorial communication lacks the ability to evoke nonexisting objects as nonexisting, and APWs as alternatives to AW. In language, we can speak about a unicorn factually ("Unicorns do not exist"), nonfactually ("I dreamed about a unicorn"), or through the fictional relocation ("Once upon a time there was a unicorn"). The need to distinguish these three possibilities prevents the equation of fictionality to nonexistence in AW. But a picture cannot acknowledge internally the nonexistence of its referent.[8] When a painting represents an imaginary object, it shows it as if it were real, and this presentation of an APW as AW is what I have defined in chapter 1 as the constitutive gesture of fictionality.

(3) A picture is fictional when pretense and role-playing are involved on the level of the scene depicted by the artist. In painting his mother, Whistler faced his real mother, and painted her as the person she was. Renoir asked a model to pose as a bather, but since the painting does not represent a specific bather, she was not adopting a foreign identity. On the other hand, when Botticelli painted "The Birth of Venus," he asked Simonetta Vespucci to play the role of the goddess. This account does not limit fictionality to portraits of imaginary beings: "The Last Supper" by Leonardo Da Vinci depicts historical individuals, but the painter's use of models makes the work fictional. When Jacques-Louis David sketched Marie-Antoinette as he saw her on her way to the guillotine, he produced an authentic historical document; when he painted the coronation of Napoleon, using the real Napoleon and Josephine as models, he produced a visual fiction because the scene he faced was not the original

coronation but a reenactment casting the original participants in their own roles. It may be argued that this account limits fiction to works painted from a model. A Madonna could be fiction or nonfiction, depending on whether or not the painter depicted a real woman or worked from imagination. An answer to this objection is provided by Searle:

> In the case of fictional or fictionalized pictures the artist need not have actually seen the object he is painting. Indeed the object may not exist, as when he paints a purely mythological figure, or even when he paints actual persons and objects he need not have seen them in the situations in which he depicts them. In such cases the artist paints *as if* he had seen such objects or had seen them in the situation in which he paints them. (1980:403)

From this observation we can derive the following generalization: a painting (sculpture, etc.) is fictional when painted partly or wholly from imagination, and nonfictional when painted from an authentic visual source. This authentic source may be provided by the artist's perception at the time of the painting, by the memory of a past perception, or by a nonfictional document derived itself from an authentic source. In a work painted from imagination there is no authentic visual perception accounting for the entire picture (though of course data derived from perception will inevitably fill out the canvas). The artist supplies the source through an act of pretense.

According to this definition, Whistler sketching his mother after her death would be producing a work of nonfiction, and so would a modern painter using his memory of historical portraits to paint Napoleon, but since no painter can claim a direct apprehension of the Virgin Mary, all existing Madonnas are fictional representations (unless society assumes that the artist was divinely inspired by a vision). While the preceding proposal limits fictionality to pictures of nonmembers of AW, this third definition accepts pictures of members of AW, when they are represented partly or wholly through an act of pretense. These fictional portraits of historical individuals constitute the visual equivalent of literary true fiction.

On this last account, the notion of pretended speech act is not as outrageous as Walton would have it. A picture does not perform direct speech acts, as does a verbal transaction, but it may be regarded as an indirect statement. A pictorial representation of an identifiable object carries an implicit message from its author: "I was there, I witnessed a scene, and I recorded it as I saw it." Or: "I have seen many objects of class P, and this is how I perceive a typical member of this class." Or: "The sight of scene S inspired this vision in me." In the class of paintings I label fictional, such speech acts are implied, but they are not literally true. Botticelli did not see Venus, David did not paint Napoleon at the very moment he put the imperial crown on the head of Josephine, Chagall did not witness a newlywed couple floating in the sky above the Eiffel Tower. The witnessing and recording act must be attributed to a substitute I, and the pictorial gesture can be analyzed as shown in figure 9.

Mixed Verbal/Nonverbal Media

The preceding account is easily extended to primarily visual media which make optional use of language, such as comic strips, cartoons, and movies. Comic strips are fictional because the characters are invented, and the artist merely pretends to have a visual and auditive source. Political cartoons represent real-world individuals, of whom the cartoonist may have a genuine visual source, but these individuals are placed in imaginary situations. Caricaturing the features of politicians is not essential to the fictionality of the cartoon: a caricature is just a portrait stylized in a such a way as to exaggerate certain features. Every representation, whether verbal or visual, involves a selection, arrangement and shaping of potentially available features, and this *mise en forme* has nothing to do with fictionality.

As for movies, they are nonfictional when the camera captures genuine events and fictional when the recorded events are simulated by actors. By this account, acted movies are fiction, while documentaries are not. Against this categorization, some theorists have argued that many documentaries record staged rather than spontaneous events. As Thomas M. Leitch observes: "The position in the often heated debate over whether Leni Riefenstahl's *Triumph of the Will* is a work of fiction or of nonfiction have characteristically been based on beliefs about whether and to what degree

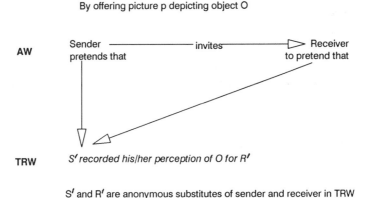

By offering picture p depicting object O

AW   Sender ———————— invites —————▷ Receiver
          pretends that   to pretend that

TRW   S' recorded his/her perception of O for R'

S' and R' are anonymous substitutes of sender and receiver in TRW

Figure 9
The communicative structure of fictional pictorial communication

the events of the 1934 Party Congress in Nuremberg were staged expressly in order to be photographed'' (1986:186). By the same reasoning, a documentary about Navajo rug weaving would be fictional, if the weavers shown in the film were not ''caught in the act'' but deliberately demonstrating their craft at the director's request. This argument fails however to distinguish staging from pretending. The woman is really weaving a rug, not pretending to do so, and for all the advance planning, the events of the 1934 Party Congress really *counted as* the 1934 Party Congress. Riefenstahl's movie would only qualify as fiction if the events had been reenacted, whether by actors, or by the original participants.

Fiction, Quote, and Verbal Icons

In fictional discourse, the signs produced by the actual speaker function as icons of the signs attributed to the substitute speaker. This mode of signification is not exclusive to fiction: in direct quote also, two distinct utterances are fused into one linguistic object, and the discourse of the quoter copies the discourse of the quoted speaker.[9] The words in quotation marks stand for the only entity that linguistic signs can depict with a reasonable degree of accuracy: another token of the same string of signs. Beyond this resemblance, however, fiction and quote are distinct modes of expression: there is quote of fiction (the literary examples in the present text), and there is fictional quote (the dialogues in a novel). An adequate theory of fiction should account not only for the similarities and differences between the two modes of expression, but also for the possibility of their combination.

The semiotic similarity between fiction and quote is acknowledged in Barbara Herrnstein Smith's division of discourse into *natural* and *fictive* utterances. She defines natural discourse as ''all utterances, spoken or inscribed, that can be taken as someone's saying something, sometime, somewhere: all utterances, that is, that are understood to be verbal acts of particular persons on, and in response to, particular occasions'' (1977:747). Through its context-bound character, natural discourse is a ''historical event,'' occupying ''a specific and unique point in time and space.'' In the conceptual framework of this book, one could add: a historical event in AW. Fictive discourse, on the other hand, is a ''depiction or representation, rather than [an] instance of natural discourse'' (8). In quoting somebody's words, as in writing a novel or poem, a speaker (writer) is not actually saying the words, but ''presenting a facsimile of them, and thus a fictive utterance'' (65).

With its two categories, however, Herrnstein Smith's model allows neither a distinction of fiction from quote, nor, within quote, of quoted fiction from quoted nonfiction. Her definition of fictive discourse as ''reproduction of natural discourse'' provides a satisfactory account of quoted nonfiction, but remains inadequate in the cases of fiction and of quoted fiction. Being in essence imaginary, the utterance of the substitute speaker of fiction is neither a historical event nor a response to an actual situation, and it fails the criteria of natural discourse. But it cannot be classified as fictive either, since in the terminology of Herrnstein Smith "fictive" means reproduction. If the substitute speaker uttered fictive discourse, fiction as a whole would be then be fictive discourse reproducing fictive discourse, which in turn would reproduce another discourse, and so on in an infinite regression.

This difficulty with the taxonomy stems from the fact that the concept of natural discourse is based on a number of disparate features. On one hand it is defined as a "historical event," which means actual and nonimaginary. On the other, it is opposed to "fictive discourse," and this dichotomy makes it noniconic, since "fictive" means for Herrnstein Smith reproductive. But being uttered in a historical context and being noniconic are separable features. A solution to the problem of contrasting fiction and quote is to distinguish the issue of iconicity from the issue of historical status, thus allowing both iconic and noniconic discourse to be themselves either actual or imaginary. This would mean a shift from a system of classification based on a single distinctive feature (the dichotomy natural/fictive being formally equivalent to +/− natural or +/− fictive) to a system of two dichotomies.

This avenue has been explored by Felix Martínez-Bonati in *Fictive Discourse and the Structures of Literature* (1981a). His theory of fictionality is based on the dichotomies real/imaginary and authentic/inauthentic. The meaning of these two pairs can be stated as follows (my interpretation, since Martínez-Bonati does not provide a formal definition):

(a) *Real/imaginary*: a real utterance occurs in a concrete context or situation, at a definite time and place. It therefore constitutes a specific historical event. An imaginary utterance presents none of these properties. In the language of modal logic, the distinction could be rephrased as: real utterances take place in AW, imaginary ones at the center of another modal system.

(b) *Authentic/inauthentic*: a sentence is authentic when it signifies "linguistically," i.e., through lexical convention; it is inauthentic (or a pseudo-sentence) when it reproduces linguistic signs and signifies in the iconic mode. (Observe that the features of Herrnstein Smith's natural discourse are distributed between the categories real and authentic: real discourse is a historical event, authentic discourse is noniconic.)

With these two pairs of features, Martínez-Bonati distinguishes three types of sentences: real authentic, real inauthentic, and imaginary authentic. The first two classes are illustrated, respectively, by "ordinary" discourse and by quote of ordinary discourse. The third category never exists on its own, since an imaginary sentence must always be transmitted by a real sentence, but "we can pronounce pseudo-sentences that represent other, authentic, but unreal sentences" (79). This last statement captures the nature of fiction. The discourse of the author reproduces the sentences of the narrator; these sentences are themselves imaginary because the speech act of the narrator never took place in AW, and they are authentic because most of the time the narrator represents facts and not discourse. Though

Martínez-Bonati does not discuss the possibility, a fourth category is readily waiting in his model for fictional dialogues: pseudo-sentences representing imaginary inauthentic sentences.

But if the two sets of features implicit to Martínez-Bonati's discussion appear promising in their ability to relate and contrast fiction with ordinary discourse on one hand, and with quote on the other, their cross-classification does not yield a viable discourse typology. Consider the system of labels shown in figure 10. In this pairing of labels and features, quote and fiction come out as polar opposites. In reality, however, both present a layered structure, created by an iconic use of language. A valid taxonomy should stress and not obscure this similarity. The misleading ascription of properties derives from the fact that fiction and quote are characterized on different levels. The matrix labeled "quote" describes the reproducing discourse, while the matrix labeled "fiction" describes the reproduced utterance, the discourse of the substitute speaker. In order to be properly compared and contrasted, quote and fiction should be specified on the level of both the embedding and the embedded speech act. On the embedding level they share the feature [− authentic], but they differ on the embedded level.

A separate specification of reproducing and reproduced discourse requires a model allowing a recursive application of its constitutive features. Only such a model would be able to deal with complex combinations of features, such as fiction within fiction, quote within quote, or quote of fiction.

Figure 10
The relation of fiction to quote
according to Martínez-Bonati (1981)

To build such a model, we need a basic dichotomy corresponding to Martínez-Bonati's distinction between authentic and inauthentic discourse. Let us call it *iconic/noniconic*. A discourse is iconic when it reproduces another discourse; it is noniconic when it represents a world. Within the iconic category, and within this category alone, a second dichotomy will distinguish fictional reproduction from the reproduction of quote. We could almost use here Martínez-Bonati's distinction between real and imaginary speech acts, since quote always reproduces preexisting utterances of AW, and most fiction embeds imaginary discourse. This terminology does not, however, capture the phenomenology of the reproduction. Moreover, in some marginal cases, an act I would call fictional reproduces a historical speech act: actors performing a dramatic reenactment of historical events, complete with the actual words of the participants; or—in the domain of fictional fiction—Borges's Pierre Mesnard authoring the *Quixote*. Rather than resorting to the feature of reality, I propose to define the dichotomy as one of *duplicative* versus *impersonative* iconicity. In a duplicative utterance the emphasis is on the difference between the original and the copy: the speaker maintains his or her real-world identity, presents the speaker of the reproduced utterance as a different individual, and implicitly acknowledges the gap between t1, the time of the original utterance, and t2, the time of its reproduction (which is always *now* from the point of view of the speaker). In an impersonative utterance, as we have seen, the actual speaker plays the role of the putative original speaker, and presents the utterance as being produced for the first time. This will be actually the case when the utterance of the impersonated speaker is imaginary: Jane Eyre's discourse did not exist before Charlotte Brontë's novel came into being.

The recursivity of the model is inherent to the feature iconic. Insofar as iconic stands for "discourse reproducing another discourse," each occurrence of the feature opens a new level of communication, which itself must be specified in terms of the dichotomy duplicative/impersonating. On the other hand, noniconic discourse leads back to raw facts, and puts an end to the chain of embedded speech acts. On the tree-shaped diagram of a recursive model, all terminal nodes must be therefore noniconic.

The taxonomy generated under the present proposal is shown in figure 11. The formal characterization of a mode of expression is composed of all the features collected on a path from the top node to the terminal node labeling this form of expression. The terminal nodes labeled 1 through 7 in figure 11 correspond respectively to:

(1) "Ordinary" discourse (nonquote, nonfiction)
(2) First-order quote of ordinary discourse
(3) First-order fiction
(4) Second-order quote of ordinary discourse (quote within quote)

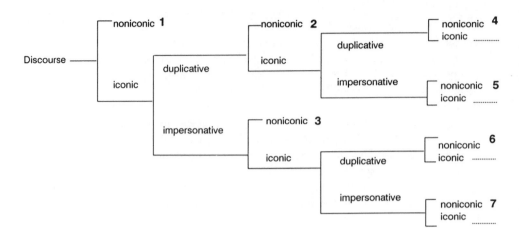

Figure 11
The relation of fiction to quote

(5) Quote of fiction (as found in critical essays or in some epigraphs)
(6) Quote of ordinary discourse in fiction (as in dialogues, or non-fictional stories told by characters)
(7) Second-order fiction (fictional story within a fictional story)

A continuation of the open branches generates more complex forms of discourse, such as the quote of a passage of a critical essay quoting a passage of a novel containing a dialogue.

Part II THE PLOTTING OF THE PLOT

6 The Modal Structure of Narrative Universes

The theory of possible worlds is applicable not only to the relation of a textual system of reality to our own native system, but also to the internal description of the semantic universe projected by the text—whether or not this universe is presented as a reflection of the system centered around AW. The concepts of modal logic provide an access to a textual semantics, and more particularly to a narrative semantics, which transcends the distinction between fiction and nonfiction.

One of the least controversial claims of contemporary narratology is that a narrative text is the representation of a number of events in a time sequence. An event, intuitively, is something that happens to an existent (character or object) and leads to changes in the overall state of a world. But if we take a close look at a typical narrative—the weekly summary of the soap opera "All My Children"—we notice that it recounts or implies many events that haven't yet, and may never actually happen, even though they form an integral part of the story:

> Tad Martin booked a one-way ticket from California to Pine Valley. On the phone, Phoebia nixed giving Tad an address where he can reach Hillary. Dixie opened Palmer's globe safe, but was disappointed to see that it only contained a cassette tape. Remy saved Frankie from getting hit by a train, but Frankie still blames Remy for Jesse's shooting death. Dixie's heart flutters whenever she's around Nico. Skye convinced Sean not to tell Tom that she isn't paralyzed. Nico warned Palmer to butt out of his relationship with Julie. Cliff told Cecily all about Sean serving time for murdering Sybil Thorne, but Sean talked Cecily into believing that he's not a bad guy. (9 Sept. 1988, by Nancy M. Reichardt. Copyright United Feature Syndicate)

Of the states and events directly mentioned or implied by the text, some are definitely nonactual:

> There is more than a cassette tape in Palmer's safe
> Frankie gets hit by a train
> Skye is paralyzed

Others are not-yet but should-be actual:

> Tad goes to Pine Valley
> Palmer gets out of his relationship with Julie

We also find must-not-be actual:

> Tad Martin returns to California
> Tad reaches Hillary
> Nico retaliates against Palmer because Palmer does not
> get out of his relationship with Julie
> Sean tells Tom that Skye is not paralyzed

and may-have-been actual:

> Remy caused Jesse's shooting death.

The narrative importance of nonfactual events was stressed more than twenty years ago by French structuralists. Bremond distinguishes two types of narrative statements: descriptive statements, which recount actual events [relatent un événement en acte, le faire effectif d'un actant]; and modalized statements, which "anticipate the hypothesis of a future event, of a virtual action" [anticipent l'hypothèse d'un événement futur, d'un faire virtuel] (1973:86). Todorov distinguishes four modal operators for narrative propositions: the *obligatory* mode, for events dictated by the laws of a society; the *optative* mode, for states and actions desired by the characters; the *conditional* mode, expressing action to which characters commit themselves if certain other events happen; and the *predictive* mode, for anticipated events (1969:46–49).

These observations are easily restated in the terminology of the present model. Bremond's descriptive statements are the states and events of the actual world of the narrative universe while his modalized statements describe the alternative possible worlds of the system. Todorov's catalog of modalities is an embryonic typology of APWs.

We have seen in the first part of this book that APWs are constructs of the human mind. The virtual in the narrative universe exists in the thoughts of characters. Narrative concerns primarily human (or human-like) action, and action is determined by the mind's involvement with external reality. Narrative semantics is rooted in an exploration of the world-making activity through which we interact with and try to shape the world we regard as actual. At the same time, a narrative semantics is a description of the cognitive categories in which readers classify the information provided by the text in their effort to make sense of the represented events. The following discussion of the possible worlds of the narrative universe should lay down the foundations for both of these aspects of narrative semantics.

To say that the cataloging of the constituent worlds of a narrative universe is an exploration of the human mind does not mean that all mental activities yield possible worlds. But it does mean that possible worlds are built from the various materials collected by the mind. Mental activity comprises two types of elements: some involve truth-functional and fact-defining propositions while some others do not. Among the former are "thinking that p," "hoping that p," "intending p." Among the latter are emotions, subjective judgments, and fleeting perceptions before they are turned into knowledge. The possible worlds of a character's domain are built out of truth-functional propositions; they are collections of facts which can be compared to the facts of the actual world. (One could of course speak of "worlds of emotions, judgments, perceptions," but this metaphorical use of the term "world" is stretched out too far to bear any meaningful relation to the theory of possible worlds.)

To form the image of a world, propositions must be held together by a modal operator acting as common denominator. In the literal sense of the term, a possible world is a set of propositions modalized by the operator of the so-called *alethic* system: possible, impossible, necessary. I have explored in chapter 2 the various interpretations that may be given to these concepts. But other operators have been proposed by logicians. Lubomir Doležel (1976a:7) enumerates the following systems of modalities:

(1) The *deontic* system, formed by the concepts of permission, prohibition, and obligation.
(2) The *axiological* system, which is assumed to be constituted by the concepts of goodness, badness, and indifference.
(3) The *epistemic* system, represented by concepts of knowledge, ignorance, and belief.

While the operators of the alethic system relate AW to TAW, the other operators relate TAW to the private worlds of characters. The epistemic system determines a knowledge-world (K-world), cut out from the general realm of perceptions; the axiological system determines a wish-world (W-world), extracted from subjective value judgments; and the axiological system determines what I shall call an obligation-world (O-world), dictated by social rules of behavior. In addition to these constructs, which are conceived as either images of TAW (K-world) or as models of what it should be (W-world, O-world), the human mind builds possible worlds as escapes from AW, as true alternatives: dreams, hallucinations, fantasies, and fictions. Let us call them fantasy-worlds, or rather, F-universes, since their structure is that of a modal system. In what follows, I propose to review the various spheres of the narrative universe, as a preliminary to a theory of narrative conflict and narrative action.

The Narrative Universe

The concept of narrative universe is best defined in contrast with a larger totality: the semantic domain of the text. The semantic domain is the sum of the meanings suggested by a text, the set of all the valid inferences and interpretations. (I leave to others the task of determining what constitutes a valid interpretation.) Within the semantic domain, the text may outline a system of reality: an actual world, surrounded by APWs. I regard this semantic dimension as constitutive of the narrative text. Narrativity resides in a text's ability to bring a world to life, to populate it with individuals through singular existential statements, to place this world in history through statements of events affecting its members, and to convey the feeling of its actuality, thus opposing it implicitly or explicitly to a set of merely possible worlds.

While the narrative universe consists of a collection of facts established for the various worlds of the system, the semantic domain accepts any kind of meanings: statements of fact, generalizations, symbolic interpretations, subjective judgments expressed by the narrator, or formed by the reader. As a subjective judgment, the statement "All happy families . . . " is part of the semantic domain of *Anna Karenina,* but not of its narrative universe. It is not a hard fact within TRW, but only the opinion of the anonymous narrator.[1] The reader may decide that the statement is invalid, not only in AW but also in TRW. Another example of the difference between semantic domain and narrative universe is the image of the pear tree in Katherine Mansfield's short story "Bliss." In the semantic domain, the pear tree is both a pear tree and what it stands for—the experience of bliss. In the narrative universe, it is just an existent, a specific pear tree. But the statement "Bertha Young experiences bliss when she sees the pear tree" yields a fact for the actual world of the narrative universe, and it is by virtue of this fact that the symbolic meaning of the pear tree reaches the semantic domain.

The Factual Domain (Actual World)

At first sight, the concept of factual domain, or actual world, is rather unproblematic for narrative semantics: it is made up of what exists absolutely in the semantic universe of the text, as opposed to what exists in the minds of characters. But how is this absolute existence established, and what authority guarantees it to the reader? Is narrative semantics concerned with the facts of the world about which the text makes predications, its reference-world (what I have called TRW in chapter 1), or with the facts presented as actual by the text itself (TAW)? Or to put it another way: should narrative semantics take a *de re* or a *de dicto* approach to the concept of actual world? It was shown in chapter 1 that TRW differs from TAW only in inaccurate texts of nonfiction (errors, lies, exaggerations). But since a truly *narrative* semantics is not concerned with the distinction between fiction and nonfiction, its concepts should be general enough to account for both types of narrative. If a fisherman narrates his last expedition, and tells us of an epic fight to catch a hundred-pound swordfish, whereas he really pulled out without problem a two-pound crappy, it is a fact in his story that the fish weighed a hundred pounds and fought an epic fight, even if the story is false in reality. Narrative semantics is concerned with what is true in the story, and not with what really happened. This supports the second of the two alternatives: a *de dicto* interpretation of the concept of factual domain, making it synonymous with TAW. To remain consistent with this conclusion, I will avoid the concept of TRW in the chapters of this book devoted to narrative semantics.

In fictional discourse, however, the *de dicto* position runs into the problem of authentication. How do we decide what the text establishes to be the case? In impersonal narration, as we have seen, the speaker has absolute authority, and his or her discourse yields directly what is to be taken as the actual world. But a personal narrator is a mind interposed between the facts and the reader, and the discourse reflects the contents of his or her mind. The reader in this case does not perceive the narrative actual world directly, but apprehends it through its reflection in a subjective world. The reader must sort out, among the narrator's assertions, those which yield objective facts and those which yield only the narrator's beliefs. When, for instance the narrator of *One Flew over the Cuckoo's Nest* declares that the orderlies of the mental hospital where he is a patient have sensitive equipment to detect his fear, we regard this belief as hallucination. But we accept as fact the statement that there are orderlies mopping the floor in the hallway. The existence of unreliable narrators in fiction demonstrates a possible gap between the world projected by the narrator's declarations (what could be called narratorial actual world, or NAW), and the facts of TAW.

This leads us to a pair of opposite observations: in nonfiction, the narrative actual world is what the speaker tells us to be the case, regardless of whether the narrator is right or wrong; but in fiction, the actual facts potentially conflict with the narrator's declarations. Who then guarantees the facts of the narrative universe? This apparent contradiction is resolved if we regard the actual speaker, rather than the narrator, as responsible for authenticating the factual domain. In fiction, the narrative actual world is determined by what the author wants the reader to take as fact (or rather, the implied author, since the authorial intent is always inferred on the basis of the text). Fictional role-playing opens the possibility for the substitute speaker to assert facts and to be overridden by the authorial projection of the factual domain. But in nonfiction, there is no doubling of the I: the narrator is the actual speaker, and what the narrator presents as fact necessarily belongs to the actual world of the textual universe.

The Components of the Actual World

As an entity existing in time, TAW is a succession of different states and events which together form a history. Each of the propositions constitutive of TAW is implicitly indexed by an absolute or relative temporal indicator (absolute: p is true at t_i; relative: q is posterior to p). TAW also comprises a set of general laws that determine the range of possible future developments of the plot out of the present situation. TAW is thus split into a factual and an actualizable domain. This latter domain is technically a possible world, linked to the present state of TAW through the relation of temporal accessibility; but it differs from the other APWs of the narrative system in that it exists absolutely, rather than being created by the mental act of a character. (In the modal system of temporal accessibility, historical events may be regarded as necessary, since they cannot be erased, future events as possible, since they may or may not happen, and counterfactual events as impossible, since they missed the chance to be actualized. A world is temporally accessible from AW if at some time in the future the history of AW may become similar to the past of this world.[2]

As we have seen in chapter 2, TAW may be either homogeneous or split into various spheres governed by different sets of laws. (Cf. Martínez-Bonati's concepts of uniregional and pluriregional narrative worlds [1983], or Thomas Pavel's concepts of flat and salient ontologies [1986:43–72].) The regions of a split ontology may be the sacred and the profane, as in medieval mystery plays, the realm of the dead and the realm of the living, as in ghost stories, the familiar and the uncanny, or more generally the natural and the supernatural, as in fantastic tales. In a narrative with a truly split ontology, the regions recognized as "other" exist as objectively as the unmarked domain of the ordinary. Readers accept their existence in TAW, regardless of whether or not their private ontologies recognize AW as divided into regions. It is important to distinguish TAWs with a split ontology from homogeneously supernatural TAWs, such as we find in fairy tales. In a narrative with a truly split ontology, communication between the different regions of reality occurs only at certain privileged moments, and is apprehended as the scandalous intrusion of a foreign element. In a supernatural but homogeneous TAW, species found in AW and species native to TAW (fairies, dwarves, and dragons) inhabit the same sphere, and the possibility of their interaction is taken for granted. It is not extraordinary for a poor girl to have a fairy godmother, or for a frog to be turned into a prince.

Different regions within the real world may be presented either as existing absolutely (as in medieval mystery plays), or as part of the private world-view of characters. Uniregional TAWs may contain individuals who adhere to a split ontology (Joan of Arc in Shaw's *Saint Joan*), or conversely, pluriregional TAWs may present characters who recognize only the realm of the profane (the myth of Don Juan).

K-World

In an epistemic system, the modal operators of necessity, possibility, and impossibility are translated into knowledge, belief, and ignorance. A K-world is realized in T/AW if it consists exclusively of known propositions; it is possible with respect to T/AW if it comprises known and believed propositions; and it conflicts with T/AW if it includes ignored propositions. (The symbol T/AW is used in this chapter whenever my remarks concern any system of reality, whether projected by a text or intuitively experienced as "our native system.") A possible K-world is an incomplete representation, and an impossible K-world involves contrary-to-fact propositions.

The meaning of the operator of knowledge is fairly straightforward: a character "knows" a p, when he or she holds it for true in the reference world and p is objectively true in this world. But because of the inherently ambiguous nature of K-worlds, the other two operators are more problematic. A K-world can be conceived from either a first-person or a third-person perspective. In a first-person perspective, K-worlds may be either complete or incomplete with respect to their reference world, but never mistaken, since we have no external access to the reference world. My own K-world consists of propositions which I hold to be true (known p's), propositions which I hold to be probable (believed p's), and of propositions which I leave indeterminate (ignored p's). In a third-person perspective, the modal operators of the K-world are computed by comparing the truth value assigned to propositions by the subject with the objective truth value in the reference world (which may turn out to be the truth value assigned by a third party). The three operators mean respectively agreement, indeterminacy, and disagreement.

Indeterminacy may stem from two sources: nonconsideration or noncommitment. A K-world may be not only correct or incorrect, and complete or incomplete with respect to its reference-world, but also total or partial. An incomplete K-world means that some of the propositions in "the book" on the reference world are left indeterminate: did the butler kill Lady Higginbotham, or did he not do it, wonders Inspector Snively. A partial K-world leaves out some of the propositions in the book: returning from a week-end with his mistress, Lord Higginbotham is unaware that Lady Higginbotham has been murdered. An incomplete K-world fits on its reference world like a cover with some holes in the middle; the location of the holes is determined, and the character knows where his or her knowledge is defective. A partial K-world is like a cover that is too small, the regions beyond the cover remaining unsurveyed.

Since the distinction between partial and incomplete K-worlds is an important one in narrative semantics, we must distinguish four epistemic categories. The objective K-world of characters is computed by taking all the true propositions in the book on the reference world (which is established by the highest narrative authority), and by assigning to each of them one of the following operators:

+ (Correspondence, knowledge): x holds p firmly for true
- (Conflict, misbelief): x holds p firmly for false, while p is true
0 (Absence, ignorance): p is unknown to x
i (Indeterminacy, uncertainty, question): x is either uncommitted to the truth of p or leans to some degree toward the truth (i.e., considers p possible, probable, unlikely, etc.) A scale of coefficients, from 1–99 (low probability) to 50–50 (indeterminacy) to 99–1 (high probability) could be used to represent the various degrees of commitment to the truth of a proposition.

The subjective K-world of characters can be derived from the objective one by taking all the + and the i propositions. Among the i propositions, those with high coefficients yield the beliefs of characters, as opposed to their unconditional commitments, and those with 50–50 coefficients yield the questions that preoccupy their minds.

The reference world of a character's K-world may not only be TAW, but any of the private worlds of the narrative universe. The possibility for a K-world to reflect another character's K-world leads to potentially infinite recursive embedding. A K-world may represent a whole system of worlds, some of which may be reflections of itself in the K-world of another individual. This cross-interception of K-worlds is an important part of strategic reasoning: "He figures I'm going to throw the curve because he thinks I expect him to think I'm going to throw something else so I'll throw the curve instead," thinks a pitcher in "Reflex Curve," a short story by Charles Einstein (1979:368). In this reasoning, the self-embedding potential of K-worlds is taken to the utmost limits of intelligibility. Was it too far or not far enough? Embroiled in his own reasoning, the pitcher throws a curve—and the batter hits it for a game-winning home run.

Prospective Extension of K-Worlds

Just as TAW contains a domain of the actualizable, the K-world of characters includes a prospective domain, representing their apprehension of the tree of possible developments out of the present situation. The propositions of this prospective domain are modalized by an operator of temporal accessibility corresponding to Todorov's predictive mode. "It is possible that Tom will find out that I am not paralyzed" reasons Skye in "All My Children." Prospective beliefs may furthermore be paired by a conditional operator *if . . . then* : "If Tom finds out that I am not paralyzed, I will be in trouble." The recursive nesting of conditionals creates a garden of forking paths into the future, a branching system of ever-increasing complexity: If A, then B, otherwise C. If B then D, otherwise E, etc. The prospective domain of a character's K-world is of crucial importance in the formation of goals and the elaboration of plans—a topic to be discussed in the next chapter.

O-World

The obligation-world, or O-world of characters, is a system of commitments and prohibitions defined by social rules and moral principles. While the social rules are issued by an external authority, the moral principles may be defined by the characters themselves. These regulations specify actions as allowed (i.e., possible), obligatory (necessary), and prohibited (impossible). A person or character's O-world is satisfied in T/AW if all the obligations have been fulfilled and none of the interdictions transgressed. (Cf. Todorov's obligatory mode.)

A variation on this deontic interpretation of modal operators classifies actions as credits (acquisition of merit), debts (acquisition of demerit), and neutral. The acquisition of merit makes characters rewardable, while the acquisition of demerit makes them punishable. For the O-world to be satisfied in T/AW, all the merits must be rewarded, and all the demerits must be paid for by punishment or penitence. An O-world with unpunished infractions is in a state of conflict with T/AW, while an O-world with unrewarded merits is compatible with T/AW without being fully satisfied.

The credits and debts of the O-world may also be acquired through commitment to future actions (what Todorov calls the conditional mode): "If you do p, I will do q." A character's O-world remains in debt until all promises are kept. Since commitments derive from interpersonal contracts, O-worlds are interactive and mutually dependent. A credit in a character's domain means that another character has a promise to fulfill toward the first. Threats present an interesting conflict: by issuing a threat, characters create an obligation, and if the precondition obtains they will be in "debt" until they execute the threat. But since the accomplishment of the threat usually constitutes a moral infraction, the character trades one kind of debt for another. The same trade-off is characteristic of revenge, as opposed to legal punishment. Characters taking revenge make themselves liable to reciprocal action by the party of their victim, and the offended party will become an offender through the very action of repairing the offense against one of its members.

These examples demonstrate the potentially conflicting nature of obligations. An individual who belongs to a number of different groups may be subjected to incompatible systems of rules. A classical example of conflicting obligations is the predicament of Rodrigue in Corneille's *Le Cid*: he either challenges his father's insulter and violates the king's law, or he lets the insulter go unpunished and violates family rule.

W-World

The wish-world of characters is defined over propositions involving the axiological predicates good, bad, and neutral. The first of these predicates corresponds to Todorov's optative mode. While moral laws define goodness and badness relatively to the community, the law of desire defines these predicates relatively to the individual. The constitutive propositions of a W-world are of the form

$$x \text{ considers that} \begin{bmatrix} \text{state} \\ \text{action} \end{bmatrix} p \quad \text{is} \begin{bmatrix} \text{good} \\ \text{bad} \end{bmatrix} \text{for } x$$

A desired state is typically the possession of a certain object. A desired action is an intrinsically rewarding activity such as making love, eating, or playing games.

A W-world is theoretically satisfied in T/AW if all the propositions labeled good are true in T/AW; it conflicts with T/AW if one of the dysphoric states or unwanted actions is actualized; and it stands in a neutral relation to T/AW—the character judging the state of T/AW acceptable—if the nonrealization of the desires does not lead to dysphoric situations. A neutral relation occurs when all coefficients of desirability remain in the middle range. Should an action or state be intensively desired, its nonrealization would be the object of an equally strong fear. But a character's W-world may be flexible enough to offer alternatives, so that the nonrealization of the highest wish can be partially made up by a less desirable but still positively valued state.

This potential flexibility of W-worlds suggests that the axiological operators "good" and "bad" are not binary categories, but the poles of a continuum. W-worlds are layered structures in which various situations are ranked according to their degree of desirability. In the course of a narrative, characters may aim successively at various layers of their W-world, settling for lower levels as the higher ones become unattainable. Or, on the contrary—like the fisherwoman in Grimm's fairy tale of "The Little Golden Fish"—they may start at the lowest level, and pursue higher and higher wishes. The system of values may furthermore be modified during the course of the action, so that what appears desirable at one time no longer seems so when it becomes reality.

The layers of a W-world differ not only through their degree of desirability, but also through their degree of compatibility with T/AW. A W-state defined over few propositions is compatible with a greater number of possible worlds than a W-state defined over few propositions, and T/AW has a greater chance to be one of these worlds. Another factor in this compatibility is of course the nature of the individual propositions. The W-state defined over the single proposition "x is king" may for instance be harder to realize than another state defined over forty.

Like O-worlds, W-worlds may be internally inconsistent. An individual may desire p on a level of consciousness, and ~p on another. The result is a chimeric W-world which will never be realized in T/AW. Examples of fictional characters living in such a world include Julien Sorel and Emma Bovary.

Pretended Worlds

The private domain of characters is not exhausted by sincere beliefs and desires, or genuine obligations. A character may forge a private world in order to deceive another. In the fable "The Fox and the Crow," for instance, the proposition "the fox finds the crow beautiful" belongs to a pretended world of judgment, and the proposition "the fox wants to hear the crow singing" to a pretended W-world. The complete semantic description of a character's domain thus includes both authentic and inauthentic constructs—beliefs and mock beliefs, desires and mock desires, true and faked obligations, as well as genuine and pretended intents.

F-Universes

A last type of private sphere involved in narrative semantics is formed by the mind's creations: dreams, hallucinations, fantasies, and fictional stories told to or composed by the characters. These constructs are not simply satellites of TAW, but complete universes, and they are reached by characters through a recentering. For the duration of a dream, the dreamer believes in the reality of the events he or she experiences, and the actual world of the dream takes the place of T/AW. The recentering of dreams, fantasies, and hallucinations differs from fictional recentering in that the basic identity of the subject is preserved through the relocation. Like the primary narrative system, F-universes consist of an actual F-world surrounded by the private worlds of its inhabitants. By virtue of the inherent recursivity of recentering, the members of F-worlds have at their disposal the entire array of world-creating activities: the characters in a dream may dream, the heroes of fictional fictions may write fictions. This type of recursive embedding differs from the one we have observed in K-worlds in that it does not propose ever new points of view on the same system, but transports the experiencer to ever new realities. Whereas K-recursion is like putting a new mirror in a room to reflect it from another angle, F-recursion is like crashing through the wall to enter another room.

While F-universes offer escapes from TAW, they may fulfill metaphorically the function of K-worlds or W-worlds with respect to the primary narrative system. The novels read by Don Quixote or Emma Bovary are selected by these characters as models of the world in which they wish to live. A character's knowledge is often made to expand into the future or into a sacred layer of reality by a dream sent from these other regions. Hallucinations can tell characters something about their real selves, as does the apparition of the devil to Ivan Karamazov. And finally, a fictional story may be told within a story as parable reflecting on TAW ("Die Wunderlichen Nachbarskinder" in Goethe's *Elective Affinities*). But not all F-universes lead back to the primary narrative system. In *Alice in Wonderland,* Alice's dream is not only introduced for its own sake, it even draws TAW into its own orbit. Once Alice awakes, she narrates her dream to her older sister, and the sister follows her, through daydreaming this time, on the paths of Wonderland.

Relations between Worlds

The relations among the worlds of the narrative system are not static, but change from state to state. The plot is the trace left by the movement of these worlds within the textual universe.

From the viewpoint of its participants, the goal of the narrative game—which is for them the game of life—is to make TAW coincide with as many as possible of their private worlds (F-universes excepted). The moves of the game are the actions through which characters attempt to alter relations between worlds. A narrative move, writes Pavel, "is the choice of an action among a number of alternatives, in a certain strategic situation, and according to certain rules" (1985:17). The alternatives are the forking paths of projections; the strategic situation is the relative position of worlds on the board of the textual universe; and the rule of the game is to move one's pieces closer to the center.

For a move to occur and a plot to be started, there must be some sort of *conflict* in the textual universe. Plots originate in knots—and knots are created when the lines circumscribing the worlds of the narrative universe, instead of coinciding, intersect each other. In order to disentangle the lines in their domain, characters resort to plotting, with the almost inevitable effect of creating new knots in some other domain.

The best of all possible states of affairs for a system of reality is one in which the constitutive propositions of all private worlds are satisfied in the central world. In such a system, everybody's desires are fulfilled, all laws are respected, there is a consensus as to what is good for the group; what is good for the group is also good for every individual, everybody's actions respect these ideals, and everybody has epistemic access to all the worlds of the system. We can represent this situation as a number of coinciding circles. Whenever some proposition in a private world becomes unsatisfied in the central world, the system falls into a state of conflict. This event can be visualized as a satellite of TAW leaving its orbit.

By this definition, conflict is not simply the complication or thickening of the plot that occurs between exposition and resolution, but a more or less permanent condition of narrative universes. The denouement of a narrative is not the elimination of all conflicts, since the resolution of the hero's problems usually creates conflicts in his opponent's domain, but only the disappearance of the productive ones. A conflict is productive when its experiencer is in a position, and is willing, to take action toward its resolution. For conflict to disappear completely from a narrative universe the ending should be either eschatological or apocalyptic: all the villains should join the ranks of the good guys, or everybody should die.

Depending on which world strays away from TAW, or on the relative positions of worlds within a character's domain, we can establish a typology of narrative conflicts and narrative situations. Each type of conflict generates specific narrative themes, and a typology of narrative conflicts leads toward a typology of plots. The following discussion is an attempt to complete and systematize an earlier typology proposed by Doležel (1976a).

The primary level of conflict is between TAW and one of the worlds of a private domain. Whenever conflict exists objectively in a textual universe, it is found on this level. But other types of conflict may contribute to the further entanglement of a situation: conflict between the worlds of a character's domain; conflict inherent to one of these worlds; and conflict between the private worlds of different characters. These secondary conflicts all presuppose a basic conflict involving TAW.

Conflicts TAW/Private Worlds

The most frequently encountered conflicts of the primary level involve TAW and the W-worlds of characters. In this type of conflict, the W-world of x contains a proposition "x has y" or "x does y" which remains unfulfilled in TAW. Deficiencies of the W-world give rise to the theme of the quest. Most narratives present quest episodes, but it is in myths and fairy tales that the theme is the most dominant.

Conflicts of the O-world occur when a character's "moral account" falls in a state of debt through the violation of laws or through unfulfilled personal commitments. This type of conflict generates some of the most common thematic sequences of oral and popular narrative: prohibition-violation-punishment; mission-accomplishment-reward; favor-repayment; infraction-penitence; insult-revenge-revenge-revenge-revenge (and so on until one of the feuding parties exits from the system).

In the epistemic domain, conflict may take two forms: the error, which stems from contradictions between a K-world and its reference world; and the enigma, which stems from an incomplete K-world with well-defined areas of indeterminacy. The error may be spontaneous, as in tragedies, or the result of deceit, as in comedies and various other genres (fables, fairy tales, soap operas, and spy stories, to name a few). The enigma, characteristic of mystery stories, gives rise to the theme of investigation. A particular form of enigma, the ontologically inexplicable, defines the genre of the fantastic. The so-called fantastic hesitation pits against each other the events of TAW and the characters' (and reader's) representation of the laws governing reality. The resolution of this type of conflict requires the sacrifice either of the K-world of the hero, or of the law-defying facts. In the one case the hero modifies his private ontology and accepts TAW as essentially pluri-regional: the ghost is an intruder from the realm of the dead. In the other case, the hero expels the inexplicable facts from TAW by ascribing them to an APW created by an altered state of consciousness or by an act of forgery: the ghost is explained away as either a dream, a hallucination, an optical illusion, or as a normal person covered with a white sheet.

Conflicts within a Character's Domain

Conflict occurs within a character's domain when the satisfaction of one world of this domain requires the nonsatisfaction of another. This situation is captured by the formula

$$\sim\!\Diamond \,(\text{AW} = \text{K-world} = \text{O-world} = \text{W-world})$$

Classical examples of such personal conflict include incompatibility between W-world and O-world (the realization of the character's desires requires some forbidden or morally wrong action, as in *Crime and Punishment*); and incompatibility between K-world and W-world (the satisfaction of a character's desires is only made possible by his or her ignorance of facts, as in the myth of Oedipus).

Conflicts within a Private World

In this type of conflict, private worlds cannot be realized because of internal inconsistency (contradictory desires, simultaneous allegiance to incompatible sets of rules) or because characters are unable to outline their borders. This last situation is typical of the psychological novel of the late nineteenth and twentieth century. When the concept of the self is called into question, private worlds become so fuzzy, so unstable and problematic, that they cannot be measured against the sharply defined facts of an actual world. In popular and folklore genres, by contrast, the private worlds of characters consist of clearly defined and stable elements, and conflicts of this type hardly ever occur.

Conflicts between the Private Worlds of Different Characters

Narrative conflict occurs between domains whenever the realization of a private world requires the nonsatisfaction of some world (usually the corresponding one) in the domain of another character. The mutual compatibility or incompatibility of the private worlds of characters divides the cast into opposing factions, and defines interpersonal relations as either cooperative or antagonistic. Conflict between distinct domains is the most productive situation for narrative development. Narrative is a competitive game and cannot go on without opposition. The closest approximation of a narrative without antagonistic private domains is found when the opponent is not an individual but a natural phenomenon—as in the story pitting Hercules against the filthy stables of Augeas. But if conflict between private domains is almost inevitable in a narrative plot, it can receive various degrees of prominence. In a classical Proppian fairy tale, the conflict between the hero and the villain is productive on the macrolevel; the whole narrative can be summarized as "hero versus villain." But in a *Bildungsroman,* where the dominant structure is the progressive expansion of the hero's K-world, antagonism is most productive in the individual episodes of the microlevel.

Subjective vs. Objective Conflicts

Conflicts involving the O-world and W-world may either exist objectively, or be created by an epistemic conflict. When a character's K-world misrepresents TAW, it will also misrepresent the relationship between TAW and all the other worlds of the narrative system. The character may thus see a conflict where none exists objectively or may wrongly believe that his or her private worlds are satisfied in TAW. The first case is illustrated by *Othello,* the second by the myth of Oedipus. Othello's erroneous belief that Desdemona was unfaithful creates in his mind a triple conflict with TAW, involving his W-world, Desdemona's O-world, and his own O-world, since he feels obligated to punish her. When Oedipus marries Jocasta without realizing that she is his mother, his incomplete K-world leads him to believe that both his W-world and O-world are satisfied in TAW.

Taken as a whole, the myth of Oedipus offers a particularly good example of the changing relations of private worlds to TAW during the course of the narrative action. The story begins in a state where all of Oedipus's worlds are in alignment with TAW. His meeting with Jocasta creates both an unfulfilled W-world requirement and a K-world conflict, since he wants to possess her and does not realize her true identity. Marriage to the queen and accession to the throne brings the satisfaction of Oedipus's W-world, but creates a transgression of the O-world which is kept hidden to him by the K-world conflict. The discovery of Jocasta's identity brings the K-world back into harmony with TAW, but throws the W-world out of orbit, and makes Oedipus aware of the conflict involving the O-world. After the voluntary penitence of the hero, his K-world and O-world are again compatible with reality, but the W-world remains forever unfulfilled.

The general system formed by the domains described above can be generated by the grammar of figure 12. Optional constituents are in parentheses. Of all the terminal categories appearing in the rules, two remain to be defined: the concepts of goal and plan, which together define the intent (I-world) of characters. The exploration of goals and plans and the discussion of their contribution to the dynamics of plot form the topic of chapter 7.

```
Global universe ⟶ TAW, characters' domains
TAW ⟶ Region 1 (Region 2) (Region 3?)
Characters' domain ⟶ Authentic worlds
                    ⟶ Pretended worlds
                    ⟶ Alternative universes (F-universes)
Authentic worlds    ⟶ K-world
                    ⟶ O-world
                    ⟶ W-world
                    ⟶ I-world
Pretended worlds    ⟶ Mock K-world
                    ⟶ Mock O-world
                    ⟶ Mock W-world
                    ⟶ Mock I-world
K-world  ⟶ AW, other characters' domains
O-world ⟶ Credits, debts
W-world ⟶ Desired states, feared states
I-world  ⟶ Goals, plans
Mock worlds ⟶ [Same structure as authentic counterparts]
F-universes ⟶ Dreams
              Fantasies
              Hallucinations
              Fictions
Dreams, Fantasies,
Hallucinations,
Fictions ⟶ Global universe
```

( ) optional components

Figure 12
The modal structure of narrative universes

7 The Dynamics of Plot: Goals, Actions, Plans, and Private Narratives

How do conflicts come into being, and how are they resolved? What causes the movements of worlds in the narrative universe, and what fuels the mechanisms of the plot? The answers to these questions lie in a theory of narrative events. This chapter will explore the mental constructs responsible for the moves of characters: their intensional world, whose components are goals and plans.

Narrative as State-Transition Diagram

The most widely accepted claim about the nature of narrative is that it represents a chronologically ordered sequence of states and events, which captures a segment of history—the history of the textual universe. This segment can be modeled on a state-transition diagram, as shown in figure 13. Narrative states are expressed as distinct matrices of truth values (+ or −) assigned to a fixed set of stative propositions. Truth values are indexed by the temporal series t0 . . . tn, and reevaluated after every narrative event.

A proposition represents an event when it forms a possible answer to the question "and then, what happened?" Events are perfective processes leading to a change in truth value of at least one stative proposition. State propositions fall into two categories: some express inalienable properties, and retain the same value throughout the narrative (x was a wolf, y was the daughter of a king), while others present the potential of alternating several times between truth and falsity. Propositions of the second kind are those which distinguish a state from another. At t1 John can be rich, then poor at t2, then rich again at t3. Event propositions differ logically from state propositions in that their truth value is neither stable nor reversible. They pass invariably from F (before they happen) to T (while they are happening) to F again (after they happened). If John marries Jane between t1 and t2, then divorces her, then marries her again between t3 and t4, he participates in two distinct events. Once event propositions have become true, they are permanently etched in the history of the narrative universe, and from a timeless perspective they retain forever a positive value.

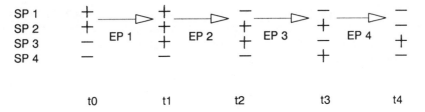

SP State propositions
EP Event propositions

Figure 13
Narrative as state-transition diagram

The model of figure 13 is a theoretical, not a cognitive one. It reflects how things are logically assumed to be in the narrative universe, but not necessarily what the reader needs to know about it. The cognitive requirements are not as rigid as the logical ones. While it is a theoretical assumption that every proposition must be either true or false at every point in the history of the narrative universe, some propositions may remain indeterminate in the reader's mind for at least certain states. We know, for instance, that the wolf is hungry at state n of "Little Red Riding Hood," when he meets the heroine. Was his appetite aroused by the sight of the little girl, or was he hungry before? Logically, the proposition "the wolf is hungry" is either true or false at state n-1; but as far as the understanding of the story is concerned its truth value can remain unspecified.[1]

Narrative vs. Nonnarrative Propositions

Filling out the model of figure 13 with semantic content requires a distinction between plot-functional and nonfunctional information, or narrative versus descriptive elements. Narratologists have long been aware of the importance of such a distinction (Barthes 1966 and Chatman 1978 under the terminology "kernels" and "satellites"; Prince 1973 under "narrative" versus "nonnarrative" events), but they tend to take the dichotomy as self-explanatory. Intuitively, narrative elements are those that contribute to the advancement of the plot, while nonnarrative elements flesh out the narrative universe and make it more vivid, without moving the plot forward. The former are usually reflected in summaries, the latter are left out.

But what does it take to move the plot forward? For a semantic element to contribute to the dynamics of the plot, it is not sufficient to be involved in a change of state in TAW, for if it were, a leaf falling from a tree would lead to a new state, and there would be no justification for excluding any event proposition from the semantic representation of a plot. The modal approach taken in this book suggests the following definition of narrative functionality for event propositions: a proposition moves the plot forward, and presents narrative functionality, when it expresses an event which affects either directly or indirectly the relations among the worlds of the textual universe. A leaf falling from a tree does not normally create a change in the relation between TAW and the private worlds of characters. It is therefore a descriptive element. On the other hand, losing all of one's money or falling in love with somebody normally increases the distance between W-world and reality. In the case of losing one's money, the distance is created by a change in TAW; in the case of falling in love, the change occurs in the W-world, but it is occasioned by an event in TAW.

This view of plot-functionality is independent of the content of the events: one could imagine a narrative in which observing a falling leaf led to a character to discover the laws of gravity, and thus increased the extension of her K-world; and another narrative in which losing all of his money does not matter to the hero because he is shipwrecked on a desert island.

A related criterion applies to the selection of plot-functional units among stative elements. The facts retained in the characterization of states should either intrinsically matter to characters, or bear a causal relation to a plot-functional event. By this definition, ''he had no friends, no job, and no money'' will normally form a narrative proposition, and ''he had long hair'' a descriptive one; but in the biblical story of Absalom the long hair of the hero eventually causes his death, and the proposition expressing this attribute acquires plot-functional significance.

By proposing a criterion for defining narrative information, I am not claiming that there exists a mechanical procedure for extracting the plot of a narrative text. The distinction narrative/descriptive is not always a clear-cut one. In a narrative text, the focus of interest may be placed on the portrayal of characters rather than on the relations between the worlds of the semantic universe. When the primary function of the plot is to reveal the state of mind and moral features of characters (as for instance in Proust's *Remembrance of Things Past*), it becomes extremely difficult, maybe even pointless, to classify states and actions as either narrative or descriptive. What, for instance, is the plot-functional status of an action of little strategic consequence, but introduced for the purpose of revealing an important mental feature of a character, a feature later reinforced by other, more important actions? It is significant, however, that narratives focused on psychological portrayal are the least amenable to summarization. The blurring of the distinction narrative/descriptive is symptomatic of a loss of narrativity, of a decline of plot as a factor of textual significance.

The layer of signification constituted by narrative propositions is not synonymous with what I have called in chapter 6 the narrative or textual universe. The narrative universe is the system of reality in which the plot occurs as a sequence of states mediated by events. Its history stretches beyond the time segment represented in the plot, and its inventory is not limited to the cast of characters and settings made visible by the story. The narrative universe comprises all the facts asserted or entailed by the text, whether narrative or descriptive, as well as an infinity of untold facts which make it ontologically complete.

The three concepts of plot, narrative universe, and semantic domain capture ever-widening, and increasingly text-specific totalities. Many different texts share the same plot (consider all the versions of "Cinderella"), but for two texts to project the same narrative universe they would have to express the same set of propositions. This occurs—in principle—in the case of translation. But insofar as some aspects of meaning are language-specific, two textual versions of the same universe would still outline different semantic domains. On the other hand, an ambiguous narrative text may project different plots, depending on the interpretation of the facts. Each of these plots presupposes a separate narrative universe, since a different configuration of facts means a different system of reality. But all these competing plots and universes are encompassed by the semantic domain, which I have defined as the totality of the meanings projected by the text. The text offers the only access to its semantic domain, while the semantic domain captures what is unique about the text.

Events, States, and Processes

The division of the continuous time-span delimited by a plot into a series of discrete states is not an automatic operation reflecting natural divisions, but one that can be performed in a number of different ways. How many narrative states there are depends not only on what changes are narratively significant, but also on the nature of the events and the interplay of the different lines of the plot. Some events, like the pulling of a trigger, are nearly instantaneous and largely deterministic, and once initiated, they will almost always reach their completion. These events create clear-cut transitions between discrete narrative states. But other events, like the firing of a time-bomb, are time-consuming processes. The temporal range between their initiation and completion leaves time for the initiation and completion of numerous other processes, some of which may prevent the bomb from going off. Events of this second type are not fully deterministic but stochastic processes, and it may be necessary to record the stages of their progression as different states in the history of the narrative universe.

Events with temporal extension introduce a dynamic element in the representation of states and blur the distinction between active and stative propositions. The definition of a narrative state may include not only stable properties, but also the specification of ongoing processes affecting existents: "the house is falling apart," "the mechanism of the time bomb is ticking away." The same type of event will sometimes be coded as an instantaneous change, sometimes as a time-consuming process. Consider these two ways of representing the action of going from place A to place B:

(a) State 0: The Queen is at the castle
Event 1: The Queen goes across the forest to get to the house of the seven dwarves
State 1: The Queen is near Snow White at the house of the seven dwarves

(b) State 0: Little Red Riding Hood is at her mother's house
Event 1: Little Red Riding Hood leaves for her grandmother's house
State 1: Little Red Riding Hood is in the forest, on her way to the grandmother's house
Event 2 [Meeting with the wolf]
State 2: Little Red Riding Hood is in the forest, further along on her way to the grandmother's house
Events 3 to n-1 [Wolf going to the grandmother's house and eating her]
States 3 to n-1: Little Red Riding Hood is in the forest, further along on her way to the grandmother's house
. . . .
Event n: Little Red Riding Hood arrives at the grandmother's house
State n: Little Red Riding Hood is at the grandmother's house

Whether an event should be represented as a singular transition or as a progressive series does not depend so much on the nature of the event as on the nature of the plot. In the case of "Snow White," the Queen's crossing of the forest is coded as an instantaneous change because no other event of lasting consequence happens between the time the Queen leaves the castle and the time she arrives at the house where Snow White is hiding. In the case of "Little Red Riding Hood," the crossing of the woods by the heroine is divided into intermediary states in order to provide a temporal space for the meeting with the wolf and for the actions of the wolf before Little Red Riding Hood reaches her destination. The progressive coding expresses the parallelism of the narrative machine: more often than not, a plot is not a single line of action, but the interaction of concurrent processes. In a narrative, as in a multitasking computer, a process may start another process, interrupt it, terminate it, slow it down, or speed it up. This interaction would not be possible if all changes in the narrative universe were induced by instantaneous events.

Transitions between States: Happenings, Actions and Moves

Transitions between states of TAW may involve two types of physical events: actions and happenings (cf. Chatman 1978 on this distinction). The difference between the two categories resides in the intention or lack thereof inhering in the event: actions are deliberately aimed toward a goal, happenings occur accidentally. Actions have a voluntary human or human-like agent, happenings have a patient but no animated agent.

Happenings

Narrative happenings are formed by unpredictable events, such as getting sick, meeting the wolf in the forest, or being freed from a prison by an earthquake. The causes of happenings are either blind natural forces (attacks by germs, tectonic activity), failures of execution (losing control of one's car and crashing into a tree), or accidental convergences of distinct processes (meeting the wolf in the forest).[2]

Like all properly narrative events, happenings change the course of the plot, steer it away from the path projected by the preceding state. To measure their impact on the history of the narrative universe, the reader must take three states into consideration:

S1: The state of the narrative universe before the happening.
S2: The state the narrative universe would have reached if the happening had not taken place.
S3: The state of the narrative universe after the happening.

(These categories are inspired by G. von Wright's model for the logic of actions [1967], even though von Wright discusses intentional actions. Further below I will distinguish actions from happenings through a fourth category.)

When state 1 consists of stable properties projecting their own continuation, S1 and S2 are similar, and the impact of the happening is to break a status quo. But happenings may also interrupt ongoing processes started by a previous event, or prevent the accomplishment of events projected by intents and obligations. In Heinrich von Kleist's story "The Earthquake in Chile" the heroine is awaiting execution when an earthquake destroys the jail where she is imprisoned, allowing her to escape. The happening mediates between the following states:

S1: Josephe is jailed and condemned by the Inquisition to be burned at the stake.
S2: Josephe is executed.
S3: Josephe is free.

By preventing a projected event, the happening creates an intersection between two roads, a virtual one leading from S1 to S2, and an actual one leading into S3. This type of happening is conceptually richer than the regular case, where the similarity of S1 and S2 prevents the projection of alternative roads into the realm of the counterfactual.

Actions and Moves

Actions are physical events motivated by two mental events: the setting of a goal and the elaboration of a plan. Goals are established by selecting one of the propositions through which some private world departs from the actual world: a desire to fulfill, an obligation to satisfy, an enigma to solve. Plans are constructed by computing a causal sequence of states and events leading from the present state to the goal-fulfilling state.

From a plot-functional point of view, actions may be divided into incidental or habitual doings, and conflict-solving moves. Habitual doings are repetitive gestures pursuing maintenance goals such as surviving in the world of everyday life. Since they are repeated daily, their execution involves a low risk of failure. Incidental actions pursue low-priority goals. They may be embedded within processes required to fulfill higher-priority goals (reading a newspaper to kill the time on an airplane during an important trip). The textual function of incidental and habitual doings is either descriptive (atmosphere-enhancing) or preparatory: the potential narrative significance of these events resides in the situations they lead into. Taking a walk on a pier with his fiancée, a man meets the woman who will haunt him for the rest of his life (*The French Lieutenant's Woman*). Hanging around the harbor after work, a man ends up killing another for no obvious reason (*The Stranger*).

The focus of narrative interest is borne by conflict-solving moves. I call a "move" an action with a high-priority goal and a high risk of failure. The higher this risk, the greater the narrative appeal of the move. From the point of view of characters, moves are responses to happenings, or to other moves, but from the point of view of the plot—or rather, of the plot-maker—all other types of narrative events are subordinated to moves. Why does the tale of "Little Red Riding Hood" describe the stratagem of the wolf disguising himself as the grandmother? Because this move is the dramatic highlight of the plot. Why does the story recount the fortuitous meeting of the two characters in the forest? Because this happening creates a new requirement in the W-world of the wolf, and provides motivation for the move in which the tellability of the tale is invested.

Since moves are driven by intents, their strategic evaluation requires four categories:

S1: The present situation
S2: What the next state would be without the move, according to the projection of the agent
S3: The state resulting from the move
S4: The state satisfying the goal of the agent

or, more concisely:

S1: The source state
S2: The state to be avoided
S3: The outcome state
S4: The goal state

If the reader failed to take these four categories into consideration, he or she would not apprehend actions, but only meaningless sequences of physical gestures. What this perception would be like is illustrated by the cognitive world of the mentally retarded Benjy in *The Sound and the Fury*.

As was the case with happenings, different relations are possible among the semantic components of moves. The minimal diversity is two distinct states represented in the four categories. This situation is found when the purpose of an action is to break a status quo. When the Greeks, deadlocked with the Trojans, resort to the stratagem of the wooden horse, the components of the move are as follows:

S1: Greeks and Trojans deadlocked.
S2: Greeks and Trojans deadlocked.
S3: Greeks victorious.
S4: Greeks victorious.

An unsuccessful move by the Greeks would have resulted in $S3 = S2 = S1$—still a two-state structure. Another type of two-state structure is preventive action. If John repairs his house to prevent it from falling apart, we have:

S1: The house is standing.
S2: The house is down.
S3: The house is standing (or down, if John fails).
S4: The house is standing.

An example of a three-state move is an unsuccessful attempt to break a status quo, where the unsuccessful action results in a new state. In Grimm's tale of "The Little Golden Fish," the fisherman's wife, having had her wishes to live in a castle and to become a queen already granted, now asks the fish to make her pope. The response of the fish to this new demand is to return the greedy woman to her former state. The structure of the move is:

S1: The fisherman's wife is a queen living in a castle.
S2: The fisherman's wife is a queen living in a castle.
S3: The fisherman's wife is a poor fisherman's wife living in a hut.
S4: The fisherman's wife is the pope in Rome.

The maximal diversity—four distinct categories—is found when a move represents an unsuccessful attempt to interrupt an ongoing process. This configuration occurs in "La Grande Bretèche," a short story by Balzac:

> One night M. de Merret, a rich country nobleman, comes home later than usual. He hears a noise in his wife's bedroom and suspects that she is entertaining a lover. He walks in and threatens to open the door of the cabinet to see if somebody is hiding inside. Mme. de Merret swears that nobody is

there. M. de Merret has a mason come over and build a brick wall to shut the cabinet permanently. He forces his wife to stay in the room, but leaves for a moment while the mason is working. During his absence, Mme. de Merret promises the mason a sum of money if he lets her lover inside the cabinet escape. At this very moment M. de Merret returns to the room, and receives the proof that his wife has been lying to him. The building of the wall is completed, and the lover starves to death in the cabinet.

The four-state move is the attempt by Mme. de Merret to rescue her lover. Its structure is as follows:

S1: The lover is alive in the cabinet; M. de Merret suspects his presence but has no proof of it
S2: The lover starves to death in the walled cabinet, but M. de Merret has no proof of his presence
S3: The lover starves to death in the cabinet, and M. de Merret has a proof of his presence
S4: The lover escapes from the cabinet, and M. de Merret has no proof of his former presence

Passive moves

While most moves require a physical gesture, some strategic decisions involve no action at all. In what may be called deliberate nonaction, or passive moves, the (non)doer's goal is to let events follow their course even though he or she is in a position to prevent this development. Passive moves are thus defined in opposition to the action that the character declines to take. The rejected action appears as MOVE in the S-categories, which are interpreted as follows:

S1: The present situation (source state)
S2: What the next state turns out to be with the agent declining to take the available MOVE (outcome state)
S3: The state which, in the character's projection, would result from taking the MOVE (state to be avoided)
S4: The state satisfying the goal of the agent (goal state)

or, in a general formulation valid for both active and passive moves:

S1: Source state
S2: Next state, with no MOVE
S3: Next state, with MOVE
S4: Goal state

Passive moves differ from active moves in the strategic interpretation of S2 and S3: active moves seek to avoid S2 while passive moves seek to avoid S3; active moves result in S3, while passive moves result in S2. Since passive moves are defined in opposition to a rejected action which itself is a potential move, they presuppose an analysis of MOVE into the S-categories of the active class.

The relation S1 to S4 is variable: S1 = S4 if there is no external ongoing process threatening to destroy S1; S1 $<>$ S4 if S1 is threatened, and the nondoer refuses to take an action which would preserve S1.

As was the case with active moves, the outcome of passive moves may or may not correspond to the nondoer's intent. If it does, S4 = S2 as opposed to S3. If not, S2 = S3 as opposed to S4. The failure of passive moves may stem from two causes: (a) The nondoer misrepresents S2 in the prospective evaluation, so that the result of doing nothing is not what was anticipated; or (b) a happening, or an unforeseen move by another person, interferes with the normal development into S2. (This second cause of failure also occurs in active moves.)

The case of a successful passive move is illustrated by "The Lion and the Rat," a fable by La Fontaine. A rat comes out of his burrow and finds himself between the paws of the King of Animals. Rather than killing this easy prey with a swat of his paw, the lion grants him life by declining to act. Later on the lion is caught in a net, and the rat repays him the favor by chewing the ropes away. In the lion's passive move, S1, S2, and S4 read "the rat remains alive," while S3, the projected outcome of the rejected MOVE, is filled by "the rat is dead." Since the MOVE of killing the rat would result in an advantage for the lion and a disadvantage for the rat, declining to take this MOVE counts as a good deed in the moral account of the lion, one which later on will be rewarded by the rat.

An example of an unsuccessful passive move is found in *La Princesse de Clèves*, the seventeenth-century novel by Mme. de La Fayette:

[The Princess de Clèves is loved by M. de Nemours, and she loves him in turn, but she tries to fight this developing passion for moral reasons. During an evening at the court of the King of France she discovers that he has just stolen a portrait of her.]
Madame de Clèves was more than a little embarrassed. It would have been reasonable for her to ask for her portrait. But in asking for it publicly she would let everyone know his feelings for her, and to ask him for it in private would be almost to invite him to speak of his love. Finally she decided that it would be better to let him have the portrait. She was happy to do him a favor when she could do it without letting him know it. The duc de Nemours, who noticed her embarrassment and who practically guessed the cause, went up to her and whispered, "If you've noticed what I've dared to do, be kind, Madame, and ignore it. I don't ask any more." (Mme. de Lafayette 1979:88)

The four categories of this passive move are:

S1: M. de Nemours has the portrait, the princess knows it, he does not know that she knows

S2: M. de Nemours keeps the portrait, and knows that the princess knows

S3: Same as S2

S4: Same as S1

Here S2 equals S3 because the visible embarrassment of the princess has the same effect as the MOVE she declines to take: to reveal her knowledge of the theft. As we have seen above, a passive move is defined in opposition to a possible active MOVE. For the nonaction to be interpreted as a strategic decision, the text must give the reader an idea of the alternatives available to the (non)agent. In the above passage, the move status of the behavior of the princess is established by contrast with the two lines of action she considers and then rejects: asking for the portrait in private, which she projects as:

S1: Same as S1 above
S2: Same as S1
S3: The princess has the portrait, but she provides M. de Nemours with an opportunity to declare his love
S4: The princess has the portrait back, M. de Nemours knows nothing about her love for him

and asking for it in public, whose goal would be the same but whose result would be:

S3: The princess has the portrait, but everybody knows that M. de Nemours loves her

In both of these projections, the cause for rejection is the anticipated discrepancy between the goal S4 and the outcome S3.

Actions and outcomes

The outcome of an action is a function of the relation between S3 and S4. If the proposition defining S4 is verified in S3, the action is technically a success; if not, it is a failure. But while the goal S4 is defined over a single proposition (or over a limited number of requirements), S3 is theoretically a complete state-description, defined over all the propositions constitutive of the semantic universe. This complete description must be compared as a whole to the private worlds of the potential beneficiary of the action. The side-effects of an action may affect aspects of TAW (or of AW, since the theory of actions is also valid for real life) other than the goal proposition, and relativize the outcome of the move: the price for success may be too high; the consequences of a failure may turn into hidden blessings. A classical example of overpriced success is the story of the Greek king Pyrrhos, who sacrificed huge numbers of soldiers in order to win meaningless battles. The case of a failure with positive results is illustrated by La Fontaine's fable "The Ploughman and His Sons": A dying ploughman bequeathes his field to his sons and tells them that a treasure lies buried in the ground. After his death the sons plough and plough, and find no treasure, but at the end of the year the field has been turned up so well that it yields a bumper crop.

The negative side-effects of actions may not only affect the private worlds of the agent/beneficiary, but also create conflicts in the domain of other characters. A case in point is the family story of the house of Atreus, as analyzed by Pavel (1985:29): Agamemnon sacrifices Iphigenia in order to placate the gods and solve the military problems of the Greeks. The move is successful, but it affects Clytemnestra's love for her daughter. Clytemnestra takes revenge by murdering Agamemnon, but in so doing, she offends the survivors of Agamemnon, Orestes, and Electra, who feel obligated to restore the integrity of their O-world by killing Clytemnestra. The chain of offenses and retaliations is finally put to an end by Athena, who pardons Orestes. Through this ability to spread conflict from one domain to another, unwanted side-effects form an important factor in the dynamics of plot.

Plans

The planning of an action by an individual involves two narrative constructs: the sequence of events leading from S1 to S2, the state to be avoided, and the sequence of events leading from S1 to the goal state S4.

The sequence S1–S2—or "passive projection"—is constructed through forward logic: the individual assesses the present situation and computes the most probable developments. If a probable development leads to the solution of her problem she can settle for a passive move. If not, she must construct an alternative to the passive projection.

This alternative—the sequence S1–S4—is the plan which specifies the nature of the actions to be taken. It is constructed through backward logic: the planner starts from the goal state, measures its difference from the current state; determines the events through which this difference may be negated; calculates the prerequisites of these events; and if they are not fulfilled in the current state, selects them as subgoa' ind repeats this operation recursively, until all the prerequisites of all th. subgoal-fulfilling events are satisfied in the current state.

The logical structure of plans can be represented by a series of units, or steps, consisting of three components: (1) a nonaccidental event, which can be a deliberate action, a gesture of sudden reaction, or an event of mental perception; (2) a set of preconditions for the accomplishment of the event; and (3) a set of postconditions capturing the result of the event. One of these postconditions represents the goal (or the subgoal) of the planner; the others correspond to the anticipated side-effects of the event. When a postcondition of a plan-unit matches a precondition of another, the two units are linked by an enabling relation. The matching element is the goal of the first unit. A sequence of events constitutes a plan for a goal if the goal is a postcondition of the last step, all steps are linked together by enabling relations, and the planner (or main agent) is in a position to take the action that will start the chain of causes and effects. It is not necessary for the planner to be the agent of every step: a plan may include actions, reactions, or perceptions accomplished by subagents. When this happens, the goal of the unit is determined from the point of view of the main planner; it does not necessarily correspond to the goal of the subagent.

The recursive/regressive character of planning reasoning is illustrated by the story of the old farmer who tries to get his donkey out of the barn: the donkey is not cooperative, so the farmer asks the dog to bark at the donkey. The dog is not cooperative, so the farmer asks the cat to scratch the dog. The cat is happy to comply, the frightened dog begins to bark, and he scares the donkey out of the barn (Mandler and Johnson 1977:127). The logical structure of the farmer's plan—whose progressive building forms the point of the story—is shown in figure 14. The interesting aspect of this scheme is that it recycles the building blocks of unsuccessful previous attempts. The farmer is not in a position to perform the physical actions necessary to the fulfillment of his goal. Obtaining the cooperation of a subagent is the critical point of the plan. For every potential helper who refuses to cooperate, the farmer adds a new step to the previous plan, in order to motivate by fear what he could not obtain through a free decision. Once a voluntary helper has been found, the plan unfolds like clockwork. Of all the subagents in the chain, only the first one acts on his own free will. The others are turned into cogwheels in a purely deterministic mechanism. This deterministic character is what makes the story so neatly illustrative of the recursive/regressive logic of planning. But it also makes the plan rather uninteresting. After the third recursion, the reader understands the building principle, and there is no point for the story to go on any longer.

When potential subagents have a mind of their own, the planning process is much more complicated—and narratively much more interesting. The free will of subagents must be exploited, manipulated, neutralized, and not simply negated. At every step involving a subagent, the planner must project the alternatives facing the subagent and foresee the subagent's reactions. This interplay of forward and backward reasoning leads to nonlinear plan construction. In sharp contrast to the farmer's purely regressive reasoning is this example of plan construction from *The Last Picture Show* by Larry McMurtry:

> [Jacy, a small-town girl whose official boyfriend is Duane, wants to conquer Bobby Sheen, a rich teenager from the "big city" (Wichita Falls, Texas) who has a well-publicized liaison with another teenager, Annie-Annie. Bobby once tried to make love to Jacy but gave up when he noticed she was still a virgin.]

> It seemed to [Jacy] that she had come off very badly with Bobby. He didn't call her for any dates afterward, and any boy who had ever been near her had promptly called for dates. The only conclusion was that Bobby found her backward and country. It was clear that she was going to have to get rid of her virginity. . . . She gave the matter much thought and came up with a plan that seemed to have multiple advantages. The week after graduation the senior class was going on what was called the senior trip. . . . They

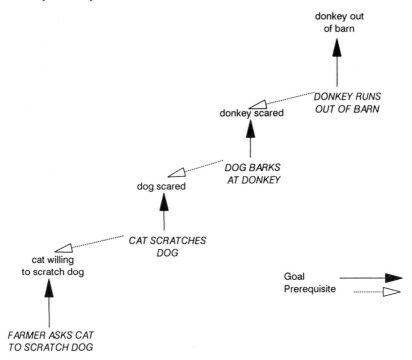

Figure 14
The farmer's plan in "The Old Farmer"

were going all the way to San Francisco and back. . . . She and Duane would thus be together practically all the time for a whole week, and it occurred to her that if she let Duane sleep with her sometime during the trip it would solve all kinds of problems. . . . She and Duane would be regarded as extraordinarily daring, and all the kids would talk about them all the way home. Also, if she slept with Duane a time or two it would make it that much easier for her to break up with him after the senior trip was over. Duane would have something beautiful to remember, and he wouldn't be able to say she had promised him anything she hadn't delivered.

Then when she got back from the trip she would no longer be a virgin and could set about taking Bobby Sheen away from Annie-Annie. If she could get him in love with her before the summer was over she might forget about the girls' schools and go to SMU, where Bobby was going. They might even pledge related fraternities.

The one flaw in the whole plan was Duane. It occurred to her that he might not want to break up with her even if she let him sleep with her before breaking the news. He was dead set on their getting married in the summer, and he was a very stubborn boy. She decided that the best thing to do would be to make an ally of Sonny [Duane's best friend]—she knew Sonny would do anything she wanted him to if she played up to him the least little bit. If Duane got ugly and wouldn't quit trying to go with her she could then date Sonny a few times. Duane would never in his life excuse that. (1966:108–9)

The construction of Jacy's plan begins with a passive projection: Bobby finds her backward and country, and instead of dating her he carries on his affair with Annie-Annie. To prevent this development, and fulfill her main goal of winning Bobby from Annie-Annie, Jacy has already decided to sleep with Bobby. She once thought that this move could be accomplished right away, but after the episode of Bobby's rejection she realizes that it carries an unfulfilled precondition: in order to sleep with Bobby she must first lose her virginity. (The number of the step corresponds to its chronological order in the finished plan, as shown in figure 16. The logical interlocking of the plan-units is shown in figure 15.)

> (5) PRE: Jacy not a virgin
> EVENT: Jacy sleeps with Bobby
> POST (Goal): Bobby in love with Jacy
> Bobby no longer in love with Annie-Annie

(It is a firm belief of Jacy, expressed throughout the novel, that whoever sleeps with her will immediately fall in love with her.)

The prerequisite of move (5) determines another step in the plan:

> (2) PRE: Jacy and Duane together
> EVENT: Jacy sleeps with Duane
> POST: Jacy not a virgin

The circumstances of sleeping with Duane are set up by taking advantage of an already scheduled event: the school trip to San Francisco. As an efficient planner, Jacy adapts her scheme to the constraints of a partially written future, rather than inventing this future on a blank page.

> (1) PRE: Jacy and Duane in San Francisco.
> EVENT: Jacy and Duane sneak away.
> POST: Jacy and Duane together.

An important part of careful planning is the computation of the side-effects of moves. Jacy decides that the consequences of the scheme are entirely to her advantage: sleeping with Duane will bring her prestige, and make it easier to break up with him later. Since she intended to do this anyway, move (2) will kill two birds with one stone and meet another criterion of planning efficiency.

Satisfied with her plan, Jacy now fantasizes about what will happen once her goal is fulfilled: going to SMU with Bobby, pledging related fraternities, and continuing the affair. But she soon discovers a potential obstacle to this projection—an obstacle created by the very solution she chose for the subgoal of losing her virginity. Far from declaring himself satisfied with what he has received from her, Duane may insist on marrying her, thus making it impossible for her to go to SMU. The continuation of the affair with Bobby becomes the goal of a new plan, and the previous plan becomes a subgoal-solving move. The new plan appends the following steps to the sequence specified by the old one:

(6) PRE: Jacy not married to Duane
   EVENT: Jacy goes to SMU
   POST: Jacy near Bobby

(7) PRE 1: Bobby in love with Jacy
   PRE 2: Jacy near Bobby
   EVENT: (and goal: this is a self-fulfilling action):
       Jacy and Bobby carry on the affair.

The first condition of move (7) has already been fulfilled by the sequence "sleeping with Duane"–"sleeping with Bobby." Now Jacy must find a solution to the precondition of move (6), which is threatened by one of the possible side-effects of step (2). These side-effects are now reevaluated as:

POST 1 (Goal): Jacy not a virgin
POST 2 (Positive side-effect): Jacy found "extraordinarily daring"
POST 3: (a) (Positive side-effect) Duane willing to break up
       OR
       (b) (Negative side-effect) Duane intent on marrying Jacy.

If postcondition 3(a) obtains, it can be matched against precondition (a) of move (4) below, and the plan is complete. The possibility of postcondition 3(b) is the flaw in the plan. To protect herself against this eventuality, Jacy constructs the following sequence, with step (3) to be executed only if necessary:

(3) PRE: - - - -
   EVENT: Jacy sleeps with Sonny and arranges for Duane to find out
   POST: Duane mad at Jacy
(4) PRE: (a) Duane mad at Jacy OR
       (b) Duane willing to give up Jacy
   EVENT: Duane and Jacy break up
   POST: Jacy not married to Duane

Step (3) has no precondition or, rather, Jacy holds the precondition for it already fulfilled by Sonny's readiness to do whatever she asks of him.

The pieces of the finished plan fit together as shown in figure 15. But the plan itself tells only part of the story: the crossroads in the future projected by Jacy (represented in figure 16) are essential to the understanding of the situation.[3] As moves are projected, new alternatives are opened on the map of the future, and new moves must be planned in order to block access to the bad roads.

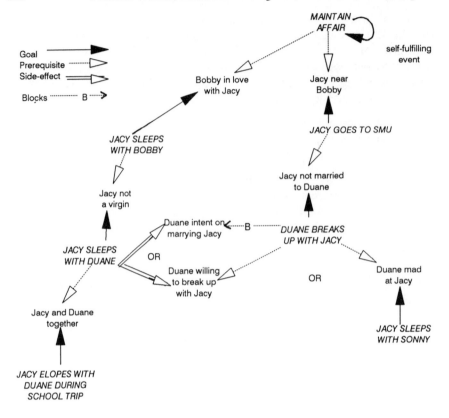

Figure 15
Jacy's plan in *The Last Picture Show*

Transfers of Control

To create narrative suspense, a plan must involve an element of risk. The examples from *The Last Picture Show* and "The Old Farmer" show that risk is located in dealing with the free will of potential subagents. Whenever the event in two subsequent plan units involve different agents, the plan requires a transfer of control. Turning over execution of the plan to another agent with an autonomous mind creates the risk of never regaining control.

Transfers of control may follow two directions: downward, from main to subagent (or rather, from superordinate to subordinate agent, since there may be a whole hierarchy of subagents); or upwards, from subordinate to superordinate agent. Upward transfers may also be called returns of control.

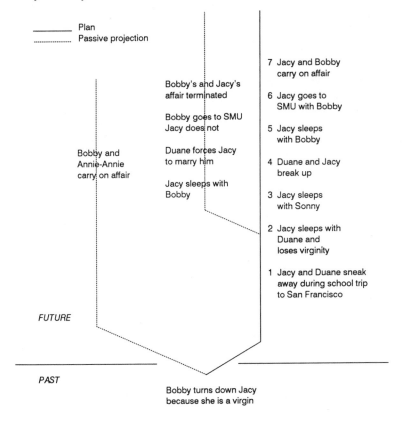

Figure 16
Jacy's map of the future

Downward transfers may be either automatic or negotiated. In an automatic transfer, the participation of the subagent is prearranged, staged by the main agent behind his or her back. The action of the subagent does not result from a free decision to participate in the plan. This case is illustrated by the dog's contribution to the scheme of the old farmer. In a negotiated transfer, the subagent must be persuaded by the main agent to take a certain action. The transition from one agent to another is effected by a speech act, such as asking for help, threatening, suggesting, bartering, or coaxing. In the old farmer's story, the transfer from the farmer to the cat is the result of a negotiation.

Projected Subagent Plans
When the contribution of a subagent to a main plan is a deliberate action, rather than an involuntary reaction, the subagent is motivated by his

own goal and plan. The main agent must project the I-world of the sub-agent, and build it into her own plan. I call the plan of the subagent, as foreseen by the main agent, the projected plan.

Subagent plans may be projected as either preexisting to the main plan, or as conceived by the subagent as a reaction to an action of the main agent. An example of a planner exploiting the preexisting plan of another agent to his own advantage is the scheme of the wolf in "Little Red Riding Hood": the actions of the wolf presuppose the execution of the little girl's plan to visit her grandmother, and the script of her plan is interwoven with the moves of the wolf in his attempt to eat her. An example of a subagent plan arising as the result of an action by the main agent is the cat deciding to scratch the dog in the story of the old farmer. This episode shows that in order to collaborate on the plan of a main agent, a subagent needs not be driven by a similar goal. The old farmer is trying to get the donkey out of the barn, but the cat has (conceivably) no other goal than annoying the dog. To support a main plan, a projected subagent plan must fulfill two conditions: represent a feasible scheme for the accomplishment of the goal of the sub-agent, and present common steps with the script of the main plan. Once these steps are accomplished, the projected plan may veer in its own direc-tion: one could imagine that the old farmer motivates the cat to scratch the dog as a way to scare the dog away from his meal, so the cat can eat it. The cat stealing the food would be part of the projected plan, but not of the main plan.

When the relation between the main and the subagent is one of cooper-ation, the plan projected for the subagent is meant to succeed by the main agent. The two agents have compatible goals, and the fulfillment of the main agent's goal depends on the success of the action performed by the subagent. But when the relation is antagonistic, the main agent counts on the failure of the projected plan, and the contribution of the subagent to the main agent's plan is involuntary. This situation occurs in narratives of plan and counterplan ("Little Red Riding Hood") and in tales of deceit. In a counterplan, the planner neutralizes the original plan by turning its main agent into a subagent in his or her own plan. In a deceptive plan, the main agent tricks the subagent into performing actions which work to the advan-tage of the main agent, and to the disadvantage of the subagent.

Overt and Virtual Plans

When a transfer of control is initiated by a negotiation, the act of com-munication between the two agents usually includes the disclosure to the subagent of the goal and plan intended by the main agent. Let us call the plan of the main agent, as disclosed to the subagent, the overt plan. The difference between the actual plan, the overt plan, and the subagent pro-jected plan is expressed by this formula (ma stands for the main agent, sa for the subagent, I for intends, B for believes):

Actual plan (AP): ma I = AP
Overt plan (OP): ma I sa B ma I = OP
Projected plan (PP): ma I sa I = PP

In a cooperative transfer, the main agent presents an accurate picture of his or her intent, and the overt plan is the actual plan. Since the subagent willingly cooperates with the main agent's plan, the projected plan is compatible with the actual and the overt plan. (Two plans are compatible when their goal can be fulfilled in the same state.) Cooperation is thus captured by the formula

$$AP = OP = = PP$$

where = stands for similarity and = = for compatibility.

In a deceptive transfer, main agents hide their actual intent from sub-agents, and the overt plan is what Bruce and Newman (1978) call a virtual plan: a pretended scheme, never meant to be fully executed. In "Puss in Boots," for instance, the cat gets rid of the giant by pretending to be genuinely interested in finding out if the giant can turn himself into an animal as small as a mouse. His fake goal is the acquisition of knowledge, while his actual goal is to eat the giant. The cat expects that in response to his request, the giant will form the goal of demonstrating the full extent of his magic power. The subagent projected plan conflicts with the actual plan but runs parallel to the overt plan: the two may differ in their ultimate goal (acquiring knowledge is the fake goal of the cat, impressing the cat is the goal projected for the giant), but the two goals can be fulfilled by the same actions. The situation of deception is defined by the formula:

$$AP <> OP, OP = = PP$$

where <> stands for incompatibility of goals.

If the projected and the overt plan were always compatible, the theoretical interest of their distinction would be negligible. But incompatibility of OP and PP does indeed occur.
The formula

$$AP <> OP, OP <> PP$$

describes a double deception. It is instantiated in the following story (quoted from Bruce 1980, who originally detected the theme of double deception):

The Fox and the Rooster

Once a dog and a rooster went into the woods. Soon it grew dark. The rooster said, "Let us stay here all night. I will stay in this tree-top. You can sleep in the hollow trunk." "Very well," said the dog. So the dog and the rooster went to sleep. In the morning the rooster began to crow, "Cock-a-doodle-doo!" Mr. Fox heard him crow. He said, "That is a rooster crowing. He must be lost in the woods. I will eat him for my breakfast." Soon Mr. Fox saw the rooster in the tree-top. He said to himself: "Ha! ha! Ha! ha! What a fine breakfast shall I have! I must make him come down from the tree. Ha! ha! Ha! ha!" So he said to the rooster, "What a fine rooster you are! How well you sing! Will you come to my house for breakfast?" The rooster said, "Yes, thank you, I will come if my friend may come, too." "Oh yes," said the fox. "I will ask your friend. Where is he?" The rooster said, "My friend is in the hollow tree. He is asleep. You must wake him." Mr. Fox said to himself: "Ha! ha! Ha! ha! I shall have two roosters for my breakfast!" So he put his head into the hollow tree. Then he said, "Will you come to my house for breakfast?" Out jumped the dog, and caught Mr. Fox by the nose. (Bruce 1980:300)

The focal point of the story is the move of the rooster. Since it is conceived as a countermove to an action by the fox, it cannot be understood without taking the original scheme of the fox into consideration. This original scheme consists of the actual plan of inviting the rooster in order to eat him; of the overt plan of inviting him in order to have breakfast with him; and of the projected plan of having the rooster cooperate in the overt plan. From the virtual character of the overt plan we can infer that the fox is trying to deceive the rooster. (Notice, however, the ambiguity of the phrase "come to my house for breakfast," which makes the plan of the fox literally nondeceptive: he tells the rooster he wants him for breakfast, and that's what he wants indeed.) Far from falling into the trap, the rooster second-guesses the fox, and responds with a counterplan. The scheme of the rooster comprises three distinct components with mutually conflicting goals:

(a) The rooster's actual plan
   1. Rooster suggests to fox to invite friend along
   2. Fox asks rooster where friend is and gets answer
   3. Fox goes to dog
   4. Fox invites dog for breakfast
   5. Dog bites fox
   6. Fox runs away from rooster and dog

(b) The rooster's overt plan toward the fox (virtual plan):
   1. Rooster suggests to fox to invite his friend along
   2. Fox asks rooster where friend is and gets answer
   3. Fox goes to friend
   4. Fox invites friend for breakfast
   5. Friend and rooster go to fox and have breakfast with
      him

(The dog is referred to as "friend" to create opacity of reference in speech acts addressed to the fox, and in projections of the fox's mind: the fox is supposed to believe that the friend is another rooster.)

    (c) The rooster's projected plan for the fox
        1. Fox asks rooster where friend is and gets answer
        2. Fox goes to friend
        3. Fox invites friend for breakfast
        4. Friend and rooster go to fox for breakfast
        5. Fox eats friend and rooster

The planning of the rooster does not end with these three projections. The actual plan (a) contains two transfers of control: a negotiated transfer to the fox; and a prearranged transfer to the dog. For every negotiated transfer, the planner must foresee both an overt and a projected plan. For every prearranged transfer, he must foresee a projected plan. When a projected plan contains itself some transfers of control, the main planner must repeat this operation recursively. In addition to the preceding plan-components, the rooster must foresee the following constructs:

    (d) The rooster's projection of the overt plan of the fox for the friend
        1. Fox learns from rooster about friend's location
        2. Fox invites friend for breakfast
        3. Friend visits fox for breakfast
        4. Fox has breakfast with friend
    (e) The rooster's projection of the fox's projected plan for the friend
        (Same as (d), without step 1)
    (f) The rooster's projected plan for the dog
        1. Dog bites fox
        2. Fox runs away from dog

The genetic relations between plan (a) and its embedded plans are shown in figure 17.

    The discrepancy of (a) and (b) makes the scheme of the rooster deceptive toward the fox. But what makes it doubly deceptive? In his overt plan (b), the rooster pretends to be willing to cooperate in the proposal of the fox, or rather, to endorse a new version of it: having not only one but two guests for breakfast. This new version serves the purpose of the fox even better, since it will give him another rooster to eat. Like the original scheme of the fox, the new version involves a deception of the rooster. The rooster pretends to be fooled by the fox, in order to fool him. The term of double deception thus denotes the act of deceiving a deceiver by faking deception.

Retrospective Constructs

    The knowledge invested in plans and goals involves not only beliefs about the present and the future, but also reconstructions of past events. These retrospective constructs may be correct or incorrect, sincere or pretended.

    An example of a plan determined by both a retrospective interpretation and a forward projection is found in "The Speckled Band," an adventure of Sherlock Holmes. The famous detective suspects that Dr. Roylott committed a murder by means of a poisonous snake, and is about to commit another.

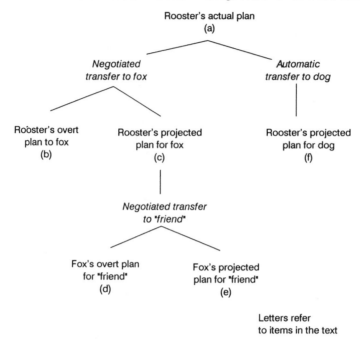

Figure 17
Relations among embedded plans in the rooster's plan
in "The Fox and the Rooster"

He sets up a trap based on these assumptions. The snake bites Dr. Roylott instead of the prospective victim, fulfilling the adage: "the schemer falls into the pit which he digs for another" (Conan Doyle 1981:188).

An incorrect evaluation of the past will cause the failure of the plan. Giving credence to Iago's calumny, Othello decides to punish Desdemona, but his tragic error turns the would-be punishment into unjustified murder. The goal is achieved in letter but not in spirit: Desdemona is dead, as Othello wanted, but because of her innocence this death loses the significance foreseen by the planner.

An astute planner may take two conflicting versions of the past into consideration, and construct a plan which will succeed no matter which one of the alternatives holds true. Such a plan is exemplified in "La Grande Bretèche." By ordering the building of a brick wall in front of the cabinet where he suspects his wife's lover to be hiding, M. de Merret will punish the lovers if indeed Mme. de Merret was unfaithful, and remain free of guilt if she was innocent.

Rather than being determined by genuine reconstructions of the past, plans may be based on fake interpretations. In "Les Deux Amis," a short story by Maupassant (analyzed in great detail in Greimas 1976), a German officer captures and kills two Frenchmen who sneaked out of Paris and went fishing into enemy territory. He pretends that they were on a spying mission, in order to masquerade their gratuitous murder into an execution required by the code of war.

Forked Plans

A plan may trace not only one, but several branching roads on the map of the future. Careful planners weigh the possible effects of every step, and foresee optional steps in order to neutralize certain outcomes. Jacy's plan was an example of such reasoning: sleeping with Sonny was like a repair kit, to be used only if the flaw in the plan should indeed create damage.

In the case of Jacy, the two forking paths lead to the same destination. But some plans are built around diverging roads not meant to meet again. The pivotal element of these plans is a conditional offer: you do this, and I'll do that; or you do that, and I'll do this. In "Rumpelstiltskin," the king makes an offer of marriage to the lazy daughter after hearing from her mother that she is able to spin straw into gold. Attached to the offer is the condition that if she accepts the proposal, and fails to produce gold, she will be executed. The purpose of the condition is to block the road leading to a marriage offering no economical advantage to the king. Two other roads are left open: the king remaining unmarried, or having a wife who makes his own fortune.

A forked plan may be conceived either sincerely or as a deceptive virtual intent. In the Maupassant story quoted above, the German officer offers the prisoners an alternative to immediate execution for alleged spying: give him the password into Paris, and be allowed to go free. Does the German officer really mean to free the two Frenchmen if he gets the password, or does he plan to kill them anyway? (The answer remains unknown, since the prisoners refuse this alternative.)

Private Narratives

The preceding discussion has demonstrated the potential complexity of the network of mental constructs that underlie human action in general and narrative action in particular. Insofar as these constructs reflect on the history, past or future, of the narrative universe, they link states and events in a temporal sequence, and they present the same structure as the narrative of which they are a part. The I-world and K-world of characters hold collections of private narratives that determine their behavior and give meaning to their actions. Whether they are verified by the actual events or remain purely virtual, these private embedded narratives weave their strands into the texture of the plot and turn it into a layered structure, a bundle of possible stories.

8 Virtuality and Tellability

Imagine that you are a writer of children's stories, and that to assist you in your job you have a computer program, called AESOP (for Automatic Experimental Story Outline Producer), which spins the plots for you. All you have to do is run AESOP until it produces a satisfying plot, and turn this plot into a text. Today you ask AESOP to generate a plot about a fox and a crow. Since there cannot be a story without a conflict, the computer asks you: what is the problem to be solved? You answer: the fox is hungry. Then the computer asks: where is food? and you answer: the crow has cheese. From this input the computer produces the following outline: Mr. Fox was hungry, so he asked the crow to give him some cheese. Okay, said the crow, let's share it and neither of us will be hungry. Moral: sharing makes good friends. You don't like this plot, so you try again. This time AESOP comes up with a plot in which the fox jumps on the crow and steals the cheese. Moral: violence prevails over legal rights. Again you don't like it, and you make a last try. For its third effort, AESOP spins a tale in which the fox, in order to get the cheese, flatters the crow, and gets him to sing. The crow opens his beak, drops the cheese, and the fox gets it. Moral: don't trust flatterers. Finally satisfied, you turn this plot into a text, and your narrative becomes a world-famous fable. Guided by intuitive reasons, you were able to do what the computer could not: assess the aesthetic potential of a story outline.

The moral of this story (which unlike the preceding stands little chance of becoming a world-famous fable) is that not all plots are created equal. Some configurations of facts present an intrinsic "tellability" which precedes their textualization. This is why some stories exist in numerous versions, survive translation, and transcend cultural boundaries. Narratologists have long been aware of this fact, but the problem of what accounts for the pretextual tellability of a narrative message is one of the most neglected areas of narratology. As Jerome Bruner observes, "In contrast to our vast knowledge of how science and logical reasoning proceeds, we know precious little in any formal sense about how to make good stories" (1986:14).

What would be the scope of a theory of tellability, and how does the project relate to the more general field of narratology? Narrative poetics is traditionally divided into a poetics of discourse and a poetics of plot. Both of these domains include a prescriptive component: how to tell a story well, and what makes a story worth telling. In the domain of discourse, the prescriptive component is a theory of performance; in the domain of plot, a theory of tellability.

One may ask at this point why I restrict the concept of tellability to properties of plot, rather than recognizing a tellability inherent to performance. My reason is that the potentiality of the suffix -able is incompatible with the concept of performance. The theory of tellability is concerned with potential narrative appeal, the theory of performance with its realization.

Some will insist that tellability cannot be isolated from performance, since the nature of performance is to enhance the features that account for tellability. It is indeed through the quality of the performance that we discern tellability. But the potential appeal of a narrative message is not necessarily realized in performance: a good joke can fall flat because of poor telling; a speaker can refuse to "display" some events thought by the hearer to be worth telling about. A concrete example of unrealized narrative potential is provided by the sociolinguist William Labov. In response to the request "did you ever experience a serious danger?" an informant produced this narrative: "Well, this person had a little too much to drink and he attacked me and the friend came and she stopped it" (quoted in Pratt 1977:44). The narrator did not invite the audience to "join him in contemplating [the experience], evaluating it, and responding to it" (Pratt 1977:136), but glossed over an episode that could have proved to be viable narrative material.

There may be a fuzzy border, an overlap between the domain of tellability and the domain of performance, but their cores are well defined—as well defined as the opposition between story and discourse, from which they are derived. The existence of a narrative text is justified either informationally or aesthetically. The justification is supported by certain properties. Among these properties, some are inseparable from the letter of the text. Others remain present in paraphrases and summaries. The former fall within the scope of a theory of narrative performance. The latter form the specific concern of a theory of tellability.

By taking plot summaries as primary data, the problem of tellability falls victim to a prejudice which may explain its discredit among literary critics. Although narratologists have come to admit the existence of a narrative level of meaning disembodied from the medium, they are reluctant to regard this level as a potential source of aesthetic value. As Wlad Godzich observes, "we are more likely to valorize those [literary texts and films] that defy plot summation and we associate the products of mass culture with plot development" (foreword to Pavel 1985:xvi).

All narratives have plots—at least in embryonic form—but plot may receive various degrees of prominence. As Godzich suggests, the texts we read for the sake of the plot are primarily popular genres: fairy tales, thrillers, soap operas, detective novels, historical romances. In the great masterpieces of the modern novel—such as Emily Brontë's *Wuthering*

Heights, Proust's *Remembrance of Things Past,* or Tolstoi's *Anna Karenina*—plot is frequently subordinated to the representation of character, setting, and ideas. Many events are not told for their own sake, but for their illustrative value: their function is to fix an atmosphere, outline a milieu, reveal the personality of characters, promote a symbolic or allegorical interpretation. This motivation is vertical, since it justifies the plot through ideas that transcend the narrative events. Vertical motivation is particular to each text, and does not lend itself to codification. (Or it is perhaps too easily codified as "x means y," where x is an event and y an abstract idea.) It is in the area of horizontal motivation that general principles of tellability may be formulated. In horizontal motivation, some events may be subordinated to others (as preparatory versus climactic), but justification remains within the plot, remains within the temporal sequence. The predominance of the horizontal type of motivation in popular genres makes them indeed more interesting—or at least, more consistently interesting—to a theory of tellability than those semantically complex literary texts which exploit the vertical significance of narrative events, sometimes at the expense of the horizontal motivation.

As an art form, however, plot is not inherently inferior to the resources for which we praise high literary narrative. It is simply less diversified and therefore more easily stereotyped. There may be a trace of the mystique of the subject in the downgrading of plot as aesthetic object: the singularity of a creative mind is far better expressed through style, message, imagery, narrative technique, and symbolism than through the rigid structures of plot. The greatest masterpieces of the plot-world—such as the archetypal plots of the detective novel, or of the tale of the dragon-slayer—are not individual achievements but collective creations.

Tellability and Narrative Points

Largely neglected by literary critics, the problem of tellability has found some attention among sociolinguists, cognitive psychologists, and specialists in artificial intelligence. The sociolinguist William Labov, who pioneered the term "tellability," also introduced the ancillary concept of narrative point. In order to be tellable, a story must have a point. The ultimate putdown for a storyteller is to elicit the response "So what's the point?" Robert Wilensky, an artificial intelligence specialist, elaborates further on the notion of narrative point:

> Points are structures that define those things that a story can be about. They characterize those contents that constitute reasonable stories and account for the existence of that story as an item to be communicated. By this I mean that a person tells or listens to a story because the story has a content that is of some intrinsic interest. The content that bears this interest value is what I term the point. (1983b:583)

Between Labov's use and Wilensky's definition, the concept of point undergoes a shift from singularity to possible plurality. Most of the utterances through which we conduct the practical business of life have a single point, or at least a very dominant one. Getting this point across is what makes the utterance a successful speech act. Among narratives produced for aesthetic reasons only jokes have their raison d'être in a single point: the punch line that ends the narrative. The study of the various types of punch lines would indeed be very instructive for a theory of tellability. But in most pleasure-oriented narratives, points of interest are varied and distributed throughout the text. "Narrative point" becomes in this case synonymous with "narrative highlight." A theory of tellability implicitly regards a plot as a sequence of peaks and valleys, and seeks out the formulae for building up the peaks.

Points may entertain various relationships with principles of tellability. Some are rooted in performance, and do not fall within the scope of a theory devoted to plot-internal tellability. An example of a point dependent on a discourse strategy is presenting the narrative as an answer to a question by topicalizing this question through a chronological reordering (Balzac, "Sarrasine"). Another is surprising the reader of a mystery novel by having the case narrated by the murderer himself (Agatha Christie, *The Murder of Roger Ackroyd*). Among the points that do concern the narrative message, some contain an implicit guideline, which contributes a concrete principle to a theory of tellability. Stating that the point of a story resides in the unusual character of the reported events leads to this principle: "To make your story tellable, select unusual events." In other cases, points are effects on the reader, and they differ from the devices through which these effects are achieved. The point of a detective novel may be said to reside in a challenge to the sagacity of the reader. This point is realized by planting clues and suggesting false leads. The principles of tellability specific to the detective novel reside in these devices, rather than in the point itself. But even when narrative points do not translate directly into concrete principles, their identification and classification constitutes an essential first step in the exploration of tellability.

Wilensky distinguishes several types of points: external and internal, static and dynamic. These categories do not form a rigorous, definitive taxonomy, but they provide a convenient frame of organization for a general overview of the question of points.

External points are "what is usually meant when someone refers to 'the point of the story.' " They correspond to "some goal a storyteller might have in telling a story," such as: convincing a listener of something, impressing someone, achieving an emotional reaction, or being informative (Wilensky 1983b:583). These examples suggest that external points reside in the relationship between text and context. They depend consequently on pragmatic principles of tellability. Filling in the category for Wilensky (who does not elaborate further on the idea), I would classify as "external points" the following reasons for telling a story:

(a) Any feature that justifies the telling of a story in a certain context, but vanishes in another. More particularly, any purpose relative to a certain speaker/hearer pair engaged in a particular situation. An example taken from fiction: in Balzac's "Sarrasine," one of the points of telling the story of a mysterious old man is to satisfy the curiosity of the narratee concerning the origin of the wealth of a prominent Parisian family.

(b) Any justification involving a departure of the facts of TAW from a standard defined within AW, such as a standard of probability or the moral standards of the society in which the story is produced. According to this principle, events are tellable if they are unusual, problematic, or scandalous. This type of point forms the essence of news and is most strikingly exemplified in the stories of tabloids.

(c) Any justification dependent on truth-in-AW. Example: the urban legend about the skier who slides down the slope backwards with her pants down loses most of its appeal if it is told as a fiction. It is tellable because it is funny, and it is funny because it is embarrassing to the woman. We love to see people being embarrassed, but we are much less likely to laugh at embarrassment experienced by imaginary people. (On a tellability scale, the story reaches its highest potential if it happened to somebody we know.)

(d) Any justification resting on a resemblance between AW and TAW. Many fictional narratives derive their point from plausibility, verisimilitude, or typicality with respect to the norms of AW. A novel may be read as a depiction of a certain milieu, as an evocation of a historical period, as the expression of real-world problems, or as the description of a human type. In these cases, character or setting, rather than plot, form the focus of interest.

(e) Any general, abstract message to be conveyed by a story. Examples: the moral of a fable; the teaching of a didactic novel; the meaning of a parable.

(f) Any narrowly defined emotion, reaction, mental or physical state to be aroused in the reader: fear by horror stories, sexual stimulation by pornography, terror and pity by Greek tragedy.

Most external points present limited interest for narrative fiction. The pragmatic approach presupposes a concrete speech situation and a personal relationship between speaker and hearer—but this is precisely what is lacking in narrative fiction. Through the roles of substitute speaker and hearer, the actual participants in the communicative event relinquish their identities, and isolate themselves from any concrete set of circumstances. The relevance of point (a) to fiction is restricted to the acts of nonfictional storytelling represented within fiction. Justification (b) is a prominent factor of tellability for information-oriented texts, but if unusual facts make good news, they rarely sustain interest in fictional communication: making up improbable events is just too easy to do. (An exception to this rule is the principle of maximal departure which operates in tall tales: the improbability of the facts is stretched so far that falsity becomes obvious, and takes over as narrative point.) That fiction and nonfiction observe different criteria of tellability is emphasized by (c): some stories must be true in order to be good. Because of our existential involvement in our native system of reality, we are more easily satisfied with stories yielding information about AW than with narratives taking their reference in a recentered system. The only elements of the list applicable to fiction are points of type (d), (e), and (f). But in (e) the message abstracted from the story is itself an instance of non-fictional communication. As for (d) and (f), their formulation offers no practical guideline for achieving the desired effect.

The second of Wilensky's categories, internal points, consist of the properties that "legitimize a story from within" (583). Wilensky distinguishes two kinds of internal points: dynamic and static. "A dynamic point is one in which a story event violates a previous expectation. Such points include irony, surprise, and humor." According to Wilensky, the violated expectations can be those of either characters or reader. While the violations of the character's expectations are a matter of content, the manipulation of the reader's expectations is mainly a matter of presentation and forms what I shall call a "strategic point." The narrative devices and figures of discourse responsible for strategic points include prolepsis, analepsis, withdrawal of information, play with boundaries (more about this in chapter 9), opaque reference, ellipsis, ambiguity, and the double-entendre of puns. But strategic points are not exclusively a matter of discourse. The narrative device responsible for the surprise of the reader may become "emplotted" as narrative event, thus challenging the distinction between narrative appeal due to performance and plot-internal tellability. A case in point is "The Shape of the Sword," the short story by Borges. The point of the narrative resides in the surprise experienced by the reader and narratee, when they find out that the narrator has told his life story from the point of view of an individual other than himself. Reader and narratee expected the narrator to be the hero, and to escape a deathly trap set up by the traitor: the narrator, after all, must survive to tell his tale. When the hero appears hopelessly cornered by the traitor, the narratee urges the narrator to continue his tale. But the story is now finished: "he" turns out to be "I," "I" turns out to be "he," and there is no rescue to narrate.

> Then a sob went through [the narrator's] body, and with a weak gentleness he pointed to the whitish curved scar.
>   "You don't believe me?" he stammered. "Don't you see that I carry written on my face the mark of my infamy? I have told you the story so that you would hear me to the end. I denounced the man who protected me: I am Vincent Moon. Now despise me." (Borges 1983:70)

The life story of the narrator could arguably be retold in a conventional manner—leaving out his temporary disguise in his transaction with the narratee. This retelling would obviously miss the point, but it would also miss the focal event in this particular plot: the revelation of the narrator's identity. It would tell the life of the same individual, but not the same story. The narrative trick responsible for the point is a communicative event within TAW, and therefore an integral part of the plot.

While strategic points illustrate the fuzziness of the borderline between theory of performance and theory of tellability, the remaining types of points are entirely located on the pretextual level. Using Hjelmslev's well-known semiotic dichotomy, I would distinguish here points involving the substance of the narrative content and points involving its form. Substantial points reside in the themes and motifs of the narrative message. A French formula for successful novels lists the following ingredients: religion, sex, aristocracy, and mystery. (The last one is a strategic point). According to this formula, the most tellable story reads: "Mon Dieu, dit la Marquise, je suis enceinte et ne sais pas de qui." (Margaret Boden proposes this English version: "My God, said the Duchess, I am pregnant. Who done it?" [1977:299]). Roger Schank (1978) provides his own recipe for bestsellers when he isolates a set of themes of "absolute interest" which comprises death, danger, power, sex, and large quantities of money. Some of these themes owe their narrative appeal to universal human concerns (love, death, sexuality), while others are heavily dependent on cultural fashion and current events (power and money). Culture-dependent principles also preside over the selection of concrete motifs, characters, and settings, gathering these ingredients into literary topoi. Past and present topoi include pastoral landscapes, fairy tale worlds, and the Wild West. The intrinsic tellability of motifs may also be due to poetic quality and originality. One of the most memorable scenes in the tale of "Sleeping Beauty" is the charming vision of the sleeping princess surrounded by wild vegetation. One could speak here of visual point: the narrative highlight is a scene which seems to have been created with the illustrator in mind. The tellability inherent to motifs is most prominent in children's literature: a hut standing on chicken feet is more memorable to a young reader than any abstract narrative unit, and a cute little rabbit provides greater narrative appeal than the most clever twists in the plot.

Substantial points cannot be left out of a theory of tellability, but their study is not particularly interesting. It begins with a catalog of themes, motifs, and topoi, and ends with the reasons for their appeal. Far more compelling, and in need of more work, is the study of the formal properties that support tellability. We can begin this project by stating the minimal conditions of narrativity: a prerequisite for making a good plot is to make a plot at all. Gerald Prince defines these conditions as "the representation of at least two real or fictive events or situations in a time sequence, neither of which presupposes or entails the other" (1982:4). A more specific formulation of the basic conditions of narrativity is proposed by Pavel: story = problem + solution. Not all of Prince's stories will satisfy Pavel's definition, but those that do will certainly be the more interesting. Hence this very general guideline: a good plot must present a conflict and at least one attempt at solving it. These very general principles, which apply to all plots, must be complemented with a repertory of particular guidelines allowing a diversification in the formal sources of tellability.

Some of these specialized guidelines can be derived from the properties that account for aesthetic effect in lyric poetry: oppositions, repetitions, and polysemy. While the canons of poetry apply to words, syllables, and individual images, their narrative equivalents operate on a semantic material consisting of states and events. Transposed to the poetics of plot, the three lyric principles become:

(1) *Semantic opposition.* This principle advocates sudden turns in the plot, reversals in the fortunes of characters, and, very generally, any kind of inversion between narrative states. These configurations are so important to the poetics of drama—as Aristotle was the first to observe—that the expressions "dramatic reversal" and "dramatic turn" have been frozen into clichés. "Dramatic" has even become synonymous with sudden turn, as in "dramatic ending."[1] Another form of semantic opposition contrasts the goals of characters with the result of their actions, leading to an effect known as narrative irony. The most potent form of narrative irony is self-contradiction. An example of this eminently tellable situation is a character being shown to be guilty of the same sin for which he or she punished another (cf. *The Decameron*: first day, fourth story, or ninth day, second story).

(2) *Semantic parallelism and symmetry.* This principle promotes the multiplication of narrative sequences presenting structural similarities but involving different participants. A character may, for instance, repeat the experience of another character, or two characters may engage simultaneously in similar action (cf. "The Gift of the Magi," by O. Henry). A well-known form of parallelism resides in the triplications of fairy tales: three wishes, three heroes, three tasks, three attempts, three dangers. Often, however, the last in the sequence contrasts with the first two, and parallelism is not an end in itself—and therefore, not a true narrative point—but a device in the service of semantic opposition. The combination of principles (1) and (2) also results in the highly tellable pattern of inverse symmetry.

(3) *Functional polyvalence.* Narrative highlights are formed by events entering into several distinct functional units. By functional unit I mean a grouping of states and events (not necessarily adjacent) presenting special strategic significance for the story as a whole. This strategic significance is captured by a label, such as retaliation, reward, deceit, test, challenge, or betrayal. An example of functional polyvalence is the marriage of Oedipus to Jocasta. This particular event functions as solution of a problem (the desire of Oedipus for Jocasta); as fulfillment of a prediction; as violation of an interdiction (the prohibition of incest); and as an infraction justifying the punishment to come. The principle of functional polyvalence is what accounts for the intrinsic elegance—and consequently, for the tellability—of certain ways of resolving problems. The most ingenius solutions are those which satisfy such adages as "to kill two birds with one stone," "to lie

without lying," or "to have your cake and eat it, too." All of these sayings ascribe multiple effects to a single action.

The Principle of Diversification

None of the principles surveyed so far tells us, however, why the stratagem selected by the crow makes a better story than the other two conceivable solutions to his problem: asking for the cheese, or taking it by violence. This is where the theory of possible worlds makes a contribution to the theory of tellability. I propose the following principle: *seek the diversification of possible worlds in the narrative universe*. We have seen in chapter 6 that conflicts are necessary to narrative action and that conflicts arise from incompatibilities between TAW and the private worlds of characters. The diversification of the narrative universe thus constitutes the most basic condition of tellability. But the involvement of this principle in the poetics of plot does not end with the creation of conflicts: if that were the case, all solutions to the problem of the fox would be equally satisfying. The demand for a diversified semantic universe also determines what kinds of resolutions and outcomes present the greater narrative interest. My contention is that tellability is rooted in conceptual and logical complexity, and that the complexity of a plot depends on an underlying system of purely virtual embedded narratives.

Embedded narratives, as we have seen in chapter 7, are the story-like constructs contained in the private worlds of characters. These constructs include not only the dreams, fictions, and fantasies conceived or told by characters, but any kind of representation concerning past or future states and events: plans, passive projections, desires, beliefs concerning the history of TAW, and beliefs concerning the private representations of other characters.[2] Among these embedded narratives, some reflect the events of the factual domain, while others delineate unactualized possibilities. The aesthetic appeal of a plot is a function of the richness and variety of the domain of the virtual, as it is surveyed and made accessible by those private embedded narratives.

According to the principle I am proposing, a string of events looking like figure 18(a) presents the lowest possible narrative potential, while a well-branched configuration like figure 18(b) provides a promising plot-line. In the two diagrams, black dots represent actualized history and white ones virtual sequences. In the configuration of figure 18(a), all private narratives are either correct interpretations of the past, or realized projections. The possible worlds of the mental domains of characters are perfectly aligned along the historical chain, and there is only one sequence of events to take into consideration. The first two versions of "The Fox and the Crow" generated by AESOP are examples of this configuration. In narratives of type 18 (b), by contrast, the private worlds of characters generate mutually incompatible courses of events, and the actual world gives access, through mental acts, to a variety of alternate possible worlds.

The conformity of the classical version of "The Fox and the Crow" to the pattern of figure 18(b) stems from the theme of deception. The system of actual and virtual events created by the scheme of the fox is shown in figure 19. As we have seen in chapter 7, a deceptive plan involves a contrast between two mental constructs: the actual plan of the deceiver and the virtual plan he or she pretends to endorse. The actual plan of the fox is fulfilled by the events of the factual domain (nodes 1–2–3–4 in figure 19). His overt plan follows a different line: asking the crow to sing in order to find out whether the beauty of his voice matches the beauty of his feathers. The crow believes the overt plan to be sincere, and he reconstructs the motivation of the fox as a genuine desire for knowledge. At point 2 in the plot, he interprets the past as the sequence 1–5–2, and he projects the future as 2–3–6. (The direction of the arrows in figure 19 indicates whether the sequence is constructed prospectively or retrospectively.) Sequence 2–3–6 represents three different mental constructs: the virtual plan of the fox, the crow's erroneous reconstruction of the actual plan of the fox, and the plan selected by the crow.[3] For the deceptive scheme to be successful, this projection must remain unrealized. The theme of deception thus weaves at least

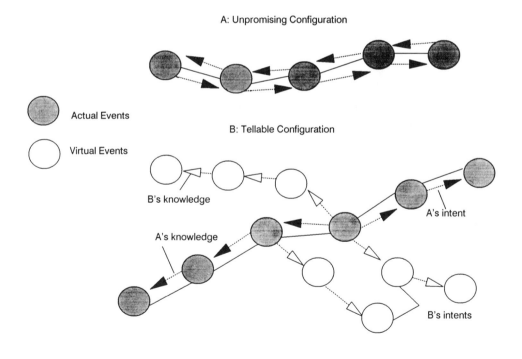

A: Unpromising Configuration

Actual Events

Virtual Events

B: Tellable Configuration

B's knowledge

A's knowledge

A's intent

B's intents

Figure 18
Two types of plot-map

two distinct threads into the fabric of the story. Therein resides a good part of its universal appeal. Stories of deception are indeed much more common, and much more entertaining, than stories involving problem-resolution through brute force or cooperation.

Among the situations that involve virtual strings of events, we find narrative themes of such common occurrence across cultures, periods, and genres as unsuccessful action, broken promises, violated interdictions, mistaken interpretation, and double as well as single deception. In an unsuccessful action, the plan differs from the actual events. In a broken promise, a character commits her- or himself to a certain line of action, but follows another line. In a violated interdiction, the behavior of the character deviates from the line prescribed by society. A mistaken interpretation of past events traces an alternative road into the present. And if simple deception involves two constructs—the actual and the pretended plan, which falls together with the projected plan—double deception traces three distinct roads on the map of the plot (as we have seen in chapter 7). The view of tellability presented in this chapter predicts the inherent superiority of these thematic configurations over the inverse possibilities—successful plans, respected interdictions, fulfilled promises, and accurate knowledge. I am not trying to say that the members of this second semantic group cannot occur

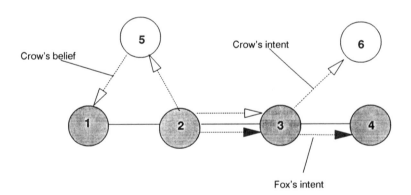

Key to events

1 Fox comes by
2 Fox asks Crow to sing
3 Crow starts singing

4 Fox grabs cheese
5 Fox wants to know how Crow sings
6 Fox admires Crow's voice

Figure 19
Plot-map for "The Fox and the Crow"

in a good plot; but when they do, they usually appear in conjunction with an element of the first category. A plan will be carried out after some failed attempts have led the agent to alter his or her original strategy; a promise will be kept against an adverse scheme; and a prediction will be fulfilled after the failure of a plan to prevent its realization. When they are not interwoven with the virtual narratives of another semantic unit, themes involving a single thread are supported by other principles of tellability. The keeping of a long-forgotten promise by a "helper character" will, for instance, save the hero from danger and create a sudden turn. Or the goal of a character will be realized accidentally, by an event satisfying the principle of functional polyvalence.

"The Fox and the Crow" is a story of almost minimal length, and it should come as no surprise that its system of embedded narratives comprises only two distinct sequences—the minimum required for a tellable story. In what follows I propose to extend the analysis of the virtual to three narratives of increasing semantic complexity.

Let us begin with the classical fairy tale of "Cinderella." The map of the plot is shown in figure 20, and the events are listed in the accompanying key. The first embedded narrative is Cinderella's wish to go to the ball and marry the Prince. She takes the first step toward its realization by making herself a dress. The stepmother pursues the conflicting goal of having the Prince marry one of her own daughters. Since her passive projection anticipates the success of Cinderella's plan, she elaborates a counterplan, by which Cinderella is prevented from going to the ball. At point 4 in the story it looks like the line of the actual events has veered away from Cinderella's goal, and is following instead the course of the stepmother's intent. Enter the Fairy Godmother, who counters the stepmother's scheme by helping Cinderella to go to the ball. Through the intervention of an external agent, the actual events thus reenter the track of Cinderella's dream, even though the execution of her plan has been terminated in event 3. (From there on, the line of her plan crosses virtual events.) When the Prince meets Cinderella at the ball he forms an intent compatible with her ultimate goal: asking her to marry him at the end of the night. This project is ruined when Cinderella is forced to leave the ball at midnight. The prince comes up with another plan toward the same goal: having the Grand Duke try the shoe left by Cinderella on all the girls in the kingdom until the owner is found. The execution of this project gives a new chance to the stepmother: fearing that the shoe will fit on Cinderella (passive projection), she locks her up in the attic, hoping that one of her daughters will manage to squeeze her foot into the slipper. The Prince's plan is now in jeopardy, but it will be finally realized, thanks to an intervention by Cinderella. To avoid the fate of being bypassed in the search, she counteracts to the stepmother's move by escaping from the attic, trying the shoe, and allowing her identification. In the end her dream is realized, though not through the course of events originally pro-

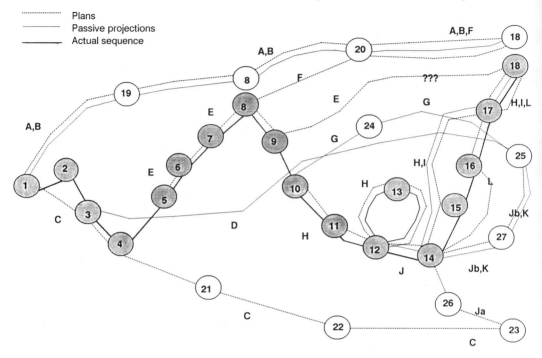

Figure 20
Plot-map for "Cinderella"

jected. The appeal of this plot resides not only in the number of virtual paths, but also in the tortuous course followed by the actual events, as they shift back and forth between the tracks of the competing plans.

In "The Fox and the Crow" and in "Cinderella," the exploration of the virtual is a business trip undertaken for the benefit of the factual domain. The purpose of the trip is to discover the psychological motivation which turns physical gestures into intelligible actions. In the next example—the first story of the ninth day of *The Decameron*—the virtual retains this explanatory function, but the trip allows sightseeing excursions. The virtual is on its way to becoming vacation-land:

A beautiful widow, Madonna Francesca, "is wooed by a certain Rinuccio and a certain Alessandro, but is not herself in love with either." In order to "rid herself of their importunities" she conceives the plan of "asking of them a service which, though not impossible, she [thinks] no one [will] ever perform, so that when they [fail] to carry it out she [will] have plausible and legitimate ground for rejecting their advances." On that day the body of a disfigured and hideous rogue, Scannadio, has been

Actual events:

    1. Cinderella and her stepsisters invited to the ball.
    2. Cinderella makes herself a dress.
    3. Stepmother forces Cinderella to stay home.
    4. Stepmother takes stepsisters to the ball.
    5. Fairy Godmother appears to Cinderella.
    6. Fairy Godmother performs magic to get Cinderella outfitted for the ball.
    7. Cinderella goes to the ball in a magic carriage.
    8. Cinderella meets the Prince at the ball and he falls in love with her.
    9. Cinderella leaves the ball at midnight, losing her shoe.
    10. Prince finds Cinderella's shoe.
    11. Prince sends the Grand Duke to look for Cinderella.
    12. Grand Duke goes to the house of every girl in the kingdom. On last iteration, he goes to Cinderella's house.
    13. Girls try shoe and it does not fit.
    14. (After last iteration of 12) Stepmother locks Cinderella in the attic.
    15. Stepsisters try shoe and it does not fit.
    16. Cinderella escapes.
    17. Cinderella tries shoe and it fits.
    18. Prince marries Cinderella.

Virtual events:

    19. Cinderella goes to the ball with stepmother and stepsisters.
    20. Prince asks for Cinderella's hand at the end of the ball.
    21. Stepsisters dance with Prince at the ball.
    22. Prince asks for the hand of one of the stepsisters.
    23. Stepsister and Prince get married.
    24. Cinderella disappears forever.
    25. Prince marries another girl, or nobody at all.
    26. Shoe fits on one of the stepsisters.
    27. Grand Duke cannot find Cinderella and goes to another house.

Virtual embedded narratives:

    A. Cinderella's intent at point 1: 2, 19, 8, 20, 18.
    B. Stepmother's passive projection at point 1: 2, 19, 8, 20, 18.
    C. Stepmother's intent at point 1: 3, 4, 21, 22, 23.
    D. Fairy Godmother's passive projection at point 5: state resulting from 3, 25.
    E. Fairy Godmother's intent at point 5: 6, 7, 9 (possibly also 8, 18).
    F. Prince's intent at point 8: 20, 18.
    G. Prince's passive projection at point 10: 24, 25.
    H. Prince's intent at point 10: 11, 12, 13, 17, 18.
    I. Stepmother's passive projection at point 12: 17, 18.
    J. Stepmother's intent at point 12: 14, 26, 23 (Ja). If not 26, then 27, 25 (Jb).
    K. Cinderella's passive projection at point 14: 27, 25.
    L. Cinderella's intent at point 14: 16, 17, 18.

Figure 20

buried in a churchyard. Through her maidservant, Madonna informs Alessandro that "for reasons he will be told later," a kinsman of hers is "obliged to convey to her house the body of Scannadio." Since she is "utterly repelled by the thought of harboring this man's corpse under her roof" she implores Alessandro to take Scannadio's place in the tomb. He will be brought to her house by her kinsmen, and for his reward he will be allowed to stay there as long as he wants. If he refuses to do her this favor she does not want to hear from him again. The maidservant is then sent to Rinuccio to inform him that Madonna needs to have the body of Scannadio delivered to her house. She is counting on him to carry out the task. Why she needs this service performed will be explained to him when the mission is accomplished. If he succeeds in delivering the body she will grant him every wish, but if he fails, she will not accept any further message from him. After long hesitations, due to the strangeness of the request and to their inability to understand its motivation, both suitors decide to comply. Alessandro takes Scannadio's place in the tomb and Rinuccio drags him to Madonna's house. Madonna stands at her window, armed "with a suitable pretext for sending them both packing" in the unlikely case they fulfill their mission. But as they come within her sight, the two suitors are challenged by an officer of the watch who happens to be looking for an outlaw. Fearing for his life, Rinuccio drops Alessandro and they both run away. The next day, the two suitors go back to Madonna to inform her of what happened, and to ask for "her forgiveness and her love," which they think they deserve since they did their best to follow her instructions. "But she [pretends] not to believe them, and by curtly replying that she [wants] no more to do with either of them, as they had failed to carry out her bidding, she neatly [rids] herself of both" (Boccaccio 1986:682–87).

The story illustrates several principles of tellability. It develops an external point by proposing a question to its audience: should the actions of the suitors be praised as a demonstration of love, or ridiculed as pure folly? It invests in the thematic appeal of the macabre—the scene of the graveyard seems to have been created with the camera in mind—and in the comic contrast between the silly courage of the lovers in the graveyard, and their cowardice under the window of the lady. The duplication of the suitors creates parallelism, and the appearance of the officer of the watch introduces a sudden turn. The plan of Madonna is a good example of functional polyvalence, since it is designed to kill two birds with one stone. Part of its ingenuity lies in the fact that if Rinuccio fails to accept the challenge there is no way Alessandro can fulfill his mission: who would then carry him to his destination? And finally, there is an ironic contradiction between appearance and reality in Madonna's excuse for not granting the suitors their wish: by pretending not to believe them, while she knows they are sincere, she is guilty of the duplicity which she attributes to them. In appearance she tells the truth and they are liars, in reality the lovers are truthful and she is the liar.

But the tellability of the tale is mostly invested in its network of virtual sequences. I will spare the reader the enumeration of the narratives formed by the plans, pretended plans, passive projections, sincere and fake beliefs of characters. Rather than repeating the analysis performed on "The Fox and the Crow" and on "Cinderella," I will focus on a type of mental construct not present in the other stories: the narratives produced by speculative activity.

Most of these narratives originate in an occulted tale: the explanations promised to Alessandro and to Rinuccio after the completion of their task. The postponement of these explanations not only covers up their nonexistence, it also stimulates the imagination of the two suitors. On his way to the graveyard Alessandro tries to explain the strange request of Madonna through a series of conjectures:

(A) Madonna's kinfolks may have discovered I'm in love with her. Perhaps they think I have seduced her, and have forced her into this so they can murder me inside the tomb. If that's the case, I shan't stand a dog's chance, nobody will be any wiser, and they'll escape scot free.

(B) Or possibly, for all I know, it's a trap prepared for me by some enemy of mine, who persuaded her to do him this favor because she's in love with him.

Even if Madonna was sincere, the outlook is rather gloomy for the occupant of the tomb. Four speculative narratives outline what Madonna's kinfolks might do with the body of Scannadio. The best possibility is dismissed as absurd—but remains of course "written" in the mind of Alessandro:

(C) It's hardly likely they would want Scannadio's body in order to embrace it or put it to bed with the lady.

What should be expected by the pseudo Scannadio is a much ruder treatment:

(D) One can only conclude that they want to wreak vengeance upon [Scannadio] in return for some wrong he has done them. She tells me not to make a sound, no matter what may happen; but what if they were to gouge my eyes out, or wrench out my teeth.

(E) And yet, if I open my mouth, they will recognize me and possibly give me a sound hiding.

(F) But even if they don't I shall have achieved precisely nothing, because they won't leave me with the lady in any case. Besides, she will say that I have disobeyed her instructions, and will never have anything to do with me again.

Even after he rejects these arguments, Alessandro continues to spin wild tales: as he lays in Scannadio's tomb,

(G) he was convinced that Scannadio would rise to his feet at any moment and slit his throat on the spot (684–85).

The imagination of Rinuccio is not as fertile as that of Alessandro, but he contributes two virtual narratives as he projects his fate:

(H) being caught red-handed by the watch with Scannadio's corpse on his shoulders, and being condemned to the stake as a sorcerer, or

(I) incurring the hatred of Scannadio's kinfolks if they should ever find out what [Rinuccio] has done. (686)

Another speculative narrative is produced by the townfolk, as they discover the disappearance of Scannadio's body:

(J) The whole town of Pistoia was alive with rumors as to what exactly had happened, the more simple-minded concluding that Scannadio had been spirited away by demons. (687)

These speculative narratives are not (psycho)logically implied by the actions of characters, and they are not subordinated to the intelligibility of the actual. Nor do they serve the strategic purpose of creating suspense, since the reader knows right away that the speculations are false. The strands they weave into the plot present no further aesthetic justification than their own contribution to the density of the semantic texture. Through its network of speculative narratives, the tale proclaims the virtual to be territory worth visiting for its own sake.

In my last example, John Fowles's novel *The French Lieutenant's Woman*, the exploration of the virtual is more than temporary vacation from the actual, it is a metanarrative move calling into question the centrality of the actual in the textual universe.

The title of the novel suggests the dichotomy of the actual and of the virtual by bringing together a representative of each of these domains: Sarah, the woman, is a member of the real world, but there is strong suspicion that the events involving the French lieutenant took place only in imagination.

The author demonstrates an intuitive awareness of the narrative character of certain mental representations, when he writes: "We are all novelists; that is, we have a habit of writing fictional futures for ourselves" (Fowles 1981:266). Though he does not mention the writing of fictional pasts, his novel explores narrative self-representation in both its retrospective and its prospective direction. Of the two main characters, one, Sarah, is a catalyzer of retrospective narratives, while the other, Charles, is an indefatigable planner who spins in the future his novels about himself. The various versions of Sarah's past include:

(1) The public version, as spoken by Ernestina. It shows Sarah as a

deranged woman who falls in love with a French lieutenant, receives a promise of marriage, gives herself to him, is abandoned, and haunts the pier in the hope that he will return.

(2) Sarah's version, as narrated to Charles. She presents herself an intelligent, educated woman, but of a low social status which dooms her to spinsterhood and to the life of a servant. In an act of revolt against the fate written for her by society she gives herself to a man she does not love, and leaves him the next day, assuming in the face of the town the shame she has brought upon herself.

(3) Dr. Grogan's version, who regards Sarah's behavior as a perverse attempt to enslave Charles, and tries to explain it as hysteria through reference to documented cases of medical history.

(4) Charles's version, after he has discovered Sarah's virginity and thus realized that versions (1) and (2) cannot be true. He interprets Sarah's fabulation of her past as a carefully planned stratagem aimed at revealing and testing his love for her. By pretending to be a fallen woman, she is asking him to sacrifice his own reputation, so as to prove worthy of her. This last narrative is shown inaccurate, when Sarah vanishes after receiving Charles's offer of marriage.

While the very essence of Sarah's character is to escape from any fabulation of her past, Charles is a determinist with a deeply rooted faith in the rational character of life. All of his actions are motivated by a reasonable plan, or at least he so believes, and he tries to write his life as a fully intelligible plot. In his efforts to determine his own future, he contemplates at least four distinct narratives. The first, a passive projection, sees him as a rich Victorian bachelor leading the rootless life of an intellectual dilettante. To escape from this fate, he forms the intent of marrying Ernestina, of founding a family, and of spending his days as a country gentleman on the estate inherited from his titled uncle. When the marriage of the uncle terminates this prospect, Charles forms another passive projection, in which, stepping down from the nobility into the bourgeoisie, he becomes the business associate of his father-in-law. In the last narrative, an active projection, he sacrifices his name and fortune in order to marry Sarah, the outcast from society, and to embark with her (despite the sacrifice of his fortune) on a life of travel and leisure, rich in sexual and intellectual pleasures. All these paths are disabled by the actual outcome, and at the end of the novel, Charles faces a future as open and shapeless as the "unplumbed, salt, estranging sea" (366).

A third group of embedded narratives consists of the fake epilogues spun around the main characters, not at the end of the story as the rules of the Victorian novel would prescribe it, but right in the middle. Since these narratives are uttered by a speaker who has so far appeared as the omniscient, omnipotent Lord of the fictional universe, their status as "actual history" cannot technically be called into question. In the next chapter, however (266), the narrator reinterprets the epilogues as a projection of

Charles's, thereby transferring them from the realm of the actual to the realm of the virtual.

Just as Charles imagines several possible outcomes, the narrator spins two contradictory endings to the novel: one in which Charles and Sarah are reconciled by their daughter; and another where they part forever. Through these two endings—both to be perceived as actualized—the novel refuses to select one path in the realm of the possible and call it the history of the one and only actual world. As in the novel described in "The Garden of Forking Paths," alternative routes are simultaneously taken. The textual universe is freed from the dictatorship of the modal structure, in which one world is singled out to rule over all the others. This refusal to organize the textual universe around a single factual sequence amounts to a rejection of plot, a rejection of the mode of intelligibility immanent to narrative organization. The subversion of the modal structure is not only suggested metanarratively by a voice from without, it is also acted out allegorically by a presence from within: Sarah, the woman without a history, who intrudes into the intelligible universe of Victorian determinism, destroys its narrative order, and brings Charles to the threshold of a life experienced outside of any plot.

Other Concepts Involving Virtuality

The notion of virtual narrative developed in this chapter presents affinities with two other concepts recently proposed by narratologists: Gerald Prince's notion of "the disnarrated," and the "ghost chapters" of Umberto Eco. How do these concepts differ, and how are they related? A detailed comparison should sharpen their definition, and reveal various manifestations of the virtual in narrative semantics.

The Disnarrated
Prince defines the disnarrated in opposition to two other, closely related concepts: the *nonnarratable*, and the *nonnarrated*. The nonnarratable is that which cannot be narrated, either because it transgresses a law (the canons of good taste, generic convention, epistemic accessibility), defies the power of language ("one cannot express what M. de Nemours felt at that moment"), or simply "because it falls below the so-called threshold of narratibility" (what I call tellability): it is "not sufficiently unusual or problematic" (1988:1–2). As for the nonnarrated, it is left out of the narrative representation for strategic reasons: "something is not told not so much because of narratorial incapacity, but because of some narrative call for rhythm, characterization, suspense, surprise, and so on."

Taken together, the nonnarratable and the nonnarrated form the difference between what exists in the reference world and what is told about this world. The *disnarrated* consists, on the contrary, of the surplus of what is told over what exists in TRW. It is indeed verbally expressed, but this narration represents that which did not happen, that which is not part of the narrative facts:

> Whereas the first two categories cover all the events that happen in the world represented but are, for any number of reasons, unmentionable or unmentioned, the category [of the disnarrated] covers all the events that *do not* happen but, nonetheless, are referred to (in a negative or hypothetical mode) by the narrative text. (2)

Within the global concept of the disnarrated, Prince accepts a variety of semantic phenomena. His examples suggest the following typology:

Type 1: Outline of an unrealized possibility imagined by a character. Prince mentions this passage from Maupassant's *Bel-Ami*:

> How easy and unexpected it had been! Until then, he had imagined that to approach and conquer one of these creatures he so much desired, infinite attentions were required, infinite waits, a skillful siege made up of gallantries, words of love, sighs, and presents. And suddenly, after the slightest of attacks, the first one he met gave way to him so quickly that it left him dumfounded. (Translated and quoted by Prince, 6)

Type 2: Outline by the narrator of a forking path in the realm of the possible not taken by the events: "this could have happened but did not." This type of disnarrated—which amounts semantically to counterfactual statements—is particularly prominent in reports of sports events: "The turning point in the game was the ball that went through Buckner's legs. If it had been caught, the Red Sox would have won the World Series." Here is a made-up narrative example:

> You would imagine that after learning of Jim's latest infidelity Luann would be fed up and ask for divorce and ruin his political ambitions. But no! If the whole affair could be covered up he had a good chance of being elected president, and she would be first lady, and that would repay her for all these years of silent humiliation.

Type 3: Outline of a narrative possibility not chosen by the creator of the textual universe. This passage from Diderot's *Jacques le fataliste* cannot be attributed to the narrator in TAW, since the narrator who tells the story as true fact has no control over the course taken by the events. It is therefore a metafictional comment, uttered from the point of view of the puppeteer in the actual world who holds the strings of the characters:

> it depends only on me to make you wait a year, two years, three years, for the story of Jacques's loves, by separating him from his master and making each meet with whatever accidents takes my fancy. What prevents me from having the master marry and be a cuckold? from sending Jacques off to the colonies? from leading his master there? from bringing both of them

back to France on the same ship? How easy it is to make up tales! (Translated and quoted by Prince, 5)

The relationship between the disnarrated and my own concept of virtual embedded narratives is one of overlap. My proposal accepts type 1 as virtual narrative, rejects type 3, and classifies type 2 as marginal. The possible differences reside in two areas:

(1) *Verbal status.* The definition of the disnarrated insists on an explicit representation. In order to attract the reader's attention the disnarrated must in fact be narrated. Virtual embedded narratives are much less dependent on linguistic manifestation. They may be spelled out in great detail, suggested by a few words, or left entirely implicit. The description of Jacy's plan in *The Last Picture Show* quoted in chapter 6 occupies a full page, the failed plan of the crow in "The Fox and the Crow" must be reconstructed on the basis of a terse mention of the goal ("to show off his beautiful voice"), and the complex system of virtual embedded narratives in the doubly deceptive plans of the rooster in "The Fox and the Rooster" is entirely inferred by the reader. An even better example of fully implicit virtual narrative is found in a short story to be discussed below, "Un Drame bien parisien" by Alphonse Allais.

(2) *Ontological status.* Embedded narratives, as we have seen, are mental representations produced by characters. They are called virtual when they are not verified in the factual domain. The mental act in which they originate assigns them to one of the private worlds of the textual system of reality. Insofar as this mental act is an event in TAW—even when narrative n is not verified, character x *really* did contemplate n—it functions as accessibility relation between TAW and the world projected by the narrative. Through their roots in TAW, virtual embedded narratives form an objective part of the plot. These conditions are fully satisfied by the first type of the disnarrated.

The second type also outlines a virtual sequence, a "way TAW could have been," but the narrative does not originate in the mental act of a character. It is not, therefore, rooted in a fact of TAW, nor is it inscribed within a private world. The mind that contemplates the unrealized possibility of Luann divorcing Jim belongs to an impersonal narrator—and as a purely logical entity, the impersonal narrator does not project a personal domain. (It would of course be different if the narrator were individuated.) Since they are not produced by the mental act of a participant in the plot, disnarrated elements of type 2 have no influence over the development of the narrative events. Virtual narratives, by contrast, are almost always influential: they provide the psychological motivation that determines the behavior of characters. The possible worlds projected by the disnarrated of type 2 present an ambiguous status within the textual universe. As "that which could have happened," they are accessible from TAW through natural and logical laws (though not through temporal relations: they have already missed their chance of actualization). This logical accessibility integrates them conceptually into the textual universe as "alternatives to TAW." But insofar as they are not accessed by any individuated member of TAW, they remain in a sense external to the plot. The disnarrated of type 2 could be deleted from the text without consequence for the logical coherence of the narrative events.

The third type of disnarrated element is not only external to the plot, but also external to the narrative universe. The metafictional perspective adopted by the speaker offers glimpses into entirely different systems of reality, projected by different narratives. By telling the reader "I could have *made* Jacques do this and that," the speaker evokes the unlucky candidates for the position of actual world in the narrative system. If selected by the creator, each of these unlucky candidates would have been surrounded by its own universe. These universes are rejected, yet made visible within the semantic domain globally projected by the text. The disnarrated of type 3 thus explodes the semantic domain from a system of worlds to a system of universes. This wider system presents, however, the same modal structure as a system of worlds: one of its elements is opposed to all others as the textual universe of the one and only story being *actually* told. The modal structure is also respected within the universes of the disnarrated stories: as a possible narrative, each of the rejected tales presupposes a unique actual world.[4]

While the first type of the disnarrated expresses a semantic dimension inherent to the plot, the second and third types are discourse strategies. As such they are not produced by what I have called a principle of tellability, but rather, by the demands of narrative performance. But they fulfill, within the global semantic domain, the same aesthetic purpose as does within the plot the principle calling for the multiplication of virtual narratives: they trace forking paths on the textual map, thereby increasing the size and diversity of the territory traveled in imagination.

Ghost Chapters

Eco's notion of ghost chapter is based on the postulation that "a text is made of two components, the information provided by the author and that added by the Model Reader, the latter being determined by the former—with various rates of freedom and necessity" (1978:18). Ghost chapters consist of the propositions through which the reader fills in the informational gaps in the story. The criterion of validity is that a ghost chapter must be determined by the text. It may complement the facts asserted for TAW, but it may not contradict them, nor introduce new existents into the textual universe.

The concept of ghost chapter is demonstrated through the analysis of a very elliptic story: "Un Drame bien parisien," by Alphonse Allais. The following summary adheres strictly to what is explicitly stated:

> Marguerite and Raoul are a young couple with a tendency to fight. One
> day, Raoul receives an anonymous letter: "If you want to catch your

wife in a happy mood, go to the Ball of the Incoherents. She will be there, disguised as a Pirogue." The same day, Marguerite receives a similar letter: "If you want to catch your husband in a happy mood, go to the Ball of the Incoherents. He will be there, disguised as a Templar." Both husband and wife find an excuse to explain to each other their absence from the ball. On the night in question, a Templar and a Pirogue sneak away for a private supper. They unmask themselves and cry out in surprise: the Pirogue is not Marguerite, the Templar is not Raoul. Marguerite and Raoul learn a lesson from this misadventure, and from this day on, become a model couple.

According to Eco, the tale is a "textual trap": the text lures readers into incorrect inferences for the pure pleasure of exposing their tendency to jump to conclusions. The trap is prepared in ghost chapter 1, is sprung in ghost chapter 2, and releases its victim in ghost chapter 3.

Ghost chapter 1: At t1, after reading about the reception of the letters, the reader forms these beliefs and expectations:

> Raoul and Marguerite have lovers; they were planning to meet them at the ball as described in the letters; they believe furthermore that their spouse is going to meet his or her lover at the ball. Despite their claims to the contrary they both plan to attend the ball. It is not clear at this point whether they intend to do so in order to meet their respective lovers, or to catch their spouse in the act.

Ghost chapter 2: At t2, after being told that a Templar and a Pirogue have discreetly eloped from the ball the reader expects one of three possibilities based on the truth or falsity of the letters.

> (a) The letter to Raoul was false. The Templar is Raoul, he believes that the Pirogue is Marguerite, but the Pirogue is somebody else.

> (b) The letter to Marguerite was false. The Pirogue is Marguerite, she believes that the Templar is Raoul, but the Templar is somebody else.

> (c) Both letters were correct. Raoul is the Templar, knows that the Pirogue is Marguerite, and believes that she believes that the Templar is her lover. Vice-versa, Marguerite knows the identity of the Templar, but believes that he believes that the Pirogue is his mistress.[5]

Nothing in the text justifies possibility (c): as Eco observes, the two letters do not mention the disguise of the alleged lovers. Raoul has no reason to believe that the lover of Marguerite will be there as a Templar. Why then would he choose the disguise of a Templar, and expect in this way to catch Marguerite in the act? Similarly, Marguerite only knows that Raoul is supposed to be a Templar, not what his mistress will be. Eco claims nevertheless that the text coaxes the reader into believing that Marguerite-as-Pirogue wants to surprise Raoul-as-Templar by being his wife and not his mistress, and vice versa.

The actual outcome inverts to some extent branch (c): the Templar is not Raoul, but he expected the Pirogue to be Marguerite. Vice versa, the Pirogue is not Marguerite, but she expected the Templar to be Raoul. At this point the reader realizes that ghost chapter 2 must be thrown away. But how can the surprise (and expectation) of the Pirogue and Templar be rationalized? Eco proposes a ghost chapter 3 which does not resolve the contradiction, but rather acknowledges the nonsense of the surprise.

Ghost chapter 3, first version:

The Templar, who is not Raoul, expected the Pirogue to be Marguerite; the Pirogue, who is not Marguerite, expected the Templar to be Raoul. This expectation is contradictory. If the Templar and Pirogue are not Raoul and Marguerite, they have no reason to expect their partner to be Marguerite and Raoul.

If ghost chapter 3 is the final interpretation, the me~~~~ of the story is something like "I am absurd, and so are you" (for building ghost chapter 2). In order to confound the reader's gratuitous assumptions, the story destroys its own logic. Eco recuperates this failure as the point of the story. But the claim that the reader is forced into constructing ghost chapter 2 seems rather gratuitous. If readers do not fall into the trap of the gratuitous inference, the story's sacrifice of its own sense will be in vain. The logical capitulation of ghost chapter 3 in the version mentioned above is not, however, an inevitable conclusion. The surprise of the Templar and the Pirogue is fully rationalized in another version of ghost chapter 3.

Ghost chapter 3, second version:

Marguerite and Raoul do indeed have lovers, and through an extraordinary coincidence, the two couples have agreed on the same disguises. After receiving, and believing, the anonymous letters, both Marguerite and Raoul decide to stay away from the ball for fear of being faced with two Pirogues or two Templars. The Pirogue and Templar at the ball are the two lovers, and they elope in the belief of being with Raoul and Marguerite.

If the facts of TAW are as in this second version, "Un Drame bien parisien" is no longer an allegory of reading and misreading, but a narrative riddle whose point is to challenge the reader's sagacity. The text presents seemingly unmotivated events, daring the reader to find a rationalization.[6] Or if the point is to encompass both possibilities—one cannot after all dismiss the interpretation of a reader as expert as Eco—what the text really does is face the reader with the question: am I absurd or am I logical? The point of the text, in other words, resides in this ambiguity.

Eco's reading of "Un Drame bien parisien" reveals considerable fuzziness—or is it versatility?—in the concept of ghost chapter. On the basis of the four specimen detected in the story, a ghost chapter can be:

— A prediction or a retrospective interpretation.

— A provisory construct, to be replaced by another ghost chapter or a definitive image of the textual universe.

— A complete rationalization or a partial filling in of informational gaps, leaving areas of indeterminacy (cf. the branches of ghost chapters 1 and 2 above).

— A valid or an invalid inference—provided the invalid inference is programmed by the text.

— An attempt at rationalizing the plot, or an acknowledgment of unresolved contradictions. (Personally, I would not label this second possibility a ghost chapter, but a metanarrative interpretation).

— A necessary or a possible interpretation. In this second case, a ghost chapter may present several competing versions outlining mutually incompatible narrative universes (cf. the variants proposed for ghost chapter 3, above).

The most obvious differences between ghost chapters and embedded narratives reside in their origin and verbal status. Ghost chapters are conceived by the reader, embedded narratives by characters. Ghost chapters are by definition unnarrated; embedded narratives are either explicit or implicit. In this second case, they are reconstructed by the reader as part of a ghost chapter.

Ghost chapters, however, do not consist exclusively of embedded narratives nor of virtual elements. Consider the second version of ghost chapter 3. The proposition "Marguerite and Raoul both have lovers, and by an extraordinary coincidence the two couples have agreed on the same disguise" is a factual event, while "Marguerite and Raoul decide to stay away from the ball" captures the nonvirtual narrative of a realized plan. The true virtual narratives contained in the ghost chapter are the passive projection of Raoul and Marguerite: "for fear of being faced with two Pirogues or Templars," and the expectations of the disguised lovers: "the Pirogue and Templar elope in the belief of being with Raoul and Marguerite."

Embedded narratives further differ from ghost chapters through their definitive character. Ghost chapters are often provisory explanations, possible at some point in the text, but supplanted at a later point by another rationalization. A discarded ghost chapter belongs to the history of the reading process, but not to the history of the narrative universe. The private narratives conceived by characters may also change during the time span encompassed by the plot, but even as they replace one another, they remain inscribed within the history of the textual universe. Against the thesis that embedded narratives are always definitive, it could be argued that when a ghost chapter is discarded by the reader, so are the intents and beliefs it attributes to characters. My answer to this objection is that the reader's hypotheses concerning the private worlds of characters do not yield embedded narratives until they pass the test of the entire text. As a type of reader expectation, a ghost chapter remains a ghost chapter even after its falsification. But as an integral part of the plot, an embedded narrative must conquer its status in the face of textual evidence. Rejecting a ghost chapter formed as the result of a textual trap means that the narratives it attributes to characters weren't accurate representations of their private worlds— weren't after all embedded in the plot.

These observations raise the questions of the possibility of ambiguity within a textual universe. If virtual narratives originate in the actual mental acts of characters, and cannot be erased from the history of the textual universe, they do not tolerate competing versions. But it is conceivable that the behavior of characters may be compatible with different sets of private narratives. In "The Fox and the Rooster," for instance, the reconstruction of the rooster's plan as a scheme involving double deception is not the only possible rationalization: Bruce (1983:258) mentions readings by children in which the rooster really wants to have breakfast with the dog and the fox, and does not realize that the dog is opposed to the project. From the point of view of tellability this explanation is vastly inferior to the deceptive interpretation, but it is logically compatible with at least some versions of the text. How, then, can the factual character of a particular set of virtual narratives be defended? Isn't it preposterous to claim that character x conceived p and not q, when actions could be explained by ascribing the narrative q to his or her thoughts or intent? My position on this question is that, once we have reconstructed a set of narratives to rationalize the behavior of characters, we imagine a universe in which these narratives were indeed conceived *as fact*. If we consider another explanation, we then contemplate another narrative universe, in which characters were driven by different beliefs, desires, and plans. When we say "it is possible that character x was motivated by p," we mean that the text is compatible with a narrative universe in which x was *actually* motivated by p. An ambiguous text is compatible with several different narrative universes, each centered around its own actual world, and there is a one-to-many relation between discourse and plot. As the case of "Un Drame bien parisien" suggests, an ambiguous text may even be compatible with both a rational and an inconsistent set of private narratives— with both a logical and an absurd textual universe. The semantic domain of the ambiguous narrative text is a system of universes, rather than a system of worlds, but a system without modal structure: each of its elements makes an equally valid claim to being the universe of "the story really told."

What holds of the relationship between ghost chapters and embedded narratives is also valid for the relationship of embedded narratives to all the representations formed during the course of the reading process: hypotheses, projections, expectations, and tentative interpretations. Let us call these representations "dynamic reader constructs." (I assume that the difference between ghost chapters and dynamic reader constructs is mainly qualitative: of all reader-generated representations, ghost chapters are the most rigidly controlled by the text, the most dependent on a deliberate withdrawal of information, and they fill in the most extensive semantic gaps.) The management of the interplay between embedded narratives and dynamic reader constructs is responsible for the type of narrative point I have called "strategic." Narrative suspense derives, for instance, from the confrontation of characters of limited foresight and a reader who anticipates—correctly or not—the situations into which they should run. The reverse strategy is also an efficient way to capture the reader's interest: delaying the reader's understanding of a sequence of actions by preventing access to the set of embedded narratives that motivate the agent. While the plot sets up a field of possibilities, the strategies of narrative discourse may guide the reader along certain paths. As the phenomenon of the textual trap suggests, this guidance is sometimes deceptive: by deemphasizing crucial details, narrative discourse may deliberately lead the reader in a wrong direction. Other strategies protect the reader from dead-end paths by flagging them in advance. For instance, if a narrative begins *in medias res*, and then reports an attempt on the life of the hero, readers know ahead of time that the attempt will fail. The branch leading to success has been pruned from the tree of possibilities by the narrative technique. But within the narrative universe itself, this branch is still part of the tree. If the readers are to understand the acts of the would-be killer, they must take the virtual narrative of the intent to kill into consideration.[7] Thus, while readers may be led to expect developments, or to form retrospective interpretations which do not appear in any embedded narratives, they may, conversely, have to consider embedded narratives that run contrary to their firmest beliefs about the narrative facts.

Stendhal once compared the novel to "un miroir qu'on promène le long d'un chemin" [a mirror that one carries along a road] (*Le Rouge et le noir* 1966:288). The poetics of discourse and performance describes the many ways of manipulating the mirror, while the poetics of plot is concerned with the configuration of the landscape encountered along the road. The principle of tellability presented in this chapter derives from the claim that the appeal of the trip depends not so much on the immediate surroundings of the road actually followed as on the glimpses it permits of the back country, and of the alternative roads it invites the reader to travel in imagination.

9 Stacks, Frames, and Boundaries, or Narrative as Computer Language

On the map of narrative, as on the map of the world, boundaries are every-where: boundaries within the representing discourse, and boundaries within the represented system of reality; boundaries with gates to get across, and boundaries with only windows to look through. While geographic bound-aries divide space in a random pattern, narrative boundaries present a con-centric structure: each territory is contained within another, and as travelers cross the narrative space, they must reenter in reverse order each of the territories encountered on the way.

This concentric structure is reflected in the family of metaphors through which narratologists have traditionally attempted to deal with the divisions of discourse and story: framing, embedding, and Chinese boxes (cf. Todorov 1971, Stewart 1978, Chambers 1984, Bal 1985, Young 1987, McHale 1987). The concepts of the frame family have become so deeply ingrained in our thinking about narrative that we tend to forget their meta-phorical nature. Together with this nature, we also tend to forget their rela-tivity, and we feel no need to look any further for descriptive models. In the present chapter, I propose to complement the standard metaphors of fram-ing and embedding with another way to talk about narrative boundaries: the metaphor of the stack, which comes from the computer field and is widely used in the discourse models of artificial intelligence. (See Reichman 1985 and Hofstadter 1980 for the first use of the concept of stack relevant to narratology.)

Narrative Boundaries: A Typology

The widely accepted distinction between story and discourse generates two types of boundaries: ontological and illocutionary. Ontological bound-aries delimit domains within the semantic universe, and their crossing is a recentering into a new system of reality. Illocutionary boundaries delimit speech acts within a text or a conversation, and their crossing introduces a new speaker or a new narrator. When the utterance of this new voice is a self-sufficient text, it generates its own semantic universe and its own TAW, which may or may not be presented as a reflection of the primary reality from which the text is transmitted.[1] As the territories defined by boundaries differ in their nature, they also differ in their mode of access. A narrative can cross a boundary by selecting the "here" and "now" of the other side as a point of reference, or it may simply look through boundaries, by revealing what is beyond the line from the perspective of this side of the line. In this second case, the crossing of the boundary is only virtual. If we cross-classify the three dichotomies [+/− illocutionary], [+/− ontological], [+/− actual crossing], we obtain the table of possibilities shown in figure 21.

In case 1 there is no boundary, and the distinction between virtual and actual is not applicable. This category corresponds to the standard narrative case: contiguous sentences have the same speaker, and they describe the same level of reality.

In 2a, the boundary involves a change of speaker, but the first and second speaker are members of the same world, and their respective utterances refer to the same reality. On the micro-level, this case is illustrated by directly quoted dialogues. Macro-level instances include narratives of personal experience (such as a newly encountered character telling what circumstances have led to her present situation), or "gossip narratives" (a character telling a story about another member of the same world to satisfy the hearer's curiosity, as in Balzac's "Sarrasine"). In 2b the speech act of the

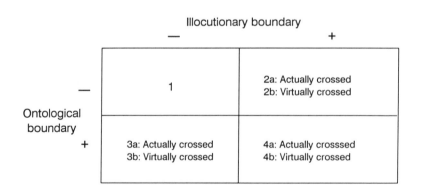

Figure 21
Types of narrative boundaries

character is presented through the speech act of the narrator, as in indirect discourse. We are informed of the storytelling act of the character, but we are denied access to her actual discourse.

In 3a, the narrative transports the reader to a new system of reality without introducing a new speaker. An example of this situation is *Alice in Wonderland*: the text moves from the primary reality of an everyday world to the dream world of Wonderland, and back to the primary reality in a continuous speech act. Another example of this situation is the technique of the "animated picture" which is used in some novels by Claude Simon and Alain Robbe-Grillet (cf. McHale 1987, chap. 8). A picture is described as an object contained within the primary reality; in the course of the description, the characters in the picture begin moving, their actions develop into a plot, and the world within the picture gradually emancipates itself from the primary reality. But there is no change in the reporting voice. The distinction between 3a and 3b is exemplified in this quote from Lewis Carroll: " 'So, either I've been dreaming about Sylvie,' I said to myself, 'and this is reality' [case 3b]. 'Or else I've really been with Sylvie, and this is a dream!' [case 3a]." (*Sylvie and Bruno*, in Carroll 1976:296). In the first part of the quote the report of the dream is anchored in reality and described from an external perspective, while in the second part the dream world is described from within its own confines, and temporarily takes the place of reality. Another example of 3b would be the description of a picture or a movie with repeated reminders of its object status in the primary reality.

Case 4a is the standard case of a fiction within a fiction: the stories told by Scheherazade in *The Arabian Nights*, or the series of novels begun but never finished in Italo Calvino's *If on a Winter's Night a Traveler*. The double crossing of boundaries is implicit to what I take to be the definition of fiction. The ontological crossing occurs in the relocation from AW to TAW, the illocutionary crossing in the sender's adoption of the narrator's voice and identity. The inherent recursivity of the fictional gesture makes this analysis repeatable in the reality centered around TAW. When Scheherazade begins telling in TAW what is for her the tale of the imaginary Ali Baba, she recenters reality around the world in which Ali Baba is a real person, and her voice fades into the speech act of the narrator who tells the story as true fact. In situation 4b, a fictional story is described rather than being actually narrated. (The description of a nonfictional narrative would fall in category 2b.) An example of this unusual situation occurs in a short story by Jorge Luis Borges to which I will return later: "Theme of the Traitor and the Hero." The primary narrator tells us that he plans some day to write a story, that the narrator's name will be Ryan, that Ryan will be engaged in writing the biography of an Irish hero, and that the hero will turn out to be a traitor; but the primary narrator never speaks as Ryan himself, and he never takes the step into the world of the projected story.

The Framing/Embedding Model

The analogical basis of the metaphors of the frame family is the idea of surrounding, transposed from the domain of the visual to the domain of the temporal. A narrative territory frames another territory when its verbal representation both precedes and follows the verbal representation of the framed territory. Figure 22 offers a concrete illustration of the frame structure of *The Arabian Nights*, a narrative known for the complexity of its system of boundaries. The different types of boundaries are represented by different kinds of lines. Scheherazade tells "Ali Baba" and "The Three Ladies of Baghdad" as fictions, and these stories are framed by a double illocutionary/ontological boundary. The porter, Amina, Safia, and Zubaida are characters within "The Three Ladies of Baghdad," telling each other about their past, and the frame of their stories is of the illocutionary variety.

We see in figure 22 that the story of Scheherazade and the Sultan frames the stories told by Scheherazade, that "The Three Ladies of Baghdad"

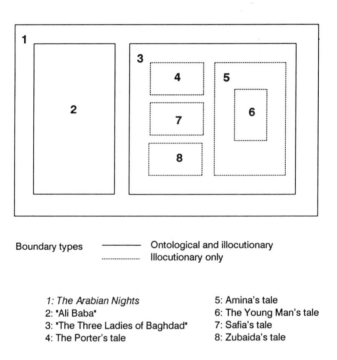

Boundary types   ———— Ontological and illocutionary
                  ·············· Illocutionary only

1: *The Arabian Nights*   5: Amina's tale
2: "Ali Baba"   6: The Young Man's tale
3: "The Three Ladies of Baghdad"   7: Safia's tale
4: The Porter's tale   8: Zubaida's tale

Figure 22
The frame structure of *The Arabian Nights*

frames Amina's tale, and so on. The mapping of fig. 22 is formally equivalent to a system of parentheses:

(( )(( )(( ))( )))

In order to be well formed the sequence must comprise the same number of left and right parentheses. The book of *The Arabian Nights* as a whole would not satisfy the conditions of narrative closure if it never returned to the story of Scheherazade and the Sultan. (Fig. 22 represents a semantic "deep structure," since in the actual narrative the return to the main story may precede the embedded stories: in some condensed versions of *The Arabian Nights*, we learn about the Sultan's decision to save the queen's life before we read the stories which motivated his decision.) The number of unmatched left parentheses crossed in order to reach a certain point is indicative of *narrative level*: "Ali Baba" is on the second level, together with "The Three Ladies of Baghdad," Amina's tale is on the third level, the Young Man's tale on the fourth, and so on. In the standard use of the metaphor, levels are considered to go down rather than up: narratologists will normally say that the Young Man's tale belongs to a deeper level than Amina's tale. The visual mapping of figure 22 not only provides an adequate account of narrative levels, it also predicts the range of acceptable transitions from a given point in the story. Boundaries must be crossed one at a time, either up or down. From Amina's story on level 3 the narrative can go to level 4 or level 2, but it cannot jump to level 1. The system also makes a distinction between "opened" and "closed" territories on the same level. A territory is closed when both its left and right border have been crossed. Boundary crossing can only lead into open territories: it would be illegal to step from Amina's tale on level 3 to "Ali Baba" on level 2, since at the point the narrative enters Amina's tale, the territory of "Ali Baba" has already been closed. The only legal transition from Zubaida's tale into level 2 is a return to "The Three Ladies of Baghdad," from where the step into level 3 had been taken.

The main limitation of the frame model lies in its inability to distinguish illocutionary from ontological boundaries. Representing the various types of boundaries with different kinds of lines, as I have done in figure 22, is only an ad hoc solution, since the meaning of the lines remains to be defined.

Another shortcoming stems from the system's implicit assumption that the ground level is the first encountered in the temporal sequence. This assumption underlies the procedure by which narrative level is calculated on the basis of the number of unmatched left parentheses. It turns out, however, that a narrative may begin on a level other than the first, and still appear well-formed. An example of this situation is the play *The Maids* (*Les Bonnes*) by Jean Genet. The play begins with a play within the play, in which the two characters of level 1, Solange and Claire, impersonate respectively Claire and Madame (their mistress). This play within the play belongs to level 2 because its semantic domain is ontologically supported by a reality in which Solange and Claire are simply Solange and Claire. This ground reality is first invisible, but it is retrospectively reconstructed by the spectator when Solange and Claire step out of their roles and return to what is for them the real world. From level 1, the play moves back to level 2, as Solange and Claire resume their act of impersonation. The same situation occurs in John Fowles's *The French Lieutenant's Woman*: the narrative begins in the world of Sarah and Charles, then crosses the ontological boundary into a world in which they are characters in a novel, and finally returns to the world in which they are real. In these two fictions, the temporal sequence leads from the second to the first and back to the second level, and the semantic level cannot be calculated on the basis of the number of boundary crossings. Since the action of level 2 surrounds the action of level 1, the system would wrongly regard the territory of level 2 as the frame of level 1. To predict levels adequately, the frame diagram should model the narrative in its logical deep structure, which inverts in this case the surface structure specified by the temporal order of presentation.

This conflict between semantic deep structure and dynamic order of presentation can be resolved by mapping narratives like *The Maids* or *The French Lieutenant's Woman* as shown in figure 23. This type of diagram is based on the metaphor of the stack. Frame diagrams and stack diagrams offer complementary views of the phenomenon of narrative boundaries: frames are static objects; stacks are dynamic; frames model a system of relations stretching over the entire semantic domain of the text; stacks capture the temporary states of this domain; frames provide a general map of boundaries; stacks model the mechanisms of the crossing of boundaries.

Stack a′ in figure 23 captures a provisory interpretation of the semantic

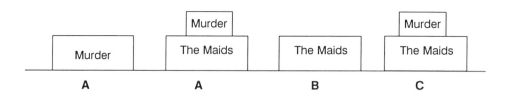

A′: First situation, provisory interpretation
A: First situation, definitive interpretation
B: Second situation
C: Third situation

Figure 23
The stack structure of *The Maids*

domain of *The Maids* in its initial state. By virtue of an interpretive convention, the spectator believes that the dramatic action begins on the ground level. But the default specified by the convention can be overridden by an obvious transition to a lower level. This transition occurs when Solange and Claire put away their disguises and step into their true identities. The sequence of stacks a, b, c shows the definitive interpretation of the three states of the semantic domain. The operations through which the system passes from one state to another are known as pushing and popping: 2a becomes 2b through the popping of the top level of reality, 2b turns into 2c through the pushing of this level back on top of the stack. (This use of the verbs push and pop is itself metaphorical. The analogy derives from a stack of trays at a cafeteria. The stack is supported by a spring, and the top tray is always level with the counter. When a customer puts a tray on top of the stack, the structure must be pushed down in order to make the top tray even with the counter; when a tray is removed, the structure pops up, and the next tray on the stack is lifted to counter level. Being on top of the stack and level with the counter makes a tray the "current tray.")

The formalism of the stack works equally well with canonical narratives beginning on the ground level such as *The Arabian Nights*. Figure 24 gives two snapshots of the current state of the semantic universe, one from within the territory of "Ali Baba" and the other from within the Young Man's tale. The top level of a stack diagram represents the currently active narrative context, and the lower levels the narratives or realities whose verbal representation is waiting to be completed. The various levels must be popped in the reverse order of their pushing: stacks are known as a "last in, first out" structure (as opposed to queues, which are "first in, first out"). The principle "last in, first out" makes the formalism of the stack equivalent to the frame diagram in its ability to predict the sequence of boundary crossings and the range of legal transitions. From the Young Man's tale the narrative must return to Amina's tale, and from there to "The Three Ladies of Baghdad." A return to "Ali Baba" is impossible, since this semantic environment is no longer present on the narrative stack. When compared to frames, however, the stack inverts the direction of narrative transitions: what is seen as going down in a frame model is regarded as going up in a stack model. Amina's tale now belongs to a higher narrative level than "The Three Ladies of Baghdad."

How does the model of the stack address the two problems encountered by the frame model, namely, the need to explain how narratives can directly reach upper levels and to distinguish illocutionary from ontological boundaries? To answer these questions, I propose to draw an analogy between narrative and a computer language. The analogy maps the statements of a program onto the semantic constituents of a narrative. A computer program consists, broadly speaking, of three kinds of elements: the name of the program, which identifies it uniquely to the computer; the list of variables; and the sequence of operations to be performed on the variables. These three

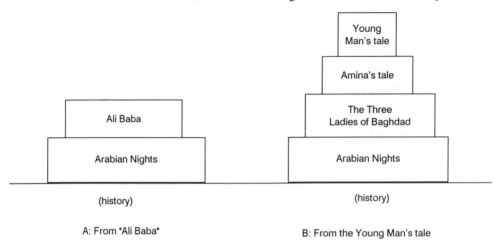

Figure 24
The stack structure of *The Arabian Nights*

components correspond, respectively, to the title of the narrative, the cast of characters, and the sequence of events that affect these characters. A further analogy resides in the fact that a computer program may activate other programs, just as a narrative may activate other narratives and other realities.

To demonstrate the mechanisms of the narrative stack, let us rewrite in the form of computer programs the history of the world, all the narratives ever written or told, and all the trips to other realities ever taken by human minds. Figure 25 shows the main program HISTORY OF THE WORLD, and the subprograms for THE ARABIAN NIGHTS and THE MAIDS. Some of the events in the program HISTORY OF THE WORLD are illocutionary and/or ontological boundary crossings. These events function as calls to subprograms. A calling statement consists of the name of the program to be activated, and of a list of variable names known in the programming jargon as the actual parameters. These parameters are variables of the calling program which will be passed into the subprogram and will become part of its semantic environment. The parameters thus establish a communication between the two units. The effect of the calling statement is to push a new semantic environment (i.e., a new set of variables) onto the top of the stack of currently active programs. When the execution of the top program terminates, its environment is popped, and control is returned to the program from which the call had been issued. We see in figure 25, for instance, that the program HISTORY OF THE WORLD contains a call to THE ARABIAN NIGHTS. The parameters of the

```
MAIN PROGRAM: HISTORY OF THE WORLD                    Title
Characters: Adam, Eve, the author of                  Variable
The Arabian Nights, U.S.A., Soviet Union, etc.           list
Begin
        Adam and Eve are expelled from Eden;          operations
        ( . . . )
        ARABIAN NIGHTS (author, reader);              Calling statement
        ( . . . )                                     with actual
        THE MAIDS ([Genet through] Actress 1,         parameters
                Actress 2, Actress 3, Spectator);
        Superpowers in nuclear war;
End.

ARABIAN NIGHTS (Narrator, Narratee)                   Subprogram title
Characters: Scheherazade, Sultan               with formal parameters
Begin
        Sultan marries Scheherazade;
        Sultan wants to kill Scheherazade at dawn;
        ALI BABA (Scheherazade, Sultan);
        THE THREE LADIES OF BAGHDAD (Scheherazade, Sultan);
        Sultan spares the life of Scheherazade;
End;

ALI BABA (Narrator, Narratee)
Characters: Ali Baba, his wife, forty thieves
Begin
        Ali Baba outsmarts: forty thieves with the help of his wife and is rich and
        happy ever after;
End;

THE THREE LADIES OF BAGHDAD (Narrator, Narratee)
Characters: Porter, three ladies: Amina, Safia, Zubaida
```

Figure 25
Narrative semantics as computer program

call are the participants in the speech act: the historical author and the reader. These parameters are matched to the so-called formal parameters which appear in the title statement of the subprogram THE ARABIAN NIGHTS, and they become members of the environment of THE ARABIAN NIGHTS under the name of these formal parameters. When the call to THE ARABIAN NIGHTS is executed, the historical author becomes in make-believe the narrator, the reader becomes the narratee, and the environment specified in the cast of characters becomes the currently active context. Adam and Eve, Hitler and Napoleon are no longer valid discourse referents, since they do not belong to the current context. The potential referents are Scheherazade and the Sultan, and all the characters of this narrative level. The same substitution occurs when a call to THE THREE LADIES OF BAGHDAD is issued from within THE ARABIAN NIGHTS, and from there to AMINA'S TALE and THE YOUNG MAN'S TALE. Figure 24b

Begin

> The Porter meets the three ladies;
> THE PORTER'S TALE (the Porter, the three ladies);
> AMINA'S TALE (Amina, the Porter);
> SAFIA'S TALE (Safia, the Porter);
> ZUBAIDA'S TALE (Zubaida, the Porter);
> All spells broken, the Porter marries Amina and the other two ladies marry good men;

End;

AMINA'S TALE (Amina, the Porter)

Begin

> Amina looking for her lost husband walks into a palace where everybody looks like a statue. She finally meets a young man;
> THE YOUNG MAN'S TALE (the Young Man, Amina);
> Amina marries the Young man, but he is killed by her jealous sisters, who are turned into dogs;

End;

The YOUNG MAN'S TALE (the Young Man, Amina)

Begin

> The Young Man was a son of a Shah and was the only one at the palace living by the laws of Islam;
> All those who did not obey the Koran were turned into stones;

End;

THE MAIDS (Claire/ Solange/ Madame, observer)
Characters not appearing onstage: Monsieur, the Milkman

Begin

> THE MURDER OF MADAME, Part I (Claire, Solange);
> Dialogue between Claire, Solange, and Madame;
> THE MURDER OF MADAME, Part II (Claire, Solange);

End;

THE MURDER OF MADAME I & II (Madame, Claire);
Characters: Counterparts of all the characters in THE MAIDS

Begin

> Dialogue between Madame and Claire, culminating
> (in part II) in the murder of MADAME

End;

Figure 25
(cont.)

shows the configuration of the stack when the program THE YOUNG MAN'S TALE is being executed. After the termination of THE YOUNG MAN'S TALE the subprogram is popped, and the execution of AMINA'S TALE resumes exactly where it had been interrupted. The same mechanism continues, changing the structure of the stack until the termination of THE ARABIAN NIGHTS and the popping of all levels except for the ongoing (and narratively always implicit) HISTORY OF THE WORLD.[2]

In the case of THE MAIDS, the impression that the action starts on the

second level stems from the fact that the calls to the subprogram THE MUR-
DER OF MADAME (as I call it) are the first and last operation of the main
play. As a result of this location, two levels are pushed in rapid succession,
and one of them is purely transitory. Since the dramatic action proper is
contained in the dialogue, it does not begin until THE MURDER OF MA-
DAME has been pushed onto the stack. When part 2 of THE MURDER
terminates, so does the script of THE MAIDS, and the last words uttered on
stage belong, like the first ones, to the dialogue of level 2.

The different types of boundaries are represented in this programming
pseudocode by the relations between the components of the subprogram
and the calling statement. An ontological boundary crossing occurs when
the subprogram has its own variable list. The characters of this list replace
the inventory of the calling program, and we have a new reality. Some
members of the list may have counterparts in the calling program: there is a
Napoleon in the program HISTORY OF THE WORLD, and another Napoleon
in the program WAR AND PEACE. In this case the character cast of the
calling program and of the subprogram will contain identical names, but as
the subprogram is pushed on top of the stack, its own referent for the name
replaces temporarily the former referent. What happens to Napoleon in
WAR AND PEACE has no influence on the Napoleon of HISTORY OF THE
WORLD.

Absence of a variable list in the subprogram means that a boundary-
crossing has no ontological consequences. To make up for the lack of native
characters, the subprogram borrows its population from the calling environment. As it borrows the characters, it also borrows their destinies: what
happens to the characters in the subprogram should reflect what happens to
them in the calling program. If a discrepancy occurs, the story told in the
subprogram is an error or a lie.

Illocutionary boundary crossings are signaled by the formal parameters.
When the names of the formal parameters match exactly the names of the
actual parameters in the calling statement, the speaker and the hearer retain
their identity across the boundary. This is the case of nonfictional embedded
narratives. When the names differ, the actual participants in the communicative act engage in the role-playing of fictional communication: Scheherazade
pretends to be an anonymous narrator, the Sultan becomes an anonymous
narratee in a recentered reality.

An absence of formal parameters indicates an absence of illocutionary
boundary. Since there is no distinct speech act, the name of the subprogram
is not a story title, but a nonverbal reality such as "dream," "movie," "picture." Insofar as it contains its own variable list, this reality differs ontologically from the calling environment.

The three boundary-crossing categories of figure 21 are translated as
follows into the programming pseudocode. (On the left is the calling statement with actual parameters, on the right the subprogram declaration with
formal parameters and variable list.)

2: + illocutionary/ − ontological:

YOUNG MAN'S TALE	YOUNG MAN'S TALE
(Young Man, Amina)	(Young Man, Amina)
	No variable list

3: − illocutionary/ + ontological:

WONDERLAND	WONDERLAND
	Characters: Alice', Queen of Hearts, Cheshire Cat, etc.

(Alice' is a counterpart of Alice in the primary reality)

4: + illocutionary/ + ontological

ALI BABA (Scheherazade, Sultan)	ALI BABA (Narrator, Narratee)
	Characters: Ali Baba, his wife, 40 thieves

The subprogram declaration of category 4 captures the standard case of impersonal third-person narration. Other types of fiction are represented by the following variations in the relation between calling statement and subprogram declaration:

Personal Narration

WUTHERING HEIGHTS	WUTHERING HEIGHTS
(Emily Brontë, Reader)	(Lockwood, Narratee)
	Characters: Cathy, Heathcliff, etc.

Fictional self-impersonation

FUNES THE MEMORIOUS	FUNES THE MEMORIOUS
(Borges, Reader)	(Borges', Narratee)
	Character: Funes, etc.

Here Borges' stands for a counterpart of the real Borges, linked to him through the principle of minimal departure: the properties of Borges' are copied from the properties of Borges as far as the text of FUNES will allow, but FUNES has the last word in changing these properties.

Performed drama

THE MAIDS ([Genet through] Actress 1, Actress 2, Actress 3, Spectator)	THE MAIDS (Solange, Claire, Madame, Observer) Characters: Monsieur, the Milkman

The list of actual parameters translates the fact that drama is a communicative act between author and spectator through the mediation of the actors. The voiding of the authorial parameter in the subprogram expresses his or her absence from the stage. While the author takes no part in the performance, the spectator plays the passive role of an anonymous witness who looks through the transparent fourth wall of the classical stage. (For the spectator's role to be individuated, the script of the play would have to invite her to step on stage and to take an active part in the performance through improvisation.) The remaining parameters match the real-world identity of the actors to their respective roles. The call refers to an individual performance and may be repeated in HISTORY OF THE WORLD with different names filling the actor slots. As for the list of characters, it contains all the members of the semantic domain who are mentioned in the play but do not appear on stage.

Epistolary novel	

LES LIAISONS DANGEREUSES
(Laclos, Reader)
	LES LIAISONS DANGEREUSES
	(Editor/Valmont/Merteuil, Witness)
	Characters: mentioned individuals who
	do not appear as letter writers
	Begin
	    Preface (Editor, Public)
	    Letter (V, M)
	    Letter (M, V)
	End.

The slashes in the subprogram declaration mean here that the formal parameter of the sender is split into various identities: Laclos pretends to be an editor addressing the public, then Valmont addressing Merteuil, then Merteuil answering Valmont, etc. In this analysis, each of the letters is itself a subprogram call of the illocutionary category, as is, on the micro-level, every turn in the performed dialogue of a play, or in the directly quoted dialogue of a novel. The same formalism of a slashed speaker parameter can be used for polyvocal fiction (such as *The Sound and the Fury*, where Faulkner speaks successively as Benjy, Jason, Quentin, and as an impersonal narrator), or for philosophical dialogues.

Adventures of the Stack

In a canonical narrative, the building and unbuilding of the stack follows a rigid protocol which restricts the range of legal operations. This protocol requires that levels be kept distinct, that they be pushed or popped on the top of the stack exclusively; that pushing and popping be properly signaled; and that every boundary be crossed twice, once during the building and once during the unbuilding. At the end of the text, the only level left on the stack should be the ground level. This protocol is respected by all standard narrative texts, but not by all the texts of literary fiction. Far from being constrained by the conditions of narrativity, the fictional text may subvert the mechanisms of the stack, thus openly taking an antinarrative stance. This subversion may take the following forms.

The Occulted Call

In the computer program representation of narratives, transitions to higher levels are effected by the calling statements. (A virtual crossing would be expressed by integrating the code of the subprogram into the body of the calling program.) Calling statements are typically manifested by boundary-signaling expressions: " 'Once upon a time,' began the Queen"; " 'This is what happened to me,' said the young man"; or "That night Joseph was visited by a dream. He saw the stars and the moon bowing in front of him." The popping of the stack is similarly signaled by specific textual devices: closing of quotation marks, description of the dreamer's awakening, reference to the story-status of the preceding section. These transition-signaling devices enable readers to properly construct the stack, identify the discourse referents, and orient themselves among the levels of the semantic domain. Like other semantic components of the plot, however, boundary-crossing events may be deleted from the narrative discourse. In *Alice in Wonderland*, the text slips without notice from Victorian England to the dream world of Wonderland: "She was considering whether the pleasure of making a daisy-chain would be worth the trouble of getting up and picking the daisies . . . when suddenly a white rabbit with pink eyes ran close to her" (Carroll 1975:13). It is only when the rabbit takes a watch out of his waist pocket that the reader realizes what Alice will ignore until the end of the story: that she has crossed the boundary into a separate reality. This impression is confirmed when strange beings make their entrance on the scene, and when the laws of nature appear to lose their hold on the events. Because of the difference between the two realities, the occultation of the boundary crossing has no disorienting consequences for the reader.

In striking contrast to *Alice in Wonderland* is the case of "The Adjourned Sorcerer" by Borges (an adaptation of a Spanish medieval text by the Infante Juan Manuel), included in the collection *A Universal History of Infamy*:

> A dean in Santiago asks a magician, Don Illan, to teach him the magic arts, and promises him a reward. Don Illan first expresses doubts as to whether the dean will keep his promise, but finally agrees to the request. They both go down into a secret room located under the river bed. As the lesson is about to begin, two messengers arrive and announce that the dean has been named bishop in Santiago. Don Illan asks for his reward but the new bishop tells him to wait. Six months later the bishop becomes a cardinal in Toulouse. Don Illan asks for his reward but he is told to wait. Three years later the cardinal is elected pope in Rome. Don Illan asks for his reward but the new pope threatens to have him burned at the stake. As he pronounces these words, the pope finds himself back in the secret room, a simple dean in Santiago, and humbly apologizes to Don Illan for his ungrateful conduct.

In this story, the events of the rise of the dean to bishop, cardinal, and pope, as well as his refusal to reward the magician, are not actually lived on the ground level of reality, but hallucinated by the dean as the result of the magician's art. Through the occultation of the passage into the world of the hallucination—which takes place at the very moment the messengers enter the secret room—the reader is no less a victim of the magic than the unfortunate hero. The transition to the hallucinated events is not only camouflaged by the deletion of the calling statement, it is further hidden by the similarity of the casts of characters: all the members of the hallucination are counterparts of the members of the ground level of reality. It is only with the sudden and obvious return to reality at the end of the story that the ordinary reader realizes the true nature of the events and the configuration of the previous states of the narrative stack. Yet as Jean Ricardou has shown (1967:26–29), an astute reader should have noticed a clue to the unreal character of the events: how could the messengers have reached the dean in Don Illan's secret underground room? The guilt expressed by the dean in the real world for what he was made to do in the world of the hallucination figures the guilt the reader should feel for missing the clues of the transition, and falling victim to the storyteller's magic.

The Endlessly Expanding Stack

When a computer program contains an unconditional recursive call to itself, or to any of its predecessors in the calling chain, the result is an ever-expanding stack of environments from which no return is possible. As soon as the same environment is pushed twice onto the narrative stack, the sequence of intermediate levels must be repeated indefinitely. The same effect can be achieved in narrative. We are all familiar with the interminable repetitions of folklore, such as:

> It was a dark and stormy night
> and Brigham Young and Brigham Old
> sat around the campfire.
> Tell us a story, old man!
> And this is the story he told:

> It was a dark and stormy night
> and Brigham Young and Brigham Old
> sat around the campfire.
> Tell us a story, old man!
> And this is the story he told:
> (Ursula K. Le Guin 1981:187)

Here the endlessly expanding stack is built by an open-ended, infinite text. If we do not step through the entire text, the possibility remains that on the next level Brigham will tell a different story, and that the whole stack will eventually tumble. This is indeed what happens in Le Guin's text: on the third recursion, we read:

It was a dark and stormy night
and Brigham Young and Pierre Mesnard, author of the
Quixote
sat around the campfire
which is not quite the way my Great-Aunt Betsy told
it
when we said Tell us another story!
Tell us, au juste, what happened
And this is the story she told:

The appearance on the third level of a new environment suggests that in the program version of the narrative the first two calls are to different stories: BRIGHAM I calls BRIGHAM II, which reads exactly like BRIGHAM I, except that it calls BRIGHAM III, which in turn calls BETSY'S TALE. If the call in BRIGHAM I were to BRIGHAM I itself, there would be no way to stop the growth of the stack after the execution of the first recursive call. All it takes for a text to establish an indefinitely expanding stack is therefore explicit self-reference. According to an essay by Borges, this phenomenon occurs in the 602d night of *The Arabian Nights*:

> On that night, the king hears from the queen her own story. He hears the beginning of the story, which comprises all the others and also—monstrously—itself. Does the reader clearly grasp the vast possibility of this interpolation, the curious danger? That the Queen may persist, and the motionless King hear forever the truncated story of *The Arabian Nights*, now infinite and circular. (Borges 1983:195)

What Borges does not tell us, unfortunately, is how this self-referential narration is implemented. A literal enactment is out of the question, for if the text of *The Arabian Nights* actually retold the framing story and all the embedded tales, it would become physically infinite and formally open, like the Brigham Young segment.[3] The only way to generate infinite recursion in a closed and finite text is suggested by Italo Calvino's *If on a Winter's Night a Traveler*. The text opens with the sentence ''You are about to read Italo Calvino's new novel, *If on a Winter's Night a Traveler*'' (1981:3). The title stands vicariously for the novel itself, and if we want to know what exactly this fictional reader, who looks so much like us, is about to read, we must replace the words *If on a Winter's Night a Traveler* with the text they refer to. Pretending that the above sentence is all there is to the novel, the text expands logically into

You are about to read Italo Calvino's new novel, ''You are about to read Italo Calvino's new novel, *If on a Winter's Night a Traveler*''

which in turn expands into

> You are about to read Italo Calvino's new novel, "You are about to read
> Italo Calvino's new novel, 'You are about to read Italo Calvino's new
> novel, *If on a Winter's Night a Traveler*'

and so on ad infinitum. The finite mirror of the self-referential title captures
the virtual image of an infinite text, and we contemplate this text as a
whole, without being caught in its endless repetition.

Strange Loops

In *Gödel, Escher, Bach*, Douglas Hofstadter defines the following violation
of the stack's hierarchy: "The 'Strange Loop' phenomenon occurs whenever, by moving upwards or downwards, through the levels of some hierarchical system, we unexpectedly find ourselves right back where we started"
(1980:10). In *Postmodernist Fiction*, Brian McHale proposes several literary
implementations of the strange loop. In Christine Brooke-Rose's *Thru*
(1975), Larissa invents Armel, who in turn is the author of Larissa (McHale
1987:120). A push into the world of Larissa's invention, then another into
the world of Armel's imagination—and we find ourselves back in the world
where Larissa invents Armel. The strange loop is a vicious circle, a stack
without a ground level, which prevents us from deciding which one, between Armel and Larissa, is "really real."

Another of McHale's illustrations is a short story by Cortázar, "Continu-
ity of Parks" (1978): "A man reads a novel in which a killer, approaching
through a park, enters a house in order to murder his lover's husband—the
man reading the novel!" (120). For the strange loop effect to arise, the level
we push into as the character begins to read must be identical, not just
similar, to the primary level. If the two levels were simply similar, the man
would be reading a novel about a counterpart of himself in an alternate
possible world, and the fate of this counterpart would remain independent
of his own. After finishing the story of his own murder, the reader would
put down the book, pop out of its system, and resume his normal life. The
text prevents this interpretation by ending abruptly, as the murderer reaches
his prospective victim. Since the narrative technique makes us apprehend
the story within the story through the consciousness of the reader on the
ground level, the simultaneous and apparently arbitrary termination of both
the embedded and the embedding text signifies the end of the mediating
consciousness, the death of the reader.

The Contamination of Levels

In a computer language, the point of calling a subprogram is to modify
the semantic environment of the main program. This communication is
achieved through the parameters: the value acquired on the higher level by
the formal parameters is transferred upon return to the actual parameters. In
all other respects, however, the various levels of the stack constitute autonomous semantic environments separated by rigid boundaries. If a variable

named x is declared in a calling program, and another variable by the same name in the called program, what happens to the x of the higher level has no influence on the value of the x on the lower level.

The same principles govern the functioning of the narrative stack. Whatever influence a higher level may exert upon a lower one occurs through the parameters. Telling a story is an act with a purpose and an effect, a consequential event for both participants. This consequentiality is showcased by Scheherazade saving her life through her storytelling magic, or by Mme. de Rochefide deciding to withdraw from the world after hearing the story of Sarrasine in Balzac's story by the same name (cf. Chambers 1984 on this topic). Aside from the changes effected in the narrator and narratee, the events of the upper level have no influence on the events of the lower level. A play about Napoleon escaping to New Orleans does not alter the fact that in AW Napoleon died on St. Helena. If there is an influence between levels, it runs from bottom to top: the textual world of a nonfictional story should ideally reflect reality, and the textual world of a fiction is assumed to be the closest possible to the actual world.

To reverse the direction of influence, the text must stage an event which denies boundaries and cuts across levels. In my two examples of level contamination, this privileged event is associated with death. In *The Maids*, the contamination of the lower level through the upper one is due to a transgression of standard acting behavior. In normal dramatic performance, the events of the actual world are protected from the events of the world of the play by a simulation of the gestures that would present lasting consequences for the actors. An action like combing a character's hair is actually performed, but a murder is represented on stage by merely going through the moves. In Claire and Solange's enactment of the murder of Madame, however, there is no simulation: Claire poisons Madame in THE MURDER OF MADAME through Solange's poisoning of Claire on the ground level of reality. Because Madame had to die in the world of make-believe, Claire must die in reality, and Solange must go to jail. But this price to pay is also a reward, since the dead Claire and the jailed Solange will be freed from their servile condition.

In *One Hundred Years of Solitude*, by Gabriel García Márquez (1967), Aureliano Buendía, last descendant of his line, deciphers the prophetic chronicle of the Buendía family by the gypsy Melquíades. As the narrative catches up with the present, it absorbs reality, and Aureliano realizes that he will never pop out of the world of the Book:

> Then he skipped again to anticipate the predictions and ascertain the date and circumstances of his death. Before reaching the final line, however, he had already understood that he would never leave that room, for it was foreseen that the city of mirrors (or mirages) would be wiped out by the

wind and exiled from the memory of men at the precise moment when
Aureliano Buendía would finish deciphering the parchment. (422)

Why cannot Aureliano survive the narration of his own death? Because the
book is not merely a prophetic but a performative utterance. Its text does
not reflect the events—whether past or future—of a more basic level of
reality; it makes events happen at the very moment of its own deciphering.
The history of the Buendía family is the product of the book, or rather, it is
the product of Aureliano's reading experience, which is as unrepeatable as
the experience of his own death.

With this performative analysis, we are led back to the case of "Conti-
nuity of Parks," which can also be regarded as an instance of reverse contamination. If reality is produced by the text of the book, then by entering
the textual universe we enter reality, and the fate of the reader cannot be
dissociated from the fate of the reader's counterpart in the book.

The Reverse Push and the Bottomless Stack

The normal procedure for constructing the stack is to push new levels at
the top exclusively. But when the hero of Borges's "Circular Ruins," after having dreamed a human being into reality, begins wondering whether he is not
himself "a mere appearance dreamt by another" (1983:50), a level is inserted
below the ground level. What we took for reality turns out to be a dream
projected from another reality, and the base of the system is shifted down one
notch. This raises the question of whether the operation is repeatable (who
dreamed the dreamer?), and whether the stack has a ground level at all.

Ontological Paradoxes and the Denial of Boundaries

The most fundamental act of self-consciousness situates the self on the
ground level of reality: I am, therefore I am real, and the world I live in is
the one and only actual world. The suspicion by Borges's hero of existing
only in the alternate possible world of his creator's dream denies this fundamental experience, and constitutes an ontological paradox. So does the
admission by characters of their own fictionality. Another form of the ontological paradox, common to modern fiction, is the meeting of author and
characters (*Six Characters in Search of an Author, The French Lieutenant's
Woman*). Since we can only meet face to face with members of our own level
of reality, the encounter of author and characters denies the imaginary status of the latter, and abolishes the ontological boundary that defines their
relation.

The Case of the Missing Level

In a well-formed stack, the top level is reached through a continuous
series of intermediary levels. No level can be supported by a vacuum. But in

a fiction by Jorge Luis Borges, "Theme of the Traitor and the Hero," a deceptive scheme leads to the occultation of intermediary levels. I will study this story in some detail, in the hope of demonstrating the usefulness of the concept of stack as an instrument of textual interpretation.

"Theme of the Traitor and the Hero" is about the making of a story. We are told that on January 3, 1944, the future author sees the plot as follows. The setting will be Ireland, in the year 1824, but the story will be told from a contemporary perspective. The narrator's name will be Ryan. He decides to write the biography of his ancestor, Fergus Kilpatrick, who died as a hero of Irish independence. Kilpatrick was assassinated in a theater, one day before the rebellion he had planned broke out and succeeded. In the course of his investigation Ryan discovers that Kilpatrick had really been a traitor to the cause of the rebels, and that the assassination had been an execution by his companions. He further discovers that the execution in the theater had been carefully planned and staged by James Alexander Nolan, a companion of Kilpatrick. Rather than revealing the leader's treason, and compromising the chances of the upcoming rebellion, the death of Kilpatrick would look like a martyr's death and inspire his compatriots to rebel. In the last days of Kilpatrick's life, all the members of the conspiracy, including Kilpatrick himself, were really acting out a script and speaking lines which had been made up by Nolan. The entire audience in the theater at the moment of the execution was performing a drama. Some of the scenes of this drama had been directly borrowed from Shakespeare.

The story ends as follows:

> In Nolan's work, the passages imitated from Shakespeare are the least dramatic; Ryan suspects that the author interpolated them so that in the future someone might hit upon the truth. He understands that he too forms part of Nolan's plot . . . . After a series of tenacious hesitations, he resolves to keep his discovery silent. He publishes a book dedicated to the hero's glory; this too, perhaps, was foreseen. (1983:75)

By extending the notion of boundary so as to include not only crossings into new worlds and into new speech acts, but also into new mental constructs, the semantic structure of the story can be mapped on the stack of figure 26.

Each of the boundaries between the levels of the stack is traced by a creative act: the creative act of conceiving a plot. The story plays on two senses of the word plot: narrative structure, and conspiracy. (These two meanings are also conveyed by the term of the original Spanish version,

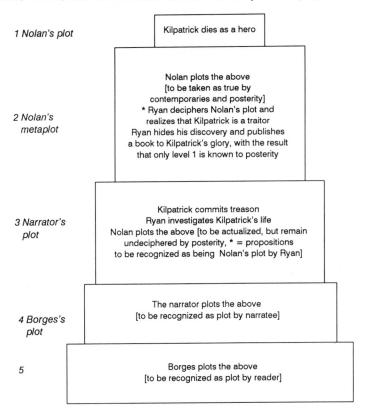

Figure 26
The actual stack of semantic environments
in Borges's "Theme of the Traitor and the Hero"

trama.) In the narrative sense, the plot is meant to be recognized by the audience as the construct of a mind located on a lower level of reality. In the sense of conspiracy, the plot is a scheme meant to be actualized by the planning mind. When the scheme is successfully executed, the planner can be regarded, at least figuratively, as the "author" of a separate level of reality—separate from the level upon which the planner's mind has no control. In a deceptive plot, this level is not only figuratively but literally distinct, since deception involves imaginary constructs defining alternative possible worlds. While the plot of narrative fiction highlights the role of the creative mind, the plot of the deceptive conspiracy keeps this role hidden, denies the existence of boundaries, and presents the imaginary facts specified by the script as actual events. In "Theme of the Traitor and the Hero," the plots conceived by Borges and by the narrator belong to the narrative category, while Nolan's plots are conspiracies involving a deception.

On the bottom level (technically outside the narrative system) we have the communicative act between Borges and his readers in the real world. The label "Borges's plot" refers to the story invented by Borges, which encompasses levels 4 through 1. (Levels are numbered from the top down, the most basic level of reality bearing the highest rather than lowest number, in order to maintain a numeric correspondence between figures 26, 27, and 28. In all three figures, levels with identical numeric labels contain the same or nearly the same events.) On level 4, a narrator who could be a counterpart of Borges proposes to write a story about a number of characters, including Ryan, Nolan, and Kilpatrick. (We know, however, that the narrator is NOT Borges because he plans to write the story some day, while the actual Borges has completed his task in sketching it.) The projected story—which begins on level 3 and extends all the way to the top—is the narrator's plot. On level 3, we have a character, Nolan, who "plots" the actions of Ryan. I call this plot—which covers levels 2 and 1—Nolan's metaplot. Within this metaplot, Ryan discovers the existence of another scheme, also imagined by Nolan: the dramatic cover-up of Kilpatrick's treason. This scheme, Nolan's plot, is found on level 1.

The construction of the stack does not follow the standard bottom-to-top order, but inserts a level in the middle after having already pushed the top level. First the narrator's environment is pushed (by Borges) in a call to THEME, then Kilpatrlck/Nolan/Ryan's environment is pushed in a call to THE FUTURE STORY, then Nolan pushes KILPATRICK'S HEROIC DEATH (= Nolan's plot), and to control Ryan's actions he builds NOLAN'S METAPLOT around KILPATRICK'S DEATH. The plot of level 2 presupposes the existence of the plot of level 1, and cannot be conceived before 1 has been defined.

The interpretation of the story hinges on the last sentence: "This too, perhaps, was foreseen." The sentence creates three paradoxes. Through its epistemic uncertainty, it contradicts the fact that the story of the Irish rebels is a fiction within a fiction. As the creator of the characters, the prospective author of level 4 is free to decide whether or not Ryan's actions were foreseen by Nolan. By expressing doubts about the facts of level 3, the speaker of level 4 abandons the privileged perspective of the author, and moves up one level on the narrative stack.

The second level of paradox has to do with the fact that Ryan is projected as the narrator of the story within the story. Most of the text describes the content of Ryan's consciousness (i.e., uses Ryan as a focalizer), and therefore makes a credible outline for a first-person narration. Most of the text—but not the last sentence: "He publishes a book dedicated to the hero's glory; this too, perhaps, was foreseen." This sentence contrasts with a preceding one: "He understands that he too forms part of Nolan's plot," to suggest that in the first case Ryan is aware of the foresight but not in the second case. And indeed, if Ryan had realized that "this too was foreseen," he would not have published a book to the hero's glory. By leaving the consciousness of Ryan, the last sentence operates an inversion in the hierarchy of focalization: formerly we saw Nolan through Ryan and Ryan through the main narrator, but now we see Ryan's actions as plotted by Nolan. The story projected by the narrator of level 4 cannot consequently be written, since it contains the illocutionary paradox of a narrator telling what he must logically ignore.

The last paradox is located within the projected story—in a system of reality grounded in level 3. As a preliminary, let me state some of the ontological principles that govern the literary production of Borges:

(1) Every reality has its ontological foundation in another reality. It is the creation of a mind, which belongs to a more fundamental level.

(2) The members of a reality can see the levels above them, but not the levels below. (The author knows about the characters, the characters do not know about the author.) From these principles follows:

(3) Reality has always one more level than what is seen of it, since it is the creation of an invisible mind.

(4) Truth and reality are located on the ground level. Each level is less real than the one below, and in the case of a contradiction the facts of a lower level override the facts of a higher level. (We can see from the stack proposed in figure 26 that Kilpatrick *is* a traitor in the projected story, because he appears as traitor on level 3, which is the ground level. It is also true that he does not exist in the actual world of the text, since he does not appear on level 4.)

From rule (4) follows that in order to achieve the ontological status of being real, Borgesian characters must push themselves onto the lowest possible level. This means being the "author" of what passes as reality, rather than a character in a plot conceived by a mind located closer to the elusive base of the system.

Figure 26 captures the objectively correct stacking of semantic environments in the textual universe. The upper levels of the stack are TAPWs created through mental acts, but the whole construct is real within the story, since its base is AW and its first level TAW. But to understand the logic of the actions of characters we must take virtual stacks into consideration: the goals of the agents, their potentially inaccurate representation of reality; or the inaccurate representations they try to impose on others when their actions are deceptive.

Let's begin this investigation with the scheme of level 1. The goal of Nolan in making up the top plot is transparent enough: he wanted to make the revolt succeed. The plot was deceitful: it was meant to hide the truth from contemporaries. But why did Nolan make the second plot—why did he make Ryan discover and conceal his role as author of the top plot? While the top plot was meant to fool Kilpatrick's contemporaries, the metaplot is meant to fool Ryan and posterity. To grasp the mechanism of the deception we must reconstruct what went on in Ryan's mind when he began to suspect that he was part of Nolan's plot. If Nolan had not "signed" his work, his authorship of level 1 would remain forever hidden. On the other hand, if he deliberately planted the clues leading to Ryan's discovery, he most likely hoped that Ryan would reveal the true nature of the plot, and that he would be recognized as author by generations to come. Should Ryan comply, the stack of reality would end up like figure 27.

In this scheme, levels 2 + 1 will be known to posterity: level 2 as the solid base of reality, level 1 as a fabulation conceived on level 2. Since these levels are both plotted by Nolan, he will again be the real "author" of the prevailing image of reality. By helping to realize Nolan's intent, Ryan will be a character in Nolan's plot. To avoid this fate—and push himself onto the ground level of the stack—Ryan must counter what he takes to be Nolan's plan. This counterplan is shown in figure 28. By hiding his discovery, Ryan hopes to step out of the role which had been foreseen by Nolan. What will pass as reality will be level 1, and Ryan's book to the glory of the hero will be the source of this image.

But according to the interpretation proposed in figure 26, the publication of the book to Kilpatrick's glory has also been foreseen. Ryan's counterplot will fail because it is based on a misreading of the plot it was meant

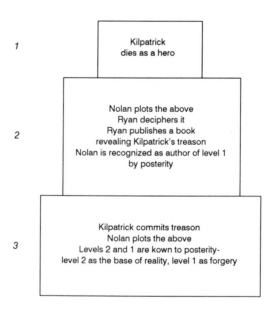

Figure 27
What Ryan believes to be Nolan's intent
(Virtual stack)

to counter. Nolan not only wanted Kilpatrick to pass as hero for posterity, he wanted Ryan to sing the praise of Kilpatrick despite his knowledge of the truth. The act of hiding the truth was itself part of Nolan's metaplot, and Ryan ends up playing his role in Nolan's scheme through the very attempt to escape from it. Nolan's plot is not only deceptive toward Ryan, but doubly deceptive, insofar as it foresees and requires its own misreading. What Nolan actually anticipated was the following: Ryan would believe that Nolan's plot was like figure 27; Ryan would try to counter this plan by forming the plan of figure 28; and by trying to execute this plan Ryan would inadvertently cause the fulfillment of the plan of figure 26. Figure 27 corresponds to what I call in chapter 7 a virtual overt plan (Nolan intends Ryan believes Nolan intends P), and figure 28 corresponds to a projected plan (Nolan intends Ryan tries to execute P). While a deceptive plot would keep one level hidden, a doubly deceptive plot causes the disappearance of two distinct levels from the narrative stack. The semantic universe of the story is three-tiered, since it consists of levels 3, 2, and 1; but what will pass as reality in the eyes of posterity is level 1 alone. By being a puppet in the metaplot of level 2, Ryan unwittingly becomes an actor in the plot of level 1. Unable to reach the third level by his failure to outwit Nolan, and having occulted the second level by denying its existence, he is lifted onto the top of the stack. Through the publication of his book, he recites his lines to the glory of the hero, just as Kilpatrick's companions had done. Far from ending in the death of Kilpatrick, the

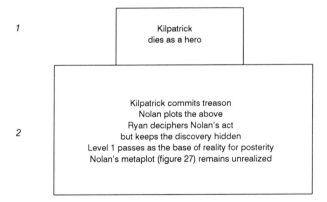

Figure 28
Ryan's counterplot to the plan of figure 27
(Virtual stack)

conspiracy of the cover-up enrolls posterity in the person of Ryan. And that is Nolan's greatest triumph: to have made Ryan act out his part in the ongoing drama to the glory of Kilpatrick, thus ensuring that level 1 will never be popped as forgery from the stack of history.

10 The Formal Representation of Plot

The problem of the formal representation of plots lies at the crossroads of several disciplines: literary theory, discourse analysis, cognitive psychology, and its favored instrument of research, artificial intelligence. By formal representation, I mean the visual mapping of the plot on some kind of graph, such as a tree, a flowchart, or a network (cf. A. Stewart 1987). What is to be gained by modeling plots on graphs? For the semiotician, a plot is a type of semantic structure—and as a spatial configuration of elements, a structure is most efficiently represented in a visual model. For the specialist in artificial intelligence the answer is more practical: a graph is an object that can be handled by a computer. An adequate system of graphic representation is therefore a prerequisite to the simulation of the mental processing of the narrative text. The purpose of a plot-graph is to capture the reader's internalization of the narrative message of the text, the way plots are stored in memory. Since the human brain is a collection of interconnected neurons, there is an isomorphism between a graph and a mind: the nodes of the graph model memory cells, and the arcs between nodes model the pathways connecting the cells. This isomorphism provides an additional reason to ground a theory of plot in a system of graphic representation.

Insofar as a plot-diagram captures the inscription of the narrative message in the reader's mind, its validity must be assessed in terms of its cognitive value. The criteria most frequently invoked by specialists of cognitive psychology include the following:

(1) An adequate system of diagramming should reveal manifestations of the same plot under differences in setting, character cast, or events. By emphasizing the functional units that account for the similarity, it should explain what we mean when we say "these two stories have the same plot."

(2) The diagram should provide a basis for answering questions about the text by giving access to the information necessary to a proper understanding, whether or not this information is directly expressed by the narrative discourse.

(3) It should model in a satisfactory way the complexity of the thought

processes that lead to the retrieval of narrative information. If a question about a story has an obvious answer, the search for this answer should be a simple operation; if a question is difficult, the answer should be retrieved at the end of an extensive search of the graph. The number of arcs and nodes traversed during the search provides the criterion for assessing the accessibility of an answer.

(4) It should allow the detection of important functional units, such as punishment, retaliation, reward, deal, promise, lie, and deceit.

(5) The graph should be able to predict patterns of summarization and memorization, by emphasizing the most important narrative units.

What a formal model of plot cannot and should not be, however, is an exhaustive and explicit coverage of all the information accessible to the reader. We do not store in memory complete semantic representations of plots, but schematic blueprints which we complete as needed, bridging informational gaps through deductive reasoning or knowledge of the world. In order to emulate the reader's performance in answering questions about the narrative, a cognitive model of plot should be able to construct answers dynamically, rather than relying exclusively on encoded information. Assisted by information-generating principles, an ideal model of narrative should extract from a minimal amount of data a maximal coverage of the semantic relations that bind the textual message in the shape of a plot.

In this chapter, I propose to submit a simple story—the fable of "The Fox and the Crow," as told by Aesop and La Fontaine—to three systems of plot representation: the story-grammar of Mandler and Johnson, as example of a tree-shaped diagram; the "plot-unit" system of Wendy Lehnert, which makes use of a network type of graph; and my own attempt to expand Lehnert's model into a "self-embedding" graph, in order to represent private worlds and virtual events. The narrative intelligence of the three models will be evaluated by trying to locate on the plot-graph the answers to the following questions:

(1) Why does the fox ask the crow to sing?
(2) Are the fox and the crow successful in the pursuit of their respective goals?
(3) Is the fox acting sincerely or deceitfully?

Narrative Grammars

In the past fifteen years, the vogue of linguistic models in the humanities has inspired numerous attempts to adapt the paradigm of Chomsky's generative/transformational grammar to the analysis of narrative structures. Story grammars have been proposed by literary theorists (Prince 1973, Pavel 1976 and 1985), proponents of textual linguistics and discourse analysis (van Dijk 1972), folklorists (Colby 1973), and cognitive psychologists (Rumelhart 1975, Mandler and Johnson 1977). Among these models, I have chosen to discuss the grammar of Mandler and Johnson (which develops the model of Rumelhart) because it offers the most detailed semantic representation of plot.

The concept of a generative grammar is no longer unfamiliar territory for literary theorists, but it will be useful to review the theoretical basis of the model. In a mathematical sense, a language is a set of strings obtained by combining the elements of a finite repertory—the lexicon—according to certain rules. A grammar is an accepting automaton for the language. Its function is to tell whether or not a given input string is a legal combination. Decisions of acceptability are made by attempting to generate the string under consideration through a set of production rules that regulate a procedure of symbol substitution. These rules take the form

$$A \rightarrow B + C \ (+ \ D, \ \text{etc.}),$$

and they are read "rewrite A as B + C." This operation can be translated graphically as

The model distinguishes three types of symbols: the start symbol, which defines the object to be generated and appears on the left-hand side of the first rule to be applied; non-terminal symbols, which correspond to analytical categories and may appear on either side of the arrow; and terminal symbols standing for lexical elements, which appear on the right-hand side exclusively. The derivational process consists of selecting a start symbol—a sentence in the case of natural languages, a story in the case of narrative—expanding it through the right-hand symbols of a rule, and repeating the operation recursively on these new symbols, until the level of terminal categories is reached. The graphic trace of the derivation is a tree-shaped diagram which assigns an internal structure to the output being generated.

A rule presenting a single symbol on the left-hand side is a context-free rule; it may be applied whenever this symbol is produced in the derivation. A rule with more than one left-hand symbol—say, $A + B \rightarrow C + D$—is context-sensitive. One of the possible interpretations of this example is that A may become $C + D$ in the environment of B, while B is deleted. According to Chomsky, natural languages cannot be generated by context-free rules exclusively. The syntactic structures produced by context-free rules—the so-called deep structure of sentences—must be modified by context-sensitive rules in order to yield the actual sentences of the language. These context-sensitive rules are the transformational component of the model. Linguists argue in favor of transformations by invoking semantic evidence: for instance our intuition that a passive and an active sentence have the same meaning. From a purely mathematical point of view, however, there is no proof that the accepting automaton for natural languages requires context-sensitive principles.[1]

The application of the model to the narrative text assimilates the set of all stories to a language, and individual narratives to sentences in that language. This assimilation will only be literal if stories can be shown to be put together out of a finite lexicon of terminal elements. This obviously cannot be the case: stories are made of sentences (or, in an abstract sense, of propositions), and the set of all sentences or all propositions is itself another language (English, French, or "propositionese") with an infinite number of strings. The elements of the first-order language do not possess a definite function in the second-order language of narrative. In natural language, the filling in of nonterminal categories with lexical elements is governed by explicit rules of syntactic categorization: we know what words qualify as nouns, verbs, adjectives, etc. In addition to these categorizations, linguists invoke selection restriction, in order to prevent the generation of nonsense sentences such as "colorless green ideas sleep furiously." The syntactic affiliation of words has no equivalent on the level of propositions: a given proposition—say, "the crow has a cheese"—can fulfill many textual functions, and fit into several of the nonterminal categories of a story grammar, no matter how these categories are selected. In a story grammar, then, the replacement of nonterminal symbols with semantic content cannot be governed by an explicit and finite set of rules.[2] The best a narrative grammar can do is generate not actual stories, but abstract story schemata. A text can be regarded as a story if it can be mapped onto one of the schemata produced by the grammar, but the mapping operation is an interpretation, rather than a mechanical procedure. For this reason, narrative grammars are more useful when used in a bottom-up manner—as a way to analyze a text—than in a top-to-bottom fashion, as a generative device. It is as bottom-up interpretive device that I will discuss here the grammar of Mandler and Johnson. What matters in this perspective is not the grammar's ability to make decisions of acceptability (these could be made by a black-box automaton deprived of semantic insight), but the internal structure it assigns to the text through the derivational tree, and the way it represents logico-semantic relations between narrative propositions.

A mapping of "The Fox and the Crow" is proposed in figure 29. It is not the only one allowed by the grammar, but the best I could produce. The derivation makes use of the following rules:

> Fable → Story and Moral
> Story → Setting AND Event structure
> Setting → State
> Event structure → Episode
> Episode → Beginning CAUSE Development CAUSE Ending
> Beginning → Event

Development → Complex reaction CAUSE Goal Path
Complex reaction → Simple reaction CAUSE Goal
Simple reaction → Internal event
Goal → State
　　 → Internal state
Goal path → Attempt CAUSE outcome
Attempt → Event
Outcome → Event
Ending → Event
　　 → State

(Adapted from Mandler and Johnson 1977.)[3]

Following the example of Chomsky, the grammar of Mandler and John-son includes both context-free rules and context-sensitive transformations. The latter operate the deletion of terminal nodes containing nontextualized information, or the chronological rearrangement of narrative propositions. The context-free rules generate the logical representation of the plot, while the transformations produce a preverbal narrative structure reflecting the textual presentation of the logical representation. In the terminology of Russian formalism, the output of the context-free rules is the *fabula,* and the output of the transformations the *sjužhet* of the text.[4] Since I am interested in the logical configuration of plots, I will limit my discussion to the output of the context-free rules.

A formal characteristic of trees is their hierarchical structure. The tree organizes the text into a series of schemata of decreasing generality, as we move from the top to the bottom. The first categories encountered correspond to generic labels (fable, story); at the next level, they capture rhetorical or discourse units (episode, setting, conclusion). From the discourse level we move to more properly semantic functions with categories such as reaction, attempt, and outcome. These are instantiated as concrete narrative proposi-tions. Missing in the hierarchy, however, are higher semantic concepts captur-ing functional units: concepts such as "promise," "sacrifice," "deceit," "treason," and "reward." How these concepts are hooked onto the terminal elements, and how they relate to the intermediary semantic categories, is one of the questions left unanswered by the grammar of Mandler and Johnson.

The structural adequacy of the tree can be evaluated according to a pair of criteria: (1) Are elements correctly grouped together? (2) Is the depth of a terminal element (i. e., its distance from the starting node) indicative of its cognitive importance?

If the grouping is correct, elements derived from the same node should present greater cohesion than elements derived from different nodes. The nature of this cohesion is captured by the label of the parent node. The mapping of "The Fox and the Crow" appears reasonably adequate in its rhetorical and semantic organization of narrative material. It opposes the initial situation (SETTING) to the narrative events (EVENT STRUCTURE);

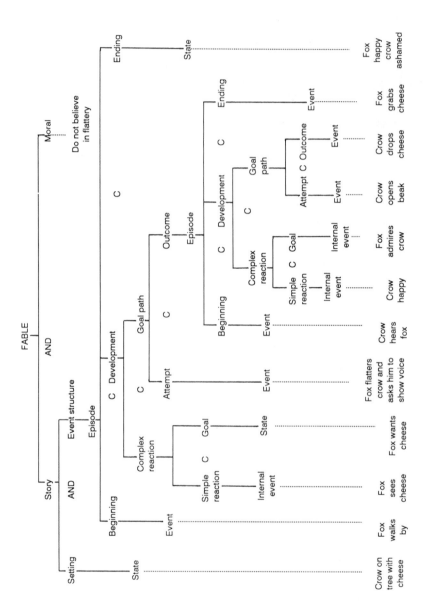

Figure 29

A story-grammar mapping of "The Fox and the Crow"
(Adapted from Mandler and Johnson 1977)

within this structure, it groups under the same node of EPISODE all the events instantiating the pattern of problem and resolution in the domain of the fox. A subset of these events appears in an embedded EPISODE. This episode captures the pattern of problem and attempt at resolution in the domain of the crow. To those familiar with the fable, the embedding of the crow-EPISODE in the fox-EPISODE reflects the fact that the plan of the fox foresees the actions of the crow, while the crow remains unaware of being manipulated. This interpretation, however, is based on what we already know about the plot, rather than on information derived from the model. Nothing tells us in the diagram what the fox explicitly wants the crow to do.

The tree fares rather poorly in predicting the relative importance of terminal elements. The length of the derivational path falls short of indicating which propositions are the most likely to be remembered. Mandler and Johnson's experiments showed that the category SETTING had the highest incidence of recall, followed by BEGINNINGS (a surprising finding: did the subjects have a short attention span?), OUTCOMES, and ATTEMPTS. SETTINGS are situated close to the root node, while OUTCOMES appear on the longest branches. REACTIONS, whose position is intermediary, rank very low in both recall and summarization. While it seems clear that certain categories are more memorable than others, the identification of these categories is not facilitated by an arborescent graph. The tree fares no better in guiding the composition of summaries. Consider this reasonably complete summary of the story:

> A crow sat on a tree with a cheese (SETTING, level 3)
> A fox asked him to sing (ATTEMPT, level 7)
> The crow opened his beak (ATTEMPT, level 11)
> to show his beautiful voice (GOAL, level 11)
> The cheese fell (OUTCOME, level 11)
> The fox got the cheese (ENDING, level 9)

Nearly every one of these elements belongs to a different level of derivation. The likelihood that a proposition will be included in a summary is more easily predicted by a simple linear schema of the form "plot-problem + solution" than by position on a hierarchical tree. Moreover, the story grammar tells nothing about patterns of semantic and pragmatic inference, which play a crucial role in the formation of summaries. The category GOAL, for instance, is omitted from most summaries because it can be inferred from the nature of the attempt.

How does the model perform on the question test? Imagine that the graph of figure 29 is programmed into the database of a computer. The mapping of the story will be considered to "know" the answer to a question if there is an explicit search algorithm leading to the retrieval of this answer. For the first question—"why does the fox ask the crow to sing?"—the answer can be obtained by asking the computer to look for an ATTEMPT node above the proposition under consideration, and to locate the goal which causes this attempt. In this particular grammar, the computer will have to move up from ATTEMPT to GOAL PATH and DEVELOPMENT, then down left to COMPLEX REACTION and down right to GOAL before coming up with the answer "the fox wants to have the cheese." The answer is correct, but the traversal seems needlessly complicated for such an obvious question. A subtree of the form "Plan → goal + attempt + result" would model more efficiently a simple mental operation.

The second question concerns the success of the two characters in the pursuit of their respective goals. This question can be answered by comparing GOAL nodes to the corresponding OUTCOME. There is, however, no pairing of GOAL and OUTCOME under the same dominating node. To find the outcome of a goal we must move up two levels from GOAL to DEVELOPMENT, then down two levels to OUTCOME. When OUTCOME dominates not just one, but a series of nodes—as is the case when it is rewritten as EPISODE—the algorithm needs a criterion for picking the appropriate event. If we instruct the machine to pick the right-most terminal node under OUTCOME, the fox goal "Fox has cheese" will be paired with the outcome "Fox grabs cheese," and the crow goal "Fox admires Crow" with the outcome "Crow drops cheese." In the case of the fox, the outcome fulfills the goal, but in the case of the crow the outcome bears no relation to the proposition expressing the character's intent. The model thus knows that the fox is successful while the crow is a loser, but here again the retrieval would be simplified by a rule rewriting plan as goal, attempt, and outcome without intermediary categories.

To answer the third question—is the fox sincere or deceitful?—we need access to the private worlds of characters. Deception was defined in chapter 6 as an agent asking a subagent to cooperate in a plan which the main agent does not intend to carry out (projected subagent plan $<>$ overt main agent plan). In a deceptive action, the overt plan of the main agent is a virtual construct. But the model of Mandler and Johnson limits the representation of narrative events to actual goals and factual events. Since there is no node expressing what the fox wants the crow to take as being his intent, as opposed to what he really wants to achieve, deceit cannot be located by a straightforward procedure. But there is an indirect way to reach the conclusion that the fox is not acting in good faith. We see on the tree that the crow fails and that the fox succeeds. We see furthermore that the crow's failure is embedded in the GOAL PATH of the fox, and determines the outcome of his plan. The automaton could thus be told that a character is deceitful toward another whenever a successful action by the first character embeds and foresees an unsuccessful action by the other: the success of the first character requires the failure of the second. But as I have observed above, the notion of foresight is not made explicit by the embedding pattern. Moreover, this definition of deceit lacks generality, since a deceptive plan does not necessarily end in success. If the crow were smart enough to avoid falling into the trap, the fox would still be acting deceitfully, but the automaton would fail to reach this conclusion.

In evaluating a formal model of narrative—or, for that matter, of any kind of object—it is important to distinguish the limitations resulting from the particular application of the model from the limitations inherent to the formalism itself. In the case of a story grammar, the first type of limitation can be overcome by modifying the rules. It may, for instance, be argued that the model of Mandler and Johnson is unable to generate accidental happenings because of the mandatory presence of causal connectors between the components of EPISODE, DEVELOPMENT, or GOAL PATH. This problem could easily be solved by turning some of the connectors into optional constituents. Similarly, the problem we have observed with efficiency of retrieval for the first two of the test questions derives from the particular definition of the rules, not from the formalism of a story grammar.

Far more substantial are the limitations rooted in the structure of trees. As a particular type of graph, a tree is subjected to the following constraints:

(1) The branches cannot be tangled. The configuration of figure 30(a) is not a tree. Now assume that two characters, A and B, are simultaneously engaged in the pursuit of their respective goals, and that A's actions alternate chronologically with B's actions. If the narrative tree respects the unity of plans, it will disrupt the chronological order, as in 30(b). The model willthen be unable to answer such questions as "did event a happen after or before b?" a task normally performed by checking the left-to-right ordering of terminal elements.[5] But if the chronological order is respected, as in 30(c), the model loses sight of which event belongs to which action sequence, and it cannot answer questions of the type "How did A realize his or her goal?"

In diagrams (a) and (b), this answer would be provided by listing all the events dominated by the node A's PLAN. The solution to the dilemma of

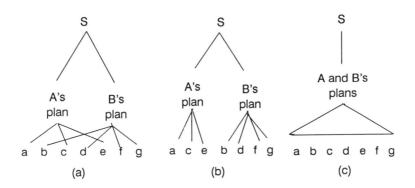

Figure 30
Tree representation
of alternating plans

alternating sequences is the tangled graph shown in 30(a), which cannot be produced by a story grammar.

(2) The arcs of trees are unidirectional, and only one arc may lead into each node. This means that trees allow no circuits, and that nodes are the children of a single parent. These constraints prevent story-trees from ascribing more than one function to a given element, when the functions are disjoint categories rather than hierarchically ordered concepts subsuming each other. Functional polyvalence, however, is a common phenomenon in narrative semantics—and as we have seen in chapter 8, an important source of tellability. Among the many semantic configurations which cannot be mapped on a tree-shaped diagram is the case of a character building a plan around the moves projected by another character. This situation is exemplified in "Little Red Riding Hood" (figure 31). To show that the event "LRR gets to the grandmother's house" is part of both Little Red Riding Hood's original plan and the wolf's counterplan, we need a double arc subsuming the event under two different headings.

Perhaps the most serious limitation of trees for the representation of narrative is their inability to model parallel processes. A generative grammar is a formalism for scanning a one-dimensional object, a strictly linear string of elements. Most narratives, however, are not linear sequences of actions, but tapestries of interwoven destinies. The lines in a plot may run parallel to each other, merge, split, or intersect, as characters pursue separate goals, become involved with each other, meet new characters, redefine their goals, or resume their involvement with an old acquaintance. To represent the interleaving of the strands in a plot we need a network-type of graph, such as the model shown in figure 32. The different lines of this network stand for the

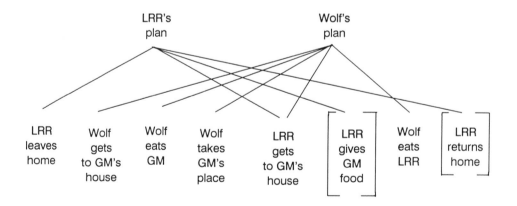

Figure 31
Plan and counterplan

individual fates of the various characters, the nodes stand for events, the left-to-right sequence signifies chronology, and the lines running into each node indicate which characters participate in each event.

The formal limitations of trees do not mean, however, that they are totally devoid of value for the analysis of narrative structures. Pavel (1985) has shown that the linking of problems and solutions and the spreading of conflict in the narrative universe is efficiently modeled on a tree-shaped diagram. Another example of the usefulness of trees is found in the graphs proposed in chapter 7 to represent the hierarchy of goals and subgoals in the logical structure of plans (cf. ''The Old Farmer'' and Jacy's plan, figs. 14–16).[6] Complete narratives may not grow on trees, but a semantically complete narrative graph (if one is ever designed) will, like any other graph, contain arborescent subgraphs, some of which should reveal patterns of signification that are lost in the forest of the global model.

The Plot-Unit Model

Our second system of plot representation was designed by Wendy Lehnert as a project in artificial intelligence. The purpose of the system is to provide an algorithm for the generation of summaries.

The plot-unit model is based on a a generalized graph with no formal restrictions on the number or direction of arcs. It differs from the grammar

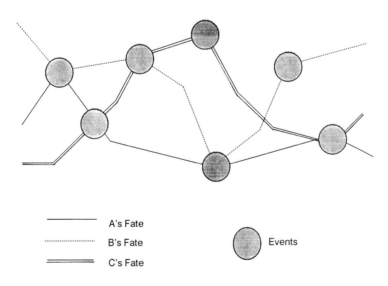

——————— A's Fate

··················· B's Fate

══════════ C's Fate

Events

Figure 32
A narrative with parallel plot lines

not only through the shape of the graph, but also through its use of labels to distinguish several types of arcs and nodes. (In the grammar, all arcs indicated a relation of instantiation between the upper and lower categories, and the type of a node was not distinct from its content).

The mapping of "The Fox and the Crow" shown in figure 33 is divided into a domain controlled by the crow (left column) and a domain controlled by the fox (right). The content of the nodes are concrete narrative propositions, and their labels indicate the "affect state" of the controlling character with respect to these propositions. The repertory of affective labels consists of three categories. Lehnert (1981:295) defines them as follows:

+ (Positive Event) Events that please
− (Negative Event) Events that displease
G (Mental State) Mental states (w/neutral effect)[7]

The repertory of arc-labels comprises four categories:

(1) m-links (motivation) lead from any node into a G-node, and represent causalities behind intents.

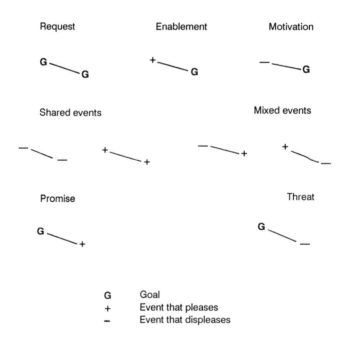

Figure 33
Interpersonal relations in the plot-unit model
(As defined in Lehnert 1981)

(2) a-links (actualization) lead from a G-node to a + or − node, and describe intensionalities behind events.

(3) t-links (termination) link nonneutral nodes (+ or −) or G-nodes between themselves. When it connects nonneutral nodes, the arc means that the affective impact of the proposition in the source node is supplanted by the impact of the target (i.e., a bad state is replaced by a good one, a good state is supplanted by an even better one, etc.) When used between G-nodes, the link means the replacement of one goal by another.

(4) e-links (equivalence) also connect nonneutral or G-nodes between themselves. Nodes are linked with e-connections when "multiple perspectives of a single affect state can be separated" (297). A concrete example of the use of the link is a state presenting both good and bad consequences. I fail, however, to grasp the meaning of an e-link between two G-nodes.

In order to represent the relations between the mental states of different characters, the model uses cross-domain arcs which may be interpreted as causal links. A cross-domain arc pointing from A's domain into B's goal means that B's goal is formed as a result of A's mental state or actions. The three possibilities, and the interpretations proposed by Lehnert, are shown on the top row of figure 33.

A cross-domain arc pointing from a + or − node to another nonneutral node specifies the affective impact of an event for different characters. Thus in "The Fox and the Crow," the event of dropping the cheese is bad for the crow, but leads to the success of the fox. The propositions in the two nodes may describe the same event, different consequences of the same event, or the event captured from different points of view (e.g., "crow drops cheese" in the crow's domain, versus "cheese falls on ground" in the fox's domain). Events are either shared or mixed, depending on whether or not they provoke the same reaction in the two characters (figure 33, middle row). Shared events indicate a cooperative relation, while mixed events occur in competitive situations.

A last possibility is a cross-domain arc leading from a goal-node to a nonneutral affect state. This configuration, which means that the setting of a goal by A provokes a positive or negative reaction by B, is interpreted by the system as either promise or threat (figure 33, bottom row).

Out of the building blocks provided by the three affect states, the four intradomain relations, and the cross-domain arc, Lehnert builds a repertory of so-called plot-units, which captures the narrative function of the propositions inscribed within the nodes. A level of primitive units is yielded by the fifteen legal combinations of affect states and intradomain relations. (The other twenty-one ways of linking the possible pairings of node-types are declared illegal.) The most important of these primitive units are shown in figure 34. The meaning of the diagrams is made transparent by the definition of their core components—the labels for arcs and nodes. The graph for problem, for instance, tells us that a problem is a bad situation motivating the setting of a goal.

The combination of primitive units yields an open-ended lexicon of complex plot-units: the system sets no limit on the size of plot-units, nor on the number of labeled configurations. Figure 35 shows complex plot-units involving a single character. (The graph for inadvertent aggravation is my own addition to the lexicon.) The diagrams offer not only a graphic definition of thematic concepts, but a semantic analysis as well: in the configuration labeled "intentional problem resolution," for instance, we recognize the subgraphs for problem, success, and resolution. A computer could easily perform this analysis by scanning the diagram and comparing it to the lexicon of figures 33 and 34. The same operation, using figures 35 and 36 as lexicon, allows the mechanical detection of complex plot-units on the level of the global narrative graph.

The greatest strategic significance for the economy of the plot is borne by those units which make use of the cross-domain arc. A sample of this kind of unit is shown in figure 36. I leave it to the reader to try to make sense out of the graphs through the definitions of arcs, nodes, and primitive

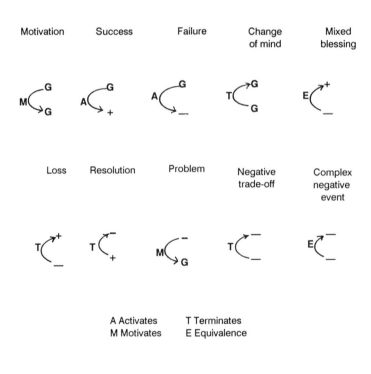

Figure 34
Primitive plot-units

units. I must personally express some reservations as to whether some of the graphs offer a viable semantic analysis of the concepts they represent, rather than an arbitrary coding.

The system thus defined overcomes the two major drawbacks of the grammar: the inability to represent parallelism, and the failure to relate narrative events to several overlapping functions. The representation of parallelism is made possible by devoting a separate column to every character. Simultaneous events appear on the same line (the vertical axis standing for chronology), but in different columns. The model's ability to handle parallelism is demonstrated by Lehnert's coding of "The Gift of the Magi" by O. Henry, a story whose central conflict and narrative point are rooted in the interaction of concurrent lines of action: a young wife cuts and sells her hair in order to buy a beautiful chain for her husband's watch, while the husband sells his treasured watch to buy an ornament for the hair of his wife.

The system's ability to express functional pluralism derives from the nonlinear character of its elements. In a model based on linear units—such as Propp's *Morphology of the Folktale*—a plot is a succession of discrete functions: the hero receives a task—the hero leaves home—the hero receives a

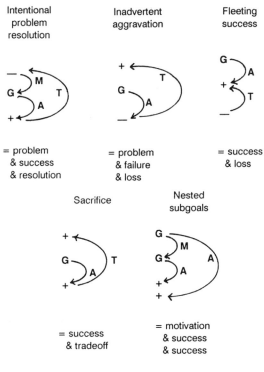

Figure 35
Complex plot-units

magical agent—the hero defeats the villain—the hero returns home—the hero is rewarded. Story-grammars combine linear sequencing with hierarchical structuring: units are strung together on the horizontal axis and embedded in each other on the vertical axis. The plot-unit model allows not only sequencing and embedding, but also overlapping. A story is constructed by interlocking the graphs of plot-units through their common nodes. Each of the labeled subgraphs using a certain node ascribes a distinct function to the proposition inscribed within this node. Since there is no limit on the number of subgraphs using a given node, there is no limit on the number of functions potentially converging around a narrative proposition.

In the graph for "The Fox and the Crow" shown in figure 37 we recognize the configurations typical of the following primitive units: problem, motivation, success, failure, loss, resolution, and enablement. The complex units include: intentional problem resolution, nested subgoals, malicious act, and inadvertent aggravation. The highest degree of functional polyvalence is presented by the node "the fox flatters the crow." This event participates in the primitive units of success and enablement, and in the complex units of nested subgoals and malicious act. Intuitively we also feel that

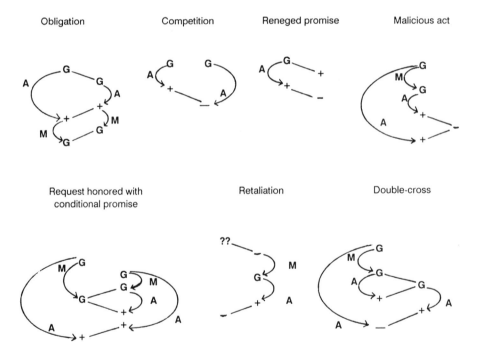

Figure 36
Complex plot-units with several characters

it participates in the theme of intentional problem resolution, though the graph listed in figure 35 for this unit is not immediately detectable. The event "The crow opens his beak and drops the cheese" participates in the primitive units of failure and loss, and in the complex units of malicious action, inadvertent aggravation, and intentional problem resolution.[8] If connectedness within the plot-graph is a sign of narrative salience, the system clearly highlights these two events.

Counting the arcs leading into a node is not, however, Lehnert's criterion for selecting the components of summaries. Her procedure involves entire plot-units, not individual propositions. The algorithm consists of drawing a derived graph based on the complex plot-units found in the primary graph. In this derived graph, nodes are filled with labels of plot-units, and arcs connect the units that share a common node in the primary graph. The resulting graph for "The Fox and the Crow" is shown in figure 38. The pivotal units for summaries are those which cannot be cut out from the rest of the graph by deleting a small number of arcs. The relations between complex units in "The Fox and the Crow" shows no pivotal components: the graph of figure 38 is a complete graph, with every element connected to every other one. According to the system, all four units are equally important. But as the following summary suggests, the theme of "nested subgoals" is easily dispensable while the others are not:

> A fox got a cheese (intentional problem resolution) by tricking a crow (malicious act) into dropping it (inadvertent aggravation).

Subjected to the three test questions, the mapping of figure 37 provides the following answers:

Why does the fox ask the crow to sing? A single a-arc, followed backwards, connects an action to its purpose: "he wants the crow to open his beak." But this is only a subgoal in the plan, not a self-sufficient purpose. The main goal can be reached by following backwards the chain of m-related G-nodes. At the top of the chain we find: "the fox wants the cheese." The three steps required for this retrieval reflect the fact that asking a bird to sing is not an evident way of gaining possession of a cheese. The path is not only shorter than the traversal needed to reach the same information on the story-tree, but also semantically more informative: while it took an 8-arc detour up and down the tree to locate the purpose of the fox, the three steps of the operation reflect the hierarchical structuring of his plan.

Are the fox and the crow successful? Take the node capturing the main goal of a character and follow the a-arc leading out of this node to see whether it ends in a + or a − node. One traversal in each case reveals the success of the fox and the failure of the crow.

Is the fox being sincere or deceitful? To answer this question the system would need access to a plot-unit of deceit. But this unit is conspicuously absent from the lexicon. In Lehnert's catalog of plot-units, the closest to deceit is what she calls double-cross. "In a double-cross, the respondent

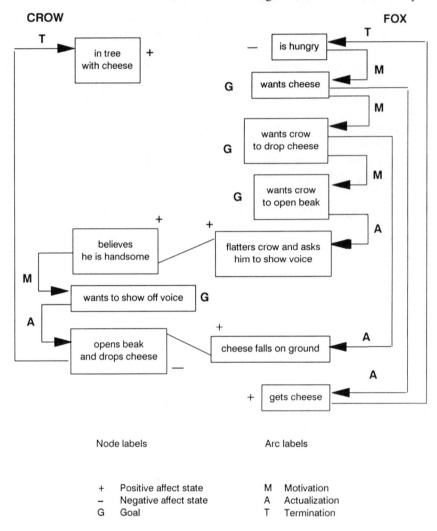

Figure 37
"The Fox and the Crow" in the plot-unit model

deceptively agrees to go along, and then intentionally does something to foil the other's goal. This unit contains subgoals, a request, a promise, and a mixed event of success and failure'' (1981:304). The deceptive element of the double-cross resides in the making of a promise with no intent to keep it. It should therefore be expressed in the subgraph for reneged promise, which does indeed appear in double-cross. But the plot-unit proposed in figure 36 for reneged promise does not express a deceptive intent. There is

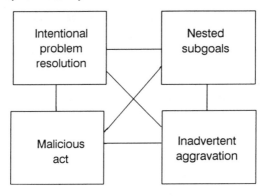

Figure 38
Relations between plot-units

only one G-node in the domain of the maker of the promise, and this unique node cannot show the contrast between actual and pretended intent. If the node is filled with the pretended intent of the promise-maker, there is no way to explain why its enactment leads to a negative affect in the domain of the recipient. And if the G-node is filled with the actual intent, the initial making of the promise should not create a positive reaction in the recipient. There is simply no way to design a satisfactory representation of a deceptive intent with the building blocks provided by the system.

Without the ability to represent the contrast between private and public intents, the system cannot detect the duplicity of the fox. This leads to an incorrect analysis of plot-unit in figure 37. The node "fox flatters crow and asks him to sing" is labeled + with respect to the fox, because the action fulfills its goal of getting the crow to believe that the fox admires him. The consequence of the flattery, "crow believes that he is handsome," is labeled + with respect to the crow since this belief pleases the crow. But a cross-domain arc leading from a + node in one character's domain to a + node in the domain of another is interpreted by the system as "shared event," indicative of a cooperative relation. This interpretation is contradicted by the relation of "mixed event" linking later on a − for the crow (when he drops the cheese) to a + for the fox. Obviously, the positive reaction of the fox with respect to the action of flattering is due to the anticipation of snatching the cheese away from its owner, not to the momentary pleasure experienced by the crow.

The difficulty the system has with the theme of deceit stems from an incomplete coverage of the semantic domain, which limits its ability to handle the distinction between the actual and the virtual. The semantic universe is divided into character-related domains, and does not include an autonomous factual domain independent of the perception of characters. The representation of the domain of characters is limited to those events or states which correspond to one of the three affect states. Beliefs, unless they lead to affective reactions, are left out of the picture. Figure 37 has a node for "crow believes he is handsome" because this belief causes pleasure in the crow, but none for the belief of the fox with respect to the appearance of the crow. Since the system does not cover systematically the beliefs of characters, and does not contrast beliefs with their reference world, it cannot identify the themes of lie and of error.

Without a separate column for objective reality, how does the system identify the facts and distinguish the actual from the virtual? A clue is provided by the labels of nodes: G-nodes contain the virtual when they are linked by an a-arc to a − situation, while nodes labeled +, −, and G linked to + yield the facts of TAW. But what if characters misrepresent the actual situation, or fail to realize all of its consequences? Will the + and − nodes contain what they believe to be the case, or what objectively happened? This dilemma is illustrated by the following example: In order to take revenge on Leon, Paul sleeps with Leon's wife. Upon hearing the news Leon is happy, for he wanted to divorce his wife, and he now has evidence of her adultery. The system would diagram this plot as shown in figure 39. But what affective value should be attached to the node "Paul sleeps with Leon's wife" relative to Paul? Paul at that time believes that the action is good for him, but objectively the situation is bad, since its effect on Leon is the opposite of what Paul anticipated. Whatever label we give to the immediate result of the action in Paul's domain, the configuration characteristic of the theme of retaliation (shown in figure 36) will not be detectable. It is only realized in the case of a successful revenge. A virtual plot-unit—projected by a character, but not actualized—leaves no traces on the narrative graph.

Until a way is found to resolve the conflict between objective reality and its interpretation, between being and appearance, the system will be unable to model such masterplots as the myth of Oedipus. In the plot-unit system, the event "Oedipus marries a woman named Jocasta" would receive a unique affective value. But in order to grasp the full strategic meaning of the situation, it is necessary to distinguish an affective value attached to the character's representation of the situation ("Jocasta is unrelated to Oedipus," + for Oedipus), from an affective value attached to the objective facts ("Jocasta is the mother of Oedipus," − for Oedipus if he knew the truth.)

Another limitation in the expressive power of the model stems from the ambiguity of some of its categories, most notably the ambiguity of the cross-domain arc. One example among many: the relation

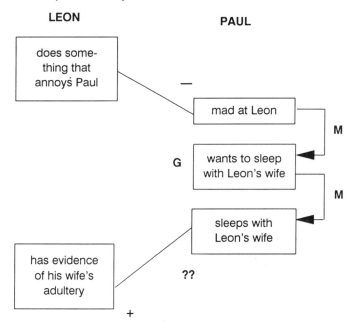

Figure 39
A plot-unit representation of failed retaliation

is used to represent several distinct situations. In the plot-unit of competition, A's success is the cause of B's defeat, and the cross-domain arc reveals a conflict of interests. In the plot-unit of retaliation, A's act presents no intrinsic benefit for A, and his rejoicing is entirely due to the trouble he causes to B. In another context, the relation could mean jealousy: B is mad at the success of A, even though A's success bears no consequences for the current pursuits of B. This ambiguity makes the system unable to express the distinction between reactions to a physical state or event, as in competition, and reactions to a mental state, as in jealousy and retaliation.

The limitations of the plot-unit model are the side-effects of its strength: the economy of its repertory and its efficiency in representing conflict situations and interpersonal relations. The diagram of figure 37 does what the grammar could not: it highlights the events that bear the focus of narrative interest. While the grammar dwelt at length on preparatory events (expressed through the categories of beginning and setting), the plot-unit model aims straight at the knots in the plot. A quick glance at the diagram reveals what the story is all about: the rivalry of the fox and the crow, the success of one character, and the defeat of the other. The repertory of analytical categories may not allow the representation of the semantic units involving error and deceit, but the model recognizes at a low cost a remarkable variety of narrative functions. It will take a considerable complication of the system to extend its coverage.

The Recursive Graph Model

To improve the representation of virtual states and events and to allow their distinction from the narrative facts, I propose a model based on a recursive graph. In a recursive graph, nodes may be filled not only with narrative propositions, but also with embedded graphs. These embedded graphs correspond to the "private narratives" discussed in chapter 6.

The model takes over from Lehnert's system the unrestricted form of the graph, the use of arc and node labels, and the division of the graph into domains related to characters. To these private domains it adds a factual domain, represented on the central column of the graph.

In the plot-unit system the domains of characters contained both physical and mental elements. In the present model, physical states and events appear in the factual domain, and the private domains of characters are entirely devoted to mental phenomena (represented in oval nodes on the graph).

Another difference with Lehnert's proposal is a systematic distinction, within the factual domain, between events (double-frame nodes) and states (single-frame). In the plot-unit model, the majority of + and − nodes were filled with action-propositions, but in most cases the affective value of the node concerned a state, the result of the action. The model got away with this simplification because the result is usually implied by the action.[9]

Characters are identified by a name, a matrix of properties (which may change during the course of the story), and a private domain. This private domain consists of two types of elements: values attached to some states and events in the name of the character, and so-called "registers" representing various aspects of mental activity. These registers correspond roughly to the private worlds discussed in chapter 6.

Among value-labels, two types are also distinguished. One type corresponds to Lehnert's affect states; it tells whether a situation is considered good (+) or bad (−) by the character. Affective values may label not only physical states and events, but also mental events; and not only mental events in one's domain, but also in the domain of another character. In the mapping of "The Fox and the Crow" in figure 40, the crow's dejection at having been had by the fox is expressed by an affective − attached to the contents of his K-register as he understands what really happened. And in the unrealized plan of the crow, shown in figure 41(c), the pleasure anticipated by the crow at being admired is expressed by an affective "+ crow" labeling the opinion to be formed by the fox.

The other type of value-label is a moral account. It tells us whether actions count as merits or demerits, and it keeps track of the credits and debts of characters toward other characters. An action by A calling for pun-

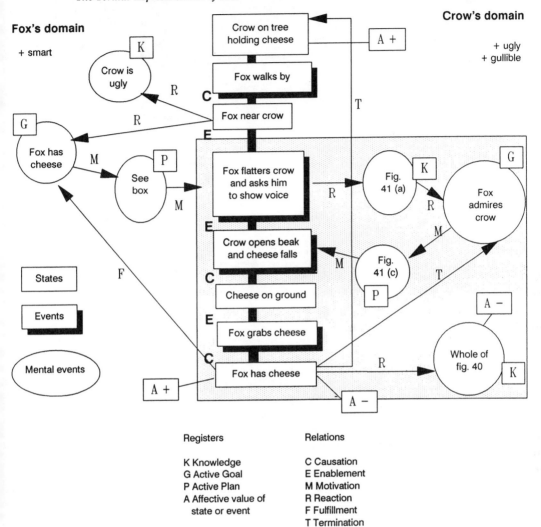

Figure 40
"The Fox and the Crow" in the recursive graph model :
Main graph

ishment on behalf of B will be labeled [− toward B] in the moral account of A. Moral labels are not needed in the mapping of "The Fox and the Crow," despite the malicious act of the fox, because this moral infraction bears no narrative consequences. It goes unpunished, and causes no attempt at retaliation on the part of the crow.

While values are labels for fact- or belief-nodes, registers are nodes in

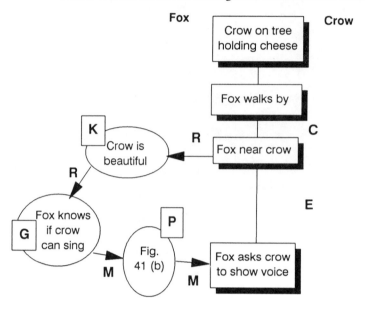

Figure 41
Embedded graphs for "The Fox and the Crow"
(a) Crow's beliefs about fox's beliefs

their own right, bearing propositional content. The name of the register functions as node-label, modalizing the propositions contained within the node. The repertory of mental registers is made out of the categories discussed in chapter 6:

K: The epistemic world of characters, containing their beliefs, projections, and retrospections

O: The private or social obligations of characters. Private obligations are specified by the contents of promises; social obligations by the laws to which characters are subjected

W: The desires and fears, likes and dislikes of characters

G: The active goals of characters

P: The plans through which characters seek to fulfill their active goals

For the sake of economy, subjective opinions are not assigned to a special register, but divided between the K- and the W-registers. A belief such as "Fox thinks the crow is beautiful" is listed in the K-register; a proposition expressing love or hate relations for other characters will appear in the W-register, since love and hate involve desire or repulsion.

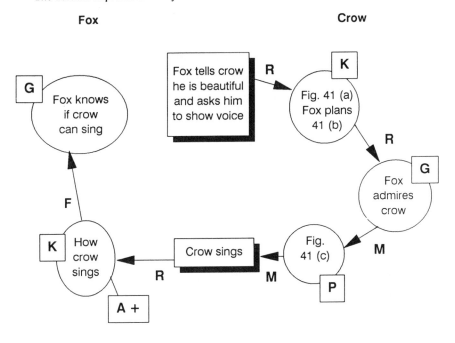

Figure 41 (b)
Fox's plan in crow's beliefs

Semantic relations between nodes are specified by six types of arc labels. Unlabeled arcs indicate chronological sequence between events without logical relation. Listed below are the labels and their meaning:

C (causation) stands for a sufficient condition. C-arcs appear between events and states.

E (enablement) indicates a necessary but not sufficient condition. These arcs typically link states to events.

R (reaction) denotes a mental response to a physical fact or to another mental event. R-arcs are found between physical facts and K-events, or K-events and W-propositions.

M (motivation) stands for a relation between a goal and a plan, or between a plan and an event, state, or mental event specified by the plan.

F (fulfillment) means that a state or event fulfills the active goal of a character. The arc usually links a node in the factual domain to a G-node, but a goal may also be fulfilled by a mental event in another character's domain (e.g. "x admires y" may fulfill y's goal).

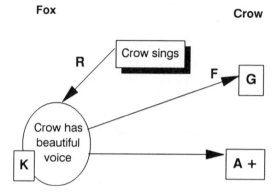

Figure 41 (c)
Crow's plan

T (termination) indicates that a state or event (physical or mental) puts an end to the pursuit of a goal. The arc can also be used between two nodes in the factual domain, indicating that the target-situation terminates the source-situation. Still another use is between two W-propositions, such as "x loves y" versus "x no longer loves y."

Since the nature of many arc-labels can be predicted from the type of node they connect, the system is not free of semantic redundancies. For maximal economy, the repertory could be reduced to three labels (in addition to the unlabeled arc): C, T, and F. The meaning of C would be narrowed down by the system according to these inference rules:

C means causation when it links an event to a state.
C means enablement when it links a state to an event.
C means reaction when it leads into a mental node (other than P).
C means motivation when its target or source is a plan register.

Given the use of T and F arcs, the specification of certain affect values could also be left to inference principles:

A state or event receives a + value for a character if it is linked by an F-arc to a goal-node in this character's domain.

A state or event receives a + value if it is linked by a T arc to a node labeled − for this character.

Symmetrically inverse principles regulate the assignment of negative affect labels. Through these principles, most affect labels could be eliminated from figure 40.

The formation of the narrative graph is governed by a certain number of rules of concatenation, which ensure the logical and semantic coherence of the plot:

(a) A happening needs no other relation to the previous node than chronological sequence, but it must be linked to a following or contemporary node through a relation of either enablement or causation. This rule provides a test for the detection of what I call in chapter 6 nonnarrative events. An event is nonnarrative when it can be deleted from the graph by cutting the two arcs of chronological sequence which link it to the previous and following nodes of the physical domain.

(b) An action must be motivated by a goal and plan, and, unless it belongs to a type that can be performed anywhere, anytime (such as opening one's beak if one is a crow), it must be enabled by a physical state. Example: the fox's desire to get the cheese motivates his discourse to the crow. This action is enabled by the physical proximity of the two characters.

(c) A physical state must be caused by an action or happening, and may be motivated by an intent. The cheese being on the ground is a result of the crow's attempt to sing, and is brought about by the fox's plan to get the cheese.

(d) A plan must be linked by an arc of motivation to a goal.

(e) A mental act other than plan must be a reaction to either a physical state, an action, or another mental act. A typical chain of mental acts is the perception of a physical situation, the extraction of knowledge, the formation of a desire, the selection of a goal, and the elaboration of a plan to fulfill the goal. In "The Fox and the Crow," we have the state of the fox being near the crow, which causes his desire to get the cheese, and the formation of his deceptive scheme.

These rules of concatenation outline a basic narrative sequence of the form:

$$
\begin{array}{ccc}
\text{new} & & \text{new} \\
\text{event} \rightarrow \text{physical state} \rightarrow \text{event} \rightarrow \text{physical state} \rightarrow \text{event} \\
\text{and/or} & & \text{and/or} \\
\text{mental act(s)} & & \text{mental act(s)}
\end{array}
$$

The sequence event→mental act, without new physical state, occurs mainly in the case of an event of linguistic communication. A sequence event→event is possible, when a physical event causes another in rapid succession, without a stable intermediary state. This situation is exemplified by the sequence "crow opens beak to sing"–"cheese falls on the ground."

To these rules of concatenation, a macro-rule of narrative closure must be added. For a sequence of mental and physical events to form a complete plot, every G-node must form the target of a T- or an F-arc. This rule insures that no goal pursuit is left dangling, and that no narrative comes to an end while a plan is still being executed.[10]

The rules of concatenation and closure capture the basic conditions of narrative intelligibility. Through their formulation, I am making the claim that a collection of propositions only forms a plot if they are properly connected in the narrative graph.

Within the model of an entire text, some groups of nodes may be easily detachable from the rest of the graph, yielding subplots or episodes. The formal test for the detection of subplots is the possibility of isolating a subgraph by cutting two links of chronological sequence. If the isolation of a subgraph requires the deletion of arcs of enablement in addition to those of chronological sequence, the resulting unit may be called an episode. While subplots are logically independent of each other, and may occur in any order, episodes set the material preconditions for other episodes and are bound to a specific chronological sequence.[11]

The registers of the private domains may contain either singular propositions or networks of propositions forming embedded graphs. The mental constructs represented by embedded graphs are the projections and retrospections of the K-register, the commitments of the O-register, and the plans of the P-register. Embedded graphs may also appear in the factual domain as part of an event of linguistic communication. If a character narrates a story, reveals past events, makes a promise, or predicts the future, his or her action will be represented in the factual domain as "x speech acts p," where p is represented by an embedded graph. Since embedded graphs represent narrative clusters of propositions, they are built from the same elements as the primary graph, and they present the same self-embedding potential.

In order to remain economical, the representation of the K and P registers is guided by the principle of minimal departure. Rather than listing all beliefs and intents, the system only specifies virtual elements: inaccurate beliefs and nonactualized plans. Correct beliefs and executed plans duplicate information appearing elsewhere on the graph, and they are implicitly represented by a pointer to this information. In the mapping of "The Fox and the Crow" shown in figure 40, the P-register in the domain of the fox consists of a pointer to the segment of the plot-graph contained within the box.

To complete the representation of knowledge, it may be necessary to specify epistemic holes, in a negative complement of the K-register. The myth of Oedipus demonstrates the importance of providing access to what a character ignores. The global knowledge of a character at time t is construed by assuming that the character knows everything in the semantic universe up to t, subtracting from this picture the facts listed in the negative K-register, and amending it according to the false beliefs listed in the positive K-register. If a K-register remains unspecified (as is the case for the fox), this means that the character maintains as time goes on a complete and correct representation of present and past situations. The only case where a correct representation must be specified by a pointer to another part of the graph is when an event of discovery dispels a former misrepresentation. This occurs at the end of the story in the K-world of the crow.

Virtual narrative elements appear in the K- and the P-registers of the crow. The flattery of the fox creates a false propositional belief: "The fox finds the crow beautiful," and a mistaken interpretation of past events. This interpretation is captured by the narrative graph of figure 41(a). It embeds another virtual narrative, shown in figure 41(b): the plan of the fox, as inferred by the crow. Since the node holding the false beliefs of the crow is contained within the box, these beliefs are foreseen by the actual plan of the fox. The scheme of 41(b), wrongly attributed by the crow to the fox, is what I have called an overt plan in chapter 7. The plan of figure 41(b) embeds another narrative construct: the plan presumably projected by the fox for the crow. In the mind of the crow, the fox is asking for his cooperation. The role specified for the crow in the fake fox-plan of 41(b) is shown in 41(c). This narrative captures not only what the crow believes the fox wants him to do, but also what the crow actually decides to do. When he opens his beak to sing, the crow is adopting 41(c) as his own plan, thus conforming to the role ascribed to him in 41(b).

It should come as no surprise that the mapping of figure 41 improves the performance of the previous two models on the three test questions, since it was designed to this very purpose.

Why does the fox ask the crow to sing? Follow back the M-arc from this event to the motivating plan, then take another M-arc back to the goal node, and retrieve the answer: because the fox wants to have the cheese. An alternative method is to locate the plan-node, then look at the final state in the embedded graph representing the plan. For the immediate goal of the action, look at the next physical event in the sequence specified by the plan: "so that the crow will open his beak." The retrieval of the immediate goal was easier in the plot-unit system (it required only one traversal), but the present model provides easier access to the main goal.

Are the fox and the crow successful? Take the goal-node of each character, and determine whether the arc leading back into it is an F-arc or a T-arc. As was the case with the plot-unit system, the model requires only one traversal to reveal the failure of the crow and the success of the fox. Failure and success could also be located through the redundant value-labels ascribed to the last state in the story: having the cheese is good for the fox and bad for the crow. In a minimal mapping, however, these labels would be left out.

Is the fox being sincere or deceitful? There are two ways to detect the deceptive intent. One is to locate the discrepancy between the speech act of the fox ("your feathers are beautiful") and the content of his K-register: "the crow is ugly." This comparison identifies the theme of lie. The other way is to look at the embedded graph for the plan of the fox. Does this plan involve the creation of false beliefs, or is it meant by the fox to be correctly deciphered by the crow? The actual plan of the fox, as we have seen, is the graph within the box. Within this graph is embedded the graph of the beliefs to be formed by the crow (41[a]). Within 41(a), in turn, is embedded 41(b), the plan which a gullible crow will attribute to the fox (the overt plan of the fox, in the terminology developed in chapter 7). The fox wants the crow to believe that he intends 41(b). The discrepancy between the overt plan and the actual plan holds the key to the detection of deceit. But to locate the node holding the overt plan the system needs a set of instructions. I propose the following algorithm: Take a plan-graph, look for an event of linguistic communication creating a transfer of control from main agent to subagent, and look at the K-register of the subagent resulting from this event. If the K-register holds a copy of the plan of the main agent, the main agent is inviting cooperation. If the K-register of the subagent conflicts with the plan of the main agent, the main agent is deceitful. This procedure is independent of the success or failure of the would-be deceiver, since the discrepancy between the actual plan and the overt plan is inscribed within the actual plan. The system looks at the crow's beliefs as projected by the fox, not at these beliefs themselves. Had the events turned out differently, the sequence within the box would not be realized in the factual domain, but it would still appear as the plan of the fox.

The procedure for the detection of deceit demonstrates how the model can be taught to recognize functional units. As was the case with the plot-unit system, the present model defines higher semantic units as specific configurations of arcs and nodes. Each unit is associated with a search algorithm. (In Lehnert's model, the algorithm was implicit to the subgraphs proposed as plot-unit definitions). Here is a repertory of procedures for the identification of major narrative themes:

Successful action: A sequence action-resulting state in the factual domain instantiates a similar sequence in the plan-register of the agent.

Action with accidental effect: The resulting state of an action conflicts with the result foreseen in the plan-register of the agent.

Fortuitous problem resolution: A goal actively pursued by a character is fulfilled by an event not specified in his or her plan-register.

Mixed blessing and negative side-effects: An action planned and executed by a character causes a new state, defined over two or more propositions. One of these propositions is linked by an F-arc to the goal of the planner, but another receives a negative affect value for the same character.

Aborted plan execution: The execution of a plan is interrupted by an event that destroys the preconditions for the next step. The state resulting from the interrupting event is linked by a T-arc to the goal of the planner.

Counterplan: A plan by a character A aims at the abortion of a plan by B. The plan of B is known to A, and A's plan integrates some elements of B's plan.

Promise: An event of linguistic transaction between A and B creates an entry in the O-register of A. This entry is a sequence of actions initiated by A, and ending in an affective + situation for B. The K-register of B holds an image of the O-register of A. The promise is kept if later on the O-construct is reproduced in the factual domain, reneged otherwise. If the promise is conditional (i.e., depends on the accomplishment of a certain action by B), the O-register of A contains a forked projection, offering as alternative to the promise an empty branch leaving A free of obligation.

Threat (from A to B): A conditional promise, with the specified branch in A's O-register leading to a state labeled − for B.

Promise never meant to be kept: A sequence appears in the O-register as the result of a verbal transaction, but the P-register of the same character holds a conflicting construct.

Deal: A double conditional promise, from A to B and B to A.

Punishment: An action by A creates an affective − for some other character, and leads to a − in A's moral account. Later on, an action by B leads to a state with an affective − for A, but erases the − in A's moral account. Since the punishment is legal, the action creates no − in B's moral account.

Retaliation: An action by A creates an affective − for B. B performs an action which leads to an affective − for A, and a "− toward A" in his own moral account. As a consequence, B will be liable to further retaliation by A.

Pardon: A's moral register contains "− toward B." This − is erased in an event of communication between A and B, without B taking an action leading to an affective − for A.

Violation: An action by A conflicts with a specification in her O-register, and creates a − state in her moral account.

Prediction: The K-register of a character contains a projection with no alternatives beyond a certain point: an event occurs on all branches of the future following the critical point. The unconditional part of the projection is transmitted to other characters, and becomes part of their K-register (provided they believe the prediction).

By keeping track of the reflection of the whole plot in the K-register of characters, the system is able to handle the situations that created problems for the plot-unit model: ambiguities due to conflicts between the objective value of a state of affairs and its subjective evaluation. Consider the made-up case of the unsuccessful revenge: Trying to harm Leon, Paul inadvertently causes a situation favorable to Leon. Paul's plan-register would contain a sequence "Paul sleeps with Leon's wife"—"Leon's wife is adulterous." This last state would receive a negative affective label for Leon, expressing Paul's belief that the plan will hurt his enemy. After the action has been performed, the sequence specified by the plan would also be inscribed in Paul's K-register: Paul believes he has succeeded. Once the state "Leon's wife is adulterous" becomes known to Leon, however, Leon realizes that he now has a way to fulfill his longstanding wish to divorce his wife. He constructs a plan taking advantage of the adultery, and the old wish is turned into an active goal. Since Leon is able to make use of the state "wife is adulterous" in the pursuit of his own interest, the state receives for him a positive value label, which conflicts with its evaluation in Paul's K-register.

For the myth of Oedipus, the system would record "Oedipus is married to Jocasta, his mother" in the factual domain, and value this state as − for Oedipus in the moral account. But in the K-register of Oedipus, the state "Oedipus is married to Jocasta" would be valued positively because the K-register does not contain the proposition "Jocasta is the mother of Oedipus."

In the domain of summarization, the model offers no marked improvement over the previous ones. The importance of a narrative proposition for a summary could be assessed from the number of higher semantic units in which it is found to participate; or it could be computed on the basis of its degree of connectedness within the graph. As we have seen above, connectedness is measured by the number of arcs leading into or out of a node. I believe, however, that an algorithm of summarization cannot be based on a plot-graph alone. Summaries are built around narrative points, and their formation should be guided by a theory of tellability. It is, for instance, because of the principle favoring semantic polyvalence that the number of functional units involving an event can be used as an index of importance for summaries.

The complexity of the mapping of such a simple narrative as "The Fox and the Crow" in the recursive graph model raises the question of its applicability to longer narratives with more intricate plots, such as fairy tales, soap operas, tragedies, or comedies of errors. Parallel lines of action require the factual domain to be braided into multiple strands, and large casts of characters require private domains to be organized into several columns, rather than conveniently assigned to the left and right side of the factual domain. (This problem was also encountered by the plot-unit model: none of the examples involved more than two parties.) Dividing the graph into several columns results in tangled lines which affect the legibility of the model. A three-dimensional graph, arranging the domains of characters in a circle around the factual domain, would be easier to read but impossible to print. A computer, however, would have no difficulty finding its way through the crowd of characters and the jungle of entangled relations, since the machine can follow arcs from node to node without being distracted by intersecting lines. The visual problem is not indicative of logical limitations, and does not affect the ultimate intelligibility of the model.

What we have produced, then, is not so much a visual mapping as a model for a purely mental object. The recursive graph system is an attempt to represent every species of tree in the narrative forest, but if all these trees are put together, the forest may be hidden to the naked eye. Except for the very simplest cases, the mappings produced by the model are not meant to be printed on a two-dimensional page, but entered into the potentially n-dimensional space of computer memory. A semantically complete representation of plot is a structure of such complexity that it can only be held and manipulated by the neural network of the brain—or by an artificial simulation of this neural network.

11 The Heuristics of Automatic Story Generation

When Pierre Mesnard, the hero of the famous parable of Borges, died without completing what would have been the masterwork of his lifetime—rewriting the *Quixote*—he could not anticipate that it would take a technological revolution for his legacy to bear its fruits. Nowadays specialists in artificial intelligence are busy trying to generate literary masterpieces, and one of the most impressive achievements so far has been the production, by a program named TALE-SPIN written by James Meehan, of a story in which a fox, trying to get a cheese held by a crow, flatters the crow into singing, and causes him to drop the cheese. What should make the modern version of "The Fox and the Crow" radically different from the fables of Aesop and La Fontaine is that it was produced by a brain aware of its own operations, using explicitly defined procedures, whereas the naturally written stories were the product of obscure intuitions about art. Therein also was supposed to reside the infinite superiority over the text of Cervantes of the chapters of *Don Quixote* written by Pierre Mesnard.

To the skeptic, however, the fact that something resembling the plot of a well-known fable came out of a computer is no proof that the machine actually displayed what Paul Ricoeur (1982) aptly calls "narrative intelligence." If a program received as input the lexicon of the Spanish language, it would eventually come up with the text of *Don Quixote* by simply trying out all the possible word combinations. But this program would have no understanding of the plots it generates, and it would be unable to weed out, from its massive output, the unsuccessful tries from those which resulted in viable stories. What this program would lack is a heuristic method "able to direct the search [for the story] along the paths most likely to succeed" (Boden 1977:347). Alternatively, one could imagine a program that would receive no input at all, but would consist of such specific procedures that all of its runs would inevitably produce the text of *Don Quixote,* together with an explicit semantic representation of the narrative events. This program would achieve a perfect understanding of its output; and since it would exclude all texts other than *Don Quixote,* it could be credited with a high degree of aesthetic judgment. But the significance of these achievements would be negated by the complete lack of generative power of the principles compiled into the program. The heuristics would be so constraining that the system would be totally deprived of creative freedom.

These examples suggest three criteria by which the "intelligence" of story-generating programs may be evaluated: creativity, aesthetic awareness, and understanding. *Creativity* is measured by the active role of the system in producing the stories, and by the variety of the output: the greater the creativity, the fewer the limitations imposed on the structure of the story. *Aesthetic awareness* is a function of the system's ability to aim at preferred plot structures, and to sort out good and bad narratives. *Understanding* resides in the system's ability to construct a graph that will provide a basis for summarizing the plot or answering questions about its internal logic. Requirements for the latter have been covered at length in chapter 10, and will receive only passing mention in the discussion to come. What I propose to do in this chapter is to evaluate the principal approaches taken in recent years to automatic story generation in terms of their creativity and aesthetic awareness. This last criterion will serve as testing ground for the principles of tellability proposed in chapter 7.

Transition Networks

The simplest way of generating stories may be called the "choose your own adventures" algorithm, by analogy with those children stories in which the reader is asked on every page which one of several possible branches the story should follow. In this algorithm, the knowledge of the program is a graph of narrative choices. The nodes of the network stand for the events of the story, and the arcs connecting the nodes indicate the logical possibility that an event may be followed by another. (A different but equivalent way of laying out the graph would be to have the nodes stand for the states of the narrative universe, and the arcs for the mediating events.) Figure 42 reproduces an attempt by Pierre Maranda (1985) to arrange the functions of Propp's *Morphology of the Folktale* into such a network.[1] Given this system of transitions, both existing and new Russian fairy tales can be generated by following the various paths between entrance and exit points, picking up along the way the events stored in every node.

It is clear, however, that this algorithm fails all criteria of narrative intelligence. Stories are obtained by chaining ready-made chunks of plot, without attempting to assess the importance of each function "for the story as a whole" (to use Propp's expression). The system is unable to identify the goals of characters, and has no access whatsoever to the causal network which confers intelligibility upon the narrative events. The active role of the

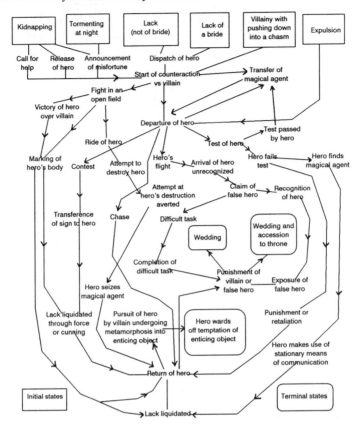

Figure 42
State transition diagram for the generation of Russian fairy tales
(Adapted from Maranda 1985)

program is limited to an ability to blindly enumerate all possible traversals of the graph. The fact that all complete traversals result in well-formed stories is determined by the contents of the graph, not by decisions made during the traversal. The system plays no role in the construction of the graph, and has no knowledge of the aesthetic principles which may have determined its configuration.

To see how an embryo of narrative intelligence could be imparted to the program, consider the loop in figure 42 leading from "departure of the hero" to "transfer of a magical agent." In Maranda's model the loop can be taken any number of times, but after too many iterations the patience of the hearer is exhausted, and the run ends in failure. We could make the program aware of this danger by having it check the number of iterations. Even better, we can build into its knowledge a guideline recommending either one or three iterations. There is no need to stress the importance in story-telling of the number three as a retarding device favoring the building of suspense. As the model stands, however, the inclusion of a guideline favor-ing three iterations of the loop would open room for the generation of unbalanced story structures. Another important aesthetic principle at work in fairy tales forbids events devoid of consequences: every episode, every detail should have a bearing on the final outcome. If the hero receives three magical agents, he should later on encounter three dangers, so that he can find use for each of the three gifts. To allow a match between acquisition and use, a second loop should be included on Maranda's graph around the node "hero seizes magical agent." Coming to this point, the program should re-member how many times it traversed the first loop, so that an equal number of iterations would be generated. The necessity of imparting to the program some sort of memory means that a reasonably intelligent story-generating algorithm can neither be based on a simple transition network (that is, on a Finite Automaton), nor even on a context-free grammar, but requires the more powerful formalism of a context-sensitive grammar, whose corre-sponding automaton is known as the Augmented Transition Network. In such a mechanism, conditions can be imposed on transitions so that the range of possible developments is not entirely determined by the current state of the network. In narratological terms, the conditions translate the fact that what can happen at any point in a story may depend as much on the distant past as on the most recent events.

Grammar-driven models

A significantly more powerful model is the top-down, schema-driven approach. The computer develops a narrative pattern specified by the rules of a grammar, instantiating the various slots with appropriate elements, and creating along the way a tree-shaped representation of the story structure. A concrete implementation of this algorithm is Alfred Correira's program TELLTALE (Correira 1980). The rule base of the program is represented in tables 43(a) and 43(b) in the form of an AND/OR tree. In this particular model, each rule consists of three slots, which may be full or empty: a precondition, an expansion, and a postcondition. The three slots in turn may consist of any number of elements. An AND connector means that every component must be instantiated, while an OR connector limits the rewriting of the rule to one possibility within a paradigm: the expansion of the node ACTION imposes, for instance, a choice between ASK-FOR-HAND, RESCUE, QUEST, or PRAY. It is the paradigmatic richness of the OR nodes which determines the variety of the output.

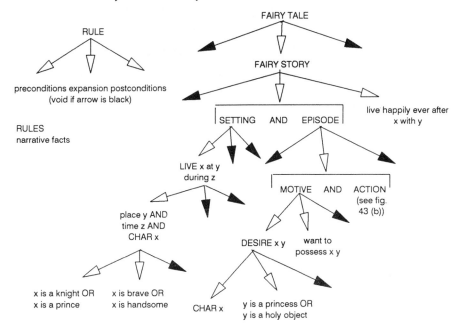

Figure 43 (a)
Rule base for TELLTALE
(Adapted from Correira 1980)

The generative procedure consists of trying to expand the rules, starting at the top of the implicit tree. When a rule is expanded, its terminal elements are integrated as facts in the developing story. A rule is applied if its preconditions can be satisfied, and rejected otherwise. Satisfaction occurs when a precondition corresponds to an established fact, or when it can be asserted without creating contradictions with already generated elements. When a precondition names another rule, the program delays its decision until it has found whether or not this other rule is itself applicable.

For a concrete example of the procedure, imagine that the program, in its application of the rule DESIRE, has chosen the alternative "y is a holy object." Now it develops the node ACTION, and chooses the branch leading to RESCUE through THREATEN and CARRY. To satisfy the precondition of these three rules, it must create a y who is a princess. But this binding of variables conflicts with the decision made at the DESIRE level, so the program must backtrack and investigate another branch. The system of preconditions creates a network of interdependencies among the rules which confer on the model the power of a context-sensitive grammar.

How does this model perform with respect to the three criteria of narrative intelligence? The limitations of TELLTALE with respect to creativity,

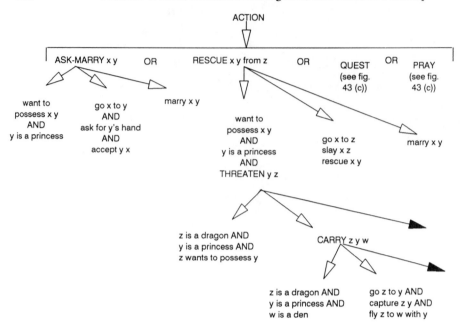

Figure 43 (b)
Detail of rule base for TELLTALE

understanding, and aesthetic awareness are those inherent to the story-grammar approach and its tree-shaped diagrams. As we have seen in chapter 10, these limitations include an inability to generate parallel story-lines and events fulfilling more than one strategic function. The first limitation restricts the program's creativity, while the second prevents it from implementing the principle of tellability calling for semantic polyvalence. In the domain of understanding, the tree of TELLTALE falls short of fulfilling the claim of the author: "A summary of the text can be extracted from any level, becoming less specific as the level approaches the root. The lowest level summary is the original text itself; the highest level (the root) is a title for the story" (1980:136). As we have seen in chapter 10, it would take a tree with branches of even length to substantiate this claim. The program's understanding is further limited by its failure to compute a systematic representation of the successive states of the semantic universe. The story-tree yielded by TELLTALE is unable to answer questions pertaining to the logical relations between plot components.

One decisive improvement of the algorithm over the preceding model is the way in which the pieces of the developing plot are fitted together. Constructing a story on the basis of a simple transition network is like working

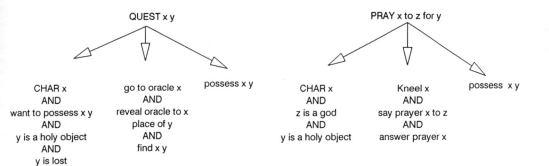

Figure 43 (c)
Detail of rule base for TELLTALE

on a jigsaw puzzle whose pieces are labeled with numbers, so that the player can pick the next piece to be fitted without any false tries. Developing the story tree in the TELLTALE algorithm requires the examination of many rules, and the checking of preconditions. When the program rejects a rule because of a precondition failure, it demonstrates what could be called an awareness of the contextual requirements for an event to happen: the program knows for instance that one cannot come into possession of the Holy Grail by asking it in marriage.

Simulative Algorithms

The ability to develop an in-depth representation of the changing attributes of the narrative universe is the strength of a class of algorithms known as simulative. In a simulation, the semantic representation of the story is implicitly divided into a static and an active component. The static component lists the members of the narrative universe and describes their properties, while the active component contains the historical events that alter these properties. After a universe has been created, the system enters a loop of generating events, computing their consequences, and creating new states to reflect these effects. The resulting picture is a trace of the changes that affect the narrative universe as a function of the passage of time. A strictly chronological generation of events is thus essential to the simulative approach.

The earliest story-generating program based on the idea of simulation is Sheldon Klein's Automatic Novel Writer (described in Klein et al. 1979). The program produces a repertory of mystery stories whose diversity is captured by the flow-chart of figure 44. The rules and subrules responsible for the creation of episodes are complex packages of instructions, including preconditions to be checked; actions to be taken; and text to be generated if the rule is applied.[2] Actions concern essentially the updating of the semantic representation of the story, and the addition or deletion of elements from a number of lists maintained as registers by the program. Since the content of these registers may determine the flow of control at a later stage, the model is formally equivalent to an Augmented Transition Network. For a concrete illustration of its functioning, consider the rule "blackmail." As shown on the flow-chart, it can only apply after x and y have become lovers, and have been caught in the act by z. A conceivable precondition of "blackmail" is that z be the spouse of neither x nor y. The rule generates two textual statements:

> z accosted x
> z blackmailed x

and inserts two implicit propositions in the semantic representation:

> z decided to blackmail x
> x and y left the room

Since the semantic representation comprises both the narrated and the implicit facts, the program's knowledge of the narrative universe is far more extensive than the printed output suggests.

A third component of the rule defines the following actions on registers:

> Add x to potential killers
> Add z to x's potential victims
> Add "get rid of blackmailer" to x's reason-to-kill

These statements do not update the state and history of the narrative universe, but specify narrative possibilities which may or may not be turned into actual events. Every time the program loops through the love-making/caught-in-the-act sequence, selecting different characters to replace the variables, new potential killers and victims are added to the registers. When the program finally exits the top loop and comes to the point where a murder has to be generated, it will pick randomly a member of the potential killer register, and select accordingly the victim and the reason to kill. Depending on these choices, one of several possible murder scenes will be imple-

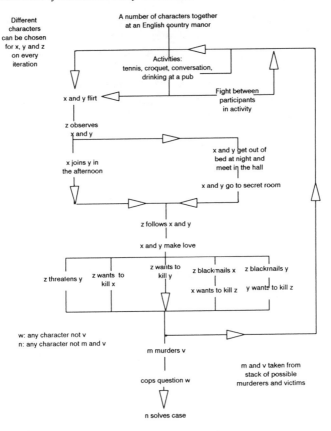

Different
characters
can be chosen
for x, y and z
on every
iteration

A number of characters together
at an English country manor

Activities:
tennis, croquet, conversation,
drinking at a pub

Fight between
participants
in activity

x and y flirt

z observes
x and y

x joins y in
the afternoon

x and y get out of
bed at night and
meet in the hall

x and y go to secret room

z follows x and y

x and y make love

z threatens y

z wants to
kill x

z wants to
kill y

z blackmails x

z blackmails y

x wants to kill z

y wants to kill z

w: any character not v
n: any character not m and v

m murders v

cops question w

m and v taken from
stack of possible
murderers and victims

n solves case

Figure 44
Flow-chart for the generation of mystery stories
(Adapted from Klein et al. 1979)

mented. Similar dependencies obtain between the murder scene and the
solution.

In its present state of development, the program's creativity suffers from
severe restrictions. The uniformity of the output is not only due to the rather
specific semantic requirements of the mystery genre, but also to the fact that
the program works with concrete building blocks, specified in great detail,
rather than with abstract categories. It does not, for instance, depart from a
category "setting," which would allow a choice of concretizations, but instantiates right away the particular setting of an English country manor.
And rather than dividing an episode such as "amorous encounter" into

subcomponents which could be filled in various ways, the program selects a rigid script to determine a lengthy sequence of actions. But these limitations do not concern the simulative method per se. They are peculiar to Klein's implementation—and as the early date of the program indicates, the author had to contend with much greater hardware limitations than did the authors of the other projects discussed in this chapter.

The (dubious) aesthetic quality of the stories is totally independent of the program's operations. If you happen to like English country manors, idle aristocrats, and torrid bedroom scenes you may appreciate the stories' daily routine of tennis and croquet, engaging in conversation, flirting and slipping out for an amorous encounter, while being followed by a jealous observer, but the credit for your pleasure should go to the natural imagination of the programmer, and not the artificial intelligence of the program. On the other hand, the deficiency of the output as a mystery story is clearly due to the approach. Since the murder is narrated before it is solved the stories lack suspense, the essential ingredient of the genre they are supposed to represent. The program produces the historical sequence of events underlying a detective story, but not a well-formed textual rendition. In order to do this the system should make two passes over the history of the narrative universe. The first would generate the events preceding the murder, whether or not they are causally related to it: a good mystery story plants the false clues of possible but unrealized explanations. The second would generate the events responsible for the discovery of the facts asserted during the first pass and for the construction of the causal network connecting some of these facts to the murder. It is during the second pass that the narrative text should be generated.

In the domain of understanding, the strength of Klein's algorithm is not limited to the computation of the background of untold facts necessary to the understanding of the narrative events. The real breakthrough resides in the program's ability to represent the modal structure of the narrative universe. The simulative algorithm decomposes this universe into a plurality of worlds, and assigns each narrative proposition to a specific domain. The characters of a story are not only defined by their physical, objective properties, but also by their correct and incorrect beliefs, their system of affective values, their goals, plans, fears, and rules of behavior. The sum of these mental constructs forms a self-enclosed subsystem within the global narrative universe. Klein observes that the mechanisms that produce the story by manipulating the data and rules of the global universe can easily be made to operate within the confines of a private domain. When a subsystem related to a particular character momentarily takes the place of the global semantic universe, the program's operations reflect the point of view of the character in question. By generating stories in the mind of characters, a program can simulate the mental processes of looking ahead, imagining, dreaming, and hallucinating.

But because its algorithm looks exclusively forward, the program is unable to simulate those mental activities that involve backward logic. From a narrative point of view, the most important of these activities is the formation of plans. When we design a solution to a certain problem, we compute in reverse chronological order the intermediary states and the mediating steps linking the target state to the present situation. The lack of a planning mechanism prevents the program from specifying the intents of characters, and from deciding whether their actions ended in success or failure.

Problem-Solving Algorithms

A combination of forward-oriented event simulation with problem-solving techniques is found in the most famous of all story-generating programs, James Meehan's TALE-SPIN (described in Meehan 1981). Implicit to the program is the rudimentary macrostructural pattern: "story = problem + attempted solution." As internal data, the program receives not only a list of characters with their physical properties and private semantic universe, but also a number of inference rules which represent the practical knowledge of characters (and thus form the procedural component of their private domain). One of these rules may state that if an object is deprived of support it will fall on the ground. Another, that in order to sing one has to open one's mouth (or beak). A third, that opening one's mouth deprives of support whatever was held in it. These inference rules enable the program to simulate the reasoning of characters in elaborating solutions to their problems. In a first stage, the program selects a goal of a character as the central problem, and a plan is constructed on the basis of the character's knowledge. In a second stage, the program undertakes the execution of the plan, updating after every event the state and history of the narrative universe, and assigning propositions to the private worlds of characters. The semantic representation computed during the run of the program is roughly equivalent to the third of the formal models of plot discussed in chapter 10, and reaches a similar level of performance in answering questions.

Whether the story will end in success or failure is determined by the accuracy of the planner's knowledge: out of mistaken beliefs arise plans which are doomed to go wrong. By making the crow indifferent to compliments, contrary to the fox's expectation, TALE-SPIN could for instance generate a tale in which the fox would learn that flattery is not dependable as a source of income.

The principal limitation of the algorithm resides in its lack of aesthetic purpose. While it is true that the energy applied by characters toward the solution of their problems is the most fundamental of the forces that move a plot forward (cf. Pavel 1985), the mere fact that an attempt at a solution was made does not in itself guarantee narrative interest. As I have argued in chapter 7, the various plans that solve the same problem may differ widely in their coefficient of tellability. An intelligent program should be able not only to construct solutions, but also to decide whether or not a given line of action is sufficiently imaginative to present an intrinsic narrative appeal. Existing plan generators aim toward the production of practical, cost-efficient solutions, and not toward the kind of convoluted schemes that captivate the reader of such tales as "Puss In Boots" or "Ali Baba and the Forty Thieves." To produce plans of intrinsic narrative interest, a program would need to follow guidelines such as: avoid standard solutions; favor cunning over violence; try to kill two birds with one stone. Until this recipe is perfected, the only way to ensure imaginative solutions to the characters' problems will be to select them from a library of ready-made plans borrowed from existing stories.

Another shortcoming of the algorithm concerns the variety of the output. Since most events are planned actions, and since the outcome of an action depends on the accuracy of the planner's knowledge, the fate of the narrative universe is almost entirely sealed in the initial situation. The closed character of the narrative system limits the output to one type of pattern: x has a goal, x makes a plan, x succeeds or fails depending on the soundness of the plan. In real life, however, as well as in good stories, perfectly well conceived plans can be derailed by accidents, coincidences, or the actions of other agents. External interference is limited in TALE-SPIN to accidents written into some of the rules. For instance, the program generates a story in which George ant tries to drink and falls into the water; Wilma bird then flies to his rescue, and George is thankful ever after. But the accident is used to create a problem; the story is still about the successful execution of a plan (Wilma's rescue of George).

The structural limitations on the output are due to the strictly horizontal progression of the simulative algorithm. The program moves the plot blindly forward without a global apprehension of the structure it is generating. The diversity of the output could be increased through the top-down guidance of global schemata. For instance, if its repertory of possible story structures contained the pattern "problem-plan-accidental failure," the program would select a goal, construct an appropriate plan, begin its execution, and then choose from a list an external event susceptible to destroy the preconditions for the next action specified by the plan. Of even greater interest are story schemata calling for the blocking of a character's goal through the interfering actions of another agent. All tales of rivalry between a hero and a villain are based on this principle. One among the many variations of the pattern could be generated through the following protocol (adapted from de Beaugrande and Colby 1979):

(1) Create a protagonist and give him a goal.
(2) Create an antagonist and give him a goal incompatible with the goal of the protagonist.
(3) Create a plan for the goal of the protagonist.

(4) Create an event which will make the antagonist aware of the plan of the protagonist.
(5) Have the antagonist create an interfering plan.
(6) Execute the plan of the protagonist up to the point where the antagonist is scheduled to take action.
(7) Execute the plan of the antagonist.

In this story-frame, the antagonist is the winner. Another protocol could reverse the situation by having the protagonist construct a new plan and defeat the antagonist.

By giving the program access to a rich library of protocols from which to choose from, some improvement could be made in the domain of creativity. But this combination of top-down guidance with forward-oriented simulation would not resolve the problem of aesthetic awareness. A program consulting a library of frozen schemata may know that certain templates are good, but it does not know why. Lacking any kind of productive principles, it would not be able to generate dynamically the frames of good stories. Moreover, the selection of a frame specified exclusively in terms of goals and outcomes does not guarantee the success of the story. From the same pattern of goals, plans, accidents, and outcomes we can derive the classical tale of "Little Red Riding Hood," or a completely flat version in which the wolf eats the little girl in the woods, then runs to the grandmother's house, eats her for dessert, and is killed by hunters. Interestingly enough, from a practical point of view the plan of the wolf is far superior in the flat version than in the actual tale: why should the wolf delay his meal by going first to the grandmother, when he could find immediate satisfaction in the woods?

This points to an important difference between the point of view of the wolf, who is a member of the narrative universe and confronts it from the perspective of real life, and the point of view of the author who shapes and contemplates the narrative universe from the perspective of art. While the goal of the wolf is to solve a practical problem, the goal of the author is to create a successful story. The selection of the convoluted scheme of the wolf is dictated by the need to create some future rebounding of the plot which will result in a climactic situation. The tellability of the story is invested in the dramatic encounter of Little Red Riding Hood with the wolf disguised as the grandmother, and in the sudden turn leading from the success of the wolf to his undoing by the guns of the hunters. The narrative climax is not generated by the preceding events; it is rather the preceding events that are generated by the climax. In the authorial perspective, logic operates backwards and there are no accidents. Events are created with a foresight which is radically foreign to the blind progression of pure simulation. While the purpose of simulation is to discover what will happen in a world under specific circumstances, story-generating programs should rather pursue the goal of finding out how a world must be set up, so that certain events can be made to happen.

Authorial Perspective

An attempt to generate stories from the perspective of the author rather than that of characters is found in UNIVERSE, a program currently being developed by Michael Lebowitz (1984,1985). As its name indicates, UNIVERSE was designed for the purpose of creating extended stories of the type found in TV soap operas: stories with a large cast of characters, numerous interleaved subplots, and the potential of being indefinitely continued. The program is based on a library of ready-made "plot fragments" which function as possible plans for the goals of an imaginary author. A concrete example of a library entry is the fragment "forced marriage," shown in figure 45.[3] Here is an example of a plot derived from the fragment:

> Liz was married to Tony. Neither loved the other, and, indeed, Liz was in love with Neil. However, unknown to either Tony or Neil, Stephano, Tony's father, who wanted Liz to produce a grandson for him, threatened Liz that if she left Tony, he would kill Neil. Liz told Neil that she did not love him, that she was still in love with Tony, and that he should forget about her. Eventually, Neil was convinced and he married Marie. Later, when Liz was finally free from Tony (because Stephano had died), Neil was not free to marry her and their trouble went on. (Lebowitz 1985:484)

The basic algorithm consists of picking one or several authorial goals, of selecting a suitable plot fragment, and of executing the plan embodied in the script. The process is recursively repeated for each of the subgoals specified by the plan, until a ground level is reached. For instance, if the goal is "keeping lovers apart," the program may have a choice between the plot fragments "forced marriage," "lover drafted by the army," and "lover stricken with amnesia." Having selected "forced marriage," the program finds a series of subgoals, including "together * ?him" (where * stands for any suitable female character). This particular subgoal may be realized by "seduction," "job-together," or "drunken sneak-in." Just as a goal may be fulfilled by several distinct plans, a plan may be suitable for several different goals. The selection of plot fragments is guided by the policy of trying to satisfy as many goals as possible with the same element: "forced marriage" may be no better than "drafting by the army" for the purpose of keeping lovers apart, but since it involves the subgoal of getting ?him involved with another female character, it becomes the obvious choice if the author entertains simultaneously the goal of maximizing the number of couples engaged in sexual relations. Through this policy, the program is able to create numerous subplots and to interleave their strands.

In its choice of authorial goals, however, the program pursues no higher ambition than following the recipe of TV soap operas. The top-level goals are defined in terms of the themes typical of the genre: love affairs

	Pseudo-code	Comments
Plot fragment	Forced marriage	
Characters	?him, ?her, ?husband, ?parent	
Constraints	(has-husband ?her)	[the husband character]
	(has-parent ?husband)	[the parent character]
	(<(trait-value ?parent)	
	(niceness) -5)	
	(female-adult ?her)	
	(male-adult ?him))	
Goals	(churn ?him ?her)	[prevent them from being happy]
Subgoals	(do-threaten ?parent	[threaten her]
	?her "forget it")	
	(dump-lover ?her ?him)	[have ?her dump ?him]
	(worry-about ?him)	[have someone worry about ?him]
	(together * ?him)	[get ?him involved with someone else]
	(eliminate ?parent)	[get rid of ?parent (breaking threat)]
	(do-divorce ?husband)	[end the unhappy marriage]
	(or (churn ?him ?her)	[either keep churning
	(together ?him ?her))	or try and get ?her and ?him back together]

?him, ?her, ?husband, ?parent: character variables
*: any suitable female character

Figure 45
A typical UNIVERSE plot-fragment
(Lebowitz 1985)

encountering obstacles, people stricken with amnesia, or the return of spouses believed dead by their partner. Unknown to the program are the principles of tellability which may lead an author to select such episodes. In a program driven by concrete themes, "keeping lovers apart" is an authorial goal. But in a program driven by general principles of tellability, the theme would be produced as a means to achieve an effect, such as keeping the reader spellbound. This effect would form the goal, and the formula to achieve it would be integrated into the knowledge-base of the program. In the case of "keeping readers spellbound" this formula might read:

(1) Create a character with whom the reader will identify.
(2) Engage this character in a pursuit.
(3) Delay the fulfillment of the character's goal (and at the same time of the readers' wishes, since they are hoping for an outcome favorable to the character).

Whereas a program driven by a thematic goal would produce episodes with minor variations (such as the reasons for the lovers being kept apart), a program operating under the type of principles listed above would be able to generate a variety of plots: not only lovers being kept apart, but also a hero fighting to defend the rights he is being denied, or a traveler prevented from coming home. The adoption of an authorial perspective will not lead to a significant improvement in the domain of aesthetic awareness and creativity until top-level goals are specified as abstract designs and general directives, with minimal reference to thematic content.

Tellability and Story Generation: A Proposal

A truism of artificial intelligence is that a program is only as good as its theoretical foundations. But for a long time, story generation has maintained a theoretical isolation from poetics and narratology. To produce better story-generating systems we do not so much need supercomputers and programming wizards as a better understanding of the semantics and aesthetics of narrative. In this section, I will outline my conception of an algorithm capable of aesthetic discrimination by engaging in an exercise of hybrid nature: part generative criticism, inspired by the work of such theorists as Zholkovsky (1984) and Bremond (1988), and part simulation of the decisions made during a sample run of an imaginary program. The target of the generative process will be the tale of "Little Red Riding Hood." My discussion should not be taken as a polished algorithm, but as a somewhat utopic blueprint whose implementation depends as much on "issues to be resolved later" as on standard resources of artificial intelligence.

If it is true that good plots originate in climaxes rather than in frozen patterns, then story generation should begin with the center(s) of interest, and from there proceed outward, rather than follow a rigidly chronological order. The program should build one or several narrative highlights, create the preparatory events through backward logic, and take the story to the next highlight, or to an appropriate ending through a guided simulation. The task of my imaginary program will be to generate "Little Red Riding Hood" from what I take to form its narrative climax: the encounter at the grandmother's house and the ensuing reversal in the fortunes of the two main characters.

Human brains do not spin tales out of nothing, and neither do computers. Our story-generating system will operate from a bank of knowledge including the following components:

First of all the program needs a large database of world knowledge, including stereotyped descriptions of the objects found in the narrative universe, standard scripts for the actions routinely performed by its inhabitants, and rules of inference specifying the preconditions and consequences of possible events. By complying with the rules of its world-knowledge, the program will ensure the logical and pragmatic coherence of the plot.

Another indispensable component of the program's knowledge is a set of generic conventions that will impose constraints on the shape of the plot. For the genre fairy tale, these conventions may read: there must be a happy ending, good deeds must be rewarded, and bad deeds must be punished. The genre-specific database will also specify the inventory of TAW (are witches available as characters?), as well as its physical laws (can objects be turned into something else?).

Besides propositional knowledge, the program also requires interpretive abilities. Given a concrete event, it should be able to tell whether its consequences are positive or negative for the affected characters. It should also be able to relate concrete events to abstract functional concepts, such as revenge, promise, or punishment, and to assess the potential of a concrete motif to fulfill a given narrative function.

Aesthetic awareness will be achieved by consulting a list of principles and seeking to satisfy its elements. The list is headed by a meta-guideline prescribing economy and aiming toward multiple aesthetic justification. The other aesthetic goals are defined by the principles of tellability discussed in chapter 8, especially by those relating to the configuration of the plot:

(1) (Meta-principle) If an element can fulfill several aesthetic goals at the same time, it must be preferred over an element satisfying a single goal.
(2) Favor semantic opposition.
(3) Favor symmetry and repetition.
(4) Try to create suspense.
(5) Try to implement functional polyvalence.
(6) Seek the diversification of possible worlds in the semantic universe.

(These are the principles invoked in the generation of "Little Red Riding Hood"; the list may be expanded for other tales.)

Each of these principle is linked to a repertory of specific procedures for achieving the desired effect. For "semantic opposition," one of the procedures is a recipe for creating a sudden turn: assess the affective value of a situation for a character, then create an event leading to a situation of opposite value. The principle "symmetry and repetition" will activate the famous rule of three: create three manifestations of the same abstract structure. "Suspense" may be implemented through retarding devices: delay the fulfillment of the goals of characters.

Much more problematic is the implementation of functional polyvalence. Yet it is essential to the creation of narrative climaxes. The events with the greatest number of functions are likely to form the highlights of the plot. For instance, the event of the wolf eating Little Red Riding Hood functions as the solution of a problem (for the wolf); as the source of a problem (for the victim); as an infraction worthy of punishment; and as the punishment of an infraction (Little Red Riding Hood's failure to follow her mother's advice). To favor the convergence of strategic functions on certain events, the program could consult a list of preferred narrative patterns, such as interdiction/violation, prediction/fulfillment, problem (goal)/solution, infraction/punishment, merit/reward, and offense/revenge. Having created an event, the program will evaluate its potential for fulfilling a given function. It will ask for instance whether the eating of a little girl qualifies as a merit, creates a problem state, or constitutes a possible infraction. When a function is found compatible with the event already created, the program may activate it by selecting a sequence in which this function appears, and by generating appropriate events to fill in the remaining slots. Thus, having found that eating a little girl can be viewed as an infraction, and creates a problem for the victim, the program will complete the sequences potentially opened by this event by generating a punishment and a rescue. The same procedure may be applied to generate retrospectively the first element of the two sequences that close with the wolf eating the heroine.

The principle of diversification predicts that narrative highlights will be situations of maximal conflict among the private domains of the narrative universe. A way to implement these conflicts is to follow the suggestions listed in figure 46. As with other aesthetic guidelines, the principle of semantic diversification can be invoked in either top-down or bottom-up fashion. In a top-down consultation, the program sets as primary goal the generation of possible worlds differing from TAW. It chooses one of the branches of figure 46 and instantiates it in an appropriate situation. In a bottom-up consultation, the program uses the rule in order to determine which one of a number of possible candidates is the best way to fulfill another current goal. By choosing the facts with the best coefficient for the diversification of possibilities, the program will fulfill two goals at the same time, and satisfy the principle of economy.

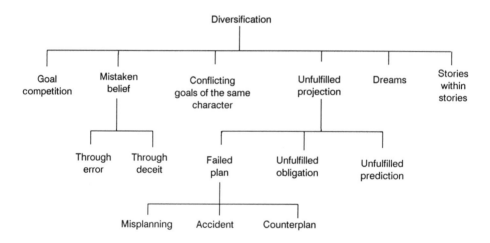

Figure 46
Ways to implement the diversification of possible worlds
in a textual universe

In order to orchestrate the various principles of its repertory, the program needs access to a system of priorities. The purpose of this system is to prevent any given principle from taking over and running wild. If no limits were set on the number of invocations of "diversification," the semantic universe would reach such complexity that the reader would lose track of the worlds to be contemplated. And if "semantic contrast" were invoked repeatedly, the tale would become a fully predictable sequence of reversals in the fortune of characters. Aesthetic balance will be maintained by keeping a record of the invocation and satisfaction of every principle. This record will determine which principle is highest on the list of priorities. If "diversification" has already been invoked a number of times, it will sink low on the list, and "functional polyvalence" may replace it as the next principle to be invoked. By specifying different priorities, different outputs will be produced. As a variable which may be entered by the user, the system of precedences makes a significant contribution to the creativity of the program.

A last piece of knowledge presupposed by our imaginary program is the list of outcomes shown in figure 47. Each of the outcomes is associated with coefficients relative to their ability to create sudden turns and semantic diversity. These coefficients tell the program which principles have been satisfied and which ones should now receive priority. Of the six outcomes listed on figure 47, (a) ranks low on both criteria, (b) is high on diversity, (c) is high on sudden turn, (d) is high on both criteria, (e) and (f) high on sudden turn.

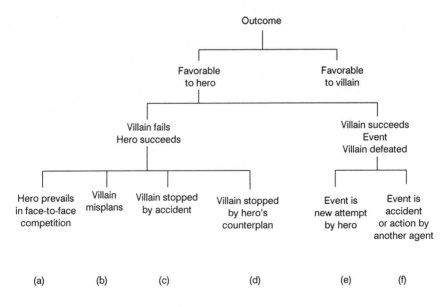

Figure 47
Outcomes of goal competition

Every run of the program begins with a pair of blind decisions, one fixed and one random. The fixed decision is the choice of the left-most branch on the table of diversification: create goal competition. If this decision seems limiting, consider that we are not yet in the business of generating *all types* of narratives. Our program is a mere subroutine in the grandiose project of a Universal Story Generator—the subroutine devoted to standard fairy tales. The ultimate Story Generator will not consist of a single unit, but of a collection of semi-independent modules devoted to various genres.

The random decision is the choice of a branch on the table of outcomes. In the case of "Little Red Riding Hood," the selection made is the right-most possibility: triumph of the hero, after a temporary triumph of the villain, through an external intervention. The coefficient assigned to this outcome tells the program that it satisfies the demand for sudden turns. As a result of this choice, the program will assign a higher priority to the principle of diversification. The system of priorities could be told that "sudden turn" needs to apply only once in a tale, but that "diversification" tolerates more frequent invocations.

The next decision in the run of the program is the selection of the characters who will be engaged in goal competition. At this point the program faces two possibilities: select a hero as dominant character, give him some goals and plans, and create a villain to provide motivation for or obstacles to these intents, or conversely, select the villain's intent as the driving force in the plot. Randomly, the program selects the second solution. Now it must define the identity of the two characters. Imagine that the program has access to a list of adequate "villains-as-dominant-character," from which it pulls a wolf. Then it consults a list of adequate goals for wolves and finds "satisfy one's appetite." For this goal to demonstrate badness the wolf must be lusting for a forbidden object—such as a little girl. Observing the metaprinciple of economy, which recommends trying to get the most use out of elements already available, the program will select as heroine the prospective victim. Since being eaten by a wolf conflicts with the universal implicit goal of preserving one's life, this choice creates the desired polemic relation between the two protagonists.

Now the program faces the task of constructing the plans of the two characters. The horizon of possible worlds will be enriched if in addition to her implicit maintenance goal of preserving her life (for which she needs no plan unless she has a reason to believe her life is in danger), Little Red Riding Hood is actively pursuing an explicit goal of her own. In a simulative algorithm, the program would first create the goal and plan of Little Red Riding Hood, and construct the wolf's stratagem as a response to her intent. But since we have decided that the wolf would be the dominant character, and that his actions would bear the focus of interest, we will adopt the opposite strategy: the program will construct a plan for the wolf, and shape the actions of the little girl to make them fit into this scheme.

To generate the plan of the wolf I propose the following line of reasoning. If the program gives high priority to the principle of diversity, it will seek to implement the suggestions of figure 46. One of the branches—the creation of false beliefs through deceitful actions—appears particularly appropriate to the purpose of eating a little girl. The main problem facing the wolf is getting close to the prospective victim: since his goal is harmful he cannot expect voluntary collaboration from her. One way to overcome the expected reluctance of the heroine to let the wolf come close is for the wolf to pass as somebody else. For the stratagem to succeed, the impersonated person must be trusted by the victim. The chances of success will further increase if the victim is already entertaining the goal of getting close to this person. The first consideration will generate the character of the grandmother, and the second will determine Little Red Riding Hood's intent of paying her a visit. The exact circumstances of the planned visit can be derived from a standard script for the action "x visits y." Y being bedridden should be available as a possible motivation for x, and x bringing presents to y as a standard component. Before the wolf can take the place of the grandmother in bed, she must of course be eliminated. The similarity between this subgoal and the main goal of the wolf should once again lead the planning mechanism to the idea of impersonation. Rather than creating a brand-new character for the wolf to impersonate, the program will once again invoke the principle of economy, and take advantage of the fact that Little Red Riding Hood already fulfills the requirement of being trusted by the grandmother. Before playing the grandmother to trick the granddaughter, the wolf will play the granddaughter to trick the grandmother. It will not be necessary to create a reason for the prospective victim to get close to the impersonated person, since this person already holds the goal of moving toward the victim. By resorting twice to the same stratagem, but with different characters filling the roles, the program makes a contribution to the principle of inverse symmetry: the wolf will play successively the parts of granddaughter and grandmother, making the two encounters similar in the realm of make-believe (Little Red Riding Hood comes to grandmother), but different in the realm of actuality (wolf comes to grandmother, Little Red Riding Hood comes to wolf).

As execution differs from intention, so does generating the actions of characters from constructing their plans. Since it has already been established that the wolf would succeed, the program will turn the actions specified in his scheme into historical events. Being doomed to failure, the plan of Little Red Riding Hood will not be executed, but some of its components are foreseen by the wolf and will therefore be actualized as a part of his plan.

In its repertory of aesthetic guidelines, our program may discover that a narrative climax must involve some suspense. It should know furthermore that the building of suspense is favored by retarding devices. To comply with this demand, the program will delay the success of the wolf by throwing in his way some temporary obstacle which will give a chance to the prospective victim and cast for a while some doubt on the outcome. A natural obstacle in a plan based on impersonation is an imperfect disguise: the ears, eyes, and teeth of the wolf showing up under the grandmother's attire. These choices will set the stage for the climactic dialogue through which the heroine, marching toward the bed, questions the identity of its strange occupant. The number of questions is specified by the famous rule of three, and their content is determined by a rule of progression: each question concerns a body part located closer to the mouth of the wolf, spatial target of the whole plan.

The creation of the climax being thus completed, the program needs to generate the preparatory events. Notice first that the plan of the wolf includes an anticipation of the little girl's arrival, and presupposes a knowledge of her goal and plan. Furthermore, a source must be found for the wolf's desire to eat the little girl. These two requirements will be satisfied by arranging a previous encounter between the two protagonists. A good location for the encounter is in the woods, the natural habitat of wolves. The geography of the narrative universe will be laid out in such a way that the task of helping the grandmother will involve the crossing of the woods. To determine how the wolf will learn about the plan of the little girl, the program will consult the tree of possibilities for the transmission of information. The choice is between direct and indirect transmission: either the little girl will reveal her plan in a face-to-face interaction with the wolf, or the wolf will learn about her intention by overhearing a conversation with another character. The first possibility presents the advantage of creating a situation of dramatic irony: a character unknowingly helping her opponent, thus becoming an instrument of her own doom. Since an act of verbal communication presupposes a reasonably trusting relation between the participants, it will be necessary to neutralize the fearsome nature of the wolf by having him engage in another act of deception: pretending to be friendly.

Before implementing this new act of deception, however, the program should check the features already entered in the description of the participants. Deception is compatible with the [+bad] feature of the wolf, and he has already engaged in deceptive behavior. If his description contained a feature [+honest], the program would have to look for another solution to the problem of acquiring information. The same procedure is applied to Little Red Riding Hood. Since no feature in her description opposes her falling into the trap, she is specified as [+naive], and the deception is implemented. By repeating this procedure every time an action is being generated, the program will not only build up the description of characters, it will also ensure the consistency of their behavior with respect to their moral features.

At this point a very intelligent program would reconsider the plan already built for the wolf, asking whether or not it constitutes the most efficient scheme for the goal under consideration. The purpose of this operation is not to replace the plan already selected—which as we have seen needs to satisfy the criteria of tellability more urgently than those of efficiency—but rather to strengthen its logical motivation by eliminating more practical alternatives. In a well-constructed tale, the wolf should not embark on a complicated and risky plan when the same result could be achieved through simple and safe action. The program should therefore compute the standard solution to the wolf's problem—eat the little girl on the spot—and create an obstacle to motivate the wolf's rejection of this possibility. A good reason for not wanting to eat Little Red Riding Hood right away is a fear of witnesses: hunters or woodcutters will be placed in the forest, and the wolf will be made aware of their presence.[4]

Extracting from its list of preferred narrative patterns a sequence interdiction/violation/punishment, and noticing that the third element is potentially implemented through the rather unpleasant experience scheduled for the little girl, the program could add another semantic dimension to the events by presenting the fate of Little Red Riding Hood as well-deserved treatment. Rather than generating a new event to function as offense, the program will create an interdiction that will confer on the independently justified episode of the conversation with the wolf the strategic dimension of a violation. The interdiction should stem from a person in a position of authority over a little girl—who could that be but her mother? At this point, the program also needs to find an origin for the mission of Little Red Riding Hood, and for the same reason the character of the mother is a natural choice for the role of dispatcher. If the mission given by the mother includes the instructions "do not waste time in the woods" and "do not talk to strangers," the tale will convey a moral entirely suited to its genre: "Do as your mother says or you will be sorry." Notice that in this line of reasoning the moral is added to the tale as an afterthought. This reflects the rather secondary importance of moral messages to the genre fairy tale. In a strongly didactic genre, such as fable or parable, the appropriate strategy would consist of selecting a moral through a high-level goal, and of generating the tale as an illustration of its message. (Cf. Zholkovsky 1984 and Bremond 1988 for examples of this approach.)

The generation of the final outcome is tightly constrained by the decisions made during the construction of the climax. We have already seen how two strategic sequences were potentially opened by the climactic episode. To bring the tale to a satisfactory conclusion it will be necessary to close these sequences in a way compatible with the type of outcome specified by the laws of the genre. The program will now pursue the goals of solving the problem of the heroine and of punishing the villain. Since the heroine has been made helpless by the success of the wolf, the reversal of fortune must be initiated by an external agent who will act like a *deus ex machina*. To comply with the rule of semantic polyvalence, the program will try to have the rescuing event support at the same time the function of punishment. This event should therefore be fatal to the villain. Consulting its world knowledge, the program will find out that hunters are the natural enemies of wolves. A group of hunters will thus be added to the cast of characters. Having condemned the wolf to be shot, the program needs to set up the stage for this event by fulfilling two preconditions: make the wolf vulnerable by putting him to sleep, and give the hunters a reason to enter the house, such as being attracted by the snores of the wolf. To reach the proper conclusion, the program will need to invoke a specialized law of the narrative universe, through which Little Red Riding Hood and the grandmother will be allowed to pop out unhurt from the belly of the dead wolf.

The skeptical reader may fail to be impressed by my imaginary program's ability to generate "Little Red Riding Hood," since the goal was known to me from the beginning—as *Don Quixote* was known to Pierre Mesnard. I have described a line of reasoning which I believe to constitute an improvement over other existing programs in the domain of aesthetic awareness, but of course this awareness should not be achieved at the cost of creativity. A truly creative program does not have a specific story preprogrammed in its knowledge base; it gradually discovers the story as it manipulates the rules of its internal knowledge. Against accusations of overdeterminism, I would argue that if we learn about tellability by studying existing narratives, then it is only natural that our programs should be biased toward the stories from which their knowledge was derived.[5] But if this knowledge consists of powerful principles, the programs will also generate variants of the archetypal stories, and these variants will present sufficient diversity to appear discovered rather than preprogrammed.

What I am suggesting, then, is that a program able to produce "Little Red Riding Hood" following this particular line of reasoning would be versatile enough to produce other viable stories not foreseen by the programmer, stories differing from each other not only in thematic content, but in structure as well. While the variations in thematic content would be obtained by selecting different elements for the low-level goals (a witch instead of a wolf, a gingerbread house as a way to attract the victim), the variations in global structure would result from a different initial choice on the table of outcomes. The branch "hero prevails in face-to-face competition" could lead to the tale of the dragon-slayer, while the branch "villain stopped by hero's counterplan" could result in "Hansel and Gretel." More variations could be obtained by modifying the order of precedence among the principles of tellability responsible for the selection of the intermediary and top-level goals. And finally, entirely different plot structures could be generated by selecting other points of departure on the table of diversification: "mistaken beliefs" would lead to comedies of errors; "stories within stories" to Chinese-box tales. These forms cannot be produced by the algorithm I have described, but other modules could be added to the Universal Story Generator that forms the ultimate goal of narrative AI. As a preliminary step in the expansion of the project toward new genres, we must subject the most representative texts of these genres to the same type of critical exercise I have performed on "Little Red Riding Hood": try to reconstitute a sequence of decisions leading to their generation.

The implementation of an algorithm driven by principles of tellability would undoubtedly require numerous reformulations of its system of aesthetic priorities. The fine-tuning of this system is one of the areas in which the speed and obedience of the computer could be a true asset to narratology. Which principles should be invoked first and which ones should come last? Will better stories be produced by maintaining a balance between the principles, or by letting one of them dominate the generative process? Will some of the principles I have postulated turn out to be useless? Will new ones be suggested by certain runs of the program? Narratology defines the aesthetic resources that guide the computer, but through trial and error, the computer may teach narratology how to manage and orchestrate these resources. The real importance of the seemingly hopeless enterprise of teaching computers the art of spinning tales does not reside in the output, but in the opportunity to test hypotheses. While the models of narrative designed by semioticians, literary theorists, cognitive psychologists, and specialists of discourse analysis will remain an important source of heuristics to automatic story generation, story-generating programs can act in return as a heuristic tool leading to new discoveries about the nature of narrative.

Conclusion

I started this expedition through textual space under the assumption that narrativity and fictionality were logically distinct phenomena, but I left open the possibility of a symbiotic relation. At the end of the journey, what happens to this hypothesis? A symbiotic relation could take two directions: one asserting the primacy of fiction over narration, the other making fiction dependent on narration. In the first case, all narratives would be fictional to some extent, but there could be radically nonnarrative fictions; in the second case, all fictions would present a narrative core, but narratives could be nonfictional. The dependency could also go both ways, so that fiction and narration, though distinct species of communication, could only develop in the environment provided by the other.

The thesis of the necessary fictionality of all narratives has received far more support in recent literary theory than the converse possibility. Its proponents argue that if there were such a thing as a truly nonfictional narrative, it would be the genuine, unretouched image of a reality existing independently of mind and language—what I call AW in this book. But reality does not present itself to immediate experience in narrative form. Narration is never a mechanical, photographic representation of events located "out there" in a reference world. Every narrative act involves selection and emplotment of data. Narrative is form—and form is imposed by the mind (or in a more radical version, by language) on the referent. According to Hayden White: "This value attached to narrativity in the representation of real events arises out of a desire to have real events display the coherence, integrity, fullness, and closure of an image of life that is and can only be imaginary" (1980a:23). Or further: "Historical narrative succeeds in endowing sets of past events, over and above whatever comprehension they provide by appealing to putative causal laws, by exploiting the metaphorical similarities between sets of real events and the conventional structures of our fictions" (1978:91). In this passage, White seems to acknowledge the possibility of absolutely existing "real events" forming some kind of raw narrative data. What is created by the mind are the causal links and the "conventional structures" which "emplot" these events. Louis O. Mink goes further toward mentalism, arguing—in White's paraphrase—"that it makes no sense at all to speak of an event *per se* but only of events under description." In other words, it is the description which "determines the kind of fact [events] are considered to be" (White 1980b:251). An even more radical version of mentalism states that events are not simply arranged into the narrative structure, but made up to fill in the slots. Every narrative representation contains forged events—and "forged" is the etymological meaning of the term "fictional." The narrative representation of a reality is consequently a fictionalization of this reality.

I reject this doctrine on two grounds. The most obvious is that by equating "made-up" events with "fictional events" the thesis presupposes a referential definition of fictionality incompatible with the intensional account defended in this book. My other objection is that the doctrine rests on a fallacy: "If it has form, it is fiction." This equation is fallacious because there is no such thing as a raw, immediate, unshaped perception of reality. The brain is a processor of data, not a mechanical recording device. The difference between active processing and raw perception is exemplified by the mechanism of visual perception: we perceive only as the brain recognizes patterns and discrete shapes; an exposed film, in contrast, "sees" only a matrix of dots bearing the imprint of various types of light waves. If the shaping of sensory data is inherent to perception, every mental representation has form, and according to the equation, every mental representation is a fiction. By embracing too much, the term "fiction" becomes a useless category.

The other alternative—regarding fictionality as rooted in narrativity—is much more in tune with the account presented in chapter 1. According to the theory of recentering, fictional discourse must project a universe structured as a modal system. For the relocation of the speaker to take place, the text must assert or imply the existence of an actual world. This world is established by means of what I have called in chapter 1 mimetic statements: utterance acts making singular existential claims, stating facts rather than opinions, proposing an image of a world existing independently from the discourse that describes it, and meant to be valued as either true or false in this world. The ability to project a universe centered around an actual world is also constitutive of the narrative text. Being narrative means: bringing a universe to life, and conveying to the reader the sense that at the center of this universe resides an actual world where individuals exist and where events take place. Narrative, like fiction, is supported by truth-functional mimetic statements. Both are rooted in the declaration: once upon a time there was an x, such that f(x). In narrative, this statement may be uttered either from AW or from the actual world of a recentered system; but in fiction, recentering is mandatory.

The narrative potential inherent to fiction is not necessarily realized as a complete plot-structure of the type described in chapter 10. In order to be narrative, a text must not only project an actual world, it must also place this world in history. Many mimetic texts ignore the temporal dimension of their referent. An example of nonnarrative mimetic discourse would be the achronic description of a primitive culture. This lack of temporal dimension is rare, but possible in a fiction: Borges's "Tlön, Uqbar, Orbis, Tertius" is a nonnarrative treatise describing an imaginary civilization. But through its core of mimetic statements, the text creates the scene of a potential story, thus laying down the logical foundations of narrativity. Some fictions may lack events, and perhaps even characters, but all present a concrete setting.

It could be objected that according to the pretense account of chapter 4, the transaction between the substitute speaker and the substitute hearer is not restricted to mimetic discourse. If every speech act that can be performed in actuality can also be performed in make-believe, there should exist radically nonnarrative fictions. Nabokov's *Pale Fire* and Lindenberger's *Saul's Fall* reveal the possibility of fictional criticism and of fictional scholarly editions of fictional literary texts. These two works happen to be pervaded by narrative elements—a whole story is told in the footnotes to Shade's poem in *Pale Fire*—but their existence suggests that a fiction could be pure expression of ideas. Plato's dialogues, which my definition accepts as a borderline case of fiction, are indeed dominated by universal statements and discussion of abstract concepts. But even philosophical dialogues include singular existential statements and ascription of properties to individuals. Consider the beginning of two of Plato's dialogues:

ECHECRATES: Were you there yourself, Phaidon, with Socrates, on the day when he took the poison in prison, or did you hear about it from someone?

PHAIDON: I was there myself, Echecrates. (*Phaidon*, Rouse 1956:460)

SOCRATES: Good morning, Ion. Where have you now come from your travels? From home, from Ephesus?

ION: Oh no, Socrates, from Epidauros; I have been at the feast of Asclepios. (*Ion*, Rouse 1956:13)

What if the dialogue avoided any kind of reference to particular events and concrete circumstances (the death of Socrates, the travels of Ion), and concentrated exclusively on such topics as the immortality of the soul, essences, truth, the nature of language, and the ideal political system? Would this be fiction in a pure form, freed at last from any narrative element? My reply to this suggestion is that the embryonic narrativity of the text does not depend on the particular contents of the dialogue. A world is established and populated with individuals through the mere mention of names, followed by an attribution of speech: SOCRATES: " . . . "; ION: " . . . " The text cannot give up this last narrative element without giving up the doubling of the I which constitutes its claim to fictionality.

If fiction is indeed rooted in a narrative soil, some considerations on the nature of narrativity should provide a suitable pendant to the definition of fictionality which launched this journey into textual space. The question of the nature—or ontological status—of narrative bears crucial implications for the validity of the classical distinction between story and discourse, which I have so far accepted uncritically.

The distinction story/discourse is supported by two arguments. The first is that the two levels may contain different information, or present information in a different order. Discourse may delete some of the constituents of story, or disrupt their chronological order. The other argument is that the "same story" can be told in a novel, filmed as a movie, acted out on stage, illustrated in a painting, or danced in a ballet (cf. Bremond 1973). From this observation Chatman concludes that narratives are "structures independent of any medium" (1978:20).

The dichotomy has encountered a variety of objections. Jonathan Culler maintains that "the distinction between story and discourse can function only if there is a determination of one by the other" (1981:186). This determination is assumed to go from story to discourse. Endorsing a definition of story as "the set of events in their chronological order, their spatial location, and their relations with the actors who cause or undergo them" (originally proposed by Mieke Bal), Culler discusses several examples of narratives in which events are introduced into the story in order to fulfill the communicative demands of discourse, rather than functioning as source of this discourse. The thesis of a one-way determination of discourse by story is easily dismissed in the case of fiction, since events do not exist independently of the narrative discourse (except, of course, in make-believe), but it will only receive a fatal blow if it is attacked in its stronghold: nonfictional narratives, in which events are displayed to the audience as predating their representation. Culler's demonstration invokes as evidence narratives of personal experience. In Labov's analysis, these texts include two types of statements: narrative clauses reporting events, and evaluative clauses through which the narrator comments upon these events. The former outline the story, the latter are produced by discourse requirements. Labov mentions, however, some narratives of personal experience in which evaluative comments are attributed to the participants and become events in the story. Rather than commenting: "This was a dangerous situation. He could have killed me" a narrator may say "Oh no, I thought, he's gonna kill me!" According to Culler, the reversibility of the determination between story and discourse confronts narratology with an unsolvable dilemma: "The analyst must always choose which [between story and discourse] will be treated as the given and which as the product. Yet either choice leads to a narratology that misses some of the curious complexity of narratives and fails to account for much of their impact" (186).

Culler's examples offer convincing evidence in favor of a bidirectional determination between story and discourse, but why should this phenomenon be detrimental to the distinction, and constitute a serious problem to narratology? It could be argued, on the contrary, that the possibility of a double perspective enriches the discipline. A one-way determination of discourse by story would only be essential to the functioning of the dichotomy if the task of narratology were to develop a reversible algorithm, through which narrative discourse could be derived from facts of TRW, and vice versa, facts of TRW inferred from narrative discourse. Such an algorithm would fail in the case of the Labov example: assuming that the narrator did not actually think "Oh no, he's gonna kill me," this event would be put into the text during the generative phase leading from the facts to the discourse—triggered, presumably, by communicative considerations. This information would not be deleted during the interpretive phase leading from discourse to facts, since it is positively asserted by the text. The end result would differ from the point of departure, and the verification of the algorithm would fail. The concern of narratology is not, however, with the facts of TRW, but with their representation in TAW and its surrounding universe. It does not matter to the analyst whether or not the narrator really thought "Oh no, he's gonna kill me." What matters is what the text presents as fact—and the thought is clearly one of the events in TAW. Whether or not the hearer accepts this information as fact in TRW stands outside the concern of narratology.

Culler's argument may call into question the possibility of establishing a clear-cut borderline between story and discourse, but insofar as it takes its point of departure in an explicit and stable definition of story, it affirms the validity of the concept as an autonomous level of signification. But the particular definition chosen is a simplistic one. In Culler's discussion of a Freudian narrative, the case of the Wolfman, story, or rather, plot is reduced to a string of actual events. The issue at stake is whether the neurosis of the Wolfman was caused by his witnessing of his parents' copulation at age one-and-a-half, or whether this event was fantasized by the patient at age four in an effort to explain his neurosis. In this case, writes Culler, "the structures of signification, the discursive requirements, work to produce a fictional or tropological event" (180). (Note the referential use of the term "fictional.") For Culler, this "fictional" event is not part of the plot: "From the point of view of narratology, and also from the point of view of the engaged reader, the difference between an event of the plot and an imaginary event is irreducible" (181). For the model of narrative defended in this book, by contrast, a virtual event inscribed in a private domain is of course as much part of the plot as one asserted as fact. The case of the Wolfman is simply an ambiguous text, compatible with two distinct plots: one in which the primal scene occurs in TAW and causes the neurosis of the hero, another in which the primal scene occurs in his K-world as an effect of the neurosis.

A more sophisticated conception of story than the definition adopted by Culler opens the door to a much more radical questioning of the dichotomy story/discourse. As Hayden White argues, a group of events listed in chronological order does not necessarily have a plot and may not form a story. A case in point is the *Annals of Saint Gall*:

709. Hard winter. Duke Gottfried died.
710. Hard year and deficient in crops.
711.
712. Flood everywhere.
713.

"Although this text is 'referential' and contains a representation of reality," writes White, "it possesses none of the attributes that we normally think of as a story: no central subject, no well-marked beginning, middle, and end, no peripeteia, and no identifiable narrative voice" (1980a:7). In a fully developed narrative of historical events, argues White, plot is not "found" in the events, but "put" into them by "narrative techniques" (20). This argument is supported to some extent by the famous example of novelist E. M. Forster. "The king died, then the queen died" is a plotless chronicle, but the same pair of physical events can be built into narrative form by connecting them through causal relations. The missing link in the causal chain is provided by an inferred mental event: "The king died, then the queen died of grief."

The nonnarrativity of some chronological reports of events leads Thomas Leitch to the following position:

> If we decide that only the nature of the discourse itself determines whether or not a given sequence of events is a story, then story itself becomes a discursive product, not a presumed anterior or prediscursive set of events. The conclusion is inescapable: since there is no way of distinguishing between stories and nonstories without reference to the discourse which presents them, story is indeed a discursive category. (1986:16)

This absorption of story by its former opposite leaves unclear, however, what is meant by discourse. In his *Dictionary of Narratology*, Gerald Prince distinguishes two aspects of discourse: the substance and the form. Substance is the medium of manifestation (language, still or moving pictures, gestures), while form is the connected set of narrative statements that states the story and determines such parameters as order of presentation, point of view or speed of narration (1987:21). Which one of these aspects does Leitch have in mind when he assimilates story to "a discursive category"? If discourse were simply the medium of expression in its physical manifestation, the argument would be based on a truism: it is obvious that we cannot decide whether or not a message is a story without looking at the material signs which transmit this message. But the truism would be built into fallacy, since the message (story) remains semiotically distinct from the material signs which transmit it (discourse). For the argument to retain validity, then, discourse must be conceived as form.

The alternative to discourse as medium of expression is discourse as the configuring mental activity that spins tales out of events. Discourse in this case would be synonymous with narrative structuring. Culler seems to tend toward this position when he equates "structures of [narrative] signification" with "discourse requirements." I object to this assimilation on the ground that it obscures the distinction between two types of motivation. Adding "of grief" to the sequence "The king died, then the queen died" turns a chronicle into a story and fulfills the requirements of narrative signification. On the other hand, adding to a story an evaluative event such as

"Oh no, I thought, he's gonna kill me" satisfies a demand for efficient communication, this is to say, a rhetorical requirement. The same type of motivation underlies those discourse strategies that leave the story intact, such as reordering and topicalizing events, emphasizing the point, summarizing or expanding a scene, setting a narrative pace, or adopting a point of view. Discursive strategies do not make a message narrative, they make an already narrative message more appealing to the audience. "The demands of discourse" are in essence rhetorical, while narrative requirements are strictly semantic ones. The claim that story is a "discursive category" involves a confusion of semantics and rhetoric.

The main source of resistance to the dichotomy story/discourse resides in the implicit belief that the absorption of story by discourse offers the only alternative to the widely discredited doctrine of an inherently narrative reality. This belief entails, however, a reductive view of language. As a type of semantic structure, story or plot is a signified, not a referent. Reality, on the other hand, is a referent and not a signified. Claiming that a distinction between story and discourse locates story in reality constitutes another case of an inability to distinguish TAW from TRW. This confusion reduces language from a triple relation between signifier, signified, and referent to a binary relation between sign and referent.

Within a model of signification involving three parameters, the concept variably labeled story, plot, fabula, or narrative structure becomes a mental representation functioning, in the terms of Louis O. Mink, as a "form of human comprehension" (1978:132). As such it is distinct from both the material signs that communicate it, and the world it is supposed to represent. In this perspective, plot is not a property "put into events by narrative techniques" (to paraphrase again White's expression), but rather, an interpretive model built by the mind as it tries to understand events—whether real or imaginary. "Narrative," writes Jon-K. Adams, "is an act of explanation: the narrator picks out and links together past [or imaginary] events in order to explain or account for what happened" (1989:149). Paul Ricoeur observes that "mise en intrigue" (literally, "putting-into-plot-shape") is a "configuring act" (1982:102). "A story should be more than an enumeration of events in serial order, it should organize these events as an intelligible totality, so as to make it always possible to ask: what is the theme of the story" (102, my translation). Peter Brooks echoes: "Narrative is one of the large categories or systems of understanding that we use in our negotiations with reality, specifically, in the case of narrative, with the problem of temporality." "Plot as I conceive it is the design and intention of narrative, what shapes a story and gives it a certain direction or intent of meaning" (1985:ix).

This view of narrativity as condition of intelligibility for time-bound phenomena is fully supported by the formal model of plot proposed in chapter 10. Within the semantic universe of the text, the model distinguishes a raw historical sequence, consisting of all the physical states and events in their chronological order, and a rationalized sequence, in which information is integrated into the graph according to the rules of concatenation. These rules define the conditions of narrativity. In the rationalized sequence, the events of the factual domain are made intelligible by the relations which tie them to mental events located in the private domains of the participants, as well as by the relations of material causality which link them to each other. Since mental events and logical relations are not directly observable, but always inferred to some degree, the rationalized sequence is a mental construct, not part of empirical reality. The rationalized sequence is the plot of the text, and a text is narrative to the extent that it invites its reader to interpret it by organizing its contents in a narrative network. It does not really matter whether or not the connected graph is explicitly represented; in fact it never is entirely. A mere enumeration of physical events, without statements of mental events nor of logical connections, can be read as a narrative text if the reader is able to supply the missing links and nodes.

As a cognitive category, narrativity does not require the presence of narrative discourse to be operative. Among the utterances we interpret narratively, some do not fulfill Gerald Prince's definition of "narrating": "the telling or relating of one or more events" (1987:57). In a dramatic performance, the story is not told by a narrator (unless there is a chorus), but lived by the characters and simulated by the actors. The plot is read by the spectator into the gestures and utterances observed on stage in an attempt to rationalize the behavior of the characters. The same interpretive activity may be performed on data from real life. Just as we read a plot into a play, we may form a story out of private experiences or out of personally recorded observations. There is no act of narration in the conversation quoted below, yet Umberto Eco suggests that an intercepter may derive from it at least the beginning of a narrative message:

> Paul: Where's Peter?
> Mary: Out.
> Paul: I see. I thought he was still sleeping.

"From this text," writes Eco, "one can extrapolate a story telling that (i) in the world of Paul's and Mary's knowledge . . . there is a certain Peter; (ii) Paul believed p (= Peter is still sleeping) while Mary assumed she knew q (= Peter is out); (iii) Mary informed Paul about q and Paul did not believe any longer that p was the case and presumed to know that q was the case" (1979:29).

The possibility of extrapolating narrative structures from both narrative and nonnarrative discourse suggests two modes of narrativity: literal and figural. Unlike its literal counterpart, figural narrativity requires neither representation of physical events, nor even singular existential statements. The characters of a figural narrative may be derived through allegorization of abstract ideas or individuation of generic concepts, and its events are inferred from variations in the properties ascribed to the entities selected as characters. This phenomenon of figural narrativity justifies an epic reading of Hegel's *Reason in History* ("The Adventures and Ruses of Reason"), or efforts to find a dramatic development in the fragment "Ithaca" of *Ulysses*.

The occurrence of a figural type of narrativity supports the thesis of the independence of narrative structures from any particular semiotic manifestation. Plots are detected in visual, verbal, even musical messages; their network interprets either communicative objects ("texts") or data acquired through life experience. But the doctrine of the medium-free status of stories is relativized by the case of literal narrativity. Plots may be suggested by various media, but only language can express the logical relations and the private worlds which hold together their semantic network. The ability of pictures—whether still or moving—to make propositional acts and existential statements has long been a subject of debate among philosophers. Even if one admits that showing on a screen, stage, or canvas an object x with a property p counts as asserting "there is an x which has p," there is no visual way to assign a modal operator to this proposition. Nonverbal media are extremely limited in their ability to express the difference between actuality and virtuality. As Shlomith Rimmon-Kenan argues: "The indeterminacy and abstract nature of language . . . renders literature more amenable [than theatre or cinema] to the representation of dreams, hallucinations, and the like" (1989:162). In cinema and theatre, shifts from TAW to TAPWs may be suggested by conventionalized techniques such as dim lights, fade-offs, or the superposition of two pictures, one showing a character in TAW, the other the contents of her mind. But these rudimentary techniques allow rather limited travel in the semantic universe. The only domain fully accessible to nonverbal communication is the central world of a system. Since nonverbal media cannot express modalities, they impart an implicit existence to whatever they represent. Language is unique among semiotic codes in its ability to assign propositions to private domains, to express the forking paths of plans and projections, to represent possible worlds in their alterity, to state what motivates agents, and even to express causal relations. Literal narrativity does not necessitate the representation of the entire semantic network of plot, but it requires the explicit expression of a core of propositions from which the network can be derived. In all but the most rudimentary narratives, only language can transmit enough of this information to make the plot accessible. From the orchestral *Peter and the Wolf* to the ballet *Cinderella*, most of the cases invoked by narratologists as evidence of the medium-free nature of story are really illustrations of already familiar plots. It is the spectator's acquaintance with a textual version of *Peter and the Wolf* or of *Cinderella* which enables him or her to read these plots into the acoustic or visual data. As A. Kibédi Varga observes: "The image is not a second way of *telling* the tale, but only a way of *evoking* it" (1988:204).

As an interpretive structure, narrativity is not a discrete category like fictionality but a model admitting various degrees of realization. It is fully represented and aesthetically dominant in those popular narrative genres which we read for the sake of plot: soap operas, comedies, fairy tales, romances, and detective stories. It competes with other layers of meaning but is still integrally realized in the classical novels of the nineteenth and early twentieth century. It may be figuratively represented in lyric poetry: a tempting way of making sense of an obscure poem is to look for a narrative scheme, even though the text does not make the existential claims necessary to literal narrativity. It is embedded in a largely plotless chronicle in such genres as family saga, (auto)biography, personal diary, and novels following the destiny of a main character: telling a life is not only the enumeration of the events which mark this life—a largely plotless sequence—but the narration of the stories that crystallize around some of these events. And finally, narrativity is exploded and fragmented in the collages of the postmodern novel: underlying the text is a proliferation of incomplete narrative graphs which tease the reader with the promise of an intelligibility never to be achieved. This promise and withdrawal should not be regarded as a new narrative form, but as the expression of a fundamentally *anti*-narrative stance: the rejection of plot as principle of textual unification. The evolution of what is called novel in postmodern literature does not affect the basic conditions of narrativity; it simply turns narrativity into an optional ingredient of the genre. As a construction kit, narrativity produces plots in many shapes, even incomplete fragments, but the kit itself, in its repertory of basic elements and specifications for connecting these elements, transcends the boundaries of time, culture, and genre.

Notes

1. Fictional Recentering

1. The rare case of a textual universe without modal structure will be discussed in chapter 8. In such a universe, all worlds are equally actual, and there is no hierarchy actual/nonactual within the components of the system. The prototypical case of a nonmodal textual universe is the universe of a novel that was never written: the work of Ts'ui Pen, as described in "The Garden of Forking Paths" by Jorge Luis Borges.

2. This definition is inspired by Martínez-Bonati's concept of apophantic sentences: " 'Apophantic sentence' seems . . . the best designation for sentences that assert states of affairs or circumstances as being facts, and are either true or false with respect to what is the case" (1981:25). For Martínez-Bonati, apophantic sentences are a subclass of mimetic utterances; the broader category of mimetic utterances also includes subjective opinions. My own definition of mimetic discourse excludes opinions ("the conduct of Emma Bovary is despicable"), universal statements ("all men are mortal"), and statements about abstract entities ("the soul is immortal"). It is consequently equivalent to what Martínez-Bonati calls singular apophantic sentences." Also among types of discourse I regard as nonmimetic are commands and performative utterances. Most texts are mixtures of mimetic and nonmimetic statements; yet one kind is usually ancillary to the other. Thus in philosophical works, mimetic statements stating individual facts are subordinated to universal claims. In literary fiction, on the other hand, universal and evaluative statements ("All happy families") interpret the facts established by mimetic statements, but it is the mimetic statements which form the core of the discourse.

3. While this fusion of TAW and TRW appears to corroborate the doctrine of the self-referentiality of the literary text (to the extent, of course, that literature is fictional), it does not support the most radical version of the doctrine, which claims that literary language can only be about itself. According to the radical interpretation, there is no room for the construct of an external reference world, not even for a make-believe one. The literary text mirrors itself as text, much in the same way the famous paradox "This sentence is false" refers to itself as sentence. I do not deny the possibility for literary language to make statements about itself (the philosophical paradox shows indeed that this option is open to nonliterary language as well), but I reject the view that literary language is *necessarily*, *exclusively*, and *literally* self-referential.

4. In the absence of a constraint preventing a minus in the second and third column, the combination $+ - - -$ becomes theoretically legal. It could be interpreted as an unreliable act of fictional narration projecting a world compatible with AW, yet felt by the reader to misrepresent TRW. Needless to say, I am unable to come up with a concrete example of this purely theoretical possibility.

2. Possible Worlds and Accessibility Relations

1. One could think of an inverse relation of compatibility, by which TAW's inventory would be a subset of AW's inventory, or intersect with it, but this relation is not productive in the semantics of fiction because it contradicts the principle of minimal departure (to be exposed in chapter 3). If TAW has France, by a law of geographic solidarity it must have Paris, even if Paris is not mentioned; if it has Napoleon, its inventory implicitly comprises all the individuals who ever lived in AW. Assuming the exclusion of any given real-world entity from TAW without specific textual directives would amount to postulating a gratuitous—and therefore less than minimal—departure from AW. For the departure to be nongratuitous, the exclusion would have to be made explicit by the text. How can this be done? One way to establish the absence from TAW of a specific entity would be to assert the fact plainly: "The scene of the story is France, but there is no Paris in this France." But this statement would constitute a metafictional comment, spoken from the perspective of AW and breaking the fictional game. Another way would be through a paradox, such as having a character exclaim "France would be so much nicer if Paris existed [as it does in AW]." Here again, the device involves an ambiguous stance with respect to AW and TAW. To remain strictly within TAW, the characters could travel to the exact location of a real-world city—as determined by unique geographic features, such as the confluence of two well-known rivers—and see nothing but forests and fields. I cannot think of an analogous device to exclude real-world individuals.

2. If two systems have identical actual worlds they are identical as a whole, since their APWs originate in actual mental events. If their APWs differed, so would the mental acts, and so would their actual worlds.

3. Reconstructing the Textual Universe

1. I first stated the principle in Ryan 1980. In a paper published in 1981, Peter Rabinowitz arrives at a very similar principle, without using the conceptual framework of possible world semantics: a "basic rule of reading" is that "all fiction, even the most fantastic, is realistic except when it signals to the contrary" (1981:342 [abstract]). For a further discussion of minimal departure, see Pavel 1986.

2. The postulation of counterpart relations between inhabitants of different possible worlds raises the question of a distinction between essential and accidental properties. It is highly doubtful that a dog called Napoleon in a novel or a counterfactual statement could pass as possessing the identity of the emperor, because it would lack the essential property of being human. We can hardly complete the expression "If Napoleon had been a dog" in a meaningful way, and a novelist could hardly convince his reader that in TAW, the emperor is a dog. But if only accidental properties are altered, the lines of transworld identity will not be severed. We may complete the expression "If Napoleon . . . " with virtually any proposition that can be made of a human being (even with " . . . had been a woman"), as long as it does not entail "If Napoleon had not been himself," which is a contradiction.

That individuals inhabiting different worlds, and possessing somewhat different properties, can be referred to by means of the same name has important implications for the semantics of proper names. To account for this fact, proponents of model theory (as the theory of possible worlds is known among logicians) reject the thesis that proper names stand for clusters of descriptions (a position proposed by Frege and Wittgenstein and defended by Searle—see Kripke's discussion [1972]), and endorse instead Saul Kripke's proposal, the "causal theory of names." (See Pavel 1986 for an application to the question of fictionality.) According to the causal theory, a name is a "rigid designator" attached to a certain individual—or rather, to the set of all the counterparts of a certain individual in all possible worlds—through an original act of baptism. As rigid designators, names refer to individuals regardless of the changes in properties these individuals might undergo. Since the function of names in model theory is to pick out one and only one individual in a given possible world (though not necessarily one in all possible worlds: worlds may be characterized by the absence of certain individuals), the causal theory precludes the existence of namesakes. Names are unique, original labels, and they designate as unambiguously as social security numbers.

4. Voices and Worlds

1. The case of "Funes the Memorious" has shown that self-impersonation is also available to fiction, but as we have seen in chapter 3 the counterpart relation between the textual I and the real I has to be artificially induced through the use of a proper name, whereas in the verbal play of oral communication it is spontaneously inferred. In fictional self-impersonation, the author steps into his own alter ego as if it were a foreign identity.

2. Another discourse strategy widely considered to be specific to fiction is the practice of presenting new information as if it had already been introduced. A text beginning with the sentence "The little girl sat crying on the stairs, holding a broken toy" is likely to be a novel or short story. Nowadays, however, this practice is more and more common in journalistic writing. The emergence of the genre of true fiction has resulted in a general blurring of the stylistic and pragmatic distinctions between fiction and nonfiction. An example of a fiction-connoting discourse strategy in a nonfictional text is this sentence, which begins a chapter of Simon Schama's *Citizens: A Chronicle of the French Revolution*: "One morning in August 1776, a rather shabbily dressed, stout gentleman stood on the dockside at Rotterdam. Puffing on a pipe, his tricorn hat planted carelessly over a perruque that had seen better days, he watched intently the slow progress of timber barges as they sailed down in the direction of Dordrecht." (Schama 1989:96). What authorizes the historian to state as fact the content of the perceptions of Chrétien-Guillaume de Malesherbes on the day in question? The next sentence holds the answer: "In his journal he described [this perfectly ordinary scene] as 'one of the most singular spectacles that I have seen in my whole life.' " The historian has appropriated the private thoughts presented in the journal, and presented them as if he had access to them though narratorial omniscience.

3. The implied speaker may in fact be divided into a pair of entities: the semantically implied speaker, who endorses the literal meaning of the uttered discourse, and the pragmatically implied speaker, who transmits the transformed meaning of ironic and figural language.

4. In modern and postmodern literature, the challenge of traditional narrative forms may take the form of a refusal to choose between personal narration subjected to the constraints of natural communication, and unconstrained anonymous narration. The following strategies enable the text to combine the properties of the two types of narration:

(1) Weakly individuated speakers who gradually turn into impersonal omniscient narrators (Flaubert, *Madame Bovary*); and strongly individuated ones who intermittently "hide" behind omniscient narrators and then show up again (Proust, *A la recherche du temps perdu*);

(2) Exploded, dispersed, or schizoid narrators speaking through many voices and manifesting what Uri Margolin calls the "disintegration of the full and unified Cartesian subject" (1986a:184): *The Unnameable* by Samuel Beckett. An extreme case of the disintegrated subject is what Margolin calls the "voided subject": "The 'I'

expression occurring in the discourse is now no longer even speaker indicative" (187). Margolin's examples of this case are Beckett's *Textes pour rien, Comment c'est,* and *Company.*

(3) Texts narrated by supernatural beings: Günter Grass, *The Flounder.*

See Margolin 1986a for a wide-ranging coverage of the "adventures of the I" in modern fiction.

5. This rule is inspired from and partly equivalent to Gregory Currie's definition of fictional utterances (U below is the utterer, O a variable ranging over characteristics of persons, and P a proposition):

U performs the illocutionary act of uttering fiction in uttering P if and only if

There exists O such that U utters P intending that anyone who were to have O

(1) would make-believe P;

(2) would recognize U's intension of (1);

(3) would have (2) as a reason for doing (1). (1985:387)

The difference between my definition and Currie's is that Currie regards fiction as "a speech act on a par with assertion," indeed as an alternative to regular assertion, while I view it as a meta-speech act, or illocutionary modality, embedding any type of speech act. Currie's first rule suggests that every proposition p encountered in a fiction is make-believedly asserted for TRW, and should be used as material for its reconstruction. But as the case of unreliable narration suggests, not all assertions found in fiction yield truths for the fictional universe. What the reader is urged to make-believe is not necessarily the fact that p obtains in the fictional universe, but the fact that a speech act with propositional content p was accomplished by a member of TRW. The reader does indeed use all the statements of the narrator in "make-believing" the fictional universe, but without systematically accepting every one of them.

The purpose of Currie's rules (2) and (3) is to make the model compatible with Grice's definition of meaning. Such rules could be easily added to proposal 4.

5. The Fiction Automaton

1. This principle does not apply to narrative poetry, nor to nonsense rhymes. For the nonsense to be felt as such, the text must be understood as making existential claims about an actual world. Its assertions must be interpreted literally and not figuratively. The "obscure light" of baroque poetry is only a way of speaking about religious experience, but the old young man of the French rhyme exists objectively in TRW. Nonsense poetry, because of this literal dimension, does create an autonomous system of reality, and does satisfy the requirements of the fictional analysis.

2. Another literary theorist who regards lyric poetry as the nonfictional expression of an inner vision is Käthe Hamburger (1968:220): "Wir erleben das lyrische Aussagesubjekt, und nichts als dieses. Wir gehen nicht über sein Erlebnisfeld hinaus, in das es uns bannt. Dies aber besagt, das wir die lyrische Aussage als Wirklichkeitsaussage erleben, die Aussage eines echten Aussagesubjekts, die auf nichts anderes bezogen werden kann als eben auf dieses selbst" (1968:220). [Approximative translation: We experience the lyrical subject of enunciation, and nothing but this subject. We do not go beyond the field of personal experience in which he draws us. This means that we experience the lyrical utterance as an utterance about reality, as a discourse uttered by a true subject, and expressing nothing but this subject.]

3. An apparent exception to this observation is the case of an actor. But an actor is not a storyteller. As Aristotle observed, the actor's mode of presentation is mimetic, while the storyteller's discourse is mainly diegetic.

4. This effect is possible when tall tales are told in an informal context, such as exchanging stories around the campfire, but not when they become part of an institutionalized event, such as the annual tall tale contest in Yellow Knife.

5. Gregory Currie discusses a similar case of retrospective assessment of fictionality in a written text: "David Lewis has drawn my attention to the following interesting case. Kingsley Amis has a short story, entitled 'Who or what was it?' in which he begins by saying that he is going to recount certain events which happened to him and to Elizabeth Jane Howard, his wife. At first one is enclined to believe that this is a piece of autobiography, but it becomes increasingly clear that what we are being offered is a fictional story of the supernatural. Amis is playing with his audience; revealing his fictional intent only late in the piece" (1985:389).

It could be argued that the title of the collection, *Collected Short Stories* (1983), exposes right away the fictional intent. But it is interesting to notice that the story was originally given as a radio broadcast by the author, where the title did not interfere with the initial illusion of reference to AW.

6. This possibility is realized in Herbert Lindenberger's *Saul's Fall*: the book is the critical edition, by an imaginary professor acting as substitute speaker, of a fictional play.

7. A different analysis of the problem of metafiction is proposed by Tamar Yacobi (1987). Whereas I postulate a role-switching and a stepping in-and-out of worlds on the part of the speaker, Yacobi distinguishes two logical types of narrator: those who commit themselves to the factuality of the tale, and those who present themselves as the creator of the narrative world (or universe, in the present terminology). The narrator of *The French Lieutenant's Woman* belongs to this second category, together with the Scheherazade of *The Arabian Nights* who "frankly spins her tales for the Caliph's entertainment" (361), and the narrator of Gide's *Counterfeiters* who openly wonders what to do with some of the minor characters of the novel. In the present account of fictionality, telling the story as true fact is essential to the narrative act—whether fictional or not—and there is only one logical type of narrator. If the narrators of fictional stories could tell their tales as invention, there would be no need to distinguish them from the author. Whereas for Yacobi it is the same speaker who asserts in *The French Lieutenant's Woman* "He [Charles] took the path formerly used by Sarah" (192) and "These characters I create never existed outside my own imagination" (80), for me they are separated by an ontological gap, and only the speaker of the first sentence is internal to the narrative universe (though both, of course, belong to the global semantic domain of the text). As for Scheherazade, she may spin invented tales for the caliph in the world of the framing tale of *The Arabian Nights*, but as soon as she utters "Once upon a time," she steps into a new system of reality, where she trades her identity for the role of impersonal narrator. Since Yacobi would regard the narrator of the framing tale as committed to factuality, her distinction between two types of narrators obscures the parallelism in the relations author of *The Arabian Nights*/narrator of the framing tale and Scheherazade/narrator of "Ali Baba." By regarding Scheherazade herself as narrator, Yacobi denies ultimately the recursivity of the fictional relocation.

8. The painting may suggest that the unicorn is an image, not a real object, by picturing it as a picture in a frame, but in this case the primary referent is the picture of the unicorn, and this picture is itself presented as a real object.

9. While this parallelism assimilates the quoter to the author, and the quotee to the narrator, there is also an inverse relation quoter/narrator and quotee/author. As

Uri Margolin observes: "If we now look at the *narrator* of a FPN (first person narration] and imagine him as an individual existing in some alternate, non-actual world, then we realize that his speech about himself comes from outside of himself, and he is a mere quoter or repeater of the first-person speech of another/author about him" (1986a:205). Author and quotee are free to invent discourse, while narrator and quoter must reproduce the discourse of another speaker.

6. The Modal Structure of Narrative Universes

1. If the narrator were individuated, the proposition "x [narrator] thinks that all happy families are happy in the same way" would yield a fact for the narrative universe. But in impersonal narration, the statement cannot be attributed to the belief world of a particular member of TAW, nor can it be regarded as an absolute fact in TAW.

2. Another temporal interpretation of possibility and necessity is evitability and inevitability. Given a tree of the future developments allowed by the physical laws of a world, a state or event is temporally necessary if it occurs on all the branches, possible if it occurs on some of them, and impossible if it is excluded from all branches.

7. The Dynamics of Plot

1. Another respect in which figure 13 appears semantically overspecified is the temporal indexing of states and events. This indexing system reflects the logical assumption that every state and event occupies a certain point in the history of the narrative universe. But the absolute dating of events is usually not important to the reader. What matters is the relative ordering of states and events (captured by the series t0 . . . tn). When a narrative presents several parallel sequences concerning different characters, however, the serial indexing becomes too specific. Imagine a narrative that recounts the life of John until he meets Mary, then move back to recount the life of Mary up to the meeting. The states and events in both Mary's and John's life can be ordered with respect to each other in self-contained subhistories, but the narrative may not allow the reconstruction of a global chronological sequence encompassing both of these narrative lines. From a cognitive point of view, parallel narratives are more efficiently modeled by a diagram in which all the lines in the plot are separately indexed, so that t1 in Mary's life is not necessarily simultaneous with t1 in John's life.

2. The distinction actions/happenings is not as clear-cut, however, as the criterion of intentionality suggests. Within unplanned events, a distinction can be made between purely accidental happenings, events resulting from the coincidence of an intent-driven action and an accidental happening, and events resulting from the miscalculation of an agent. If Francesca tries to shoot Romeo, but she is pushed as she pulls the trigger, and she kills Alessandro instead, the event "Francesca shoots" is an intent-driven action, "Francesca is pushed" an accidental happening, and the event "Alessandro dies" an event of hybrid intentional/accidental origin. If Francesca deliberately aims at Alessandro, believing he is Romeo, the unplanned event "Alessandro dies" is entirely caused by Francesca's intent to kill Romeo, though it does not fulfill this intent.

3. The ordering of events in figure 16 is not the only one possible. The relations of presupposition on plan 4 indicate that the sequence "sleeping with Sonny"–

"breaking up with Duane" must follow the move "sleeping with Duane" and pre-cede "going to SMU," but they may either precede or follow "sleeping with Bobby." Instead of 1-2-3-4-5-6-7 there could be 1-2-5-3-4-6-7.

8. Virtuality and Tellability

1. Reversals of fortune are not only an important factor in narrative tellability, they also play a central role in what may be called the "poetics" of sporting events: a good script—or plot—for a game involves several changes in the lead, and the greater the deficit that is finally made up, the more aesthetically satisfying the out-come of the game.

2. This use of the term "embedded narrative" is idiosyncratic. For most nar-ratologists, embedded narratives are the stories told by characters. (cf. Bal 1985 or Chambers 1984). My own concept requires no speech act, no verbalization: an em-bedded narrative is simply a mental representation involving a temporal dimension, and presenting therefore the same semantic structure as the story of which it is a part.

3. There is actually a slight difference between the plan of the crow and the plan attributed to the fox, since the fox pretends to be interested in any answer to the question "can the crow sing," while the crow wants this answer to be positive. But the fulfillment of the plan of the crow presupposes the fulfillment of the fake plan of the fox. Hence, the divergence does not make a significant contribution to the diver-sification of the narrative universe.

4. This situation contrasts with the case of *The French Lieutenant's Woman*: whereas the passage from *Jacques le Fataliste* suggests a semantic domain composed of numerous universes, each of which respects the modal structure, *The French Lieuten-ant's Woman* projects a single universe in which the modal structure is subverted by competing actual worlds.

5. Note that Eco does not include in this ghost chapter a branch in which both letters are false. In this situation, the Pirogue would not be Marguerite, the Templar would not be Raoul, and the individuals disguised as Pirogue and Templar would not expect their partner to be Raoul or Marguerite. At this point in the text, however, nothing precludes this possibility. Why should the ghost chapter exclude this possi-ble inference, when it includes the incorrect inference of branch (c)?

6. Eco considers this possible explanation, but rejects it as cheap: "This sounds repugnant to our sense of narrative etiquette" (1978:67). The self-deconstructing interpretation is much more appealing to the contemporary taste! His main argu-ment against the rational version of ghost chapter 3 is that the text has never as-serted the existence of the lovers. It is therefore illegal to introduce them into TAW. But if the text never states as fact that there is in TAW an x-mistress of Raoul and a y-lover of Marguerite, it certainly raises the question of their existence. Contrary to what Eco claims, the text gives clues to a liaison, and the revised version of ghost chapter 3 does nothing more than develop suggestions immanent to the text. In my opinion, there is no valid textual reason to exclude the rational explanation.

7. This argument is inspired by Culler's discussion of Bremond's narrative model in *Structuralist Poetics* (1975:211).

9. Stacks, Frames, and Boundaries

1. The illocutionay boundary does not always coincide with the textual bound-ary of the story. If a speaker in a conversation narrates an anecdote, after some preliminary statements, the illocutionary boundary is crossed when the speaker

takes the floor, but the textual universe only comes into being when the story begins. I assume here that the illocutionary crossing is completed when the speaker has both taken the floor and set up the textual universe as an autonomous context, separable from the previous topics of the exchange. I recognize, however, a microlevel illocutionary boundary crossing, which occurs in a text—or in a conversation—at every turn of a dialogue. See Young (1987) on the question of delineating a narrative textual universe—what she calls a Taleworld—during the course of a conversation.

2. HISTORY OF THE WORLD functions like the operating system of a computer: it runs all the programs, and it remains active until the system crashes.

3. My checking of *The Arabian Nights* to see how the text resolves this paradox provided no clue to an answer: the two editions I consulted (translations by Burton and by Madras) have different stories for the 602d night, and none of them has to do with Scheherazade and the Sultan.

10. The Formal Representation of Plot

1. Such proofs do, however, exist for other types of languages, for instance for the language formed by all the strings containing three sequences of equal length of three different symbols, where the sequences can be of any length (i.e. abc, aabbcc, aaabbbccc, etc.). (If you don't believe it, try to write the grammar!)

2. In the case of Mandler and Johnson's grammar it is actually possible to determine by rigorous criteria whether or not a given proposition fits in the next-to-terminal categories of state and event (a proposition intrinsically belongs to one or the other of these categories), but the problem of classification occurs on the next level up: in different stories, the state "the crow has a cheese" could function as setting, goal, beginning, or ending of episode. A similar phenomenon occurs with the category noun in natural languages: a given word is unambiguously a noun, but a noun can fulfill many syntactic functions: subject, object, indirect object, etc. It is significant, however, that Chomsky's grammar does not refer to categories such as subject or object: all nouns are derived from the symbol noun-phrase, without distinctions of position and syntactic function. Moreover, syntactic function can be established by formal criteria (a noun is a subject if it precedes the verb in a declarative sentence), but there is no discovery procedure by which to determine the narrative function of a proposition such as "the crow has a cheese" in a given text.

3. In the original grammar, Goal is only rewritten as "Internal state"; and Ending must include a physical event.

4. The opposition fabula/sjužhet is often translated as fabula versus plot, but in the present book I use the word plot as a synonym of fabula. As a translation of sjužhet I propose "presentational structure."

5. The model of Mandler and Johnson, as other story grammars (Prince, van Dijk) allows the disruption of the chronological order *after* the application of transformations. The output of the transformational component, however, is no longer the logico-semantic representation of the plot, but the structure of textual presentation. In the present discussion, we are not dealing with textual presentation but with a level of plot-representation on which logical and semantic relations should be made absolutely transparent.

6. When an action specified by a plan fulfills two different subgoals, however, the structure of the plan will no longer be a tree, since the graph will contain a circuit.

7. In Lehnert's original article, G-nodes are called M-nodes. Since they invari-

ably contain the goals of characters, however, I find that the symbol "G" makes the plot-graph easier to read.

8. To justify the classification of the two propositions as part of an intensional problem resolution, however, the lexical entry for this unit should present two variants: one allowing a chain of nested goals and moves in the position of the problem-solving action, and another allowing the problem-solving actions to involve the domains of several characters. Lehnert's article defines only the first variant.

9. On the mapping of "The Fox and the Crow" shown in figure 40, some state specifications are indeed redundant. It is highly doubtful that a reader would store a representation of the plot including both "Fox walks by crow" and "Fox near crow," or "Fox grabs cheese" and "Fox has cheese." For a more economical and cognitively more plausible mapping of the story, the states that can be inferred from the physical events could be represented by empty squares on the diagram. The semantic distinction between states and events would be maintained, and the model would preserve the basic narrative pattern of state/event, but the content of the empty nodes would be specified only as needed, in a dynamic construction of information.

10. An apparent counterexample to this rule is *Gone with the Wind*, which ends when Scarlett O'Hara decides to find a way to reconquer Rhett Butler. But since she has no plan to fulfill this desire, "Reconquering Rhett Butler" is a mere wish, listed in the W-register, and not an active goal. Alternatively, one could enter the proposition as goal, and declare the narrative open, as many readers have done.

11. An example of a narrative made out of logically independent subplots is the French medieval novel *Le Roman de Renart*. It does not matter in which order the fox tricks the wolf, the crow, and the hunters. But the judgment of Renart by the lion at the end of the text is a more tightly integrated narrative unit, since it functions as punishment of the mischief. A concatenation of semantically self-contained yet mutually dependent episodes is typical of the picaresque novel. If the hero is brought to a certain city by a love affair, and there meets a band of robbers, the episode "love affair" sets the material preconditions for the episode "hero joins a band of robbers."

11. The Heuristics of Automatic Story Generation

1. Maranda's criterion for including arcs on the graph is that the transition between the two functions must be found in at least two tales of the corpus studied by Propp.

2. This question is decided by assigning a "probability factor" to the rule and generating a random number. If the number is smaller than the probability factor, the rule is implemented. The nonfulfillment of preconditions will normally result in a coefficient so low that it will be automatically exceeded by the random number.

3. The formalism of the pseudo-code in figure 45 is inspired by the syntax of LISP, the standard language of AI.

4. Among the "natural" versions of the tale, some provide motivation for the wolf's avoidance of the standard solution (e.g., Perrault, who makes the wolf aware of the presence of faggot makers nearby), while others do not (e.g., Grimm).

5. Each of the programs discussed above was written with the generation of a particular story type in mind. The prototypes are respectively: "The Dragon Slayer" for Maranda's model; "The Quest of the Holy Grail" for TELLTALE; an unidentified detective novel for Klein's program; "The Fox and the Crow" for TALE-SPIN, and the TV soap opera "Days of Our Lives" for UNIVERSE.

References

Critical Studies

Adams, Jon-K. 1989. "Causality and Narrative." *Journal of Literary Semantics* 18.3:149–62.

Adams, Robert Merrihew. 1974. "Theories of Actuality." *Noûs* 8:211–31. Reprinted in Loux 1979:190–209.

Allén, Sture, ed. 1989. *Possible Worlds in Humanities, Arts, and Sciences: Proceedings of Nobel Symposium 65.* New York and Berlin: de Gruyter.

Bal, Mieke. 1985. *Narratology: Introduction to the Theory of Narrative.* Translated by Christine van Boheemen. Toronto, Buffalo, and London: University of Toronto Press.

Banfield, Ann. 1978. "Where Epistemology, Style, and Grammar Meet: The Development of Represented Speech and Thought." *New Literary History* 9:415–55.

———. 1982. *Unspeakable Sentences: Narration and Representation in the Langauge of Fiction.* London: Routledge.

Barthes, Roland. 1966. "Introduction à l'analyse structurale des récits." *Communications* 8:1–27.

Bauman, Richard. 1986. *Story, Performance, and Event: Contextual Studies of Oral Narrative.* Cambridge and New York: Cambridge University Press.

de Beaugrande, Robert. 1982. "The Story of Grammars and the Grammar of Stories." *Journal of Pragmatics* 6:83–422.

———, and Benjamin N. Colby. 1979. "Narrative Models of Action and Interaction." *Cognitive Science* 3:43–66.

Benveniste, Emile. 1966. *Problèmes de linguistique générale.* Paris: Gallimard.

Black, John B., and Gordon Bower. 1980. "Story Understanding as Problem-Solving." *Poetics* 9:233–50.

———, and Robert Wilensky. 1979. "An Evaluation of Story Grammars." *Cognitive Science* 3:213–30 .

Boden, Margaret. 1977. *Artificial Intelligence and Natural Man.* New York: Basic Books.

Booth, Wayne. 1961. *The Rhetoric of Fiction.* Chicago: University of Chicago Press.

Bremond, Claude. 1973. *Logique du récit.* Paris: Seuil.

———. 1988. "En lisant une fable." *Communications* 47:41–62.

Brooks, Peter. 1985. *Reading for the Plot: Design and Intention in Narrative.* New York: Random House.

Bruce, Bertram. 1980. "Analysis of Interacting Plans as a Guide to the Understanding of Story Structure." *Poetics* 9:195–311.

———. 1983. "Plans and Discourse." *Text* 3:253–59.

———, and Dennis Newman. 1978. "Interacting Plans." *Cognitive Science* 3:195–233.

Bruner, Jerome. 1986. *Actual Minds, Possible Worlds.* Cambridge, Mass. and London: Harvard University Press.

Brunvand, Jan Harold. 1984. *The Choking Doberman and Other "New" Urban Legends.* New York and London: Norton.

Chambers, Ross. 1984. *Story and Situation: Narrative Seduction and the Power of Fiction.* Minneapolis: University of Minnesota Press.

Châteaux, Dominique. 1976. "La Sémiotique du récit." *Semiotica* 18:201–16.

Chatman, Seymour. 1978. *Story and Discourse.* Ithaca: Cornell University Press.

_____. 1988. "On Deconstructing Narratology." *Style* 22.1:9–17.

Colby, Benjamin. 1973. "A Partial Grammar of Eskimo Folktales." *American Anthropologist* 75:645–62 .

Correira, Alfred. 1980. "Computing Story Trees." *American Journal of Computational Linguistics* 6: 135–49.

Coste, Didier. 1989. *Narrative as Communication.* Minneapolis: University of Minnesota Press.

Crittenden, Charles. 1982. "Fictional Characters and Logical Completeness." *Poetics* 11:331–44.

Culler, Jonathan. 1975. *Structuralist Poetics.* Ithaca: Cornell University Press.

_____. 1981. *The Pursuit of Signs. Semiotics, Literature, Deconstruction.* Ithaca: Cornell University Press.

Currie, Gregory. 1985. "What is Fiction?" *Journal of Aesthetics and Art Criticism* 43.4:385–92.

_____. 1986. "Works of Fiction and Illocutionary Acts." *Philosophy and Literature* 10.2:304–7.

van Dijk, Teun A. 1972. *Some Aspects of Text Grammars.* The Hague: Mouton.

_____. 1976. "Philosophy of Action and Theory of Narrative." *Poetics* 5:287–338.

_____. 1977. *Text and Context: Explorations in the Semantics and Pragmatics of Discourse.* New York: Longmans.

_____. 1980. *Macrostructures: An Interdisciplinary Study of Global Structures in Discourse.* Hillsdale, New Jersey: Erlbaum.

_____. 1983. "A Pointless Approach to Stories." (Commentary to Wilensky 1983.) *The Behavioral and Brain Sciences* 6:598–99.

Doležel, Lubomír. 1976a. "Narrative Modalities." *Journal of Literary Semantics* 5.1:5–14.

_____. 1976b. "Narrative Semantics." *PTL* 1:129–51.

_____. 1976c. "Extensional and Intensional Narrative Worlds." *Poetics* 8:193–212.

_____. 1980. "Truth and Authenticity in Narrative." *Poetics Today* 1.3:7–25.

_____. 1983. "Intensional Function, Invisible Worlds, and Franz Kafka." *Style* 17:120–41.

_____. 1988. "Mimesis and Possible Worlds." *Poetics Today* 9.3:475–96.

_____. 1989. "Possible Worlds and Literary Fictions." In Allén 1989:221–42.

Dyer, Michael G. 1983. *In-Depth Understanding: A Computer Model of Integrated Processing for Narrative Comprehension.* Cambridge, Mass.: MIT Press.

Eco, Umberto. 1978. "Possible Worlds and Text Pragmatics: 'Un Drame bien parisien.' " *Versus* 19/20:5–72. Reprinted in *The Role of the Reader: Explorations in the Semiotics of Texts.* Bloomington: Indiana University Press, 1979.

Fludernik, Monika. 1985. " 'Ithaca': An Essay in Non-Narrativity." In *International Perspectives on James Joyce,* ed. Gottlieb Kaiser. Troy, N.Y.: Whitston Publishing Co., 88–105.

_____ 1986. "Narrative and Its Development in *Ulysses.*" *The Journal of Narrative Technique* 16.1:15–40.

Frege, Gottlob. 1960 (1892). "On Sense and Reference." In *Philosophical Writings of Gottlob Frege,* ed. G. P. Geach and M. Black. Oxford: Blackwell, 56–78.

Fricke, Harald. 1982. "Semantics or Pragmatics of Fictionality? A Modest Proposal." *Poetics* 11:439–52.

Füredy, Viveca. 1989. "A Structural Model of Phenomena with Embedding in Literature and Other Arts." *Poetics Today* 10.4:745–70.

Gabriel, Gottfried. 1979. "Fiction: A Semantic Approach." *Poetics* 8:245–55.

Golden, Joanne M. 1985. "Interpreting a Tale: Three Perspectives on Text Construction." *Poetics* 14:303–24.

Goodman, Nelson. 1973. *Fact, Fiction, and Forecast.* Indianapolis: Hackett.

———. 1978. *Ways of Worldmaking.* Indianapolis: Hackett.

Gray, Paul. 1989, "Telling It Like Thackeray." (Review of *A Natural Curiosity* by Margaret Drabble.) *Time,* 9/4/1979:66.

Greimas, A. J. 1976. *Maupassant: La Sémiotique du texte: Exercices pratiques.* Paris: Seuil.

Grice, H. Paul. 1971. "Meaning." In *Readings in the Philosphy of Language,* ed. J. Rosenberg and B. Travis: Englewood Cliffs, N.J.: Prentice Hall, 436–43.

———. 1975. "Logic and Conversation." In *Speech Acts,* ed. P. Cole and J. L. Morgan. Vol. 3 of *Syntax and Semantics.* New York: Academic Press.

Hamburger, Käthe. 1968. *Die Logik der Dichtung.* Stuttgart: Klett Verlag.

Herrnstein Smith. See Smith, Barbara Herrnstein.

Hobbs, Jerry R. 1981. "Text Plans and World Plans in Natural Discourse." *Proceedings of the International Joint Conference on Artificial Intelligence,* 190–96.

———. 1988. "Against Confusion." *Diacritics* 18.3:78–92.

———, and Michael H. Agar. 1985. "The Coherence of Incoherent Discourse." *Journal of Language and Social Psychology* 4.3/4:213–32.

Hofstadter, Douglas. 1980. *Gödel, Escher, Bach: An Eternal Golden Braid.* New York: Vintage Books.

Howell, Robert. 1979. "Fictional Objects: How They Are, and How They Aren't." *Poetics* 8:129–78.

van Inwagen, Peter. 1983. "Fiction and Metaphysics." *Philosophy and Literature* 7.1:67–77.

Kibédi Varga, A. 1988. "Stories Told by Pictures." *Style* 22.2:194–208.

Klein, Sheldon, et al. 1979. "Automatic Novel Writing: A Status Report." In *Text Processing,* ed. W. Burghardt and K. Holker. Berlin: de Gruyter, 338–411.

Kripke, Saul. 1963. "Semantical Considerations on Modal Logic." *Acta Philosophica Fennica* 16:83–94.

———. 1972. "Naming and Necessity." In *Semantics of Natural Language,* ed. D. Davidson and G. Harman. Dordrecht: Reidel, 253–355.

Krysinski, Wladimir. 1987. "Poland of Nowhere, the Breasts of Tiresias, and Other Incongruities, or: Referential Manipulation in Modern Drama." In Whiteside and Issacharoff 1987:138–57.

Kuiper, Konraad, and Vernon Small. 1986. "Constraints on Fiction." *Poetics Today* 7.3:495–526.

Kuroda, S. Y. 1976. "Reflections on the Foundations of Narrative Theory." In *Pragmatics of Language and Literature,* ed. Teun A. van Dijk. Amsterdam: North Holland, 107–40.

Labov, William, and Joshua Waletzky. 1967. "Narrative Analysis: Oral Versions of Personal Experience." In *Essays on the Verbal and Visual Arts: Proceedings of the 1966 Spring Meeting,* ed. June Helm. Seattle: University of Washington Press, 12–44.

Lanser, Susan Sniader. 1981. *The Narrative Act.* Princeton: Princeton University Press.

Lebowitz, Michael. 1984. "Creating Characters in a Story-Telling Universe." *Poetics* 13:171–94.

———1985. "Story-Telling as Planning and Learning." *Poetics* 14:483–502.

Le Guin, Ursula K. 1980. "It Was a Dark and Stormy Night; or, Why Are We Huddling about the Campfire?" In Mitchell 1980: 187–98.

Lehnert, Wendy. 1981. "Plot Units and Narrative Summarization." *Cognitive Science* 4:293–332.

Leitch, Thomas M. 1986. *What Stories Are: Narrative Theory and Interpretation.* University Park and London: Pennsylvania University Press.

Lewis, David. 1970. "Anselm and Actuality." *Noûs* 4:175–88.

_____1973. *Counterfactuals.* Cambridge, Mass.: Harvard University Press. Excerpt reprinted in Loux 1979:182–89.

_____1978. "Truth in Fiction." *American Philosophical Quarterly* 15:37–46.

Loux, Michael J., ed. 1979. *The Possible and the Actual: Readings in the Metaphysics of Modality.* Ithaca: Cornell University Press.

Maître, Doreen. 1983. *Literature and Possible Worlds.* Middlesex Polytechnic Press.

Mandler, Jean, and Nancy Johnson. 1977. "Remembrance of Things Parsed: Story Structure and Recall." *Cognitive Psychology* 9:111–51.

Maranda, Pierre. 1985. "Semiography and Artificial Intelligence." *International Semiotic Spectrum* 4:1–3.

Margolin, Uri. 1984. "Narrative and Indexicality: A Tentative Framework." *Journal of Literary Semantics* 13:181–204.

_____1986a. "Dispersing/Voiding the Subject: A Narratological Perspective." *Texte* 5/6:181–210.

_____1986b "The Doer and the Deed. Action Basis for Characterization in Narrative." *Poetics Today* 7.2:205–26.

_____1988. "Dealing with the Non-Actual: Conception, Reception, Description." *Poetics Today* 9.4:863–78.

Margolis, Joseph. 1983. "The Logic and Structure of Fictional Narrative." *Philosophy and Literature* 7.2:162–81.

Martin, Wallace. 1986. *Recent Theories of Narrative.* Ithaca and London: Cornell University Press.

Martínez-Bonati, Felix. 1980. "The Act of Writing Fiction." *New Literary History* 11.3:425–34.

_____1981a. *Fictive Discourse and the Structures of Literature.* Ithaca: Cornell University Press.

_____1981b. "Representation and Fiction." *Dispositio* 5.13/14:19–34.

_____1983. "Towards a Formal Ontology of Fictional Worlds." *Philosophy and Literature* 7:182–95.

McCawley, James. 1978. *Everything That Linguists Always Wanted to Know about Logic (But Were Ashamed to Ask).* Chicago: Chicago University Press.

McCord, Phyllis. 1986. "The Ideology of Form: The Nonfiction Novel." *Genre* 19:59–79.

McCormick, Peter J. 1987. "Real Fictions." *Journal of Aesthetics and Art Criticism* 46.2:259–70.

_____1988. *Fictions, Philosophies, and the Problems of Poetics.* Ithaca and London: Cornell University Press.

McHale, Brian. 1987. *Postmodernist Fiction.* New York and London: Methuen.

Meehan, James. 1981. "Tale-spin." In *Inside Computer Understanding,* ed. Roger Schank. Hillsdale, N.J.: Lawrence Erlbaum, 197–225.

Mink, Louis O. 1978. "Narrative Form as a Cognitive Instrument." In *The Writing of History: Literary Form and Historical Understanding,* ed. Robert H. Canary and Henry Kozicki. Madison: University of Wisconsin Press.

Mitchell, W.J.T., ed. 1980. *On Narrative.* Chicago: University of Chicago Press.

Parsons, Terence. 1980. *Nonexistent Objects.* New Haven: Yale University Press.

Pavel, Thomas. 1976. *La Syntaxe narrative des tragédies de Corneille.* Paris: Klincksieck.

_____1985. *The Poetics of Plot: The Case of English Renaissance Drama.* Minneapolis: University of Minnesota Press.

_____1986. *Fictional Worlds,* Cambridge: Harvard University Press.

_____1988. "Formalism in Narrative Semiotics," *Poetics Today* 9.3:593–606.

Plantinga, Alvin. 1976. "Actualism and Possible Worlds." *Theoria* 42:139–60. Reprinted in Loux 1979:253–73.

Polanyi, Livia. 1979. "So What's the Point?" *Semiotica* 25.3/4:207–41.

_____1981. "What Stories Can Tell Us about Their Teller's World." *Poetics Today* 2.2:97–112.

——1988. "A Formal Model of the Structure of Discourse." *Journal of Pragmatics* 12:601–38.

Pratt, Mary Louise. 1977. *Toward a Speech Act Theory of Literary Discourse.* Bloomington: Indiana University Press.

——1986. "Ideology and Speech Act Theory." *Poetics Today* 7.1:59–72.

Prince, Gerald. 1973. *A Grammar of Stories.* The Hague: Mouton.

——1982. *Narratology.* The Hague: Mouton.

——1983. "Narrative Pragmatics, Message, and Point." *Poetics* 12:527–36.

——1987. *A Dictionary of Narratology.* Lincoln and London: University of Nebraska Press.

——1988. "The Disnarrated." *Style* 22.1:1–8.

Propp, Vladimir. 1968 (1928). *Morphology of the Folktale,* trans. L. Scott, revised Louis A. Wagner. Austin: University of Texas Press.

Rabinowitz, Peter J. 1977. "Truth in Fiction: A Reexamination of Audiences." *Critical Inquiry* 4.1:121–41.

——1981. "Assertion and Assumption: Fictional Patterns and the External World." *PMLA* 96.3:408–19.

——1987. *Before Reading: Narrative Conventions and the Politics of Interpretation.* Ithaca and London: Cornell University Press.

Reichenbach, Hans. 1976. Laws, Modalities, and Counterfactuals, Berkeley: University of California Press.

Reichman, Rachel. 1985. *Getting Computers to Talk Like You and Me.* Cambridge, Mass. and London: MIT Press.

Rescher, Nicholas. 1973. "The Ontology of the Possible." In *Logic and Ontology,* ed. Milton Munitz. New York: New York University Press. Reprinted in Loux 1979:166–81.

Ricardou, Jean. 1967. *Problèmes du nouveau roman.* Paris: Seuil.

Ricoeur, Paul. 1982. *Temps et Récit.* Paris: Seuil.

——1984. *La Configuration du temps dans le récit de fiction.* Vol. 2 of *Temps et récit.* Paris: Seuil.

——1985. *Le Temps raconté.* Vol. 3 of *Temps et récit.* Paris: Seuil.

Rimmon-Kenan, Shlomith. 1980. *Narrative Fiction: Contemporary Poetics.* London: Methuen.

——1989. "How the Model Neglects the Medium: Linguistics, Language, and the Crisis of Narratology." *The Journal of Narrative Technique* 19.1:157–66.

Ronen, Ruth. 1988a. "Completing the Incompleteness of Fictional Entities." *Poetics Today* 9.3:497–514.

——1988b. "The World of Allegory." *Journal of Literary Semantics* 17.2:91–121.

——Forthcoming. "Possible Worlds in Literary Theory: A Game in Interdisciplinarity." *Semiotica.*

Routley, Richard. 1979. "The Semantical Structure of Fictional Discourse." *Poetics* 8:3–30.

Rumelhart, David. 1975. "Notes on a Schema for Stories." In *Representation and Understanding: Studies in Cognitive Science,* ed. D. G. Bobrow and M. Collins. New York: Academic Press, 211–35.

Russell, Bertrand. 1919. *Introduction to Mathematical Philosophy.* London: Allen and Unwin.

Ryan, Marie-Laure. 1980. "Fiction, Non-Factuals, and the Principle of Minimal Departure." *Poetics* 9:403–22.

——1981a. "The Pragmatics of Personal and Impersonal Fiction." *Poetics* 10:517–39.

——1981b. "When *Je* is *Un Autre:* Fiction, Quotation, and the Performative Analysis." *Poetics Today* 2.2:127–55.

——1984. "Fiction as a Logical, Ontological, and Illocutionary Issue." *Style* 18.2:121–39.

——1985. "The Modal Structure of Narrative Universes." *Poetics Today* 6.4:717–56.

_____1986a. "Le Corbeau et le renard: De la sémiotique narrative à l'intelligence artificielle." *Revue des Sciences Humaines* 201:59–78.

_____1986b. "Embedded Narratives and the Structure of Plans." *Text* 6.1:107–42.

_____1986c. "Embedded Narratives and Tellability." *Style* 20.3:319–40.

_____1988a. "A la recherche du thème narratif." *Communications* 47:23–40.

_____1988b. "The Heuristics of Automatic Story Generation." *Poetics* 16:515–34.

Schank, Roger. 1978. "Interestingness: Controlling Inferences." Yale University Department of Computer Science, research report 145.

Schank, Roger, and R. Abelson. 1977. *Scripts, Plans, Goals and Understanding.* Hillsdale, New Jersey: Lawrence Erlbaum.

Schank, Roger, G. C. Collins, E. Davis, P. Johnson, S. Lytinen, and B. Reiser. 1982. "What's the Point?" *Cognitive Science* 6:255–76.

Searle, John. 1969. *Speech Acts.* London: Cambridge University Press.

_____1975. "The Logical Status of Fictional Discourse." *New Literary History* 6: 319–32.

_____1980. "*Las Meninas* and the Paradoxes of Pictorial Representation." *Critical Inquiry* 6.3:477–88.

Smith, Barbara Herrnstein. 1978. *On The Margins of Discourse.* Chicago: University of Chicago Press.

Spatz, Jonas. 1975. "The Mystery of Eros: Sexual Initiation in Coleridge's 'Christabel.' " *PMLA* 90.1:107–16.

Stalnaker, Robert C., 1976. "Possible Worlds." *Noûs* 10:65–75. Reprinted in Loux 1979:225–34.

Stewart, Ann Harleman. 1987. "Models of Narrative Structure." *Semiotica* 64.1/2: 83–97.

Stewart, Susan. 1978. *Nonsense: Aspects of Intertextuality in Folklore and Literature.* Baltimore: The Johns Hopkins University Press.

Todorov, Tzvetan. 1969. *Grammaire du Décameron.* The Hague: Mouton.

_____1971. *Poétique de la prose.* Paris: Seuil.

_____1975 (1970). *The Fantastic: A Structural Approach to a Literary Genre,* trans. Richard Howard. Ithaca and New York: Cornell University Press.

Vaina, Lucia. 1977. "Les Mondes possibles du texte." *Versus* 17:3–13.

Walton, Kendall. 1973. "Pictures and Make-Believe." *Philosophical Review* 82: 283–319.

_____1978a. "How Remote Are Fictional Worlds from the Real World?" *Journal of Aesthetics and Art Criticism* 37:11–23.

_____1978b. "Fearing Fictions." *Journal of Philosophy* 80:179–83.

_____1983. "Fiction, Fiction-Making, and Styles of Fictionality." *Philosophy and Literature* 7.2:78–87.

Warhol, Robyn. 1986, "Toward a Theory of the Engaging Narrator: Earnest Intervention in Gaskell, Stowe, and Eliot." *PMLA* 101.5:811–18.

Warning, Rainer. 1981. "Staged Discourse: Remarks on the Pragmatics of Fiction." *Dispositio* 5.13/4:35–54.

White, Hayden. 1978. *Tropics of Discourse: Essays in Cultural Criticism.* Baltimore: Johns Hopkins University Press.

_____1980a. "The Value of Narrativity in the Representation of Reality." In Mitchell 1980: 1–24.

_____1980b. "The Narrativization of Real Events." In Mitchell 1980: 249–54.

Whiteside, Anna, and Michael Issacharoff, eds. 1987. *On Referring in Literature.* Bloomington: Indiana University Press.

Wilensky, Robert. 1983a. *Planning and Understanding: A Computational Approach to Human Reasoning.* Reading, Massachusetts: Addison-Wesley.

_____1983b. "Story Grammars versus Story Points." *The Behavioral and Brain Sciences* 6:579–623.

Wolterstorff, Nicholas. 1980. *Works and Worlds of Art.* Oxford: Oxford University Press.

Woods, John. 1974. *The Logic of Fiction.* The Hague: Mouton.
Woods, John, and T. G. Pavel, eds., 1979. "Formal Semantics and Literary Theory." *Poetics* 8.
von Wright, Georg Hendrik. 1967. "The Logic of Action: A Sketch." In *The Logic of Decision and Action,* ed. N. Rescher. Pittsburgh: University of Pittsburgh Press, 121–36.
Yacobi, Tamar. 1987. "Narrative Structure and Fictional Mediation." *Poetics Today* 8.2:335–72.
Young, Katharine Galloway. 1987. *Taleworlds and Storyrealms: The Phenomenology of Narrative.* Dordrecht: Martinus Nijhoff.
Zholkovsky, Alexander. 1984. *Themes and Texts: Toward a Poetics of Expressiveness.* Ithaca and London: Cornell University Press.

Literary Works

(The list is limited to quoted texts and to works not quoted but receiving more than passing reference.)

Austen, Jane. 1933. *Pride and Prejudice.* In *The Complete Novels of Jane Austen.* New York: Modern Library.
Boccaccio, Giovanni. 1986. *The Decameron.* Translated by G. H. McWiliam. Penguin Books.
Borges, Jorge Luis. 1972. *A Universal History of Infamy.* Translated by Norman di Giovanni. New York: Dutton.
———1983 (1944). *Fictions.* In *Labyrinths: Selected Stories and Other Writings.* New York: Modern Library.
Burton, Sir Richard. (No date.) *The Book of the Thousand Nights and a Night,* vol. 6. Printed by the Burton Club.
Calvino, Italo. 1981 (1979). *If on a Winter's Night a Traveler.* Translated by William Weaver. A Harvest/HBJ Book. New York and San Diego: Harcourt Brace Jovanovich.
Carroll, Lewis. 1975 (1916). *Alice's Adventures in Wonderland* and *Through the Looking Glass.* New York, Chicago, and San Francisco: Rand McNally.
———1976. *Sylvie and Bruno.* In *Complete Works of Lewis Carroll.* New York: Vintage Books.
Chandernagor, Françoise. 1981. *L'Allée du Roi.* Paris: Julliard.
Conan Doyle, Sir Arthur. 1981 (1892). *The Adventures of Sherlock Holmes.* Penguin Books.
Cortázar, Julio. 1967 (1963). *Blow-Up and Other Stories.* Translated by Paul Blackburn. New York: Random House.
Einstein, Charles. 1979 (1952). "Reflex Curve." In Jerome Holtzman, ed., *Fielder's Choice.* New York and London: Harcourt Brace Jovanovich.
Fowles, John. 1981 (1969). *The French Lieutenant's Woman.* Chicago: Signet Books (New American Library).
García Márquez, Gabriel. 1970 (1967). *One Hundred Years of Solitude.* Translated by Gregory Rabassa. New York: Harper and Row.
Genet, Jean. 1984 (1947). *Les Bonnes.* Paris: Gallimard (Collection Folio).
Gogol, Nikolai. 1965. *The Overcoat.* In: *Tales of Good and Evil.* Translation by D. Magashack. New York: Norton Library.
Lafayette, Mme. de. 1979 (1678). *The Princess of Clèves.* Translated by Mildred Sarah Greene. University, Mo.: Romance Monographs.
Lindenberger, Herbert. 1979. *Saul's Fall.* Baltimore: Johns Hopkins University Press.
Madras, J. C. 1980. *The Book of the Thousand Nights and One Night,* vol. 3. Folio Press.
McMurtry, Larry. 1966. *The Last Picture Show.* New York: The Dial Press.

Murdoch, Iris. 1965. *The Red and the Green.* New York: Viking.

Nabokov, Vladimir. 1955. *Lolita.* New York: Putnam.

――――1982. *Pale Fire.* New York: Putnam; A Berkley Medallion Book.

Plato. 1956. *Great Dialogues of Plato.* Translated by W.H.D. Rouse and edited by Eric H. Warmington and Philip G. Rouse. Mentor Books (New American Library).

Richter, Hans. 1965. *Dada: Art and Anti-Art.* New York: McGraw Hill.

Riordan, James. 1983. *Tales from The Arabian Nights.* New York, Chicago, and San Francisco: Rand McNally.

Schama, Simon. 1989. *Citizens: A Chronicle of the French Revolution.* New York: Knopf.

Seuss, Dr. (Theodore Geisel). 1975. *Oh, the Thinks You Can Think.* New York: Random House.

Stendhal. 1966. *Le Rouge et le noir.* In *Romans et nouvelles,* ed. Henri Martineau. Paris: Pleïade/Gallimard.

Woolf, Virginia. 1925. *Mrs. Dalloway.* New York: Harcourt Brace Jovanovich.